W9-AGH-507

THE SPIRITS' BOOK

Allan Kardec

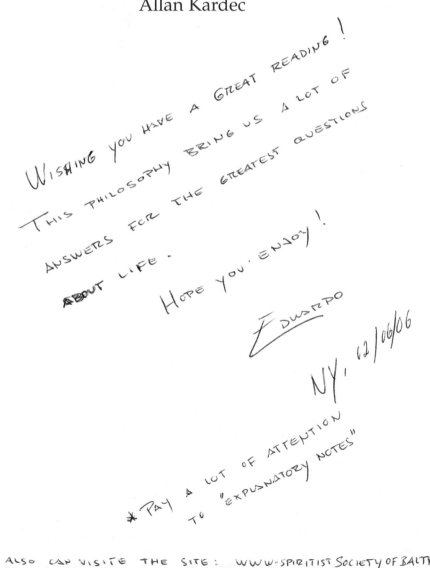

WISHING YOU HAVE A GREAT READING !
THIS PHILOSOPHY BRING US A LOT OF
ANSWERS FOR THE GREATEST QUESTIONS
ABOUT LIFE.

HOPE YOU ENJOY !

Eduardo

NY, 02/06/06

* PAY A LOT OF ATTENTION
TO "EXPLANATORY NOTES"

YOU ALSO CAN VISITE THE SITE : WWW.SPIRITIST SOCIETY OF BALTIMORE

Copyright @ 2003

Published by:
Allan Kardec Educational Society
P.O. Box 26336
Philadelphia   PA 19141
Phone (215) 329 4010

Scripture taken from the HOLY BIBLE, NEW INTERNATIONAL VERSION, Copyright @ 1973, 1978, 1984, by International Bible Society. Used by permission of Zondervan Publishing House. All rights reserved.
The "NIV" and "New International Version" trademarks are registered in the United States Patent and Trademark Office by International Bible Society.

Manufactured in the United States of America

Library of Congress Control Number: 95-83481

Main entry under title:

The Spirits' Book

1. Spirituality 2. Spiritist Doctrine   3. Christianity. I. Kardec, Allan, 1804

ISBN 0-9649907-0-9

(translated from *Le Livre des Esprits*, 1857)

TABLE OF CONTENTS

PART I - THE FIRST CAUSE

CHAPTER I

CHAPTER II

CHAPTER III

CHAPTER IV

TABLE OF CONTENTS

TABLE OF CONTENTS

TABLE OF CONTENTS

PREFACE TO THE NEW ENGLISH EDITION

Since its original publication in France in 1857, Allan Kardec's *The Spirits' Book* has been an inexhaustible source of spiritual discernment and comfort for millions of readers throughout the world. Its clear exposition of our physical and non-physical realities, and the constant interaction between the two, makes *The Spirits' Book* a must-read for the questioning soul. Organized in over a thousand intriguing questions and answers, the book shows that the key to spiritual growth lies in a better understanding of the cause and effect relationships that govern our present lives: relationships that were often established before we were even born.

With this New English Edition of *The Spirits' Book*, we hope to make Kardec's masterpiece easily accessible to the English-speaking world. Truly fundamental ideas, such as the ones presented here, are supposed to withstand the test of time, to inform both evolving social institutions and new scientific advances. A language, however, is as dynamic as the people who use it, and the expressions that give life and relevance to an idea in one era tend to lose currency in the next. It is for this reason that, at a time when even the Bible has been subject to several new translations to bring its text into line with contemporary usage, we could no longer continue to ignore the urgent need to provide a new edition of *The Spirits' Book*. To continue relying on the century-old, first English edition would be a grave injustice—to modern readers of the work, to Kardec's impeccable reasoning, and to the guides' illuminating insights.

In modernizing the language, we have taken great care not to compromise the ideas. Our overriding concern has always been to retain the book's substance while doing everything possible to improve its form. This new translation was carefully checked against the original French, the first English version, and the Portuguese text. In the few instances where Kardec's choice of terms has become obsolete, we have added footnotes to place them in historical context. In some cases, too, we found that the work was served better by replacing nineteenth century terms with their modern equivalents; this was especially the case for some scientific references. If anything, this renewal of the language only emphasizes the timelessness of the book. The words may have changed; but the ideas remain the same as when Kardec wrote them down.

For historical reasons, we are much indebted to Ms. Anna Blackwell, the nineteenth-century British writer who undertook the first English translation. We are especially thankful, however, to the scores of volunteers who unselfishly gave of their time and energy along the many stages that this new translation required. Their valuable assistance came from all corners of this country; their willingness to do whatever we asked of them has been a source of inspiration to all of us. Our heartfelt gratitude goes to Daniel and Marcia Benjamin, Kimberly Bomfim, Ed Crespo, Dr. Sonia Doi, Zaida Knight, Graziela de Marzio, Rev. Iclea Halton, Maria Hanna, David and Brenda Haney, Sandy Jaime, Michael Highsmith, the late Marta Hinkle, Maria Payas, Jemarie Sanchez, Jody Rohner-Brown, Lucia Machado-Schedig, Miriam and Chris Wilcox, Aldalucia Zerio, and to the many others who provided us with encouragement and assistance along the way. Dr. Robert Champ carefully edited the first draft and proofread the final manuscript. Dr. John Zerio was the originator of this project, to which he dedicated uncountable hours and all the resources at his command.

For us, it is a great honor to make this new edition available to the English-speaking public. To our readers we say: take your time. Read this book slowly; divest yourselves of any preconceived notions; do not rush to any conclusions before thoroughly meditating on what is being said. If you approach it in this way, we are confident, *The Spirits' Book* will guide you further along on your path of inner growth.

A. Bomfim, Ph.D.
Allan Kardec Educational Society

PREFACE TO THE SECOND EDITION

Following publication of the first edition of The Spirits' Book (1996), in its new English translation, the translation team undertook various other projects, including Allan Kardec's *The Gospel---Explained by the Spiritist Doctrine*, translated from the French; and A. Luiz and F.C. Xavier's *And Life Goes On* and *Nosso Lar – A Spiritual Home*, translated from the Portuguese. The first was of special importance to the present work. The rich and elegant language of The Gospel compelled the team to build a new, more congenial and probing relationship with the thought and life of nineteenth-century France and sowed the seeds of the collaborative endeavor that culminated in the book you now hold in your hands.

This new, revised edition of The Spirits' Book speaks with a clearer and more precise voice, and benefits from a richer palette of colors built by the editorial team over the past seven years. The team was much enriched by the addition of two respected linguists, experts in nineteenth-century French literature: Dr. Jean-Pierre Lafouge, of Indiana University, and Dr. Didier Maleuvre, of the University of California-Santa Barbara. Both were instrumental in helping the team navigate through the dynamic nuances of the French language as it was spoken and written during Alan Kardec's lifetime. In addition, the scientific sections of the book gained substantially from the scholarly insights of Dr. Andrea Dessen, a scientist with the *Institute de Biologie Struturale* , Grenoble, France.

This second edition also introduces some promising tools for the inquiring reader. A new glossary, a more complete and thorough index, and updated footnotes and references, should help establish The Spirits' Book as an important reference in the literature of spiritual thought in English-speaking communities.

The translation team benefited enormously from the untiring work of a truly worldwide network of friends of the Spiritist cause. We are especially grateful to the boundless commitment and encouragement of the following new contributors: Mr. Marcelo de Almeida, Dr. Vanessa Anseloni, Ms. Leda Cristina, and Ms. Elza d'Agosto, Mr. Luis Del Nero, Mr. Alexandre Goncalves, Mr. Jayme Hanna, and Ms. Jussara Korngold.

We hope you enjoy reading this inspiring and though-provoking masterpiece by Allan Kardec. Your comments and questions are welcome at www.allan-kardec.com.

The Translation and Editorial Team

iv

PREFACE TO THE REVISED EDITION

Published in March, 1860

In the first edition of this work, we announced our intention to publish a Supplement to deal with points for which we could find at the time no room, or that might be suggested by succeeding investigations. When these new materials presented themselves, however, they proved to be so closely connected with the published work that issuing them in a second volume seemed inappropriate. We decided then to wait for the reprinting of the book, at which time we could take the opportunity to unify all the materials, omit needless repetitions, and make a more methodical arrangement of the contents. Consequently, this new edition may be considered a new work, although the original principles are unchanged (in a very few cases, we have provided enhancements and explanations rather than modifications).

This uniformity in the transmitted teachings, despite the many different sources from which they arose, is a fact of great importance in establishing the truth of Spiritist doctrine. As our correspondence has shown us, communications—identical in substance, if not in form, to the ones we offer in this work—have taken place in various quarters, and in some instances, even before the publication of *The Spirits' Book*, which has served to systematize and confirm them. Lastly, history proves that most of the ideas we present here have been held by the finest thinkers of both ancient and modern times, and so gives them the additional authority of its testimony.

ALLAN KARDEC

PROLOGUE

Phenomena, inexplicable by any known laws, are occurring all over the world and revealing, as their cause, the action of a free and intelligent force.

Reason requires that an intelligent effect must have an intelligent force as a cause. In this case, the facts tell us that this force can communicate with human beings through physical actions.

Asked about its nature, this force claimed to belong to the realm of spiritual beings who no longer occupy human bodies. (This is how the existence of spirits was revealed.)

Communication between the physical and non-physical realm is part of the natural order, not a supernatural occurrence. Records of it are found among all peoples and in every age, and it is becoming increasingly more general and evident. The spirits tell us that the time appointed by Providence for a universal recognition of their existence has now come. They have stated that their mission, as messengers and instruments of God, is to inaugurate a new era of regeneration for the human race.

This book is a compilation of their teachings, written at the request and under the dictation of advanced spirits for the purpose of establishing a rational philosophy, free from prejudices and pre-conceived notions. It contains nothing that is not the expression of the spirits' thought and that has not been submitted for their approval. The arrangement of its content, the explanatory comments, and the form of certain sections are the sole contributions of him to whom the duty of publishing this work has been entrusted.

Many of the spirits who have undertaken this task declare that they have been well-known personalities who have lived during different epochs on Earth, preaching and pursuing virtue and knowledge. Of others, history has preserved no trace; but the sublimity of their ideas and their association with those who bear venerated names attest to their ascendancy.

The mission of compiling this work was presented, in writing and through various mediums, with the following words: "Be zealous and persevering in the work you have undertaken jointly with us, for this work is ours. In the book you are to write, we will lay the foundations of the new edifice that is destined to unite all human beings in a common sentiment of love and charity. But before making it public, we will go through it with you to ensure its accuracy. We will be with you whenever you request our presence and will aid you in all your labors.

"As you have already been informed, the preparation of this book is only a part of the mission that has been given to you. Of the transmitted teachings, you are to keep some to yourself for the time being. We will tell you when to release them to the public. Meanwhile, make them the subject of your meditations, so that you will be ready to work with them when the proper time comes.

"The vine-branch we have drawn for you represents the work of God. You are to place it at the beginning of this book. The vine-branch symbolizes the physical body; the juice of the grape denotes the spirit; the grape itself represents the union between the body and spirit. The grape matures in the branch until the juice acquires its quintessential properties. Likewise, the soul 'matures' in the physical existence until it has acquired sufficient experiences to attain plenitude.[1]

"Do not allow yourself to be discouraged by hostile criticism. You will have rancorous opponents, especially among those who benefit from the status quo. You will find enemies even among spirits, since those who are still earth-bound often try to scatter seeds of doubt. Have trust in God, always move forward. We will always be near to sustain you. The time is close when the truth will shine forth on all sides.

"The vanity of some people who imagine they know all and are capable of explaining everything, will give rise to conflicting opinions. However, those who have embraced the ideals of Jesus will be united in the same desire for goodness and brotherhood that will eventually spread the world over. Putting aside useless disputes about semantics, they will devote their energies solely to matters of practical importance. In the end, the essence of the teachings of the enlightened spirits is always the same.

"Perseverance will render your endeavor fruitful. In the future, the pleasure you will feel at the spreading of the Doctrine and its right appreciation will be a rich reward for you. Do not be troubled by the thorns and stones that incredulous and wrong-minded persons will place in your path. Hold your confidence fast—it will ensure our help. With faith, you will reach the goal.

"Remember that good spirits aid those who serve God with humility

....

1 *The vine-branch shown in the beginning of this prologue is a likeness of the drawing made by the spirits.*

and without self-interest. They desert the proud and ambitious, and dis-own those who use heavenly gifts as a stepping-stone for earthly advancement. Pride and ambition are barriers between God and humankind, for they blind humans to the splendors of celestial existence and God cannot use the blind to spread the light."

John the Evangelist, St. Augustine, St. Vincent de Paul, St. Louis, Socrates, Plato, Fénélon, Franklin, Swedenborg[2], the Spirit of truth[3]."

....

2 *Translator's Note: see entries for individual figures in the Biographical Appendix at the end of this book.*

....

3 *Translator's Note: Such a collection of highly regarded names could be a source of concern. We refer the reader to section XII of Explanatory Notes, particularly the discussion on the difficulty of establishing positive identity. As for the name Spirit of truth, as explained by the spirits themselves, it was adopted as a symbolic form of identifying the broad assembly of enligthened intelligences (rather than an indi-viduality) ultimately responsible for unveiling to humanity the Spiritist Doctrine.*

A NOTE FROM THE EDITORS

The "Explanatory Notes" section contains a broad-based discussion of the etymology of certain key words, as well as Allan Kardec's rebuttal to criticisms raised against the Spiritist Doctrine in its early phase in Europe. If your intention is to learn about the Spiritist philosophy, you should save this section for later reading and start immediately with Chapter 1. The soul of this book is contained in the 1019 dialogues that define the Spiritist Doctrine. The exposition contained in the "Explanatory Notes" will have more significance if you read it for supplementary understanding.

EXPLANATORY NOTES [1]

For new ideas we need new words, both as a way of ensuring exactness of expression and of avoiding the use of the same word for ideas that are, in fact, quite different. Now, the words "spiritual," "spiritualist," and "spiritualism" already have a commonly understood meaning; and to introduce a new one to describe the doctrine set forth by spirits would be to multiply the causes of linguistic confusion unnecessarily. Strictly speaking, (from a philosophical perspective) Spiritualism is the opposite of Materialism. Everyone is a Spiritualist who believes that there is in him or her something more than matter, although such a person may accept neither the existence of spirits nor their communication with the visible world.[2] Here we have adopted the words "Spiritist" and "Spiritism" to refer to the system that admits both of these phenomena. These words have a similar root and thus should be easily assimilated by the reader. Thus, we reserve the words (philosophical) "spiritualism" and "spiritualist" only to convey the meanings usually attached to them, whereas we define *Spiritism* as a doctrine that has its foundation in the relationship between the material world and spirits, i.e., the beings of the invisible world. We designate the followers of the Spiritist Doctrine then as

....

1 *Translator's Note:* The Spirits' Book *was originally published on the 18th of April, 1857 in Paris by the publisher E. Dentu. A second edition, expanded and revised, was published in March of 1860. It became the final and central work of the Spiritist Doctrine. This New English Edition is based on the second edition of the original work.*

....

2 *Translator's Note: The author's emphasis on the different meanings of spiritualism and spiritism is particularly relevant for the French language, in which the book was originally written. In English, the distinction between these two words is less clear. For instance, according to* The Oxford English Dictionary (O.E.D.), *spiritism and spiritualism are synonyms in the specific sense of indicating "the belief that the spirits of the dead can hold communication with the living, or make their presence known to them in some way, especially through a 'medium'; the system of doctrines or practices founded on this belief." Nonetheless, the O.E.D. does indicate a more general definition of spiritualism as the "... advocacy of a spiritual view or estimate of things, especially as a leading principle in philosophy or religion," which is more in line with the definition offered by Kardec. Moreover, it also points out that those interested in the study of spirit communication tend to prefer the term spiritism "as being more distinctive than spiritualism" (*The Oxford English Dictionary, 2nd Ed., Oxford: Clarendon Press, 1989).*

Spiritists.

In a special sense, *The Spirits' Book* contains the Spiritist Doctrine. In a general sense, it is related to the Spiritualist school, of which it represents one perspective.

II

Here we find it prudent to define another significant word, not only because it is the keystone of every metaphysical and philosophical system but also because the lack of a precise definition has made it the subject of numerous controversies. We refer to the word "soul." The use of this word in a wide range of contexts has resulted in a medley of meanings, whereas ideally every idea should have a term especially and succinctly expressing it (an enormous amount of discussion and many misunderstandings would certainly be avoided thereby).

Some writers have defined the soul as being the principle of organic life, as having no independent existence and as disappearing on the death of the body. Thus, the death of the body is comparable to an out-of-order device that no longer works: the device, like a lifeless body, no longer has its "soul." According to this purely materialistic belief, the soul is an effect, not a cause.

Other writers have considered the soul to be the principle of intelligence, a universal agent of which each being absorbs a portion. According to this view, there is in the universe a primary soul, which distributes its sparks to all intelligent beings during their life time. After the death of the body, each spark returns to the common source, merging back into the whole as brooks and rivers merge into the ocean. This view differs from the preceding one in that it recognizes that something lives on after physical death. Nonetheless, it is predicated on the proposition that at death the consciousness, the person's individual identity, is permanently lost. For all practical purposes, then, nothing remains after death. Each being, according to this hypothesis, is a portion of God, who is seen as the Universal Soul—a notion akin to pantheism.[3]

Other thinkers still have regarded the soul as a distinct being, independent of matter and preserving its individuality after death. This conception of the word "soul" is the one most commonly accepted. Indeed, the idea of a being that survives the body is an instinctive belief, independent of teaching and found among peoples everywhere, regardless of their degree of civilization. This doctrine—which states that the soul is a cause rather than an effect—is maintained by philosophical spiritualism.

....

3 *Translator's Note: Pantheism: A doctrine that identifies the Deity with the various forces and workings of nature. See also questions 14-16 in chapter 1.*

Without discussing the value of these opinions and considering the subject only in its philological context, we can say that these three uses of the word "soul" constitute three distinct ideas, each of which needs (but does not have) a different term. "Soul" has, therefore, a triple meaning, and is used by each school according to the special meaning that school gives the word. To avoid the confusion resulting from the use of one word to express three different ideas, we would have to confine the word to one of the three—it would not matter which, as long as the choice is clearly understood. In our case, we think it only natural to take it as it is most commonly understood; and for this reason, we use the word "soul" to indicate the immaterial and individual being that resides in us and survives the body. It should be clear, however, that, even if this being were not an objective reality and were only an image of speech, a specific word would still be needed to designate it.

Lacking more precise words for each notion associated with "soul," we use the term "vital principle" here to designate the material and organic life common to all living things—from plants to human beings. The vital principle is distinct from and independent of the intellectual faculty. In the view of some, it is a property of matter and, under certain conditions, can be observed in matter. Thus, for many scientists, the vital principle expresses itself in a particular form of energy, one that is universally diffused. Every living body absorbs it, much as inert bodies absorb light. It has been equated with the vital force, animalised electric force, magnetic force, nervous energy, etc.

In any case, these facts are certain: organic beings contain within themselves a force that, as long as it exists, produces the phenomenon of life; physical life, independent of intelligence and thought, is common to all organic beings; intelligence and thought are faculties peculiar to certain organic species. Finally, among the organic species endowed with intelligence, one alone is endowed with moral conscience, an attribute that gives it an incontestable superiority over the others—we mean, of course, the human species.

The indiscriminate use of the word "soul" has given rise to interminable disputes and will undoubtedly give rise to many more. Obviously, the loose manner in which the word "soul" is sometimes used excludes neither the materialist nor the pantheist perspectives. Even philosophical Spiritualists themselves often use it when speaking of the one idea or the other. It has become, in fact, a Protean concept, with each person free to define it after his or her own fashion. As a way out of this confusion, we might consider adding qualifying words that would characterize a given perspective. These qualifiers would represent the concepts of the material life, intelligence, and the moral faculty. Each would distinguish an attribute—as is the case, for example, with the words "hydrogen," "oxygen," etc., which describe specific properties of the general term "gas." Thus we might say—and it would perhaps be the best approach—"vital soul" for the principle of material life, "intellectual soul" for the principle of intelligence, and "spiritual soul" for the principle of individuality after death. In this case, the "vital soul" would be common to all organic beings—plants, animals, and humans; the "intellectual soul" would be the peculiar property of animals and humans; and the "spiritual soul" would belong only to human beings.

We have thought it all the more important to be explicit in regard to this point because Spiritist philosophy is based on the existence in each person of a non-material element that survives the body. As the word soul frequently occurs in the course of this work, accordingly, we found it wise to define its meaning accurately.

We now come to the principal object of this explanation.

III

Like all new theories, the Spiritist Doctrine has its supporters and opponents. We will endeavor here to reply to some of the objections of the latter by examining the basis of their arguments. It is not our intention to convince everybody, but we hope to address the concerns of sincere seekers, i.e., those who operate without prejudices or preconceived ideas. These explanatory notes will show that objections to the Spiritist Doctrine result mainly from hasty conclusions drawn from imperfectly observed facts.

Among the first of these facts was table-turning, or the movement of objects. This phenomenon was first observed—or rather, first came back into the world's awareness—in America in the late 1840s.[4] Actually, history shows that the phenomenon has been produced since the remotest times. But in its new manifestation, it combined with other strange occurrences—for example, unusual noises, raps produced without any ostensible cause, etc. It created a public sensation, and from America, table-turning quickly spread throughout Europe and the rest of the world. At first

....

4 Translator's Note: On Friday, March 31, 1848, in Hydesville, New York, the sisters Margaret and Katherine Fox had the first psychic experiments in what became known as table-turning or table-tipping, initiating a modern phase of human paranormality. On their own, the two girls developed a system of communication with the "rapping force" consisting of raps and snaps. The phenomena became popular in the United States very quickly and spread to Europe. The sisters were later surrounded by controversy, seemingly because one of them confessed, under pressure, to having committed fraud; she afterwards recanted the confession. This initial misstep did not affect the reality of the phenomena and other gifted individuals appeared in the United States and Europe, and other more sophisticated and reliable forms of communication have since evolved. The entire class of paranormal phenomena attracted considerable attention and became the subject of scientific studies by research organizations on both continents.

it met with incredulity. But so many produced the phenomenon that it soon became impossible to doubt its reality.

Now, if the phenomena had been limited to the movement of inert objects, it might have been explicable in purely physical terms. We are far from knowing all the powers of nature and even from understanding all the properties of the powers we know. The benefits to humanity brought about by electricity, for instance, multiply daily—to the point where electricity seems ready to illuminate the whole field of science with a new and extraordinary light. Hence, it appeared reasonable, on the part of many, to assume that electricity, modified by some unknown agent, was actually causing the movements in table-turning—an assumption all the more easily accepted because the intensity of the phenomena was seemingly affected by the number of persons in the room. According to this view, the human subjects formed a battery of sorts so that the larger the number of persons in the room, the more potent the "battery."

The movement of the tables was circular, which should hardly be surprising: circular movements are common in nature. Observing this, some proposed that the movement of the tables might be a reflex on a small scale of the circular path of the stars or the fortuitous effect of some hitherto unknown force similar to the one that keeps the planets in orbits.

But the movement was not always circular. It was often irregular. The table was sometimes wildly shaken, overturned, moved about in various directions. Sometimes, in defiance of the laws of physics, it rose and remained suspended in the air. Still, there was nothing here that might not be explained by the action of some unperceived physical agent; for instance, we have all seen electrical phenomena, in the form of lightning, knock down buildings, uproot trees, and hurl heavy bodies considerable distances. As for rappings and other unusual noises—if not due to the expansion of the wood that made up the table or some accidental cause, they might very well be produced by the accumulation of some mysterious form of a completely natural energy. Electricity, too, causes loud noises.

Up to this point everything might be considered as belonging to the domain of physics and physiology. And within the confines of these sciences, scholars should have considered these phenomena well worth serious study. Why didn't they? It is disturbing to acknowledge it, but the neglect of the scientific world was due to causes that only reaffirm the superficiality of the human mind. The disdain of scientists came largely from the unglamorous nature of the table itself. What power a mere name tag has in shaping our ideas of even the most serious matters. They didn't even consider that the movement under observation could be imparted to any object (not just to tables, which just happened to be the most convenient objects with which to experiment). Prejudice blinded inquiry.

Individuals too proud of their intellectual superiority were sometimes shallow enough that we can imagine a good many keen and cultivated minds considered it beneath them to take notice of what was commonly known as "the dance of tables." If the phenomenon observed by Galvani[5] had been noticed by some unschooled person and dubbed with some absurd nickname, it would probably have been consigned to the lumber-room, too, along with the divining-rod. For where is the scientist who would not have regarded it as beneath him to pay attention to "the dance of the frogs"?

However, a few individuals of enough modesty to admit that nature might have not yet revealed all her secrets, decided to investigate the matter for themselves, if only to satisfy their consciences. Unfortunately, either because their attempts at replication were not completely successful or because the phenomena did not take place at their pleasure, they arrived at negative conclusions. Despite their conclusions, the tables continued to turn. (We might say with Galileo "Nonetheless, they move!") We assert further that these occurrences have multiplied to such an extent that the phenomena have become commonplace, so that the question now is only to come up with a rational explanation for them.

Here we might ask ourselves whether the fact that these phenomena are not always reproduced in exactly the same way, and according to the wishes and requirements of the individual observer, can be reasonably regarded as an argument against them. Are there not certain electrical and chemical phenomena that are subject to the existence of special conditions? Would it be right to deny them because they do not occur when the required conditions are not present? Is it any stranger that certain conditions should have to be met for the levitation of objects? Or that a phenomenon sometimes fails to occur when the investigator insists on personally devising rules during experiments or on adopting rules from other disciplines, and yet never considers the necessity of a new way of understanding? To make sense of a new order of phenomena one needs to understand its laws clearly. Without sustained and attentive observation we can never arrive at such an understanding.

"But," it is often objected, "some of these occurrences obviously involve trickery." We might reply to this objection by asking whether the objectors are really sure that what they take for tricks are not simply an order of facts they cannot account for as yet—i.e., if they are not putting themselves in the same position as the unlearned who mistook the experiments of a learned physics professor for the sleight-of-hand of a clever conjurer. But even if we admit that trickery exists in some cases, can we

....

5 Translator's Note: Luigi Galvani (1737-1798), Italian physician and physicist, best known for the discovery of electricity and for his experiments (with frogs) that established the presence of bioelectric forces in animal tissue.

then deny the reality of all the facts? Would we discard the contributions of physics just because a few imposters call themselves physicists? Moreover, the character of the persons involved should be taken into account. What do they have to gain by staging a hoax? Would they do so simply as a joke? A joke that is played for too long becomes as dull for the joker as for the audience. And a prank carried on from one end of the Earth to the other—with the participation of scores of serious, honorable, and lucid people—would be at least as extraordinary as the phenomena in question.

IV

As we have said, if these phenomena had been limited to the movement of objects, the subject of table-turning would have remained within the domain of physical science. But this was not the case. Table-turning became the forerunner of events still more extraordinary. It was soon found that the movement of inert objects was not the product of blind mechanical force. The force gave, rather, every evidence of having an intelligent source. This discovery opened up a new field of observation and promised solutions to many fundamental questions. From the primary question—Is this force generated by an intelligent power?—came a number of secondary ones: If such a power exists, what is it? What is its nature? What is its origin? Is it superhuman?

Yes-No answers to questions were the earliest intimations of an intelligent force. At first the "table" interacted with the participants by knocking one leg on the floor according to a pre-set code. But even here, we must confess, there was nothing very convincing, since skeptics could always object that the answers were produced by accidental movements. Fuller replies were soon forthcoming. The "table leg" in motion started striking a succession of blows that corresponded to the number of each letter in the alphabet. Questions were answered in words and sentences, and the precision of the answers caused astonishment. Questioned about its nature, the mysterious force declared itself to be a "spirit." Further, it gave itself a name and disclosed various details about itself. This was an important and noteworthy circumstance, since no one had ever suggested that spirits might be behind the phenomena. In scientific research, hypotheses are usually established to frame the argument the researcher will prove or disprove. This was not the case in this instance. The idea was proposed by the force itself.

Since the method of alphabet communication proved tedious and inconvenient, the invisible agent suggested another (again, a point worth noting). It proposed that a pencil should be fitted to a small basket. This basket, placed on a sheet of paper, was then to be set in motion by the same invisible force that moved the tables. The pencil would trace letters that formed words, sentences, and entire discourses on philosophy, ethics, metaphysics, and psychology, writing as quickly as the human hand.

The same recommendation was made simultaneously in America, France, and several other countries. In Paris, on June 10, 1853, it was made, in the following terms, to one of the most fervent supporters of such experiments: "Fetch the little basket from the next room, fasten a pencil to it, place it upon a sheet of paper, and put your fingers on the edge of the basket." When this was done, the basket began to move a few moments afterwards, and the pencil wrote this quite legible sentence: "I expressly forbid your repeating to anyone what I have just told you. The next time I write, I shall do it better."

The real benefit of this device was its convenience; the form it took was only incidental. Shortly afterwards, a similar contraption that made use of a small board, a planchette, was widely adopted in place of the basket. In either case, the object moves under the influence of certain persons gifted with a special power who act as intermediaries between spirits and humans. These persons are called mediums. Although we know little at this point about the origin of their gift, we have learned that its intrinsic qualities are modulated by certain physical and mental factors operating in the medium. Furthermore, these qualities are independent of age, gender, or even the degree of schooling. The gift may also be developed simply through exercising it.

V

The basket and planchette, it was soon realized, were just extensions of the hand. Taking the pencil, the medium's hand was compelled to write feverishly by a power independent of his or her will. Through this method, communication became easier and more complete, so that it is now the one most frequently used. The number of persons who have demonstrated this gift is considerable, and it constantly increases. At the same time, experience has gradually revealed other psychic means of communication involving speaking, hearing, seeing, touching, and even direct writing by the spirits themselves, i.e., without the conscious help of the medium's hand or pencil.

The essential points remaining to investigators were the nature of the medium's intervention and his or her influence, both mental and physical, in obtaining the replies.

Two factors help clarify these points. First, the manner in which the basket moves under the influence of the medium, who merely lays his or her fingers on the edges, shows how impossible it would be to guide the basket in any direction. This becomes even more evident when two or three persons place their fingers on the basket at the same time. If no single intelligence were guiding the basket, the production of a single, coherent reply would require a truly phenomenal coordination of movements and thoughts among these persons. In addition, the writing often changes completely, depending on the communicating spirit; whenever a certain spirit replies, it usually does so in a distinctive style. In short, in the absence of an exterior intelligence, the medium would not only have to train him or herself in different handwritings but also to remember the particular writing of each spirit.

Second, answers were often obtained to questions on philosophical or scientific matters beyond the intellect and training of the medium. Indeed, in many cases the medium was not even aware of the content of the message he or she received. Or the question was proposed in a foreign language unknown to the medium, or only formulated mentally. In other instances short tracts were written spontaneously on matters about which the medium had no awareness.

The messages transmitted in this way are on occasion marked by such discernment and depth, and convey thoughts so lofty and sublime, that we can only conclude that they emanate from a superior intelligence imbued with the highest moral values. At other times the replies are so frivolous and trivial that we cannot suppose them to come from the same source. Such diversity in the answers can only be explained as a diversity among the spirits themselves. We must also ask whether these spirits belong to the human realm or if they are beyond the pale of humanity. A more thorough examination of this question, given by the spirits themselves, is found in the present work; but we will address it briefly here.

Although these phenomena are outside the usual parameters of our observation, none of them occur mysteriously. They take place, rather, in broad daylight. Furthermore, they are not limited in their manifestation to the productions of a single individual; tens of thousands of persons experience them every day, so that anyone can determine their reality. Such effects must necessarily have a cause. And since the invisible cause displays intelligence and will beyond the known abilities of the medium, the phenomena must come from beyond the physical domain.

Many theories have been introduced concerning this subject. We will examine here the most prominent of these and evaluate the extent to which they account for all the facts. Our requisite assumption throughout is that non-physical beings exist—a proposition, made by the intelligences themselves, with which we have tried to bring our arguments into accord.

VI

The beings call themselves "spirits." In many cases they indicate that they were once human beings and lived on Earth. According to them, they constitute the spiritual world—as we, during our life on Earth, constitute the physical world.

In order to address the most common objections, we will now briefly sum up the most important points of the doctrine they have transmitted.

- God is eternal, immutable, immaterial, unique, all-powerful, sovereignly just and good.

- God created the universe, which comprehends all beings, animate and inanimate, material and immaterial.

- Physical beings constitute the visible or incarnate world; non-physical beings constitute the invisible or spiritual world, i.e., the spirit-world.

- The spirit-world is the normal, original, eternal world; it is pre-existent to and survives everything else.

- The physical world is secondary. It could cease to exist, or even never have existed at all, and not affect the essence of the spirit-world.

- Spirits temporarily assume a perishable physical body, the death of which restores them to liberty.

- Among the different kinds of physical beings on Earth, God has chosen the human species for the incarnation of spirits who have arrived at a certain degree of development. This characteristic gives the human species a moral and intellectual superiority over other living species.

- The soul is an incarnate spirit, the body its material envelope.

- Human beings consist of the following: (1) a body, or physical being, similar to that belonging to animals and animated by the same vital principle; (2) a soul, an immaterial spirit incarnated in the body; (3) an intermediate link which unites the soul and body.

- Human beings have two natures: animal and spiritual. Through the body, humans participate in the nature of animals, with which they share instincts. Through the soul, they participate in the nature of the spirits.

- A link, known as the perispirit (or spiritual body), unites the body and the spirit. It is a semi-material envelope, as opposed to the fully material envelope of the body. At death, the spirit sheds the physical body, the grosser of the two, but preserves the perispirit, the spiritual body. The perispirit constitutes an ethereal body that the spirit can render visible, or even tangible, as in the case of spirit-sightings.

- A spirit is not, therefore, an abstract being, a concept of thought. Rather, it is a real and well-defined entity that, in certain situations, can be perceived by sight, hearing, and touch.

- Spirits belong to different orders; they are not equals either in power, intelligence, knowledge, or moral excellence. Those in the highest order are distinguished by purity, knowledge, and love of good-ness—they are often called "angels" or "pure spirits." The others are relatively more distant from this perfection. Those in the lower orders are inclined to most of our human passions (hate, envy, jealousy, pride, etc.) and may still take pleasure in wrong-doing. Among them are those who are neither very good nor very bad, but have frivolous, mischievous or irksome natures. These might be classed as giddy and foolish spirits.

- Spirits do not belong perpetually to the same order. They are destined to attain perfection and, as they do so, progress up through the dif-ferent orders. This advancement is achieved through incarnations, which are undertaken either as special missions or as trials leading to purification. Physical life is an experience spirits must undergo many times before reaching this goal. These lives can be understood as cleansing exercises from each of which spirits generally emerge in a more purified state.

- On leaving the body, the soul returns to the spirit-world, where it exists as a free spirit (i.e., free from the limitations of the physical world) and where it will stay for an indeterminate time until it enters a new incarnation.[6]

....

6 *There is a fundamental difference between this view of reincarnation and the notion of metempsychosis, the belief held by certain groups that allows for human souls to incarnate in the bodies of animals. (See questions 611 - 613 for a more detailed discussion of the distinction between these two notions.)*

- Spirits have many incarnations. From this we can conclude that we have all had many existences, and will have many others on Earth and elsewhere.

- The incarnation of spirits only takes place in human beings. Spirits do not incarnate in animal form.

- The chain of incarnations is always progressive. The spirit's speed of progress depends on its efforts, but it cannot regress.

- The qualities of the person are a reflection of the incarnate spirit's. Consequently, a good person is the incarnation of a good spirit, and a bad person of a less advanced one.

- The soul possesses its individuality before incarnating and will preserve it after the death of the body.

- On returning to the spirit-world, the spirit meets those it has known on Earth. In addition, it gradually recalls the actions, both good and harmful, of its former lives.

- An incarnate spirit is under the influence of matter. Those who surmount this influence through inner transformation raise themselves nearer to the higher spheres. Those who give in to instinctual tendencies and pursue solely the gratification of physical desires are closer to the inferior realm.

- Incarnated spirits live on different worlds throughout the universe.

- Free (or discarnate) spirits do not occupy a circumscribed space. They are everywhere, and both perceive and regularly associate with human beings. They constitute an invisible but active society that constantly interacts with our own.

- Spirits constantly exert an influence on both the physical and mental environments of the Earth. They constitute one of the powers of nature, since they can act equally upon matter and thought. They are the cause of many sorts of previously unexplained or misinterpreted phenomena, which now find a compelling rationale in the Spiritist Doctrine.

- Spirits constantly interrelate with human beings. The good ones inspire people to take the high road, sustain them through trials, and instill in them courage and acceptance. The less advanced ones inculcate sordid ideas and depressiing thoughts. They take pleasure in our troubles and strive to make us like themselves.

- Spirit interactions with human beings can be either subtle or direct. The subtle communications happen without our awareness, generally in the form of inspiration. We need to exercise discernment, however, in distinguishing between the uplifting and the malevolent kinds. Direct exchanges occur through writing, speech, and other physical manifestations, usually with the intervention of a medium who acts as a link between the two worlds.

- Spirits communicate either spontaneously or when called forth by those on the physical plane. Generally speaking, it is possible to evoke all free intelligences—from the most obscure to the most illustrious, from loved ones to enemies—regardless of the epoch in which they lived. If permitted, they may share information about their new situation, their thoughts regarding us, and any insights they feel like imparting.

- Spirits move by laws of affinity. It is the similarity of values that attracts them to an assembly. Advanced spirits take pleasure in assemblies with serious purpose, wherein members are animated by love and a sincere desire to learn and progress. Their presence repels less advanced spirits. The latter, in turn, find themselves at ease among frivolous minds who come together solely out of curiosity or other harmful motives. In such assemblies nothing useful is produced. The spirits' suggestions are trifling, ill-natured, and deceptive. To make matters worse, they often borrow venerated names to impose their ideas more effectively.

- It is easy to distinguish between advanced and less advanced spirits. The language of higher spirits is dignified, high-minded, and free from every trace of human passion. Their counsels breathe wisdom. Their aim is always the advancement of humanity. On the other hand, remarks by less advanced spirits make use of commonplace, sometimes coarse, language and often contain substantial inconsistencies. Although they sometimes make true and worthwhile statements, their observations are usually ethically flawed and full of false arguments. They play upon the naiveté of their audience by feeding false hopes and swelling their listeners' egos. Obviously, enlightening communications can only be obtained in assemblies of a serious character where participants are united in thought and desire by the pursuit of love and truth.

- The ethics of the higher spirits may be summed up in the words of Christ: "Do to others what you would have them do to you."[7] In brief, do good to all and wrong no one. This principle of action furnishes humanity with a rule of conduct that has universal application, from the most trivial to the most critical matters.

- Enlightened intelligences teach that self-centeredness, pride, and exaggerated sensuality keep human beings engrossed in their animal natures. Accordingly, the person who detaches him or herself from worldly things and who practices "love thy neighbor" grows more spiritual. The spirits advise that we always serve others, as our means allow us, and that the strong and powerful owe assistance and protection to the weak. They caution that the person who misuses power to oppress fellow beings violates the laws of God. They also teach that in the spirit-world nothing can be hidden; that the hypocrite is unmasked and all wrong-doing revealed; that the unavoidable presence of those we have wronged on Earth is one of the trials we must face in the spirit-world; and that the moral state of spirits, depending on how advanced or unadvanced they are, gives rise in that world to enjoyments or suffering and regrets.

- Further, they teach that there are no unpardonable faults and that there is no misdeed that cannot be redressed. Men and women find the means of redemption and progress through reincarnation. Their desire and effort set the pace of their advancement toward the ultimate aim of all—perfection.

This is the essence of the Spiritist Doctrine, as contained in the teachings of spirits of high order. Let us now consider the objections to this doctrine.

VII

Many persons regard the scholarly world's opposition to the Spiritist Doctrine, if not as proof, then at least as a very strong implication of its falsehood. As much as we might esteem these scholars and value their judgment, however, we cannot consider their opinion final and conclusive in all matters.

In the physical sciences, when theories are proposed to explain an observed phenomenon, it is not uncommon to see strong debates among

....

7 Translator's Note: Matthew 7:12

scientists defending different explanations. In defense of their position they fight with might and main. As a result, we see the most conflicting theories brought forward and rejected every day—at one moment cried up as incontestable truths, at the next cried down as absurd errors. But in the end the sole criteria of reality are facts; they are arguments that admit of no reply. In the absence of facts, the sensible person suspends judgment.

In regard to fully researched questions, the verdict of scientists is authoritative, since their knowledge is unquestionably more complete than that of others. But where new phenomena—matters beyond their field—are concerned, their opinions can only be speculative and may be no better than anyone else's. Indeed, scientists may even be more prejudiced than the rest of us because they generally explain things only from the perspective of their particular areas of expertise. Thus, the mathematician admits nothing but mathematical proofs, the chemist considers only demonstrations of the actions of elements, and so forth. In this way, thinkers who háve developed a narrow specialization often reason falsely on matters beyond their specialty. While we can, then, confidently consult a chemist about questions of chemical analysis, a physicist about electricity, a mechanical engineer about hydraulic power, and show a proper respect for their knowledge, we should attach no more weight to their unfavorable opinion of the Spiritist Doctrine than we would to the judgment of an architect on a question concerning musical theory.

The physical sciences are based on the properties of matter, which can be manipulated through controlled experiments at the will of the researcher. The class of paranormal phenomena the Spiritist Doctrine concerns itself with, on the other hand, occurs through the action of intelligences who have a will of their own and are not subject to anyone. Systematic observation cannot, therefore, be conducted as it is in the physical sciences. To insist on using similar methods of investigation is to assume the existence of analogies that do not exist. Research into paranormal phenomena requires special conditions and methods. Science as it currently exists cannot, then, determine the truth or falsehood of the Doctrine. Its positive or negative assessment of the Spiritist Doctrine carries little weight. Of course, Spiritist belief may be a conviction held by individual scientists. But submitting the Spiritist Doctrine to the judgment of physical science would be similar to inviting a team of physicists and astronomers to produce a definitive ruling on the question of the existence of the soul. In a fundamental sense, the Doctrine deals with the existence of the soul and its state after death. To assume that a renowned mathematician or pathologist is necessarily an expert in this realm is simply unreasonable. Because the pathologist does not find the soul or see it evaporate during a dissection, it does not follow that his or her views on immortality are more valid than anyone else's. It is in light of this fact that we argue that the task of deciding the truth or falsehood of the Doctrine is not within the scope of physical science. As with all new ideas that have encountered scorn and opposition before becoming widely accepted, Spiritist principles will grow in acceptance until the scientific community ends up yielding to the force of evidence. Until then, it is premature to turn scientists away from their specialized investigations and occupy their minds with matters foreign to their way of thinking and areas of expertise. Meanwhile, those who express negative views without a careful investigation of the issues, and who ridicule those persons who do not think as they do, forget that nearly all great human discoveries have met the same obstacles. Indeed, they run the risk of having their names added to the list of the misinformed enemies of new ideas, of being classed with the members of that scientific community which, in 1752, received Benjamin Franklin's paper on lightning-rods with peals of laughter, voting it unworthy of mention in the proceedings. Or with those of the French Academy, whose members declared Robert Fulton's[8] project on steam shipping impracticable, effectively denying France leadership in this new field. These blunders came about even though the matters under discussion were strictly within the area of the scientists' competence. Thus, when we read of eminent scientists treating these discoveries contemptuously, and when we find that within a few years the same discoveries revolutionizing science, industry, and daily life, can we hope that a question entirely foreign to the work of similar thinkers today would meet with any more favor at their hands?

The scientists' judgment against the Spiritist Doctrine, though incorrect and certainly regrettable, does not of course invalidate their other contributions. But is common sense always associated with a diploma? Are there only incompetents and simpletons outside the walls of scientific institutions? Let our opponents glance over the ranks of the supporters of the Spiritist idea. Let them see whether these ranks contain only persons of mediocre intelligence, and whether the character and education of its adherents do not require us to say, "When such persons profess a view, there must be something in it."

We repeat that, if the facts we are considering had been limited to the movement of material bodies, physical science would have been competent to research its causes. The facts, however, are beyond known laws and necessarily beyond the expertise of physical science. When the facts are novel and not within the scope of any known science, a scientist who wishes to study them productively must leave aside all ingrained preju-

....

8 *Translator's Note: Robert Fulton (1765-1815), American inventor of the steam boat. In this paragraph, Allan Kardec also mentions Benjamin Franklin, whose life and main contributions are summarized in the Biographical Appendix at the end of the book.*

dices and conventional models of thinking.

Obviously the person who considers his or her reason infallible is very mistaken—just as mistaken as persons who claim that reason supports their wildest ideas and who, in the name of reason, reject anything that appears impossible to them. Not surprisingly, those who spurned many of the great human discoveries did so in the name of reason. Often, too, what a person calls reason is only pride in disguise. And isn't the claim of infallibility akin, really, to declaring oneself the equal of God? We address ourselves, therefore, to those who are reasonable enough to suspend judgment until they have sufficient exposure to the facts and who believe that humanity has not reached the pinnacle of knowledge or that nature has not turned over to human inspection the last leaf in her book.

VIII

The study of a philosophy such as the Spiritist Doctrine, which introduces such novel ideas, can only be fruitfully pursued by persons of serious mind—persevering, free from prejudice, and sincerely committed to the truth. In this category, we cannot include individuals who have formed a prior opinion of the subject and failed to give it an exhaustive examination. We cannot include, either, those who have brought to the investigation neither the method nor the necessary discipline to do it justice. Still less can we place in the catagory of serious mind those who, interested only in building up a reputation for wit, ridicule matters of serious import. Let those who consider these facts unworthy of their attention abstain from dealing with them; no one will interfere with their choice. But let them likewise respect the beliefs and preferences of those who think otherwise.

As we have said, method and perseverance are characteristics of serious inquiry. Is it strange, then, that we do not always get sensible answers from spirits when we intersperse serious questions with many trivial and foolish ones? Complex explanations must sometimes be preceded or followed by a series of logical considerations, since the discussion of a scientific matter requires sufficient background information. When an untrained individual, lacking the elementary facts in a field of study, questions a scholar in that field, can the scholar ever give him or her a satisfactory answer? Under such conditions, any particular answer the scholar gives will either be incomplete or sound unintelligible. To an extent, this is exactly what happens in our relationship with the advanced spirits. If we want to learn from them, we should go through a complete course of study with them. Moreover, as in our earthly endeavors, we must choose our teachers wisely and study with diligence.

We have said that advanced spirits are attracted to gatherings in which they find harmony, lofty ideals, and high moral principles. On the other hand, frivolity and idle curiosity repel them. When these attitudes are in evidence, the path is open to unaware and mischievous spirits who are always looking for ways to entertain themselves. What becomes of any serious question in such a gathering? It will certainly find responses, but by whom? It is just as though, in the midst of a dinner party, one should suddenly propound such questions as "What is the atom? What is light?" or others equally out of place. To obtain sound answers, we must approach the investigation with diligence and put ourselves in the frame of mind required for accurate observation. We must be industrious and persevering in the work, seeking by our right attitudes to preserve the support of enlightened beings. Otherwise, they may stop troubling themselves about us, as a professor stops concerning him or herself with the idle members of a class.

IX

The movement of material bodies is a demonstrated fact. The only remaining questions are whether the movement is produced by an intelligent force and, if so, what the origin of that force might be. We are not speaking here of the intelligence displayed in the movement of certain objects, in verbal communications, or even in psychic messages handwritten by a medium. These phenomena, the spirit-origin of which is evident to anyone who has studied the matter seriously, are not at first sight sufficiently independent of the will of the medium to bring conviction to the new observer. Therefore, we address now only messages obtained with the aid of a pencil attached to an object, e.g., a small basket, a planchette, etc. In this kind of experiment, the fingers of the medium touch the edges of the object so lightly as to prevent any attempt to influence the tracing of letters. Let us suppose, however, that by some wonderful bit of chicanery, the medium succeeds in fooling even the most observant eye. Even then, how can the nature of the replies be explained, since they are completely beyond the scope of the medium's knowledge and ideas? And these replies are not monosyllabic either; rather, they are sometimes long essays dashed off with astonishing speed. Sometimes, they regard specific subjects or a topic chosen by the spirit. At other times, they are poems of great character and refined style, produced sometimes by the hand of an illiterate medium. Even stranger, these phenomena are occurring all over the world as the number of mediums constantly increases. Are these facts real or not? To this query we can only reply: "See for yourselves—opportunities are not lacking. But give yourself enough time and be willing to adapt to the conditions required for serious investigation."

To the evidence we produce, our opponents will often object "You are being fooled by charlatans; it's nothing but an illusion." In reply, it must first be noted that, where there is no profit to be made, deceit is unlikely; charlatans do not stage their acts for free. If there is deceit then, might not these effects be created for the sake of a joke? But it defies reason to suppose that a conspiracy could exist among jokers all over the world and that the conspirators would agree to produce similar phenomena and give, on the same subjects, remarkably similar replies. Second, why would honorable and educated persons bother with such trifling matters—and to what end? And how is it that the ability to deceive in ways so complex can be found even among children? Third and finally, this hypothesis, if true, would require that a medium combine the highest erudition with a complete mastery of illusion—demands totally at odds with the age, education, and social position of most of them.

"But if there is no trickery involved," the critics argue "both parties—medium and observers—have to be the dupes of an illusion." In this case we reply by asking whether the character of the witnesses should not be considered of value in determining the strength of the evidence. We might ask whether the adherents of Spiritist philosophy, several millions by now, come only from among the uneducated and undiscerning. Unquestionably, these phenomena are so extraordinary that doubt is legitimate. However, what we can hardly accept is the pretense of certain critics to a monopoly on common sense, and the arrogance with which the same critics charge anyone of a different, regardless of their ethical character, opinion with being deluded or stupid. The fact that honorable and highly accomplished individuals, after extensive inquiry, have come forth in defense of the new ideas, makes those ideas at least a distinct possibility.

X

Among the objections brought forward, some deserve special consideration because they are based on a more serious analysis of the issues.

One of these objections states that the language of spirits does not always seem worthy of the elevation we attribute to beings beyond the pale of humanity. As a matter of fact, the spirits themselves have informed us that they are not all equal, either in knowledge or moral values, and that not all spirit accounts are to be taken at face value. Unfortunately, some people have been exposed only to the worst side of the spirit-world. If they had had acquaintance with gatherings patronized by illuminated spirits, they would not hold such views. We do not mean to imply that such people attract materialistic and deceitful spirits as the result of possessing similar faults themselves. But it is possible that, in some cases, the inquirers may not be so principled that they can repel negative thoughts easily and that, taking advantage of their curiosity, imperfect spirits use this weakness to approach them.

In any case, we cannot reasonably conclude anything about spirits based on exchanges like these—any more, for instance, than we can validly assess the character of a people by the language and actions of a gang of toughs, which most of the society tries to avoid. Persons who make this objection are like the traveler who enters a great capital by one of its worst suburbs and proceeds to judge the entire citizenry by the residents of that one quarter. In the non-physical, as well as in the physical world, there are higher and lower classes of people. Let critics make a study of what goes on among spirits of the higher orders; they will soon be convinced that the celestial realm is not peopled solely by unaware and malicious spirits. "But" someone will ask, "do spirits of high degree really come to us?" To which we reply, "Don't stay in the suburbs. See, examine, judge. The facts are within easy reach of anyone, including those described by Jesus as having eyes but not seeing, having ears but not hearing." [9]

A variant of this objection consists in attributing all spirit communications and unusual physical phenomena to the intervention of some diabolical power—some new Proteus that will assume any and every form in order to deceive us. Without pausing for a more extensive discussion, we will remark that, if this were the case, it has to be admitted that either the devil is sometimes very wise, reasonable and morally good, or that there are good devils as well as bad ones.

But is it likely that God would allow only the spirits of wrong-doing to carry on their harmful actions without giving human beings the counsel of good spirits to counter-balance them? To argue that God cannot do it is to limit Divine power; to agree that God could do it but will not is incompatible with God's perfect goodness. Both contentions are equally irreverent. Once the communication of wrong-doing spirits is admitted as a possibility, though, it implicitly affirms the plausibility of spirit communications. If spirit communication does take place, it can only be with the permission of God. Why, then, would it occur only for harmful reasons, to the exclusion of all uplifting possibilities? Such a position is indefensible whether the appeal is to the simplest dictates of religion or to common sense.

XI

Another suspicious feature, the critics say, is that only the spirits of well-known persons come through in communications. Why should they

....

9 *Translator's Note: Matthew 13:13-17.*

Explanatory Notes

be the only ones? This query is due to a mistake in observation. Among the spirits who present themselves to us spontaneously, most are unknown. Still, with the exception of loved ones, the spirits we evoke naturally come from among the Earth's acclaimed and celebrated ones, since the lives of these individuals have had a great impact on us and since their names are familiar.

But, the critics counter, why should such eminent personalities respond to our call? Why should they bother themselves with things that, compared to the things that occupied them in their previous lives on Earth, are insignificant? Actually, there is nothing surprising here: the power and consideration an individual may have possessed in this life guarantee no privilege in the spirit-world. The spirits have confirmed the Gospel passage "the last will be first, and the first will be last"[10] as it concerns rank in the spirit-world. Someone who was first on earth may be one of the last in the next world. The person before whom everyone bowed during one life may find him or herself beneath the humblest artisan in the next. The most powerful leaders, in fact, may be lower than the lowest of their subjects.

XII

One observable fact, confirmed by the spirits themselves, is the practice adopted by less advanced spirits of borrowing illustrious names. How can we be sure, then, that a spirit claiming to be Socrates, Julius Caesar, Charlemagne, Fénélon, Napoleon, or Washington,[11] is really that individual? This issue naturally concerns Spiritists. Where psychic communication is admitted, the seeker cannot help looking for some certainty of a spirit's true identity. The claim of identity cannot, of course, be settled with the certainty of a publicly notarized document. But it may at least be established presumptively through many other indicators. Complete certainty is difficult to obtain in any matter.

In any case, when a psychically manifested spirit is that of someone known to us—a relative or friend—and especially when it has only recently departed from the physical realm, we find that its language is

....

10 *Translator's Note: Matthew 20:16*

....

11 *Translator's Note: Julius Caesar (c.100-44BC), Roman general and statesman; Charlemagne (768-814), also called Charles the Great or Charles I, king of Franks (768-814), king of Lombards (774-814) and emperor (800-814); Napoleon Bonaparte (1769-1821), or Napoleon I, Emperor of the French; George Washington (1732-1799), American general, first president of the United States. See the Biographical Appendix for entries on Socrates and Fénélon.*

generally in keeping with what we know of its character. This, certainly, is a strong indicator of its identity. But the indication advances almost to the point of absolute certainty when the spirit speaks of private matters and refers to family affairs known only to the family member to whom it is responding. A son could hardly mistake the language of his father and mother, nor parents that of their child. The most striking incidents often occur in evocations of this intimate kind—things and revelations of a nature to convince the most incredulous and astound the most skeptical.

Handwriting is still another indicator in establishing identity. The handwriting of the medium generally changes as the spirit comes through, and the same writing is reproduced exactly each time a particular spirit communicates. In addition, in the case of persons recently deceased, the style often bears a striking resemblance to that of the person during life, especially the signature. This is by no means a rule, but it is a point worth noting.

Only when spirits arrive at a certain degree of purification are they entirely free from material influence. To the extent that they are not completely dematerialized (to use their own expression), they retain most of the ideas, tendencies, and even mannerisms they had on Earth. Systematic observation of these and other details furnish very reliable means of identification. Spirits who have been authors are seen to discuss their own works, sometimes even pointing out their flaws; others allude to various circumstances connected with their lives or deaths. Such indications give us what we must consider strong corroboration of an identity—the only one possible under such circumstances.

Although these means of identification may be less effective in the case of more distant deaths, language and character nonetheless remain valid means of determining a spirit's advancement. A good and sensible person will not express him or herself like a malicious or immature one. As for less advanced spirits who assume well-known and honorable names, the character of their language quickly betrays them. For instance, if a spirit calling itself Fénélon made remarks at variance with the highest ethical standard, the imposture would be immediately detected. On the other hand, there would be no reason to question the spirit's identity if the ideas were clearly worthy of Fénélon. Otherwise, we would be forced to admit that an advanced spirit could knowingly make false statements.

Experience shows us that spirits of the same order, character, and attitudes are united in groups or families, but their number is so large that the names of the immense majority are unknown to us. It is possible, therefore, that a spirit of the same order as Fénélon might come to us in his name or be sent by him as a representative. In addition, in order to establish a better rapport with us, the representative might even present himself as Fénélon. After all, what does it matter whether a spirit is really Fénélon, if all it says carries the same moral excellence? Names are just earthly means of identifying the origin of ideas. While names are of secondary importance in spirit communication, however, this sort of substitution would not be acceptable in evocations of a personal character. In this case, as noted above, we must use other means of verifying identity.

Unquestionably, the assumption of false names is one of the most serious difficulties experimental Spiritism faces, since it presents the potential for considerable error. Like others, this field of investigation is not exempt from obstacles. We cannot stress enough that it requires serious and persevering efforts, and as a new field of investigation, it demands long and assiduous exploration. The student, unable to produce the phenomena at will, is obliged to wait patiently until they happen. And sometimes they happen when the student least expects them. Nonetheless, the attentive and patient student can find abundant material, since he or she can discover in the facts already established thousands of particulars representing an endless source of essential reference points. It is the same in almost every other branch of science: while the superficial observer sees in a flower only an elegant form, the botanist discovers in it a mine of fact for continued study.

XIII

The foregoing remarks bring us to another difficulty—the divergence of views that exists among the spirits. Spirits differ where knowledge and moral intelligence are concerned. Consequently, reflecting their various levels of advancement, their views on the same question may be at odds with each other. The same would hold true on Earth if a question were alternatively proposed to a person of science, an uneducated peasant, and a mischievous wit. The important point, as we previously remarked, is to know to whom the question is being addressed.

But, it can be argued, why don't spirits that allegedly belong to a higher order all hold the same view? We reply that there are innumerable causes that influence the nature of the replies, irrespective of the quality of the spirits themselves. This is a point of the highest importance, and it requires continuous study. That is why we reiterate the need for unwavering attention, in-depth observation, and perseverance. Years of study are required to make even a second-rate physician. Three-quarters of a lifetime can go into the making of a scholar. Yet people fancy that a few hours will suffice to acquire knowledge of the Infinite! Let there be no mistake regarding this matter. The subject of the Spiritist Doctrine is immense. It is a new world opening before us, and it involves all other fields—physical, metaphysical, and social. Should we be surprised by the fact that time, and a good deal of it, is needed to develop a sound acquaintance with its principles?

The contradictions in spirits' replies are not always as absolute as they may seem at first glance. We frequently see scientists give different definitions of the same thing. Their fundamental idea may be the same, but the use of different terms and alternate methodologies generate diverse perspectives on the subject. Let any one count up, for instance, the numerous definitions that have been given of "grammar"! We should also remember that the form of an answer often depends on the way in which the question was framed. We would be naive, then, to regard as a contradiction what is often only a semantic difference. The thought is everything for evolved spirits; they pay no attention to forms of expression.

Let us take, for example, the definition of soul. Since the word "soul" has no fixed and definitive meaning, both humans and spirits use it in a variety of contexts. One will say that the soul is "the principle of life," another will call it the "spiritual spark," a third will argue that the soul is within us, while a fourth will contend that it is outside, etc. And each may be right from his or her own point of view. It is the same regarding the word "God." According to some, God is "the principle of all things," according to others, "the creator of the universe," "the sovereign intelligence," "the Infinite," "the great Spirit," etc. All these terms indicate God, even if they do not define "God." Yet God is always God. This has happened, too, with the classification of spirits. Since spirits constitute a continuous progression from the lowest to the highest, all classification attempts are naturally arbitrary. We can view them, without being in error, as making up three, five, ten or twenty classes. In establishing a classification system, every field of science encounters similar variations in detail and difficulty in structure. But, while every researcher seems to adopt a different system, and their systems constantly change, science remains the same. Whether we study botany according to the system of Linnaeus, Jusseau or Tournefort, what we learn is nonetheless botany. Let us stop overestimating, then, the importance of matters of convention and devote ourselves to truly important things. By so doing, we will often discover, on reflection, similarities of meaning in statements that first appeared hopelessly mired in contradiction.

XIV

We would pass over the objection of certain critics concerning the faulty spelling of some spirits, except that it affords us the opportunity to call attention to a point of great significance. Though the spirits' orthography is not always flawless, a critic must be very short of arguments to present it as a serious hurdle to belief that, "since spirits know everything, they ought to be well up in spelling." We might retort by pointing to the numerous grammatical errors committed by scientific luminaries, although these in no way detract from their authority. A more important issue stems from the facts to which we have already alluded. For spirits, especially advanced ones, the idea is everything, the form nothing. Moreover, spirits communicate by thought, which no sooner exists than it is transmitted instantaneously. Consider the difficulty this poses in communicating with us, when they must use human speech with its tedious and awkward forms. They often refer to this as an inconvenience—understandably so. We would find it so, too, if we had to speak a language in which the words and locutions were longer, and the inventory of expressions more scant. The same difficulty is felt by persons of genius, who feel impatient at the progress of the pen, which always lags behind their thoughts. It is easy to see, then, why the spirits place so little importance on grammatical proprieties. Still, they express themselves, when necessary, precisely and according to the accepted forms of all languages—as, for instance, when dictating poems, their writing is of a correctness and elegance that defy the severest criticism, despite the fact that the medium might be ignorant of literary matters.

XV

Some people see danger in everything that is new to them. And more than one has drawn a negative conclusion about the Spiritist Doctrine from the fact that a few adherents, from among hundreds of thousands, have showed symptoms of mental instability. In fact, these supposedly sensible people have, with no proof whatever, pronounced instability to be a particular hazard of Spiritism. Mentally frail people, however, fall into instability when they give themselves to any intense endeavor. Who can say how many mathematicians, medical researchers, musicians, philosophers, etc., developed manias that led to mental illnesses? But what does this prove? Should those disciplines be banned?

To make use of a simple analogy, strenuous physical activity may place excessive demand on a frail person and, for instance, lead to bodily injuries. Now, just as the body is the means for physical activity, the brain provides the incarnate spirit with the means for intellectual pursuits. Therefore, intense mental activity of any kind may occasionally adversely affect mental instability. In any case it is only the body that is affected, not the spirit. Once free from its defective physical envelope, the spirit regains full control over its faculties. This is what happens when an incarnate spirit takes on more than its physical body is equipped for.

Mental illnesses have traumatized people in science, art, religion, and all walks of life. Likely, the problem has its roots in a predisposition that leads the individual to pursue a certain interest with fanatic zeal. In the case of those who have embraced the Spiritist Doctrine, the person's thought will naturally turn on spirits and spirit-life—just as, in other areas, thoughts may fix on angels, devils, God, wealth, power, the arts, a scientific subject, or a social theory. In other instances mental illness may be triggered from seemingly innocuous events such as childbirth, a stressful social environment, etc. Thus persons who are obsessed with religious ideas could go mad on the subject of Spiritism if that's where their minds have chosen to focus. Someone whose mental imbalance was apparently set off by the study of Spiritism would, under other circumstances, lose his or her sanity over something else. The point is that a person with such a predisposition is no more likely to become obsessed with Spiritism than with any other subject.

Indeed, when correctly understood, the Spiritist Doctrine may be a protection against insanity. Among the most common causes of mental distress can be counted frustrations, misfortunes, blighted affections, and the many anxieties of human existence, which are the frequent causes of suicide. But a true Spiritist sees the things of this life from a point of view so elevated that they seem petty and immaterial in light of the future. Life appears so short and fleeting that its tribulations are, in the Spiritist's eyes, merely the unpleasant incidents of a journey. Events that induce violent emotions in the mind of others affect the Spiritist only slightly. The sorrows of life are, the Spiritist knows, trials that will aid his or her advancement if borne willingly and will end in reward depending on one's fortitude. The Spiritist's convictions are a source of strength, a guarantor against despair, mental illness, and even suicide. Moreover, through psychic communications, the Spiritist becomes aware of the implications of suicide—knowledge that leads to serious reflection and that has stopped many who were on a downward spiral leading to self-destruction. This is one of the more positive results of Spiritist Doctrine. The incredulous may laugh. We only wish they could experience the same consolation the Doctrine has afforded us, who have sounded its depths.

Fear is also a potent cause of mental illness. Dread of the devil, for instance, has deranged many a mind. Untold numbers have fallen victim to the hideous images and illusory power of Satan. It is sometimes said that tales of the devil, like werewolf and bogeyman tales, are only used to frighten little children, to make them docile and well-behaved. But when the horrible images lose their grip on the imagination, the child's behavior may be even worse. There is still another possibility that the advocates of such methods apparently overlook: the danger of damage to the child's delicate psyche. Religion would be weak indeed if its power could only be sustained by fear. Fortunately, this is not the case. The Spiritist Doctrine has come to furnish religion with a more efficient basis than superstitious terror. It unveils a more logical reality and substitutes a healthy appreciation of the consequences of wrong-doing for the vague apprehensions of an induced and totally baseless fright.

XVI

Two objections remain to be examined. These are founded on stronger rational grounds than the above and so deserve more particular answers. Both objections begin by admitting the reality of paranormal phenomena. Both deny that the intervention of spirits produces these phenomena.

The first proposes that phenomena that are commonly attributed to the action of spirits are really produced through self-hypnosis. According to this theory, mediums go into a hypnotic or trance state that is analogous to a state of lucid somnambulism—a phenomenon frequently observed in studies of human hypnotism. During the trance, the theory's proponents claim, the medium's sensory faculties expand, his or her intuitive perceptions extend beyond ordinary limits, and the ability to call up information from within the self—even information the medium does not know when awake—markedly increases. Now we would not contest here the potential of hypnotic trance. We would be the last to do so after studying it for thirty-five years; and we agree that hypnotic trance undoubtedly presents a plausible explanation for some types of psychic phenomena.[12] We contend, however, that in many instances, any intervention of the medium, other than as a passive instrument, is absolutely impossible. Investigation has proven this to be the case; and we say, to those who attribute the phenomena to hypnotism, "Observe and investigate—you have certainly not seen everything." In addition, we must offer a few interesting points for these critics to ponder. First, where does the hypothesis of spirit-generated action come from? Is it an explanation invented by a few individuals to account for those phenomena? No, not at all. Who, then, brought it up? The very mediums whose awareness the critics extol! But if their awareness is so acute, why should mediums attribute to spirits what they have derived from themselves? Furthermore, how could mediums give information about the nature of extra-human intelligences

....

12 *Translator's Note: The author used the French words for "magnetism" and "somnambulism" instead of "hypnotism" and "hypnotic trance," which is the terminology adopted in this translation. While they were perfectly adequate for the jargon of the nineteenth century, we thought Kardec's choice of words could be confusing for the contemporary reader. To be sure,* The Oxford English Dictionary *indicates that magnetism, in the sense used in this book, means "the process or practice of inducing ... a hypnotic state." (See also questions 424 - 455 for an expanded discussion of this topic.)*

with such precision and logic? Either mediums are lucid, or they are not. If they are lucid, and if we trust their veracity, we cannot suppose them to err on this point. Finally, if all phenomena had their source in the mediums themselves, the phenomena would always be identical for each individual; and the same medium would not use different styles of expression or make contradictory statements ever. The lack of unity so often observed in the communications received through the same medium proves the diversity of the sources. Since the cause of this diversity cannot be found in the medium, it must lie elsewhere.

The second objection holds that the medium is really not the source of the manifestation but, in fact, calls up information from the persons around him or her. In this view, the medium acts as a mirror reflecting the thoughts, ideas, and knowledge of others. Consequently, nothing should come through the medium which is not known to at least some of a gathering's participants. Now, the influence of other persons is a true possibility, and it is taken into consideration by the Spiritist theory. The extent of this influence, though, differs considerably from what is implied here. In fact, the evidence is heavily weighted against the notion that the medium is a mere echo of the thoughts of those in the immediate vicinity. This notion, we should state, is primarily the result of hastily arrived-at conclusions and often reflects the personal opinions of people bent on rejecting arbitrarily the notion of spirits and anything that transcends the science of the day. The theory seems appealing at first glance, but is unable to explain too many of the relevant facts. It has been shown frequently that the communications produced by the mediums are often entirely foreign to those present and sometimes even contradict prevailing ideas. Our critics are not discouraged by so slight a difficulty. The radiation of thought, they say, extends far beyond the medium's immediate circle—the medium is the reflection of the human species in general. Thus, when not deriving inspirations from those in the gathering, he or she derives them from others farther off—in another town or country, from the rest of humankind, and even from beings on other planets.

We do not think that this theory provides a simpler or more probable explanation than the Spiritist Doctrine, since it assumes the action of a cause far more incredible. In any event, the idea that universal space is peopled by beings who are in continual interaction with us is no less reasonable than the hypothesis that radiation converges from every point of the universe onto a single individual.

We repeat—and cannot insist on it too strongly—that the hypnotic trance and reflection theories were devised by human beings; the theory of spirit-agency was given by the spirits themselves. At that time no one thought of spirits as an explanation; the general opinion was clearly contrary to such a hypothesis. Hence, we ask, how did mediums, scattered the world over and unknown to each other, agree in asserting the same thing? Where did the mediums find a theory that was in no one's mind? If the first French medium was influenced by facts from America, by what strange guidance was the medium made to search for ideas, not from among his or her own acquaintance at home, but across the length of an ocean and among a foreign people speaking a different language?

There is still another circumstance that deserves attention. The earliest manifestations, in Europe as well as America, came neither through writing nor speech but through raps indicating the letters of the alphabet that were then used to form words and sentences. Through this means the causative agents declared themselves to be spirits. We admit the possibility that the medium might exert an influence in the production of verbal or written communications. But in the case of raps, this possibility is eliminated.

We might bring forward any number of facts to demonstrate the existence of an individuality and of an independent will in Spiritist phenomena. Our critics, however, must verify it for themselves, and we renew our invitation for them to observe thoroughly, without prejudice and without drawing conclusions until they have acquired an in-depth knowledge of the issues.

Concerning these two alternative theories, we would like to propose two further questions. First, why does the entity coming through the medium so often refuse to answer questions pertaining to matters that are perfectly known to the questioner—such as the questioner's name and age, what object the questioner has in his or her hand, what the questioner did yesterday, what he or she intends to do tomorrow, etc.? If the medium is simply a mirror reflecting the thoughts of people within the same circle, nothing should be more natural than to answer such questions. The critics respond to this question with another one: "How come the spirits, who should be all-knowing, allow such trivial questions to go unanswered? After all, if you know the forest well, you should also know the trees." Thus, from this presumed inability to address such simple questions, the critics conclude that the phenomenon cannot be caused by spirits. On our part, we would counter by asking whether a learned gathering would react to thoughtless questions any differently. From the gathering's derision or silence, would it be correct to conclude that its members are merely a group of morons? With their silence, the spirits are tacitly advising us to consider more serious subjects.

Second, we would like to ask why spirits come and go at their own pleasure; and why, once they have departed, neither prayers nor entreaties will bring them back. If the medium were influenced solely by the mental force of persons nearby, the focusing of the wills of those persons ought to stimulate the medium's abilities. But frequently the medium is unable to yield to their collective will. Why? It is because he or she is reacting to an influence apart from the self and apart from the other-persons present. By acting in this way, this influence clearly and emphatically asserts its own independence and individuality.

XVII

When it does not result from prejudice, the skeptic's view of the Spiritist Doctrine often has its source in a poor knowledge of the facts. Unfortunately, many well-meaning people have tried to settle the question as though they had perfect knowledge. Their excessive belief in their own infallible judgment only shows how little discernment they have. Some persons, on the other hand, have regarded spiritual communications as only a matter of intellectual curiosity. Let us hope that the reading of this book will present the former with sufficient evidences and the latter with sufficient facts that they will conclude that spirit communication is more than just a pastime.

The Spiritist Doctrine consists of two parts: the experimental, which deals with the phenomena per se; and the philosophical, which examines the intellectual content of the phenomena. Anyone who has known only the first is in a position similar to the person whose knowledge of physics is limited to a series of amusing experiments and who therefore lacks a comprehension of its scientific principles. The Spiritist philosophy consists of teachings imparted by spirits, and the knowledge conveyed is of a character far too serious to be mastered without earnest and persevering attention. These teachings should be meditated upon. Only then will the student be able to have an informed opinion and grasp innumerable nuances and facts that would otherwise go unnoticed. If this book has no other result than to show the serious nature of the subject, and to induce inquirers to approach it in the proper frame of mind, it will have justified its existence. We take no credit ourselves for this work. The principles it contains are not of our own creating; and whatever honor the book comes to deserve, the merit belongs entirely to the spirits who dictated it. We hope that the book will achieve yet another result—that of serving as a guide to those who seek enlightenment. The book shows the sublime end of individual and social progress, and points out the right road for attaining both.

Let us end these remarks with some intriguing analogies. Astronomers, sounding the depths of the sky, discovered some curious hollow spaces—spaces seemingly empty, although this conclusion did not accord with known physical laws. Accordingly, the astronomers conjectured that these spaces must be occupied by planets that had escaped their observation. When certain inexplicable physical effects came to their attention, they reasoned that a void could not exist and planets must be in that region. Reasoning from the effects to the cause, they calculated the elements of the planets whose presence they had inferred. The facts subsequently supported that inference. We can apply the same method of reasoning to this new order of ideas. If we observe natural forms, we find that they make up a continuous chain from crude matter to human beings. But between humans and God, who is the alpha and omega of all things, what an immense hiatus exists! Is it reasonable to suppose that the links of the chain stop with us and that we can vault over the distance that separates us from the Infinite Perfection? Reason suggests that, between God and ourselves, there must be other links—just as reason showed the astronomers that between the planets known to them were others that must exist, although they were imperceptible. The Spiritist Doctrine fills this hiatus. It shows us that all things are linked together from one end of the chain to the other; that beings, existing on an infinite number of levels, fill the void between God and ourselves; and that these beings are spirits like ourselves, each at a different point on the path of progress. Let those who deny the existence of spirits propose a better purpose for the endless universe. Let those who scoff at the idea of spirit-teachings devise a nobler plan than the one the spirits present of God's handiwork—one that presents a more convincing demonstration of the Divine wisdom and goodness.

ALLAN KARDEC

PART I
THE FIRST CAUSE

I

GOD

God and the Infinite

1. What is God?[1]

▲ *"God is the Supreme Intelligence, the First Cause of all things."*

2. How should we define Infinite?

▲ *"As that which has no beginning and no end."*

3. Can we say that God is the Infinite?

▲ *"In this case, your definition is incomplete. Unfortunately, human language is incapable of expressing ideas that transcend human intelligence."*

Discussion: In perfection God is infinite. But God is also more than the Infinite, and we make an error in logic when we equate the two. A quality possessed by a being cannot be considered identical to the being itself. Furthermore, "Infinity" is an abstraction. To define something unknown, like God, by reference to something equally unknown is, once again, to make an error in logic.

Proofs of God's Existence

4. What are the proofs of God's existence?

....

1 *Translator's Note: The quoted text that follows a question is the answer provided by the spirits. The indented "discussion" paragraphs that follow the answers are notes and explanations provided by Allan Kardec. In some instances Allan Kardec's remarks take up a full chapter or were assigned a "question" number of their own. In these cases, the comments are printed without special indentation.*

▲ *"An axiom in science states, 'There is no effect without a cause.' Look for the cause of things which are not the work of human beings, and your reason will provide the answer."*

Discussion: To assure ourselves of the existence of God, we have only to look at the works of creation. The universe exists; therefore, it must have a cause. To doubt the existence of a First Cause is to deny the axiom that every effect has a cause and to assume that something can be created from nothing.

5. God's existence seems to be universally intuited. What can we conclude from this fact?

▲ *"That God exists. Ask yourself how and why the human mind would possess this intuition if it has no basis in reality. This is simply an extension of the axiom that there is no effect without a cause."*

6. Can't our intuitive sense of God's existence be explained as the result of formal education and cultural influence?

▲ *"If that is so, how does it happen that even primitive cultures possess a sense of God?"*

Discussion: If the intuition of the existence of a Supreme Being were due solely to education, this intuition wouldn't be universal; like certain scientific notions, it would be found only among those peoples who were educated to it.

7. Can we find the First Cause of things in the essential properties of matter?

▲ *"What, in that case, would be the cause of those properties? There must be a First Cause."*

Discussion: To credit the beginning of all things to the essential properties of matter is to mistake an effect for a cause, since properties are themselves effects.

8. What about the view that the creation of all things resulted from chance combinations of matter?

▲ *"Another absurdity! Can any thinking person regard chance as an intelligent agent? What is chance? Nothing."*

Discussion: The harmony that regulates the workings of the universe reveals a plan which, by its very nature, posits the existence of an Intelligent Power. Consequently, it makes no sense to attribute the origin of all things to chance. Chance cannot produce anything like the creations of intelligence. If chance had the properties of intelligence, it wouldn't be chance.

9. What proof is there that the First Cause of all things is a Supreme Intelligence, superior to all other intelligences?

▲ *"You have a proverb that says, 'The workman is known by his work.' Look at the work around you. From it alone you can assume the presence of a workman. Some people have such a high opinion of themselves that they can't grasp the simple truth in this proverb. For them, the notion of a superior being is simply inadmissible. Poor souls, who could be felled by the mere breath of God!"*

Discussion: We judge the power of an intelligence by its works. Since no human being could have created the natural environment around us, the First Cause must, therefore, be an intelligence superior to ours; and human intelligence must itself have a cause. The greatness of our intellectual achievements only emphasizes the extraordinary quality of this Cause, of which our intelligence is an effect. Whatever names we choose to give it, this Supreme Intelligence is the First Cause of all things.

Attributes of God

10. Can any individual understand the essential nature of God?

▲ *"No, human beings lack the capability for such understanding."*

11. Will we ever be able to comprehend the mystery of God?

▲ *"When human beings have advanced sufficiently—that is, when they have overcome the yoke of matter—they will be better able to comprehend God."*

Discussion: The limited nature of our human faculties prevents us from having an understanding of God's essential nature. As a result, in the early stages of human development, we often confused the Creator with the creation and attributed to the former the qualities of the latter. However, as we progress spiritually, we are able to penetrate the nature of things more deeply and form a more just and rational idea of God, though our ideas will always be incomplete.

12. If we cannot understand the essential nature of God, can we have at least some idea of God's perfections?

▲ *"Yes, some of them. You will understand them better as you raise yourself above matter, and naturally your mind will have glimpses of them."*

13. When we say that God is eternal, infinite, unchangeable, immaterial, unique, all-powerful, sovereignly just and good, aren't we expressing a complete idea of the qualities of the Divine?

▲ *"Yes, from your point of view. But don't think that you sum up everything in these terms. You must understand that there are things that transcend the capacity of even the most intelligent person and that outstrip the power of language to express. However, your reason tells you correctly that God must possess the perfections you mention in the supreme degree. Lacking one of them or having less than the absolute degree in any of them, God would be less than perfect; and in order to be above all things, to be almighty, God must have no imperfections."*

Discussion: God is infinite and eternal. If we assume a beginning to God's existence, we must mean that God either sprang from nothing or was created by some other being. Our realization that this is not true leads us to our ideas of Infinity and Eternity.

God is unchangeable. If this were otherwise, universal laws would have no stability.

God is immaterial and by nature differs from everything we call matter. Without this quality, God would not be unchangeable and would be subject to the transformations of matter.

God is unique. If there were more than one God, there would be neither unity of plan nor unity of power in the ordering of the universe.

God is all-powerful. The possession of anything less than sovereign power would indicate the existence of something more powerful than or equally powerful to God. Without sovereign power, God could not have created all things, and those things not created by one God would be the work of another God.

God is sovereignly just and good. The wisdom of the divine laws is revealed as clearly in the smallest things as in the greatest. This wisdom makes it impossible to doubt either God's justice or goodness.

Pantheism

14. Is God a being distinct from the universe or, as some people believe, the result of all the forces and intelligences of the universe?

▲ *"The latter view makes God an effect and not a cause. But, as we have stated, God is the First Cause, and it is impossible to be both cause and effect at the same time.*

"But do not doubt God's existence. This is the one essential point. To go beyond it is to lose yourselves in a maze. Nor in the end will such explorations make you better persons. They might, in fact, do harm by adding to

your pride and leading you to believe, incorrectly, that you know something others do not. Don't waste your time on these theories. You have enough to think about in the here and now, beginning with yourselves. Study your own imperfections, and try to get rid of them. This course is far more profitable than trying to penetrate the impenetrable."

15. What is your view concerning pantheism, which states that all natural bodies, beings, and planets are parts of God and, taken together, make up the essence of God.

▲ *"Humanity, unable to become God, is eager to become at least a part of God."*

16. Pantheists claim that their belief demonstrates some of God's qualities. They argue that since worlds are infinite in number, God must be infinite; and that, since empty spaces do not exist, God must be everywhere. Then they conclude that, since God is everywhere, God must be everything and thus the intelligent cause of the universe. How can we counter this argument?

▲ *"With the dictates of reason. Think of the assumptions behind this notion and you will have no trouble seeing its fundamental flaws."*

Discussion: The pantheist doctrine makes God into a material being. While crediting God with supreme intelligence, the pantheist actually sees the Divine as a human being drawn on a vast scale. What is the result? If constituted of matter, God would have no intrinsic stability, since matter is constantly being transformed. Furthermore, lacking changelessness, which is one of the essential qualities of Divinity, God would also be subject to all the frailties and needs of human beings. In reality, using the properties of matter to describe God degrades our idea of the Divine. Ultimately, however, such subtle arguments fail to solve the problem of God's essential nature. We do not know all that God is; we do know what God is not. Pantheism, on the other hand, confuses Creator with creation. This is the equivalent of considering an ingenious piece of equipment to be an integral part of its inventor.

    The intelligence of God is revealed in the work of God, just as the painter's appears through the picture on a canvas. The works of God are no more God than the picture is the artist who conceived and painted it.

II

THE GENERAL ELEMENTS
OF THE UNIVERSE

The Beginning of Things

17. Can we ever know how everything began?

▲ *"No. Not everything can be revealed in this world."*

18. Will we ever be able to penetrate the mystery of things we don't understand now?

▲ *"As you achieve purification, this veil will be lifted. But in order to understand some things you need faculties you don't yet have."*

19. Can't we penetrate some of nature's secrets through science?

▲ *"Scientific research is a means of advancing in every direction. But you still face natural limitations."*

Discussion: The more we explore nature's mysteries, the greater our admiration should be for the wisdom of the Creator. But our shortcomings, especially when coupled with our pride, often make us susceptible to illusions. We heap theories upon theories. Yet every day we uncover errors in theories we mistakenly took for truths, and find truths in ideas we once dismissed as errors.

20. Outside the domain of scientific research, can we receive teachings about matters that transcend the physical senses?

▲ *"Yes, at times the Creator may find it useful to reveal things that are beyond the competence of science to explain."*

Discussion: It is through such revelations that, within certain limits, we obtain knowledge of both our past and future.

Spirit and Matter

21. Has matter, like God, existed from all eternity, or was it created at some specific point in time?

▲ *"God only knows. Nonetheless, there is an essential point to consider. God, the eternal fountain of love, must never have been idle. No matter how far into the past you reach, you can't imagine a single moment when God wasn't active."*

22. Matter is generally defined as something that occupies space, that can be perceived by one or more senses, and that is impenetrable.[1] Is this definition correct?

▲ *"Yes, from your point of view. But matter exists in other states that are unknown to you; and while this matter may be too ethereal and subtle to make an impression on your senses, it is still matter."*

—What definition would you give of matter?

▲ *"Matter is the element that surrounds the spirit, and upon which the spirit exerts its action."*

Discussion: From this point of view it may be said that matter is the intermediary through which, and upon which, the spirit operates.

23. What is spirit?

▲ *"The intelligent principle of the universe."*

—What is the essential nature of spirit?

▲ *"This is impossible to explain in human language. For you, the spirit is nothing; it isn't a real entity because it isn't tangible. For us, it's an objective reality as substantial as the body is to you. There is, however, no such thing as nothingness."*

24. Are the words spirit and intelligence synonyms?

▲ *"Intelligence is an essential quality of spirit. The two merge, however, in a unitary principle. So, from your perspective, they can be said to be the same."*

25. Is spirit independent of matter, or is it only one property of matter, as colors are a property of light and sounds a property of air?

▲ *"Spirit and matter are distinct from one another; but the union of spirit and matter is necessary to give intelligent activity to the latter."*

—Is this union equally necessary to the manifestation of the spirit? (We mean, in this context, the intelligent principle, rather than a spiritual being per se.)

▲ *"It is for you, because your senses aren't designed to perceive spirit apart*

....

1 *Translator's Note: Impenetrability is the inability of two bodies to simultaneously occupy the same space. This is not to be confused with extension, which is simply the ability to occupy space.*

from matter. They weren't developed for such an order of perception."

26. Can spirit be conceived of without matter, and matter without spirit?

▲ *"Certainly, as objects of thought."*

27. There are, then, two general elements of the universe—matter and spirit?

▲ *"Yes. Above them is God, the Creator of all things. These three—God, spirit, matter—are the essence of all that exists, the universal trinity. We should also add here the Cosmic Principle² which is an intermediary between spirit*

....

2 *Translator's Note: Cosmic Principle: The original French text uses the word fluid instead of principle. According to the Oxford English Dictionary, it was not unusual in the physics of the mid-1800s to use fluid to mean subtle, imponderable, all pervading substances, whose existence had been assumed to account for the phenomena of heat, magnetism and electricity. Nowadays, however, fluid is more commonly defined as a substance that is characterized by low resistance to flow and the tendency to assume the shape of its container, such as liquid or a gas.*

The spirits' chosen terminology was definitely in keeping with the scientific jargon of the mid-nineteenth century, but human language is dynamic and words that are current today may easily become obsolete in a matter of a few decades. Thus to dwell on the old terminology (fluid) would be a grave injustice to the spirits' insight, which is as fresh and current today as it was over a hundred fifty years ago when it was first presented. Throughout this book, then, we have chosen to substitute principle for fluid, a choice that was motivated by the spirits themselves, who, in reference to the vital principle, use these two words interchangeably (see Chapter Four). Thus, by Cosmic Principle we mean the subtle, fundamental, unifying substance that gives rise to phenomena such as heat, magnetism, and electricity, and to matter itself.

Interestingly enough, the notion of a fundamental element, transcending the known structures of matter can be traced back to Newton's Law of Universal gravitation [Sir Isaac Newton (1642-1727)]. According to this law, every particle of matter attracts every other particle, everything is interconnected. What the high spirits seemed to indicate was that the gravitational force could not arise from the particles of matter themselves; instead it would be a transformation of, or have its origin in, the Cosmic Principle.

One can also draw insightful parallels between the spirits' notion of Cosmic Principle and the work of James C. Maxwell (1831-1879) and of Albert Einstein (1879-1955). In the mid-1860s Maxwell's theory of electromagnetism brought magnetism, electricity, and light into an integrated mathematical framework and introduced to physics the concept of fields, which he thought of as modifications of a subtle structure, the aether. The fact that the aether eluded detection in laboratory experiments motivated Einstein to propose the theory of relativity in 1905, which, while abstracting from the notion of aether, accounted for electromagnetic phenomena in terms of fields alone. In Einstein's view, fields are non-material in nature. One important question remained, however: Is it plausible to have fields occurring within nothingness? The discovery of this subtle medium, in which fields take existence, and which the high spirits denominated the Cosmic Principle, is to this day a central objective of theoretical physics.

More recently, quantum mechanics has offered an alternative view to the theory of relativity. In investigating the innermost secrets of matter, quantum physicists found an immense quantity of smaller particles within the atom. They

Footnote continued page 42

and matter as you know it. Earthly matter is too dense for the spirit to act upon directly. Yet you can distinguish the cosmic principle and the matter found on earth by their properties. You should understand that if the Cosmic Principle were simply classified as an element of matter, the spirit would necessarily have to be defined as material, too. This Cosmic Principle is, however, intermediate between spirit and matter; its essence is imponderable; it is the irreducible and fundamental constituent of all matter. Under the guidance of spirit and in combination with denser matter, the Cosmic Principle can be used to produce an infinite number of things about which you now know very little. As the agent used by spirit in acting on matter, the Cosmic Principle is the force without which matter would remain in a perpetual state of division. Without it, matter would never acquire the properties given to it by gravity."

—Is this the energy we call electricity?

▲ *"The Cosmic Principle is susceptible to innumerable combinations. What you call electric energy, magnetic energy, etc., are simply modifications of it. It is essentially a more perfect and refined form of matter with an independent existence of its own."*

28. Since spirit itself is something, wouldn't it be clearer and more correct to call these two general elements by the terms inert matter and intelligent matter?

▲ *"These verbal distinctions have little importance to us. You need to formulate your definitions in a way that will make you intelligible to one another. Your disputes, we have noticed, almost always arise from your lack of agreement over the meaning of words. Your language is incomplete where anything that doesn't strike your senses is concerned."*

···························

Footnote 2 continued from page 41
discovered, too, that each particle has its own matter field. Thus, the fields of so-called fundamental particles of matter may be considered fundamental fields and, together with gravitational and electromagnetic fields, the fundamental fields of nature. In this sense, living forms constituted of atoms, cells, organs and bodies would be a complex system of hierarchical fields. However, the knowledge that these particles are neither matter nor vibration, or that they are perhaps both, brings the challenge of identifying the force which maintains the "activity" within the fields. Einstein's unfulfilled vision was unified field theory which encompasses the known fields of physics: gravitational, electromagnetic, and quantum matter. Like the Cosmic Principle, this superforce would have the property of bringing the universe into being and furnishing it with light, energy, matter, and structure.

It is against this background of knowledge that one must understand the concept of Cosmic Principle. The high spirits presented this notion in a form that could fit the scientific knowledge and language of the time (1850s), but in a way that also allowed it to be comprehended in the future (today). Certainly, it was their hope that each generation would create its own bridges to interpret the concept and in so doing be part of the pursuit of "understanding life."

Discussion: One fact, evident to everyone, dominates all our hypotheses. We see matter that is not intelligent; we see the action of an intelligent principle that is independent of matter. The origin of and connection between these two things are unknown to us. We don't know if matter and the intelligent principle have a common, preordained source and thus points of contact. We don't know whether intelligence has an independent existence of its own or if it is only an effect. We don't even know if intelligence is, as some believe, an emanation of the Divine. Matter and intelligence appear to us to be distinct, and we therefore speak of them as being two constituent elements of the universe. We do see, above these, a higher intelligence that governs all things, and that is distinguished from them by essential qualities peculiar to itself. We call this Supreme Intelligence, God.

Properties of Matter

29. Is ponderability an essential property of matter?

▲ *"Yes, of matter as you understand it. The Cosmic Principle, however, cannot be weighed, though it is the fundamental building block of what you call matter."*

Discussion: Weight is a relative property. Beyond the gravitational spheres of suns, planets and other universal bodies, there is no such thing as "weight," just as there is no up or down.

30. Is matter formed of one element or several?

▲ *"Of one basic element. The elements you regard as basic really are not: they are transformations of a more fundamental matter."*

31. Where do the different properties of matter come from?

▲ *"Elementary molecules undergo changes both because of their interaction with other molecules, with which they combine, and in response to environmental pressures. From these changes arise differing properties."*

32. According to this view, flavors, odors, colors, sounds, the poisonous or medicinal qualities of certain substances, are only the result of changes in one basic, universal element?

▲ *"Yes, undoubtedly. And furthermore, the existence of these qualities is dependent on the sensory organs that perceive them."*

Discussion: The latter principle is proved by the fact that not everyone perceives the qualities of certain substances in the same manner. An object that looks blue to one person will appear red to another. The same food that tastes good to Person A will be disliked by Person B. The old saying, "One man's meat is another man's poison," can be literally true.

33. Is this same basic matter capable of undergoing all possible changes and thereby acquiring all the properties we associate with matter in our world?

▲ *"Yes. This fact is implied in the saying that everything is in everything."*[3]

Discussion: Oxygen, hydrogen, nitrogen, carbon and all the other substances that we regard as fundamental are only transformations of one basic substance, the Cosmic Principle. But because we can't at present study this basic force, except through intellectual deduction, we continue to regard the other elements as matter's primary constituents.

—Doesn't this theory confirm the view that matter has only two essential properties, force and movement, and that all other properties—since they are conditioned by the intensity of force and the direction of movement—are really only secondary effects of the two?

▲ *"Yes, this view is correct, though you should add 'according to' the different molecular arrangements of matter. Consider, as an example, an opaque body that can become transparent and vice versa."*

34. Do molecules of matter have a defined form?

▲ *"Unquestionably, they do—but not one your senses can detect."*

—Is this form constant or variable?

▲ *"Constant for basic, elementary molecules; variable for secondary molecules, which are only combinations of the basic ones. What you call a molecule is still very far from being the elementary unit of matter."*

Universal Space

35. Is the universal space infinite or limited?

▲ *"Infinite. Assume for a moment the existence of boundaries in space. You can*

....

3 *Given that there is only one primitive material element, the Cosmic Principle, and that the properties of different substances are only modifications of this element, we can conclude that the basic essence of all substances, regardless of their properties, is the same. This notion offers a possible explanation for a unique phenomenon, the ability of a few individuals to use their psychic/mental power to alter the properties of a given substance, such as imparting a specific flavor or odor to water. This phenomenon resembles magnetic healing (see Chapter Four), except that, instead of acting on a patient, the person acts, say, on a glass of water. Thus, just as the addition of an extra atom of oxygen to a molecule of water turns it into hydrogen peroxide, a strongly oxidizing liquid, the focused thought/energy forms radiated by a human being may conceivably alter the inherent properties of a given sub-*

see how this idea confounds human reason. Reason tells you something must exist beyond those boundaries. Under any aspect that you care to consider, this always holds true with the idea of the Infinite. But in your narrow sphere of understanding, Infinity is incomprehensible."

Discussion: If we imagine a limit to space, no matter how far off our thought may place this limit, our reason tells us that there must still be something beyond it. In this way, moving step by step from one supposed limitation to the next, we arrive at our idea of Infinity. After all, even if it were an absolute void, this "something beyond," would still be space.

36. Does an absolute void exist in any part of space?

▲ *"No, there is no void. What appears to be a void to you is occupied by matter in a state that escapes detection by your senses and scientific instruments."*

III

CREATION

The Formation of Planets

Discussion: The universe consists of innumerable planets, both seen and unseen. It contains all animate and inanimate beings, and all the stars and energies that fill space.

37. Was the universe created, or has it existed from all eternity, like God?

▲ *"Of course, the universe cannot have made itself. And if, like God, it has existed from all eternity, it could not be the work of God."*

Discussion: Reason tells us that since the universe could not have made itself, and since it did not appear by chance, it must be the work of God.

38. How did God create the universe?

▲ *"To use a well-known expression, through the Divine Will. Nothing will give you a better idea of God's all-powerful Will than the grand words of Genesis, 'God said, "Let there be light", and there was light.'"* [1]

39. How are planets formed?

▲ *"All that can be said on this subject, within the limits of your understanding, is this: Planets are formed by the aggregation of matter disseminated in space."*

40. Are comets, as we currently believe, celestial bodies in the early stages of formation, i.e., are they constituted of newly condensed matter?

▲ *"Yes, but it would be a stretch to believe that comets have the influence that*

· ·

1 Translator's Note: Genesis 1:3

popular beliefs often ascribe to them. All heavenly bodies share in influencing the production of certain physical phenomena."

41. Is it possible for a completely formed planet to be destroyed and its matter disseminated again in space?

▲ *"Yes. God renews planets as well as the beings that live on them."*

42. How long does it take to form a planet—Earth, for instance?

▲ *"We do not know the precise amount of time. We would be making fools of ourselves if we presumed to tell you, for example, the exact number of centuries required for the formation of each planet. Only the Creator truly knows."*

The Creation of Living Beings

43. When did living beings start to appear on Earth?

▲ *"In the beginning everything was chaos. All the elements were mixed up and in a confused state. Gradually, though, the elements settled; and living beings, when Earth became ready to support them, began to emerge."*

44. Where did the living beings who appeared on Earth come from?

▲ *"The prototypical structures² of these beings were contained in the Earth, where they waited for favorable conditions to develop. When the force that had been holding the primitive organic principles apart ceased to exist, they united and formed the biological prototypes of all living beings. Like a chrysalis or the seeds of plants, these prototypes remained dormant, though full of potential, until environmental conditions were right for the birth of each species. The beings of each species then came together and multiplied."*

45. Where were the organic elements before the formation of Earth?

▲ *"They existed as archetypal forms in space, in the realm of spirit, or on other planets. There they waited for the creation of Earth where they could give rise to a new cycle of life."*

Discussion: Chemistry shows us molecules of inorganic bodies that, under the right conditions, combine to generate regularly formed crystals. The slightest change in these conditions may affect the formation and the uniformity of the crystals. Similar reactions, we assume, occur with organic elements. After all, certain animal and plant embryos have been con-

---

2 Translator's Note: The author used the word "germ" with the intention of indicating "an essential unit, one that serves as the source or principle of the living forms." As such, it may correspond to both physical and non-physical concepts. To avoid confounding the reader with biology's definition of the word germ—a small organic structure of a cell from which a new organism may develop—we opted to translate "germs" as "prototypical structures." We employ this terminology in the sense accepted by biological sciences—an archetype, or a primitive form regarded as the basis of a group.

served for years and only develop at the right temperature and circumstances. Haven't we seen grains of wheat harvested centuries ago germinate? This is possible because the vital principle remains latent in the grains. Now, can't something that takes place today also have taken place during the Earth's formative stages? Does this view of creation in any way detract from the glory of God? In reality, it supports our sense of the greatness of the Divine power. It reveals to us a God who commands the infinite worlds by acting through universal laws rather than by fiat. This theory doesn't solve the problem of the origin of the vital elements; but we need to remember that God has some mysteries that extend well beyond the limits of our current ability to investigate.

46. Do any living beings come into existence spontaneously?

▲ *"In order for life to come to existence, organic prototypes (archetypal forms) must already be in a state of potentiality. You see this phenomenon constantly. Consider, for example the billions of germs that exist in a human or animal body. Under the right conditions, these germs will spring to action and affect the process of organic decomposition upon the death of the body. The life of these microorganisms was latent until the proper conditions were created."*

47. Was the human species among the organic elements present in the primitive Earth?

▲ *"Yes, it emerged when the conditions were appropriate. This is the origin of the statement that the first human was 'formed out of the dust of the ground.'"*

48. Can we establish, then, the period when human beings and the other living beings on the Earth first appeared?

▲ *"No, your scientific calculations are only speculative."*

49. If the biological prototypes of the human species were among the Earth's first organic elements, why don't we see humans being produced spontaneously today?

▲ *"Only God has the blueprint of creation. All we can say for certain is that from the beginning humanity was given everything it needed to survive and flourish. It was also given, as a way of ensuring the continuity of the species, the ability to pass on these elements through reproduction. We can say the same for all other living species."*

The Population of Earth - Adam and Eve

50. Did the human species begin with only one person?

▲ *"No, the one you call Adam was not the first man to inhabit Earth."*

51. Is it possible to know when Adam lived?

▲ *"About the period that you assign to him; that is, about 4000 years before Christ."*

Discussion: The name "Adam" is given to the survivor of one of the great cataclysms that at various times have convulsed and changed the surface of our planet. Adam simply was among those who founded one of the races that now inhabit Earth. Many have correctly regarded stories of Adam as parables, personifying the early stages of human-ity. In fact, life on Earth had to exist long before the period assigned to the accounts of Adam. The most fundamental laws of nature make it impossible to admit that the enor-mous amount of progress accomplished on Earth before the birth of Christ could have been attained in a matter of about 40 centuries.

The Diversity of Human Races

52. What caused the physical and intellectual differences that distinguish our human races?

▲ *"Climate, modes of life, and social habits. If you raise two siblings apart, in different societies, and subject them to differing influences and conditions, they will likely harbor no psychological resemblance."*

53. Did the human species come into existence in various places?

▲ *"Yes, and in various eras. This is one cause of the diversity of human races. Individuals traveled, endured different climatic conditions, integrated with people from other areas. In time, they formed new groups with various phys-ical differences."*

—Do racial differences constitute distinct species?

▲ *"Certainly not. All of the races make up a single family. Do the differences among varieties of the same fruit prevent them from belonging to the same species?"*

54. If the human species hasn't all evolved from one common ancestor, can we still regard each other as brothers and sisters?

▲ *"All of you are related by your common relation to the Creator. You are all brothers and sisters in God. You are all animated through spirit and share the same goal. You have to guard against the tendency to be too literal in these matters."*

The Multitude of Planets

55. Are other planets inhabited?

▲ *"Yes. And the people of the Earth are far from being, as you suppose, the leaders in intelligence, goodness, and enlightenment. Many people, some very erudite among them, believe that only Earth is inhabited by intelligent beings and that God has created the universe only for them. It is a presumptuous idea."*

Discussion: God has peopled the planets of the universe with living beings, all of whom work to do the Divine Will. To think that all beings would be created to function only within the narrow limits of the human reality, is to grossly underappreciate the Divine Wisdom. All celestial bodies serve a purpose, they do not exist solely to gratify us on a starry night. There is also nothing in the position or composition of Earth that would lead us to suppose that it alone, in the midst of a multitude of planets, is inhabited.

56. Is the physical composition of all planets the same?

▲ *"No, they may differ greatly."*

57. Since planets are physically different, can we assume that their inhabitants are differently constituted?

▲ *"Absolutely. The situation is similar to one on your planet where fish are organized for living in water and birds for living in air."*

58. Are the planets farthest removed from the sun deprived of light and heat, given that the sun is like a distant star to them?

▲ *"Do you think there are no sources of light and heat other than the sun? Would you discount, for instance, the action of electricity, which on certain planets plays a very much more important part than it does on Earth? How do you know that the beings on those planets have an organic structure that resembles yours? The matter that composes their bodies could well be of a nature completely unknown to you."*

Discussion: We must assume that the conditions of existence for beings who inhabit the various planets are appropriate to the sphere in which they live. If we had never seen fish, we would be at a loss to explain how any living beings could exist in the sea. Likewise, we should consider that other planets contain elements and life forms that are unknown to us. As we on Earth experience the electrical displays of the Aurora Borealis, it is very possible that beings on planets with a greater supply of electricity than ours might use electricity in ways we don't yet understand and might be able to generate their own heat and light.

The Biblical Account of Creation

59. Throughout the ages, human beings have held many disparate ideas about creation, always reflecting their level of understanding. With the passage of time, logical reasoning, with the support of science, has rendered some of these ideas untenable. The explanation of the subject given here through spirit communication confirms the views advanced by modern science.

Many, no doubt, will object to this explanation on the grounds that it contradicts statements in the Bible. Yet a careful examination of Biblical statements proves the contradiction to be more apparent than real, the result of an interpretation of phrases that were meant to be understood allegorically. Thus, the question of the existence of Adam, regarded as the first man and sole progenitor of the human species, is only one instance in which religious convictions have changed in order to accommodate the facts. At one time, for instance, the hypothesis that the Earth rotated around the sun appeared to be in utter opposition to the Bible. Official religion abhorred the idea and directed every kind of persecution against its defenders. Yet, despite all this anathema, the Earth continued to move in its orbit. Today, anyone denying this fact would run the risk of being thought crazy.

The Bible also tells us that God created the world in six days and interpretation fixes the time of the event at about 4000 years before the Christian era. Prior to this 4000 year period, the Earth did not exist; then, miraculously, God called it forth out of nothing. Such is the categorical affirmation of the sacred text. Yet, positively and inexorably, science has advanced proof to the contrary.[3] The history of the formation of our planet is written indelibly in the fossil record, which proves beyond all doubt that the six days of the creation were successive periods, each of which may have lasted millions of years. This is not merely a statement or an opinion. It is a fact as incontestable as the motion of the Earth, and one that theology itself must admit. This admission shows us again the danger of treating figurative speech as literal truth. Should we then consider the Bible inaccurate? No, but we must be very careful with our interpretation of it.

Scientists now know the order of succession in which the different species appeared on Earth. The order corresponds largely to the sequence offered in the book of Genesis, with this difference: the Earth, instead of issuing miraculously from the hand of God in the course of a few days, developed over impressively long periods under the impetus of the Divine Will, and according to the laws and forces of nature. Does this view make God appear less great and powerful? Are the results any less sublime for not having been produced instantaneously? Evidently not. Even the smallest mind must recognize, when considering the evolution of the universe, the grandeur of the

....

3 Translator's Note: Scientific research has determined that Earth is approximately 4.6 billion years old, that life has been evolving on its surface for over 4 billion years, that the primate order emerged about 70 million years ago, and that hominid forms have stood erect on land and walked upright for at least 4 million years. (J. Birx, Interpreting Evolution, Prometheus Books, 1991, 16.)

Almighty Power that is implied in the action of eternal laws. Science, far from diminishing the work of God, reinforces our sense of God's power and majesty by showing how all the work occurred and continues according to the laws of nature.

Modern science is also in keeping with one Mosaic account when it places the human species last in the order of creation of living beings. Moses, however, places the Flood in the year 1654 from the formation of Earth, whereas geological findings suggest that the universal deluge, of which the Noah story is supposedly a literal account, occurred before the appearance of the first humans. The latter is apparent from the fact that the geological strata[4] show, so far, no evidence of human life or even of related animal life-forms at the time of the universal deluge. Still, there are points open to dispute. Recent discoveries, for instance, suggest that the human species is considerably older than was once thought. Such findings, if true, would prove that the Bible, in assigning a date to the creation of humankind and in other similar matters, can only be understood allegorically. We accept then that Noah's flood cannot have been the universal deluge of geology because of the time required for the formation of fossil-bearing strata. If, on the other hand, scientists should eventually discover traces of the existence of the human species before the geological deluge, it would be even more evident that Adam could not have been the first human, since the creation of humankind would be pushed back to a more distant period.[5] If so, there would be no arguing against the facts. The great age of the human species, if proved by geology, would have to be admitted, in the same way that we now accept the solar orbit of the Earth and the six "days" of the formation of Earth would have to be accepted as symbolic time.

Whether or not the human race existed before the universal deluge still belongs to the domain of hypothetical considerations, but here are some thoughts we can be more sure about: If we suppose that human beings first appeared on Earth 4000 years before Christ, and that the whole of the human species with the exception of a single family was destroyed 1650 years later, we must believe, too, that the population of the Earth dates only from the time of Noah—i.e., from 2350 BC. Yet when the Hebrews emigrated to Egypt in the eighteenth century before Christ, they found a country densely populated and already enjoying a high degree of civilization. History also shows that, at the same period, India and various other countries were equally pop-

···································

4 Translator's Note - In the Precambrian (4.5 billion years ago), the oldest geological strata, only the fossils of rudimentary organisms (e.g., algae and bacteria) were found.

···································

5 Translator's Note - Modern discoveries indicate the earliest ancestor of man walked on Earth between 6 and 7 million years ago. According to discovery by French researchers, Michel Brunet and Patrick Vignaud, this early hominid lived in the Central African nation of Chad.

ulous and flourishing; and the chronological tables of other peoples go back to even more remote periods. Consider the difficulty this poses for a literal interpretation of the Biblical account. We would have to assume that, from the twenty-fourth to the eighteenth century before Christ—that is, in the space of 600 years—the descendants of a single individual were able to populate all the immense countries that had been discovered, as well as lands then unknown but that we have no reason to believe were uninhabited. We would also have to believe that during this brief period humankind was able to raise itself from a completely undeveloped state to the highest degree of intellectual attainment—assumptions totally irreconcilable with anthropological laws.

The existence of diverse racial groups also supports an allegorical interpretation of Genesis. Climate and modes of life undoubtedly change the physical characteristics of human beings to some degree. But physiological examination of human remains proves conclusively that there are constitutional differences among the races too profound to have been produced by climatic differences alone. The interbreeding of races results in a dilution of racial characteristics; it does not engender original racial types. But racial interbreeding itself presupposes the existence of races already distinct from each other. This clearly would have been impossible if humanity had originated from a single individual, i.e., Adam. It is even less likely if we restrict the evolution of these races to a very brief period. Can we really believe that the descendants of Noah could have been transformed into Ethiopians, for example, within a few hundred years? Such a metamorphosis is almost as inadmissible as the idea of a close common ancestor for the wolf and the sheep, the beetle and the elephant, or the bird and the fish. In the long run, the force of the facts has to prevail. Everything becomes logically apparent if we assume that human beings existed in a period before the one commonly assigned to their creation. One might then postulate that, some 6000 years before the present, Adam began populating a country until then uninhabited; and, that the Flood of Noah, which became a metaphor over time for the universal deluge of geology, was a local catastrophe. In this way one makes due allowance for the allegorical form of expression characteristic of the Oriental style, and common to the sacred books of all peoples.[6]

It would be unwise to hastily discard scientific hypotheses simply because they appear to contradict certain theological positions. Some of these hypotheses might sooner or later become facts born out by the data. But religion does not lose ground when it admits scientific advances. Rather, it grows stronger by becoming less vulnerable to the attacks of skeptics.

··························

6 Translator's Note: In 1929, while searching for Ur near the Persian Gulf, British archeologist Sir Charles Leonard Woolley (1880-1960) undertook excavations that uncovered geological evidences of a great flood that occurred 4000 years before Christ, possibly the flood referred to in the Bible (Vol. 21 of The World Book Encyclopedia, 1995, 403). Further research confirmed this fact, showing that there had been a local flood in the delta of the Tigris and the Euphrates Rivers in the period mentioned in the Bible.

CHAPTER IV

THE VITAL PRINCIPLE

Organic and Inorganic Beings

Discussion: Organic beings have within themselves a source that produces life. They are born, grow, reproduce their own kind, and die. These beings also have organs that are adapted to the performance of certain activities, e.g., the satisfaction of needs and the preservation of life. Among these beings are human beings, animals, and plants.[1]

Inorganic beings lack both vitality and the power of self-movement. They are not formed of animal or vegetable matter. Examples include minerals, air, water, etc.

60. Is the force that unites the elements of matter in organic and inorganic bodies the same?

▲ *"Yes, the law of attraction is the same for both."*

61. Is there a difference between the matter found in organic and inorganic bodies?

▲ *"The matter in both contains the same elements. In organic bodies, however, matter is vitalized."*

....

1 Translator's Note: *The word* organic *is used here in its general sense, i.e., "characteristic of, or pertaining to, living organisms." The special sense of the word in chemistry—"pertaining to compounds that are hydrocarbons or their derivatives"—does not apply to the discussion that takes place in this chapter. Likewise, the definition of* inorganic *here is "not characterized by vital process."*

62. What causes this vitalization?

▲ *"The union of matter with the vital principle.²"*

63. Is the vital principle found in a particular agent, or is it only a property of organic matter? In other words, is it a cause or an effect?

▲ *"It is both. Life is an effect produced by the action of an agent on matter. This agent, without matter, isn't life, just as matter has no life without it. The vital principle gives life to all beings that absorb it."*

64. We have seen that spirit and matter are the two constituent elements of the universe. Is the vital principle a third?

▲ *"The vital principle is a necessary element in the structure of the universe. But it has its source in a special modification of the Cosmic Principle. For you, it is an element, like oxygen or hydrogen, although these elements are not basic at all. In fact, all the elements known to you, however simple they seem, are modifications of the Cosmic Principle."*

—Simply put, the vital principle is not a distinct primitive agent; it results from a special modification of the Cosmic Principle.

▲ *"Correct. This follows from what we have just told you."*

65. Does the vital principle exist in any one of the bodies known to us?

▲ *"The vital principle has its source in the cosmic principle. You have referred to it as animal magnetism or animal electricity. It enables the union between the spirit and the physical body."*

66. Is the vital principle the same for all organic beings?

▲ *"Yes, but modified according to species. It is the principle that gives a species its power of movement and activity and distinguishes it from inert matter. After all, the movement of matter isn't life. Matter is moved, it doesn't originate movement."*

67. Is vitality a permanent quality of the vital principle, or does it only develop through the interactions of the organs in which we see it operate?

·····························

2 *Translator's Note: Vitalism's fundamental concept is that the functioning of living organisms is due to the existence of a vital principle that infuses matter with life, and that living organisms are more than merely the systematic organization of nonliving parts. This view of the origin and evolution of life can be traced to the Greek philosophers, and it has been adopted in modern times by well-known natural philosophers such as Jean Baptiste de Lamarck, Teilhard de Chardin, and Henri Bergson. At its core is the idea that there is a force, with origin in God, that sustains life. Modern science, however, has taken the view that life is solely the result of biochemical processes and organic evolution. The Spiritist Doctrine, is committed to accompanying (and changing with) the findings of science, however, it affirms unequivocally the notion that God, and not random biochemical and genetic events, is the fundamental source of life.*

▲ *"It is developed only in connection with a body. As we have just said, the vital principle, without matter, isn't life. It's the union of the two that brings forth life."*

— When the vital principle is not united with matter, is it right to say that vitality is latent?

▲ *"Yes, this is the case."*

Discussion: All the body's organs comprise a sort of mechanism that receives its impetus from the vital principle that exists in each organ. This principle is the generating force of all life. Moreover, while the vital principle sustains the organs, the interaction of these very organs develops and keeps up the activity of the vital principle, just as friction develops heat.

Life and Death

68. What causes the death of organic beings?

▲ *"The exhaustion of bodily organs."*

—Might we compare death, then, to the cessation of movement in a machine that is out of fuel?

▲ *"Yes, when a machine has no fuel, it stops running. When the body falls into a fatal illness, the vital principle withdraws from it."*

69. Why is death from heart problems more likely to occur than when other organs become diseased or damaged?

▲ *"The heart is a life-sustaining mechanism. But remember—the heart isn't the only organ that, when diseased or damaged, can stop the body from functioning. It is only one of the mechanisms the machine needs to keep working."*

70. What happens to matter and the vital principle after death?

▲ *"The inert matter decomposes and becomes part of other bodies; the vital principle returns to the general mass of the Cosmic Principle."*

Discussion: When an organic being dies, the elements which comprise its body break down and its various elements undergo new combinations that form new forms of life. These, in their turn, draw the principle of life and activity from the universal source. They absorb and assimilate it, and restore it again to that source when they die.

     The bodily organs are saturated with vital energy. This energy communicates to all the organs the activity that causes them, for instance, to respond to disease and injury by reestablishing bodily functions that have been temporarily suspended. But when the vital organs have been destroyed, or too deeply injured, the vital energy is powerless to animate them, and the being dies.

The body's organs interact more or less actively with each other. The body is in a state of harmony when the interaction is reciprocal and balanced. But harmony is destroyed when the organs become deficient. The body, in other words, is like a machine that comes to a standstill when one or more of its mechanisms is out of order. You might compare it to a clock that eventually wears out through constant use or that someone accidentally breaks, so that the spring can no longer keep it going.

An even better image of life and death is the battery. Like all natural bodies, a battery contains electricity in a state of potentiality. When this potential energy is set in motion by a special cause (the completion of a circuit, for instance), we become aware of electricity's particular effects. Metaphorically speaking, the battery comes alive. Remove the cause, however, and the electrical phenomena stop: the battery once again becomes inert. An organic body can be thought of as a kind of battery in which the flow of energy produces the phenomenon of life and the cessation of the flow means death.

The amount of vital energy varies by species. It is not the same either for the members of a species as a whole or for particular individuals within the species. Some species, as a result, appear to be saturated with it. In others, it is proportionately very small. Wherever it is abundant, the species will be more active and tenacious of life.

The reserves of vital energy in a given organism can be exhausted, and thus become incapable of sustaining life. These reserves can, however, be replenished through the absorption and assimilation of substances that contain this energy. Vital energy can, for instance, be transmitted from one individual to another.[3] An individual in which it is more abundant can pass it on to another in which it is lacking, in some cases rekindling, so to speak, the vital flame that is on the point of going out.

······························

3 Translator's Note: Laboratory evidences of transfer of energy were obtained through the use of Kirlian photography. The Kirlian process was discovered in Russia; the first series of experiments conducted in Russia is described in Ostrander, S. and Lynn Schroeder, Psychic Discoveries Behind the Iron Curtain, Bantam, 1970.

Intelligence and Instinct

71. Is intelligence a quality of the vital principle?

▲ *"No. For instance, plants have organic life, but they only live; they don't think. Intelligence and matter are independent of each other. A body may live without intelligence; but intelligence can only manifest itself in the physical world through a physical being. Organic matter can only produce intelligent activity by its union with spirit."*

Discussion: Intelligence is a faculty appropriate to certain classes of organic beings. It gives these beings the power to think, the will to act, consciousness of their existence and individuality, and a means of establishing relations with the external world. It also allows them to satisfy the special needs of their way of life.

We can distinguish three classes of beings: (1) inanimate beings, formed of matter but without life or intelligence—e.g., minerals; (2) animate and non-thinking beings, formed of matter and possessing vitality, but without intelligence; (3) animate and thinking beings, formed of matter and possessing vitality, but also having an intelligent principle that generates thought.

72. What is the source of intelligence?

▲ *"We have already told you: the universal intelligence."*

—Does every intelligent being draw a portion of intelligence from a universal source and assimilate it, just as it draws and assimilates the vital principle?

▲ *"The comparison isn't exact. Intelligence is an attribute particular to thinking beings. It is integral to a person's moral individuality. But, as we have said, there are things humans can't fully understand yet. This is one of them."*

73. Is instinct independent of intelligence?

▲ *"No, not exactly. Instinct is a form of non-reasoning intelligence through which all beings provide for their needs."*

74. Can we draw a line of demarcation between instinct and intelligence? In other words, can we define precisely where one ends and the other begins?

▲ *"No, because they often blend into one another. But instinctive and intelligent actions are more easily distinguishable."*

75. Do the instinctual faculties diminish as the mental faculties grow?

▲ *"No. Though humans pay less attention to them, the instinctual tendencies continue to exist. Moreover, instinct (intuitive behavior) can lead us in the right direction as well as reason. We can usually feel instinct's guidance, sometimes more powerfully than reason's. It more rarely goes astray."*

—Why isn't reason an infallible guide?

▲ *"Because it is distorted by defective education, egotism, selfishness. Otherwise, it would be infallible. Note that, unlike instinct, reason leaves room for choice and for free will to make decisions."*

Discussion: Instinct is a rudimentary form of intelligence, a guidance system that differs from reasoning intelligence in that its actions are almost always spontaneous. Intelligent acts, by contrast, come from thought and deliberation.

Instinctive actions vary according to the needs of specific species. In beings with self-consciousness and the mental awareness of things outside themselves, instinct is allied to intelligence, i.e., to freedom of will and action.

PART II
THE SPIRIT–WORLD

CHAPTER

V

SPIRITS

The Origin and Nature of Spirits

76. What is the definition of spirits?

▲ *"Spirits can be defined as the intelligent beings of creation. They populate the entire universe and can be found well beyond the boundaries of the material world."*

Discussion: The word "spirit" is used here to mean the individuality of incorporeal beings. In the first part of this book we used it to designate the intelligent element of the universe.[1]

77. Are spirits called "children" of God because they are parts of God, or are they distinct beings?

▲ *"Spirits are the work of God, just as a machine is the work of the engineer who makes it. The machine is the engineer's work, however; it isn't equivalent to the engineer. This can also be said of spirits and God. When somebody makes something original they call it their 'child'; in the same way, we are God's 'children' because we were created by God."*

78. Have spirits, like God, always existed, or did they have a beginning?

▲ *"If spirits had no beginning, they would be like God. However, they were created by God and thus are subject to God's will. The Creator has existed from all eternity; this we know. We don't know how and when the work of creation started. What we can say is that God, having existed for all eternity, has created for all eternity. In this sense, the creation of spirits had no beginning.*

....

1 Translator's Note: The concept of spirit as "the intelligent element of the universe" was introduced in question 23.

But we have no information on how and when each of us was created. That remains a mystery."

79. As the intelligent and material principles are the two general elements of the universe,[2] is it safe to say that spirits are formed out of the former and physical bodies out of the latter?

▲ *"Exactly! Spirits are the individualization of the intelligent principle, much like physical bodies are the 'individualization' of the material principle. Again, what we ignore is the 'how' and 'when' of the spirits' formation."*

80. Is the creation of spirits always going on, or did it only take place at the beginning of time?

▲ *"It is always going on. God never ceases to create."*

81. Are spirits formed spontaneously or do they evolve from each other?

▲ *"Spirits are created by God's will, like everything else. However, we reiterate, the origin of the spirit is one of those things that transcend our comprehension."*

82. Are spirits immaterial?

▲ *"Human language has no exact words to describe the essence of spirit, as a person who is born blind has no conception of how to define light. Immaterial is not quite the term; incorporeal would be a better word. Once a spirit is created it must be 'something,' but your senses can't grasp the essence of spirit any more than your language can satisfactorily define it."*

Discussion: We say that spirits are immaterial because their essence differs from everything we know under the name of matter. In the same way, a nation of blind people would have no terms to express light and its effects. Someone blind from birth imagines that hearing, smell, taste, and touch are the only sensory modes, and won't understand ideas communicated by the sense of sight. Where the essence of spiritual beings is concerned, we are the blind ones. We can only define them by means of comparisons that are imperfect, that is to say, by an effort of the imagination.

83. Do spirits ever die? We understand that the universal intelligent principle from which spirits come is eternal. What we're asking is whether the spirits' individuality has an end. We know, for instance, that material bodies eventually return to the natural element. Does something similar happen to spirits? After all, if something has a beginning shouldn't it also have an end?

▲ *"As a child doesn't understand all that its parents do, or an uneducated person doesn't grasp all that a scientist does, so you can't understand every-*

....

2 *Translator's Note: See question 27 on the general elements of the universe.*

thing about spirits because your intellectual reach is limited. At present, all
we can do is to reiterate that the existence of spirits has no end."

Essential World

84. Do spirits constitute a different world from the one we see?

▲ *"Yes, the world of spirits, of incorporeal intelligences."*

85. Is the spirit-world the principal one in the order of things?

▲ *"Yes, it is pre-existent to, and survives, everything else."*

86. Then would the essence of the spirit-world have remained unchanged even if the material world had never existed, or if it ceased to exist?

▲ *"Yes, because the two worlds are independent of each other, although they*
continually interact with and react upon each other."

87. Do spirits occupy a defined and limited region in space?

▲ *"Spirits are everywhere. The infinite reaches of space are peopled with them*
in infinite numbers. Usually imperceptible to us, they are constantly beside
us, observing and influencing. Spirits are one of the powers of Nature. They
are the instruments God uses to accomplish the designs of Providence. But
not all spirits can go everywhere. There are regions to which access is limit-
ed, depending on the individual spirit's degree of advancement."

The Form and Omnipresence of Spirits

88. Do spirits have a well-defined and consistent form?

▲ *"Not for human eyes. You imagine them only vaguely as a flame, a gleam,*
an ethereal spark. But for us they have a form."

—Is this flame or spark of any color?

▲ *"If you can see it, it will appear to you to vary from a dull gray to a perfect*
brilliance, according to the degree of the spirit's purity."

Discussion: Spirits are sometimes depicted with a star or flame on their
                foreheads. This allegorical representation of their essential
                nature depicts the head as the seat of intelligence.

89. Do spirits use up measurable time when transporting themselves through space?

▲ *"Yes, but their motion is as rapid as thought."*

— As the spirit thinks, does it transport itself to the object of its thought?

▲ *"Wherever an intent thought is, that's also where the spirit is. After all, it is*
the spirit who thinks; thought is only an attribute. The spirit is wherever the

thought focuses with intent."

90. When a spirit travels from one place to another, is it conscious of the distance covered, or is it suddenly transported to the place it wants to go?

▲ *"A spirit can travel either way. It can, if it wants, become aware of the space it traverses, or it can rid itself entirely of the sense of distance. It all depends on the spirit's will and its degree of purity."*

91. Does matter obstruct a spirit's movement?

▲ *"No, spirits can pass through anything: the air, the earth, water, even fire, are equally penetrable to them."*

92. Do spirits have the gift of omnipresence? In other words, can a spirit divide itself or exist at several points of space at the same time?

▲ *"No. A spirit cannot experience self-division. Each, however, is a center which radiates in all directions; and because of this, it may appear to be in several places at once. You might compare it to the sun, which also radiates in all directions, sending out rays across great distances. The sun, though, isn't divided. It is one body."*

—Do all spirits have the same power of radiation?

▲ *"There's considerable difference among them in this respect. It depends on the degree of their purity."*

Discussion: Each spirit is an indivisible unit. But, while unable to divide itself, the spirit can extend its thoughts in all directions. It is like a spark that sends out its brightness far and wide and can be seen from every point on the horizon, or like a person who sends orders and signals to various locations while remaining in one spot. Only in this special sense can we speak of the gift of omnipresence.

Perispirit[3] (Spiritual Body)

93. Are spirits enclosed by an envelope of some sort?

▲ *"From your perspective, the spirit is enveloped by a vaporous substance fine as a mist. For us, this substance is much denser. Nonetheless, the spirit's envelope is fine enough to allow it to float in the atmosphere and transport itself through space at will."*

·····························

3 *Translator's Note: Perispirit: equivalent to the concept of spiritual body as indicated by St. Paul (1 Cor. 15:44), Theosophy's astral body or etheric double, and bioplastic body as described by Russian scientists (in Ostrander and Schroader, Psychic Discoveries Behind the Iron Curtain).*

Discussion: Just as the seeds of some fruits are covered by a special plant tissue, called the perisperm, the spirit is enveloped by a vaporous substance, which we will call the perispirit.

94. Where does the spirit get this ethereal substance?

▲ *"From the modified Cosmic Principle present in each planet. The Cosmic Principle is differently organized on each planet, obliging the spirit to adjust its envelope as it moves from one world to the next, just as you ordinarily change your clothes."*

—Do spirits from a more advanced planet than ours need to assume a denser perispirit to visit us?

▲ *"Yes, they must take up a perispirit or spiritual body that is sufficiently dense to enter our atmosphere."*

95. Can a spirit's perispirit assume definite form and can we see it?

▲ *"Yes! As the spirit can choose the form of its perispirit, it can occasionally make itself visible and even palpable to you in dreams and sometimes even when you are awake."*

The Different Orders of Spirits

96. Are all spirits equal, or does a hierarchical ranking exist among them?

▲ *"They are of different degrees or ranks depending on their level of purification."*

97. Are the orders or degrees of purification among spirits fixed at a certain number?

▲ *"The number of orders is limitless, though there's nothing like definite lines of demarcation among them. Because fixed divisions among spirits don't exist, the number of orders can change depending on the point of view from which they're being considered. Nonetheless, if we consider the general characteristics of spirits, we can reduce them to three principal orders or ranks.*

"In the first and highest rank are the spirits who have reached the degree of relative perfection; they constitute what may be called pure spirits. In the second rank are those who have reached the middle of this ascending ladder; they have arrived at a degree of purification in which the love of good is the ruling desire of their existence. In the third and lowest rank, occupying the lower rungs of the ladder, are the less advanced spirits; they are in a state of unawareness and so tend toward mistakes, wrong-doing, and base sentiments, everything that retards their advancement."

98. Are spirits of the second order actually able to express their "love of good" through their actions?

▲ *"It depends on their degree of purification and desire. Some of them are distinguished by scientific knowledge; others by thoughtfulness and kindness. Still, all of them have trials to undergo."*

99. Are all spirits of the third order essentially bad?

▲ *"No. Some of them are apathetic and neutral; they perform neither good nor unwholesome acts. Others take pleasure in doing harm and are delighted to find an opportunity to bring it about. Still others are frivolous, indiscreet, extravagant, mischievous. While not tricky or positively malicious, these spirits entertain themselves by mystifying people who fall under their influence, causing them various petty annoyances just for the fun of it."*

The Spirit Hierarchy

100. Preliminary Observations

The classification of spirits is based on their level of advancement, the qualities they have acquired, and the imperfections from which they still have to free themselves. This classification is by no means absolute. It is only in its totality that the character of each category is distinctly shown, since each category merges by imperceptible degrees into the one above it. At their boundaries especially, the peculiarities of the successive categories blend together—which is also the case in nature, as we can see from the colors of the rainbow and the phases of a human life. Consequently, spirits can be divided into a number of classes; and even then the number will vary depending on the point of view from which we observe the classes. As in all other systems of scientific classification, the system we finally adopt will be more or less complete, rational, and easy to understand. But, whatever the form of classification, nothing is changed regarding the pertinent scientific facts. It isn't a matter of great importance, then, that the answers of spirits, when questioned on this point, sometimes vary as to the number of categories into which they are divided. Far too much weight has been given to this apparent contradiction by those who forget that disincarnate intelligences attach no importance whatever to the conventions of human language. For them, the meaning of a statement is the only important point about it. They leave the question of its form, the choice of terms and of classification—i.e., everything that pertains to developing a system—to us.

We should also never lose sight of the fact that there are less advanced spirits, just as there are immature human beings, and we can't be too much on our guard against the tendency to believe that spiritual beings know everything simply because they are spirits. The work of classification demands method, analysis, and a thorough knowledge of the subject investigated. Accordingly, inhabitants of the spirit-world who possess only a small amount of knowledge are as incapable of grasping a subject completely or formulating a system as any uneducated person would be. They have no idea, or only a very imperfect one, of any sort of classification. All spirits superior to them appear to be of the highest order, since they cannot differentiate among the many degrees of knowledge, capacity, and ethical development that distinguish spirits. And even the ones who are capable of this discrimination will vary in their appreciation of the details. It all depends on their particular point of view—which should come as no surprise, given a subject that by its very nature has nothing fixed or absolute about it.

Linnaeus, Jusseau, Tournefort[4] each had his own particular system of botanical classification. Yet the nature of botany has not been changed by the diversity of systems among botanists. These scientists haven't invented plants or their characteristics: they've simply observed certain likenesses and developed certain groups or classes based on them. We have proceeded in the same way. We have not invented spirits or their characteristics. We have seen and observed them; we have judged them by their words and acts; and we have classed them according to their similarities, basing our classification on data they have furnished themselves.

The spirit-instructors generally admit the existence of three principal classes among the inhabitants of their world. Occupying the lowest division, at the bottom of the ladder, are the imperfect spirits who are characterized by the predominance of their instincts over their moral nature, and by their propensity for harmful acts. Those of the second division are characterized by the predominance of their moral nature over their instincts, and by their love of good. They form the category of good spirits. The first or highest category consists of those who have reached the state of pure spirits and have attained the highest degree of perfection.

This division of spirits into three well-marked categories appears perfectly rational to us. And having arrived at this general classification, it only remains for us to bring out, through a sufficient number of subdivisions, the principal differences in the classes we have established. We have done this with the aid of the spirits themselves, whose friendly instructions have never failed to carry us forward in the work we have started.

The following classification system will help in determining the rank and degree of superiority or inferiority of the spirits with whom we may communicate. It will also allow us to determine the degree of esteem and confidence to which they are entitled. The power of determining these points constitutes the key to Spiritist research. It alone can enlighten us

---

4 Translator's Note: Joseph Pitton de Tournefort (1656-1708), French botanist and physician; Bernard Jusseau (1699-1777), French botanist; Carolus Linnaeus [Carl von Linné] (1707-1778), Swedish botanist.

regarding intellectual and moral inequalities among spirits and explain for us the anomalies presented by spirit communications. We have to remark, however, that spirits don't in all cases belong exclusively to such-and-such a class. Their progress occurs only gradually, and at times, inconsistently. As a result, they may exhibit in themselves the characteristics of several sub-classes—a point easily understood and confirmed by observing their language and acts.

Third Order—Imperfect Spirits

101. General Characteristics

Influence of matter predominates over spirit. There is an inclination toward wrong-doing. Spirits of this order are unaware, proud, self-centered, and exhibit all the negative sentiments that result from such traits.

They intuit the existence of God, although they have no comprehension of God. They are not all thoroughly bad. In many of them, there is more frivolity, lack of thought, and love of mischief than downright badness. Some do neither good nor evil, but the very fact that they do no good denotes their lack of advancement. Others, take pleasure in wrong-doing and are gratified when they find an opportunity of working harm.

Among spirits of this order, a certain amount of intelligence is often allied with malice and love of mischief. But whatever their intellectual development, their ideas are lacking in elevation, and their sentiments are more or less abject.

Their knowledge of the things of the spirit-world is narrow, and the little they know is confused with the ideas and prejudices of their former incarnate life. They can give only false and incomplete notions of the spirit-world; but the attentive observer can often find in their communications, however imperfect, confirmation of the great truths proclaimed by spirits of the higher orders.

Their character is revealed in their language. Every spirit who betrays a wicked sentiment in its communications may be ranked in the third order; consequently, every harmful thought suggested to our minds comes to us from a spirit of that order.

They see the happiness enjoyed by good spirits, and this sight causes them to burn with jealousy and envy.

They hold onto the memory and the impressions of sufferings in the incarnate life, which often creates more painful feelings in them than did the reality. They suffer both from the ills they have endured themselves and from those they have caused others to endure. And as these sufferings continue for a very long time, they believe themselves to be destined to suffer forever. When God allows such beliefs to persist, they are a form of atonement for the offending spirit.

The spirits of this order can be classified into the five lowest classes:

102. Tenth Class - Impure Spirits

They are inclined to wrong-doing, and make it the object of all their thoughts and activities. As spirits, they give human beings unwise advice, stir up conflict and distrust, and assume every sort of disguise in order to mislead more effectively. They besiege those with less developed characters, hoping to win acceptance for their suggestions and thus divert people from the path of progress. They rejoice greatly when their victims give way under the appointed trials of incarnate life.

Spirits of this class can be recognized by their language, since they use coarse or trivial expressions—always a sign of an unevolved moral sense. Their communications show the baseness of their inclinations; and though they may try to impress us by speaking with an appearance of reason and propriety, they are incapable of keeping up false appearances and finally betray their true selves.

Certain cultures have regarded them as infernal deities; others give them such names as "demons," "evil genii," or "evil spirits."

When they incarnate, they display in their lives all the faults brought about by debased sentiments; they are the sex addicts, the rogues, the brutal, the greedy, the insincere. They do wrong for its own sake, without any clear motive. And because they hate all that is good, their targets are generally decent and honorable people. Regardless of their social status, they are a burden to society. Not even the varnish of civilization can hide their true instinctual nature.

103. Ninth Class - Frivolous Spirits

They are unknowing, mischievous, irresponsible, addicted to mockery. They meddle with everything and answer questions with no regard for the truth. They love to cause petty annoyances, raise false hopes of immediate rewards, and deceive people with hoaxes. The spirits in this class have the characteristics commonly attributed to goblins and elves. They often work under orders from other spirits.

In their communications with human beings their language is usually witty and humorous, but shallow. They are quick to discern the oddness and absurdity in people and things, on which they comment sarcastically. If they borrow distinguished names, as they are fond of doing, it is for the fun of it rather than from any malicious intention.

104. Eighth Class - Pseudo-Authorities

Their knowledge is often considerable, but they imagine themselves to know a good deal more than they really do. Since they've made a certain amount of progress from various points of view, their language has about it an air of importance that may easily give a false impression of their real capacities and knowledge. Their ideas are generally nothing more than reflections of the prejudices and false reasoning of their earthly lives.

Their statements contain a mixture of truth and absurdity, along with easily spotted traces of presumption, pride, jealousy, and stubbornness, from which they haven't yet freed themselves.

105. Seventh Class - Ordinary Spirits

They are neither advanced enough to take an active part in doing good nor bad enough to be active in doing wrong. They sometimes lean toward one or the other but they are not, morally or intellectually, above the ordinary level of humanity. They are strongly attached to material things and miss the satisfactions they derived from them.

106. Sixth Class - Noisy and Boisterous Spirits

Strictly speaking, these spirits don't really form a distinct class based on personal qualities. They can be found among all the third-order classes. Often they reveal their presence by producing sensory phenomena, such as rapping sounds, blowing a soft air current, the moving and throwing of objects, etc. More than any other class of spirits, they seem to be attached to matter. They also appear to be active agents in certain environmental occurrences, acting on air, water, fire, and the underground. The phenomena produced may seem logical, but it is hard to assign them either a random or a physical cause. All spirits, of course, can produce physical phenomena. Spirits of the higher orders, however, usually leave them to the lower order of spirits since the latter are better fit to act on matter than to pursue affairs requiring intelligence. When higher spirits find it useful to produce physical manifestations, they enlist the help of this class of spirits.

Second Order—Good Spirits

107. General Characteristics

Spirit predominates over matter. Second order spirits desire the good. Their qualities and their power for good are relative to their current level of advancement. Some of them possess scientific knowledge; others have acquired knowledge and charity. The more advanced ones combine knowledge with moral virtue. Since they aren't completely dematerialized they preserve traces of their incarnate existences that, depending on their level, are more or less noticeable. These traces can be seen in their way of expressing themselves, in their habits, and in some cases, even in characteristic eccentricities and mannerisms which they still retain. Without these weaknesses and imperfections, they could pass into the category of spirits of the first order.

They comprehend the idea of God and of Infinity, and they already share in the bliss of the higher spheres. They find their happiness in doing good and preventing evil. The affection that unites them brings them inexpressible delight, and they are untroubled by envy, remorse, or any of the other negative emotions that torment spirits of the lower degrees. Nonetheless, they still must undergo the discipline of trials until their purification is complete.

As spirits, they instill good and noble thoughts into the minds of human beings, keep them from wrong-doing, and protect those whose life course makes them worthy of aid. These spirits also neutralize, through their suggestions, the influence of lower spirits on the minds of individuals.

The human beings in whom they are incarnated are upright and benevolent. They are not motivated by pride, self-centeredness, or ambition; nor do they feel hatred, rancor, envy, or jealousy. They do good for its own sake.

To this order belong the spirits who are often popularly called "good genii," "protecting genii," "good spirits." In primitive societies they were regarded as beneficent divinities.

They can be divided into the middle four principal groups:

108. Fifth Class - Benevolent Spirits
Their dominant quality is kindness. They take pleasure in serving and protecting human beings, but their knowledge is somewhat narrow. Their moral advancement is greater than their intellectual progress.

109. Fourth Class - Learned Spirits
They are especially distinguished by the extent of their knowledge. They are less interested in spiritual and ethical issues than in scientific investigation, for which they have a greater aptitude. However, their scientific pursuits are for the common good. They are entirely free from the negative emotions that mark spirits of the lower degrees.

110. Third Class - Wise Spirits
The highest ethical qualities form their character. Without having arrived at the possession of unlimited knowledge, they have reached a development of intellectual capacity that allows them to judge human beings and situations with insightful clarity.

111. Second Class - High Spirits
They combine, to a very great degree, scientific knowledge, wisdom, and goodness. Their language, inspired only by the purest benevolence, is always noble and elevated, and often sublime. Their superiority makes them, more likely than any others, to give us just and true ideas about the spirit-world (that is, within the limits our knowledge allows). They willingly enter into communication with persons who honestly and sincerely seek truth, and who are free enough from material bonds to appreciate their teaching. But when questions are prompted only by curiosity and

questioners are motivated more by material than spiritual concerns, they withdraw.

When under exceptional circumstances they incarnate themselves on Earth, it is always to undertake a mission that will lead to our progress. In this way they show us the highest type of perfection to which we can aspire in the present world.

First Order—Pure Spirits

112. General Characteristics

The influence of matter is nil. The superiority of these spirits, both intellectual and moral, is so absolute as to constitute what, by comparison to spirits in all the other orders, can be called perfection.

113. First and Highest Class

These spirits have passed up through all the degrees on the scale of progress and freed themselves from all the impurities of the material world. Having reached the height of perfection for created beings, they no longer undergo trials or purifications. And since they aren't subject any longer to reincarnation in perishable bodies, they enjoy a life of bliss in the immediate presence of Divinity. In other words, with the desires and needs of material life behind them, they exist in a state of unalterable blessedness. But this state doesn't mean that they rest idly in perpetual contemplation. Rather, they are God's messengers and ministers, executors of the Divine Will in the maintenance of universal harmony. They exercise a sovereign command over all spirits lower than themselves, help these spirits accomplish their work of purification, and inspire them in their endeavors. They find it congenial, too, to assist human beings in their distress, encourage the love of good in them, and help them overcome the imperfections which hold them back on the road to supreme happiness. They are sometimes spoken of as "angels," "archangels," or "seraphim."

They can, when they choose, enter into communication with humans. But it is a presumptuous person indeed who thinks they can be summoned at will.

The Progression of Spirits

114. Are spirits good or bad by nature, or do the same spirits advance through their own efforts?

▲ *"The same spirits advance through their own efforts, passing from a lower to a higher order."*

115. Are some spirits created good and others bad?

▲ *"God creates all spirits in a state of simplicity and unawareness—that is, without knowledge. To each one God gives a mission: self-enlightenment and gradual progress toward perfection through the pursuit of knowledge and truth. In this way, they are drawn ever nearer to the Divine presence. This perfection is, a condition of pure and eternal happiness. Spirits acquire knowledge by passing through trials. Some accept these trials with submission and achieve their goal sooner; others endure them with bemoaning and consequently widen the distance that separates them from the perfection and happiness reserved for them."*

—At their origin, then, spirits are like children, unaware and inexperienced, but gradually acquiring knowledge by passing through the different phases of human life. Is this correct?

▲ *"Yes, that's a good analogy. You might say, too, that the willful child remains immature while the more good-natured one progresses quicker. There is this difference, of course: human life comes to an end; that of spirits stretches out into Infinity."*

116. Do any spirits remain forever in the lower ranks?

▲ *"No, all of them reach perfection. It may take a long time, but all eventually progress. Just as a good parent can't condemn a child out of hand, God, Who is the infinite source of goodness and justice, will always be merciful. God's standards couldn't be lower than yours."*

117. Are spirits themselves responsible for hastening their progress toward perfection?

▲ *"Certainly. The length of time it takes them to reach their goal depends on their desire to do so and on their observance of the Law. Don't compliant children learn quicker than idle, stubborn ones?"*

118. Can spirits regress?

▲ *"No. As they advance, they understand the things that hinder their progress. When a spirit finishes a trial, it learns a lesson it will never forget. It may remain in the same place for a while but it never regresses."*

119. Could God exempt spirits from the trials they undergo to reach the highest rank?

▲ *"If spirits were already created perfect, they wouldn't have the merit and joy of sculpting their perfection. We appreciate things more when we have to struggle for them. Besides, toiling and sharing with spirits of different orders is an important factor in a spirit's learning during each stage of growth. Also important is the fact that, as a spirit masters each learning experience, it cooperates with the Divine Plan and contributes to the harmony of the universe."*

Discussion: A good analogy is found in our everyday life. In principle, all persons are able to climb to the highest social ranks. Yet it's no wonder heads of states don't make generals of all of

their soldiers, or department directors of all their civil servants. They must earn it by their own merit. One must be a
student before becoming a teacher. However, there is one
important difference between the human and spirit hierar-
chies. In the former, not all ascend to the highest ranks;
after all, human life is finite. But in the spirit life, which is
eternal, they will all eventually rise to perfection.

120. Do all spirits have to taste evil to arrive at good?

▲ *"Not evil, but unawareness."*

121. Why do some spirits follow the road of good, and others the road of wrong-
doing?

▲ *"God creates all spirits simple, unenlightened, and equally disposed toward
good and bad. That is, God gives them free-will. The wrong-doers choose that
path for themselves."*

122. How can spirits who don't have self-consciousness initially possess freedom
of choice? Do they have some inner principle or tendency that inclines them
toward one road and not the other?

▲ *"The spirit develops free will as it gains self-awareness. If its decisions were
cued by internal pre-programmed principles, the spirit wouldn't have any
free will. On the contrary, the relevant cues are external to the spirit, they are
the scores of influences in its milieu. How it chooses to respond to the different situations determines how it progresses. The significance of this choice is
depicted in the parable of 'the fall of man and original sin': some spirits make
better decisions than others."*

—Where do the negative outside cues that act on a spirit come from?

▲ *"Temptation is allegorically portrayed in the figure of Satan. Actually it
comes from imperfect spirits who try to influence other spirits, to tempt and
cause them to give in."*

—Do these influences act on a spirit only in its early, unaware stage?

▲ *"The spirit may be vulnerable to lower influences in any phase. However, as
it progresses it becomes less and less vulnerable."*

123. Why does God allow for the possibility that a spirit will take the wrong road?

▲ *"Why do you think that God owes you an explanation? The wisdom of God
is shown in the freedom of choice given to every spirit, since everyone has to
earn advancement."*

124. Are there many degrees between those of spirits who from the beginning
chose a path of good and those who chose a path of wrong?

▲ *"Yes, certainly. In these intermediary degrees you will find the vast majority of spirits."*

125. Will the spirits who've chosen the wrong road ever reach the same degree of elevation as the others?

▲ *"Yes, but their journey of redemption will be a longer one."*

Discussion: These spirits advance so slowly that many of them believe that their misery is eternal. This belief is reinforced every time a valuable opportunity for transformation is wasted.

126. Are spirits who reach the supreme degree after wandering into the wrong road less deserving than others in God's sight?

▲ *"God regards the spirits who have returned to the right road with the same approval and affection as the others. They were classed, for a time, among the less advanced orders because they misused their free will. But prior to choosing the wrong road, their predisposition for one way or another was no greater than the others."*

127. Are all spirits created equal intellectually?

▲ *"They are created equal and without knowledge of their origin. As their free will develops, they progress, both morally and intellectually, at their own pace."*

Discussion: Spirits who follow the right road from the beginning do not attain a state of perfection immediately because they still have to acquire the knowledge and experience that goes with this state. Spirits, just like children, however good they may be, need time and experience to develop into maturity. But although spirits, like children, can be good or bad from the start, we need to remember that while children are born with their instincts already formed, a spirit is formed in a state of neutrality—that is, without a predisposition toward either good or evil—and that it uses its free will to determine its path.

Angels and Demons

128. Do the beings we call angels, archangels, and seraphim form a special category different from that of other spirits?

▲ *"No, angels are spirits who have purified themselves of all imperfections and reached the highest degree on the scale of progress."*

Discussion: The word "angel" is generally supposed to imply the idea of ethical perfection. Nonetheless, it is often applied to all beings, good or bad, outside the human realm. We say, "a good angel," "a bad angel," "an angel of light," "the angel of darkness," etc. In these cases, the word is simply a synonym for spirit. Here it is used in its highest sense, a purified spirit.

129. Have the angels passed up through all the degrees of progress?

▲ *"They've passed up through all the degrees, but with the difference that we've already mentioned: that is, the ones who have accepted their mission without complaining have reached the same goal quicker than others."*

130. If the view which claims that some beings are created perfect and superior to all others is wrong, why is it found in the tradition of almost all peoples?

▲ *"Your world hasn't existed from all eternity. Long before it was created, hosts of spirits had already attained the supreme degree; therefore, the people of your Earth naturally supposed those perfected spirits to have always been at the same degree of elevation."*

131. Are there any demons in the usual sense of that term?

▲ *"If demons existed, they would be the work of God. But would it be just on God's part to have created beings condemned to eternal wrong-doing and misery? If demons exist, it is in your unadvanced world and in worlds of similar degree. They are, in fact, the human hypocrites who represent a just God as being cruel and vindictive and who imagine that the bizarre deeds they commit in the name of the Divine Will can make them more acceptable to God."*

Discussion: Only in its modern interpretation does the word "demon" imply the idea of evil spirits. The Greek word *daimon*, from which it is derived, signifies genius, intelligence, and is applied indiscriminately to all immaterial beings, whether good or bad.

Demons or devils, as these words are usually understood, are supposed to be a class of beings who are essentially evil. But if they exist, they must necessarily be, like everything else, a creation of God. And God, who is sovereignly just and good, cannot have created beings predestined to evil by their very nature and condemned beforehand to eternal misery. If, on the contrary, they are not a creation of God, they must, like God, have existed from all eternity; otherwise, there would have to be several creators.

The first requirement of any theory is internal consistency. But the theory that asserts the existence of demons, as the word is popularly understood, essentially lacks this requirement. It is understandable that the religious belief of peoples who knew very little of God's attributes would also admit the existence of malevolent deities and therefore the existence of demons. But those of us who acknowledge perfect goodness to be God's distinguishing quality find it illogical and contradictory to suppose that God could have created beings doomed to evil, and destined to do wrong forever. Such a supposition is the negation of Divine goodness. In answer, those who believe in devils appeal to the words of Christ to support their doctrine. We certainly don't wish to challenge His teachings; but we would rather see them take root in the human heart than be used loosely. Are these people, for instance, quite sure of the meaning Christ attached to the word "devil"? We all know that He uses allegories as a means of teaching and that the Gospels contain many things which aren't to be taken literally. To prove our case, we need only quote the following passage:

"Immediately after the distress of those days the sun will be darkened, and the moon will not give its light; the stars will fall from the sky, and the heavenly bodies will be shaken. At that time the sign of the Son of Man will appear in the sky, and all the nations of the Earth will mourn. I tell you the truth, this generation will not certainly pass away until all these things have happened"[5]

Haven't we seen that the literal form of the biblical text in reference to the creation and movement of the Earth, is contradicted by the discoveries of science? Might it not be the same regarding certain figurative expressions used by Christ as a way of adapting His teachings to the time and scene of His mission? Christ couldn't have made a statement knowing it to be false. If, therefore, His sayings contain statements that appear to be contrary to reason, it is evident that either we don't understand their meaning or that we've misinterpreted them.

Humans have done in regard to devils what they have done in regard to angels. Just as they imagined that there are beings who were created perfect from all eternity, so they imagine that spirits of the lower degrees are beings essentially and eternally evil. But the words demon and devil ought to be understood as indicating impure spirits who are often no better than the imaginary beings called by those names. There is this difference: for spirits, the state of impurity and inferiority is only temporary. We are speaking here of the imperfect spirits who rebel against the learning experiences to which they are subjected and who must undergo those experiences for a longer period. (They will, nonetheless, reach the goal when they are ready.)

5 *Translator's Note: Matthew 24:29,30,34.*

"Demon" and "devil" might possibly indicate rebellious spirits. But because these words have come to be understood exclusively in the false sense—i.e., as descriptors of beings created exclusively for evil—their continued use as a designation for the lower degree of spirits is unjustified.

As for the term "Satan," it is no more than the name given to an allegorical personification of the principle of wrong-doing. Logically, we can't admit the existence of a being who fights against God as an independent and rival power, and whose sole business in life is to contravene the Divine plan. But because images and figures have always fired the human imagination—and necessarily so— humanity has constantly pictured the beings of the spiritual world as having material form, and depicted them as having certain characteristics that have become symbolic of good or evil qualities. Thus the ancients, in personifying the idea of time, represented it as the figure of an old man with a scythe and an hour-glass. To have used the figure of a youth would have been contrary to common sense. The same can be said of the allegories of Fortune, Truth, etc. Today, angels or pure spirits are represented in the form of radiant beings with white wings, an emblem of purity; Satan, on the other hand, is shown with horns, claws, and other animal-like attributes, which can be seen as emblems of negative and instinctual feelings. Unfortunately, many people, confronted with these allegorical figures, have taken them literally and believe them to be real personalities. This is no real advance on the ancients, who accepted the allegorical personifications of the old mythology as absolutely real.

THE INCARNATION OF SPIRITS

The Purpose of Incarnation

132. Why do spirits incarnate?

▲ *"God has established incarnation as the means through which spirits eventually become perfect. Spirits themselves experience incarnation in different ways. For some, it is a process of purification; for others, an opportunity to fulfill a mission. But whatever the individual experience, reaching perfection requires that every spirit undergo the entire range of experiences particular to existence in a material form. The value of the purification process resides in accumulating these experiences.*

"Besides purification, incarnation has a second and no less important function. It allows spirits to perform their proper share in the work of creation. To accomplish this work, the spirit takes on bodily form; a form that enables it to function in the environment in which it is called to live. Under these conditions, the spirit benefits doubly. It contributes to the universal good through performing its own special work, and at the same time, it furthers its own advancement through the process of purification."

Discussion: The work of the universe is served by the actions of incarnated spirits. Wisely, God has also willed that this action should furnish spirits with the means of advancement through which they will eventually come into the Divine presence. As a result of this admirable law of Providence, all things are interconnected, and unity is established among nature's different realms.

133. Is incarnation necessary for spirits who have followed the right road from the beginning?

▲ *"When spirits are created, they are simple and in a state of unawareness. To attain knowledge they must pass through the trials and struggles that attend incarnate life. God, being just, would not grace them with bliss from the beginning. Without experiencing troubles, without exertion on their part, spirits would lack real merit in their own eyes and in God's."*

—Then if no spirit is spared these trials and struggles once it is incarnated, what do spirits have to gain by following the right road?

▲ *"They arrive sooner at the goal of perfection. A spirit's sufferings in life result, more often than not, from its own imperfections. Following the right road ensures that imperfections will be fewer and that the spirit's anguish will be less. Obviously, if a spirit isn't envious, jealous, greedy, or ambitious, it won't have to go through the anguish that inevitably arises from these faults."*

The Soul

134. What is the soul?

▲ *"An incarnate spirit."*

—What was the soul before it united with a body?

▲ *"A spirit."*

—Souls and spirits, then, are the same thing?

▲ *"Yes, souls are only spirits. Before uniting itself with a body, the soul is one of many distinct intelligent beings inhabiting the invisible world. In uniting with the body, the soul temporarily assumes a material form as a way of bringing about its purification and enlightenment."*

135. Is there anything in human beings besides a soul and a body?

▲ *"Yes, there is the link by which the soul and the body are connected."*

—Can you describe this link?

▲ *"It is semi-material. In other words, it is by nature midway between soul and body. Without it, soul and body could not communicate with each other. This is the purpose of the link: it enables the spirit to act on matter and matter to act on the spirit."*

Discussion: A human being is formed of three essential elements. The first element is the body, which humans have in common with animals. As such, the body is animated by the same vital principle that exists in animals. The second element is the soul or incarnate spirit, of which the body is the habitation and means through which the spirit acts. The third element is an intermediary between the body and the spirit; it is a semi-material form called the perispirit. It constitutes the spirit's innermost envelope and unites the spirit with the body. They are similar to the parts of a fruit: core, perisperm, and flesh.[1]

136. Is the soul independent of the vital principle?

▲ *"As we have repeatedly said, the body is only the envelope of the soul."*

—Can a body exist without a soul?

▲ *"Yes, clearly the body continues to exist for a time after the soul has left it. It is also true that prior to birth the union between the soul and the body is incomplete. Once the union has been definitively established, however, only the death of the body can destroy it. Then and then alone can the soul withdraw. Nor can the soul inhabit a body deprived of organic life, although in certain cases organic life can vitalize a body without a soul being present."*

—What would the body be like without the soul?

▲ *"A lump of flesh, lacking intelligent activity. You could call it anything you like, except a human being."*

137. Can the same spirit incarnate itself in two different bodies at the same time?

▲ *"No, the spirit is indivisible and cannot animate two different bodies simultaneously."*[2]

138. What about the assertion that the soul is the principle of material life?

▲ *"This is a matter of terminology. You should begin by agreeing among yourselves about the exact meaning of your words. We don't, among ourselves, attach great importance to them."*

139. Certain spirits, and certain philosophers before them, have defined the soul as "A spark that has emanated from the Great Whole." Why does this contradiction exist?

▲ *"It isn't necessarily a contradiction. Everything depends on the meaning you give these words. Why don't you have a word that is specific to each idea and thing."*[3]

....

1 *It might help to think of this triad-like arrangement in terms of the structure of a peach or an apricot. At the core of these fruits exists a nucleus, i.e., an inner germ, which we can think of as the spirit. The nucleus is surrounded by a stone or perisperm, which in us is analogous to the perispirit. The stone, in turn, is surrounded by the edible flesh of the fruit, which is comparable to our body.*

....

2 *See the chapter "Bi-Corporeality and Transfiguration" in Allan Kardec's,* The Mediums' Book, *Samuel Weiser Inc., 1999 (reprint), Chapter 7.*

....

3 *Translator's Note: For coherence, Allan Kardec adopted the convention of using the word soul to mean an incarnate spirit; when the soul is free from the physical body it is called simply spirit. For a more complete discussion of this issue, see Part II of the Explanatory Notes, of this text.*

Discussion: The word "soul" is frequently used to express very differ-
                ent things. At times, for example, it denotes the principle of
                life itself. Explained in this way, it is correct to say, at least
                figuratively, that the soul is a spark that has emanated from
                the Great Whole. Here the phrase "the Great Whole" refers
                to the universal source of the vital principle. From this
                source, each being absorbs a portion, which it relinquishes
                back into the Great Whole after the being's physical death.
                It is important to note that this definition does not exclude
                the idea of an autonomous being which has a distinct per-
                sonality, is independent of matter, and preserves its own
                individuality. Since this is the sense in which we speak of
                the soul as an incarnate spirit, this latter definition can
                account for the being we call the soul.

                In providing different definitions of "soul," the spirits
                are often speaking in different contexts. In some cases their
                discourse still reflects the influence of their own earthly
                views. The confusion really results from an inadequacy of
                human language. Since there is not a specific word for each
                concept, a vast number of misunderstandings have grown
                up, prompting many onerous discussions. For this reason
                the higher spirits always ask us to begin by distinctly defin-
                ing our words.

140. According to one theory, the soul is subdivided. It has as many parts as there
are organs in the body. In this way, the theory proposes, the soul governs each
bodily function. What should we think of this view?

▲ *"Once again, it depends on the meaning you give the word 'soul.' If you
    define 'soul' to mean the animating force of life, the theory is right. If you use
    'soul' to mean an incarnate spirit, it is completely wrong. Remember what
    we have told you—a spirit is indivisible. The spirit controls organic activity
    through the intermediary element, the perispirit."*

—Nonetheless, there are spirits who have given this definition.

▲ *"Uninformed spirits have been known to mistake effects for causes."*

Discussion: The soul acts in the material world through the intermedi-
                ary of the body's organs. The organs, in turn, are animated

by the vital principle which is distributed among them, being concentrated especially at their centers of activity. Consequently, to equate the soul and the vital principle is incorrect when we mean by "soul" the spirit that inhabits the body during life and leaves it at death.

141. Is there any truth in the view that the soul is exterior to the body and surrounds it?

▲ *"The soul isn't shut up in the body like a bird in a cage. It radiates in all directions and manifests itself outside the body. Think of it, if you will, as a light radiating from a lightbulb, or as a sound being emitted in successive waves from a struck bell or some other resonating source. In this special sense the soul is exterior to the body. But don't conclude, as a result, that it envelops the body, too. The soul has two envelopes. The first, innermost one has a light and subtle nature; it is what you call the perispirit. The second, outer one—which is more dense, material, and heavy—is the body. The soul exists at the center of both these envelopes, like the nucleus in the stone of the fruit, as we have said."*

142. What about the theory that the "soul" undergoes a process of formation that begins in childhood and is carried on through the successive stages of human life?

▲ *"The spirit is a unit. It's as complete in the child as it is in the adult. Only the body's organs, the instruments through which the soul acts, gradually and completely develop during a lifetime. Here, again, you mistake the effect for the cause."*

143. Why don't all spirits define the soul in the same way?

▲ *"All spirits aren't equally knowledgeable about these matters. Some have still advanced so little intellectually that they have no understanding of abstract ideas. They're like the children of Earth. Others are full of false learning and use high sounding but empty words in an attempt to impose their authority on listeners. And they, too, resemble many in your world. But frequently even spirits who really are enlightened will express themselves in terms that appear to differ but that, at bottom, mean the same thing. This usually occurs when matters come up that your language is incapable of clearly expressing and that can only be communicated by means of figures and comparisons, which you often mistake for literal statements of fact."*

144. What are we to understand by "the soul of the world"?

▲ *"It's the universal principle of life that produces individual beings. But very often the people who use these terms confuse their meaning. The word 'soul' is so elastic that everyone interprets it according to his or her own fancy. Certain persons have even attributed a soul to the Earth. 'Soul of the world' can be understood as indicating the assembly of devoted spirits who steer the progress of humankind, especially when you listen to them. They are, as it were, God's lieutenants in the administration of Earth."*

145. Why have so many philosophers, ancient and modern, studied the soul without arriving at the truth?

▲ *"These thinkers were precursors of the ideas contained in the Spiritist Doctrine, for which they prepared the way. Being human and subject to mistakes, they often confused their own ideas with the true light. Still, even their errors served the cause of truth, since they brought both sides of the argument into relief. Among those errors you will find many great truths, as a comparative study of the various theories held by these philosophers will make plain."*

146. Does the soul have a definite location within the body?

▲ *"No—although, in the case of geniuses and people who think a great deal, it can be said to be more centered in the brain. In people of an emotional nature, particularly those who act primarily from compassionate motives, it can be said to reside in the heart."*

—Then what are we to think of people who locate the soul in a center of organic life?

▲ *"You might say that the spirit is more likely to inhabit that part of your organism because all the sensations converge there. But those who place it in what they consider to be the center of vitality confuse it with the vital principle. A better analogy would be to say that the soul is more apt to reside in the centers which we associate with feelings and intellectual activities."*

Materialism

147. Why are anatomists, physiologists, and scientists in general, so often materialists?

▲ *"Scientists refer everything to the senses. And then, too, there is a kind of pride that leads people to believe that they can explain everything, that refuses to admit that anything is beyond human understanding. Science itself can make some minds presumptuous. These people imagine nature has no secrets they can't unravel."*

148. It's unfortunate that studies that ought to convince us of the superiority of the Intelligence governing our world should lead instead to materialism. Is this an indictment against scientific investigation?

▲ *"Actually, materialism isn't a consequence of those studies. It results from the imperfection that leads so many to draw false conclusions from the studies. People can put the very best things to the poorest use at times. You might consider, in this regard, that a belief in absolute annihilation, which is a chief tenet of materialism, upsets its defenders far more than they'll admit. Its loudest advocates are usually more boastful than brave. Most so-called materialists come to their convictions only because they can't find a rational ground for belief in a future life. A gaping void opens beneath them. Show them that rational ground and they'll grasp at it with the eagerness of the drowning who have had a life-line thrown to them."*

Discussion: Some people, through an imperfection of intellect, can see nothing in human beings but the action of matter. Hence, they attribute all the phenomena of existence to this action. They see the human body entirely as an electro-chemical machine, and they study the mechanism of life only in terms of organ interactions. So when they see, as they often do, a life snuffed out by the rupture of a single vein, their whole focus becomes the vein. They may look to see if any other evidence of life remains. But since the only thing they find is inert matter, and since they haven't seen the soul leave the body or been able to touch it, they conclude that everything can be reduced to mere matter and that death is the annihilation of all thought. A sad inference, if true. It would mean that good and bad are exactly alike—purposeless. In that case, everyone would be justified in thinking only of themselves and in considering only the gratification of their senses. All social ties would be broken; the holiest bonds of affection would be destroyed forever. Happily for us, these ideas are not widely accepted. Their scope is narrow, being limited to subjective opinion only, and they have never been erected into a doctrinal system.[4] A society founded on such ideas would contain within itself the seeds of its own destruction, like a group of wild beasts of prey whose members tear each other to pieces.

Human beings intuitively believe that all does not end with the death of the body. We have a horror of annihilation. And no matter how strongly we oppose the idea of a future life, there are few of us who, faced with death, don't anxiously wonder what is going to happen to us. The idea of our saying good-bye to life forever will dismay the most courageous heart. After all, can anyone really feel detached at the prospect of being separated, absolutely and eternally, from everything he or she has loved? Or imagine, without feeling the terror of it, the mere nothingness in which every faculty and cherished aspiration is to be swallowed

....

4 *Translator's Note: The materialistic philosophy of Karl Marx came the closest to this concept. Karl Marx's* Das Kapital *was published in 1867, 10 years after the publication of* The Spirits' Book.

up? There aren't many who will calmly say: "After my death there will be nothing left but the void of annihilation. Everything will be over. After awhile, no memory of me will survive. Earth will retain no trace of my existence. The good I've done will be forgotten by the people I've helped. And nothing will compensate me for all this loss. Beyond all this ruin, the only future I can look forward to is the certainty that my body will be eaten by worms!"

Isn't there something horrible in that picture, something that sends a chill through the heart? Religion teaches us that this can't be our destiny. And our reason confirms this teaching. Yet vague, indefinite assurances of a life after death fail to satisfy our natural desire for some positive proof. It is the lack of this proof that causes us to doubt the afterlife's reality.

"Even if we admit that we have a soul," many naturally ask, "what are we actually talking about? Does the soul have a form? Does it have a particular appearance? Is it a well-defined being, or something undefined and impersonal? Some people call it 'a breath of God'; others insist it is a spark. Still others claim it is 'part of the Great Whole, the principle of life and intelligence.' But what do we learn from these statements? What's the good of having a soul if it's only going to be merged in immensity like a drop of water in the ocean? Isn't the loss of our individuality equal, as far as we're concerned, to annihilation? Again, some say the soul is immaterial. But the immaterial has no defined proportions, and therefore no reality for us. Religion also teaches us that our happiness or unhappiness depends on the good or bad we've done. But what about the happiness or unhappiness that we've been promised in the future life? What can it be like? Is happiness a state of blessedness in the bosom of God, an eternal contemplation that consists entirely of singing the praises of the Creator? And the flames of hell: are they real or simply a figure of speech? Traditional theology gives them a figurative meaning. But what kind of suffering does this figure suggest? And where do those 'sufferings' occur? In short, what shall we be, what shall we do, what shall we see, in that other world where all of us are said to be going?"

No one, it is claimed, has ever come back to give us an account of that world. But this statement is wrong. The mission of the Spiritist Doctrine is precisely to enlighten us regarding our future state and to enable us, within limits, to see and touch it, not merely as a deduction of our reason, but through the evidence of facts. Thanks to communications made to us by the people of that other world, the future life is no longer a matter of mere presumption or probability. We no longer have to fantasize about the world of the afterlife or read poets who embellish it with fictions and allegorical images that mostly delude us. We now have brought before us that other world itself, in its reality. The beings of the life beyond the grave come to us. They describe the situations in which they find themselves; they tell us what they are doing; they allow us to become, so to speak, spectators of their new order of life. And they show us the inevitable fate that is reserved for each of us according to our merits or misdeeds. Is there anything anti-religious in such a demonstration? Not at all. Rather, it furnishes unbelievers with a ground of belief, and inspires lukewarm believers with renewed fervor and confidence.

The Spiritist Doctrine can be seen, then, as a most powerful auxiliary of true religion. As such, it must be acknowledged to exist by accordance of God, for the purpose of giving strength to our wavering convictions and leading us back onto the right road by showing us the prospect of our future happiness.

THE RETURN TO THE SPIRIT LIFE

The Soul After Death

149. What happens to the soul at the moment of death?

▲ *"It becomes a spirit again; that is to say, it returns to the world of spirits, which it had temporarily left."*

150. Does the soul preserve its individuality after death?

▲ *"Yes, it never loses its identity. What would the soul be without an identity?"*

—How does the soul assert its individuality, since it no longer has a material body?

▲ *"It still has a semi-material body peculiar to itself, which it draws from the atmosphere of its planet and which represents the appearance of its last incarnation—its perispirit (spiritual body)."*

—Does the soul retain anything from an incarnate life?

▲ *"Nothing but the memory of that life and the desire to go to a better world. This memory can be sweet or bitter depending on the use the soul made of the earthly life it has left behind. The more advanced it is, the more clearly it sees the futility of what it has left on Earth."*

151. There are people who subscribe to the opinion that the soul returns to the Universal Whole after death? What is your reaction to this?

▲ *"Don't all spirits, considered in their totality, constitute a whole? And does not this whole constitute a world? When you're in an assembly, you form an integral part of that assembly, and yet you still retain your individuality."*

152. Is there any proof that the soul preserves its individuality after death?

▲ *"Aren't these communications proof enough? If you didn't blind yourself to us, you would see; if you didn't close your ears to us, you would hear. You are often spoken to by an 'inner voice' that gives you the intuition of an 'invisible presence' near you."*

Discussion: Those who believe that the soul returns to the Universal Whole after death are wrong if they imagine that there, like a drop of water that falls into the ocean, it loses its individuality. They are right if they mean by the Universal Whole the totality of spirit-world beings, of which each individual soul or spirit is an element.

If souls were blended together into a mass, they would have only those qualities common to the whole. There would be nothing to distinguish them from one another: they would have no special intellectual or other quality of their own. But the communications from the spirits make it abundantly clear that each spirit is conscious of itself and has a distinct personal will. The infinite diversity of characteristics the spirits reveal is both the result of, and evidence for, a distinctive individuality. Moreover, if there were nothing after death but what is called the "Great Whole," which absorbs all individuality, this whole would be uniform in its characteristics, and communications received from the invisible world would be identical. But among the dwellers of that other world we meet with some who are good, others who are bad; some who are knowledgeable, others who are unaware; some who are happy, others who are unhappy. They present us with every shade of character, some being frivolous and others serious, etc. From this, it is evident that they are perfectly distinct from one another. Their individuality becomes still clearer when they are able to prove their identity by unmistakable manifestations and by verifiable details of their terrestrial life. And it cannot be a matter of doubt when they make themselves visible to us.

The individuality of the soul has been taught theoretically as an article of faith. The Spiritist Doctrine renders it clear and distinct and, so to speak, a material fact.

153. In what sense should we understand eternal life?

▲ *"The life of the spirit is everlasting; the life of the body is transitory and fleeting. When the body dies, the soul re-enters the world of eternal life."*

—Wouldn't it be more accurate to apply the term "eternal life" to the life of purified spirits, who have attained a degree of relative perfection and no longer have to experience suffering?

▲ *"For spirits of that degree, life might be better termed 'eternal happiness.' But this is a question of words. You may call things whatever you please, as long you agree about their meaning among yourselves."*

Separation of Soul and Body

154. Is the separation of the soul from the body painful?

▲ *"No, the body often suffers more during life than at the moment of death, when the soul is usually unaware of what is happening to the body. In fact, the sensations experienced at the moment of death are often a source of enjoyment for the spirit who recognizes them as marking the end of its term of exile."[1]*

Discussion: In cases of natural death, which occurs as the result of the exhaustion of bodily organs through age, the soul passes out of life without realizing that it is doing so. The process can be compared to the flame of a lamp that goes out because of a lack of oil.

155. How is the separation of soul and body brought about?

▲ *"When the bonds that keep the soul linked to the body break, the soul disengages itself."*

—Does this transition come about instantaneously and abruptly? Is there, between life and death, a distinct line of demarcation?

▲ *"No, the soul disengages itself gradually. It doesn't escape from the body all at once, like a bird that suddenly finds its cage open. The two states touch and blend into each other. The spirit frees itself little by little from its fleshly bonds, which loosen but for a time do not break entirely."*

Discussion: During life, a spirit is held to the body by its semi-material envelope, or perispirit. Death destroys the body but not this second envelope, which separates itself from the body at death. Observations show us that the separation of the perispirit from the body doesn't happen abruptly at the moment of death but happens gradually and with various

....

1 Translator's Note: *The sense of enjoyment seems to be a natural feature of the process of death as reported by patients who suffered clinical death. The literature on near-death experience presents a wealth of evidence on the death and dying process. For some of the pioneer works in this discipline see R. Moody,* Life After Life, *Atlanta: Mockingbird Books, 1975; and K. Ring,* Life at Death, *New York: Quill, 1982.*

degrees of slowness in different individuals. In some cases it happens so quickly that the perispirit is entirely separated from the body within a few hours. In others, and especially in those whose lives have been highly materialistic and sensual, the release is much slower, sometimes taking days, weeks, even months. This delay doesn't mean that the life of the body in any way continues or that there is any possibility that the body will return to life. It is simply the result of an affinity between the body and the spirit, which is always more or less tenacious, depending on how close to material life the spirit was while on Earth. It is then only rational to suppose that the closer a spirit has identified itself with matter, the greater the difficulty it will have in separating from its material body. On the contrary, intellectual and introspective activity, and habitual elevation of thought, causes this separation to start even during the life of the body. Thus, when death occurs, the separation is almost instantaneous. The study of a great number of individuals has also shown that an inordinate identification between the soul and the body can, after death, be extremely distressing since, by resonance, such identification forces the spirit into an awareness of the horror of bodily decomposition. Such unfortunate experiences are the exception rather than the rule; it is peculiar only to certain kinds of life and certain kinds of death. It occurs, sometimes, in the case of suicides.

156. Can a definite separation of the soul and body take place before organic life stops completely?

▲ *"Sometimes the soul leaves the body before the last agony comes; in this case the last agony becomes only the closing act of its organic life. The dying person no longer has any self-consciousness, but a faint breath of vitality remains for awhile. At that point, the body is only a machine that is kept operating by the heart. It continues to 'live' as long as the heart pumps blood through its veins. It has no need of a soul to do that."*

157. Does the soul ever experience, at the moment of death, a desire or an ecstasy that gives it a glimpse of the world it is about to re-enter?

▲ *"The soul often feels the loosening of the bonds that attach it to the body, and it does its utmost to hasten and complete the work of separation. Already partially freed from matter, it sees the future unroll before it and enjoys, in anticipation, the spirit-state it is about to return to."*

158. On Earth we notice the metamorphosis of the caterpillar, which first crawls

on the ground, then shuts itself up in its chrysalis as if dead, and finally is reborn as a butterfly, taking on a new and brilliant existence. Does this give us anything like a true idea of the relationships among our terrestrial life, our experience of death, and our new existence in the spirit-world?

▲ *"An idea yes, but on a very small scale. It's a good analogy, but don't accept it literally, as you often do with these images."*

159. What sensation does the soul experience at the moment it regains consciousness in the spirit-world?

▲ *"That depends on the circumstances. If the soul has done wrong from the love of wrong-doing on Earth, it is overwhelmed with shame. For the soul who has done good, things are very different. It seems to have been relieved of a heavy burden, and it does not dread the most searching glance."*

160. Does the spirit immediately find itself in the company of the ones it knew on Earth who died before it?

▲ *"Yes, and more or less promptly depending on the strength of their mutual affection. Spirits will often come to meet a spirit on its return to the spirit-world and help to free it from the bonds of matter. Others, which a spirit knew but lost sight of on Earth, will also come to meet it. Finally, it can both see those in the spirit-world and visit the ones who are still incarnated."*

161. In cases of violent or accidental death, where the organs haven't been damaged by age or illness, does the separation of the soul take place as soon as the organic life ends?

▲ *"In general, the interval between separation and organic death is very brief."*

162. After capital punishment, for instance, does a person retain consciousness for a longer or shorter time?

▲ *"The person frequently stays conscious for a few minutes, until the organic life of the body is completely extinct. But the fear of imminent death often causes the individual to lose consciousness before the moment of execution."*

Discussion: The question asked concerns the person's self-awareness as a physical individuality. This awareness may linger a few moments after execution, but it will disappear with the death of the brain. However, brain death does not necessarily imply the complete separation of the perispirit from the body. On the contrary, in all cases of death resulting from violence rather than the gradual extinction of vital forces, the bonds that unite the body to the perispirit are stronger and the separation comes about more slowly.

The State of the Soul After Death

163. Does the soul regain self-awareness immediately after leaving the body?

▲ *"Not all at once. For a time it is in a state of confusion that obscures its perceptions."*

164. Do all spirits experience this confusion to the same degree and for the same length of time?

▲ *"No, this depends entirely on their degree of elevation. Spirits who have already achieved a certain amount of purification and freed themselves from the grip of matter during their incarnate life will recover consciousness almost immediately. Those spirits who have loved the flesh or whose consciences aren't clear, will retain the impression of matter far longer."*

165. Does a knowledge of the Spiritist Doctrine exert any influence on the length of this state of confusion?

▲ *"A very considerable influence, since it allows the spirit to understand beforehand the new situation in which it is about to find itself. But the practice of goodness during the earthly life, and a clear conscience, are factors that shorten this experience far more effectively."*

Discussion: At the moment of death, everything appears confused. The spirit takes time to recover self-consciousness. Seemingly, it is stunned, like someone who suddenly wakes up out of a deep sleep and needs a few minutes to get his or her bearings. Gradually, though, bodily impressions dissipate, the fog obscuring the spirit's perception lifts, and the spirit regains clearness of thought and its memory of the past.

The length of this confused state varies considerably. It may be only a few hours; it may continue for several months, or even years. It is least for spirits who, during the incarnate life, identified themselves most closely with their future state, since they are sooner able to understand their new situation.

This state of confusion takes on special aspects depending on individual character and manner of death. In cases of violent or sudden death—by suicide, capital punishment, accident, stroke, etc.—the spirit is often astounded, doesn't believe itself to be dead, and stubbornly persists in asserting the contrary. Nonetheless, it sees the body it has left as something apart from itself. It knows the body to be its own, although it can't understand how the body became separated from it. It then goes about among its living friends and relatives, speaks to them, and becomes puzzled when they do not hear it. This sort of illusion lasts until the separation of the perispirit and the incarnate body is complete, since only then does the spirit begin to understand its actual situation and realize it is no longer part of the human world. Since death has come by surprise, the spirit is stunned by the suddenness of the change that has taken place. For it, death may still be synonymous with destruction and annihilation.

But as the spirit continues to think, see, and hear, it doesn't seem to itself to be dead. The illusion is further strengthened by the apparent similarity between its present body and the one it has just left. At first it doesn't realize the rarefied nature of this new body, and supposes it to be as solid and compact as the other. When its attention is called to its new state, it is astonished to find the new body is of different density The phenomenon is similar to what happens to hypnotized subjects who, when they are first placed into hypnotic sleep, refuse to believe they are not awake. Sleep, for them, is synonymous with the suspension of perception. But because they can think freely and see, they don't appear to themselves to be sleeping at all.

Some spirits experience this confused state even in cases where death has been expected. But it occurs most frequently in cases where, though they may have been ill, individuals have not expected to die. The curious spectacle is then presented of a spirit attending its own funeral, as if the service were for someone else, and speaking of the event as an impersonal matter—that is, until the moment when it finally understands the true state of affairs.

In the mental confusion which follows death, there is nothing painful to the person who has lived honorably on Earth. Such a spirit remains calm, and death appears as a peaceful awakening from sleep. But for spirits with troubled consciences the awakening is filled with anxiety and distress, which become all the more poignant as the spirit recovers full consciousness.

In cases of collective death, in which many persons have died in the same catastrophe, it has been observed that they do not always see one another immediately afterwards. In the confusion that follows, each spirit goes its own way or concerns itself only with those in whom it takes an interest.

CHAPTER VIII

MANY LIVES

Reincarnation

166. How does a soul that has not reached perfection on Earth complete its work of purification?

▲ *"By undergoing the trial of a new life."*

— How can a soul start life anew? Are you referring to the changes it experiences in a new life in the realm of spirit?

▲ *"Purification does require change. But, in order to bring about true inner transformation, the soul needs the trials of a new physical life."*

—The soul, then, has lived many lives in the physical realm?

▲ *"Yes, we have all had many lives. Those who preach the contrary lack real awareness and, in this respect, misinform you with their conjectures."*

—The soul, after leaving one body, takes another one. In other words, it reincarnates itself in a new body. Is this your meaning?

▲ *"Yes."*

167. What is the purpose of reincarnation?

▲ *"Purification, to redress previous mistakes, and to effect human progress. Otherwise, there would be no justice."*

168. Is there a set limit to the number of incarnate lives, or does a spirit go on reincarnating forever?

▲ *"With each new life, a spirit takes a step forward on the path of progress. When it has stripped itself of all impurities, it will no longer need the trials of incarnate life."*

169. Is the number of incarnations the same for all spirits?

▲ *"No. The ones who advance quickly save themselves many trials. Still, a spirit commonly experiences many successive incarnations. Progress is almost infinite."*

170. What happens to a spirit after its last incarnation?

▲ *"It enters into the state of perfect happiness, as a purified spirit."*

The Justice of Reincarnation

171. What is the basis for the doctrine of reincarnation?

▲ *"The justness of God, and revelation. As we've said already, a loving parent always leaves the door of forgiveness open to straying children. Doesn't reason convince you that it would be unjust to withhold happiness eternally from spirits who haven't had the chance to improve themselves? All of us are God's children. Injustice, unrelenting hatred, everlasting punishments are concepts you find among self-centered and less advanced humans, but not in God."*

Discussion: All spirits strive toward perfection, and God furnishes them with the means of acquiring it through the trials of life in the body. But Divine justice also requires spirits to achieve, in their new existences, the things they had not been able to do or complete in previous trials.

Condemning spirits to eternal suffering would be inconsistent with God's justice and goodness since spirits meet with stumbling blocks to improvement that they haven't sought and that result from conditions beyond their control. Furthermore, if spirits' fates were conclusively determined after death, God would not be weighing all their actions in the same scale and would not be treating them all with impartiality.

The doctrine of reincarnation—that is, the doctrine that human beings have many successive lives—alone conforms to our idea of justice for individuals whose spiritual progress is just beginning. It is the only one that can explain the future to us and that, by offering us the chance to right our mistakes through new trials, can furnish us with a sound basis for our hopes. Reincarnation is supported by reason, then, as well as by the teachings of our spirit-instructors.

The person who acknowledges his or her personal imperfections can draw hope from reincarnation. If a believer in God's justice, he or she cannot hope to attain, at once and for all eternity, the same level as individuals who have made a better use of life. But the knowledge that these imperfections do not automatically exclude one from supreme happiness forever, and that one can achieve this happiness through renewed efforts, revives and sustains our courage and energy. In addition, people often regret at the end that many of their experiences have come too late to be useful. Reincarnation assures them that these experiences will not be lost and that they will profit by them in a new incarnation.

Incarnation on Different Planets

172. Do we lead all our incarnate lives on Earth?

▲ *"Not all of them. You may find that you have lived on many different planets. The one on which you live now certainly isn't the only one that can support incarnate life, though it is one of the most material and farthest removed from perfection."*

173. Does the soul pass from one planet to another with each new incarnation, or can it live several lives on the same planet?

▲ *"It can live many times on the same planet if it hasn't progressed enough to pass onto a higher one."*

—We may, then, come back to Earth several times?

▲ *"Certainly."*

—Can we come back to Earth after having lived on other planets?

▲ *"Definitely. You might have lived elsewhere than on Earth already."*

174. Are we required to live on Earth again?

▲ *"No. But if you don't advance, you may reincarnate on a planet no better than this one, or even worse."*

175. Is there any advantage in coming back to live on Earth?

▲ *"No special advantage, unless one has a mission to fulfill. But in that case the spirit advances no matter where it is incarnated."*

—Wouldn't it be better to remain in the spirit-realm?

▲ *"No, no! Then you would remain stationary, and you want to advance toward God."*

176. Can spirits come to this planet for the first time, after having been incarnated on others?

▲ *"Yes, just as you may go to other ones. All the planets are united by a common purpose. What you don't do or finish on one, you can do or finish on another."*

—Some of those now living on Earth, then, are here for the first time?

▲ *"Many of them are, and at various stages of advancement."*

—Is there any way we can know the spirits who are here for the first time?

▲ *"The knowledge wouldn't be of the slightest use to you."*

177. In arriving at perfection and supreme happiness, does a spirit have to reincarnate on all the planets in the universe?

▲ *"No. A great number of planets are at the same stage, and a spirit would learn nothing new on them."*

—How can we explain, then, the numerous lives a spirit may live on the same planet?

▲ *"It may find itself, with each return, in very different situations that still allow it to acquire new experience."*

178. Can spirits reincarnate on planets relatively less advanced than the ones on which they've lived already?

▲ *"Yes, when they have a mission to fulfill in aid of progress. In such cases they accept the trials of such a life gladly, because these will help them advance."*

—Doesn't this also happen as a means of atonement? And doesn't God send rebellious spirits to planets at lower developmental stages?

▲ *"Spirits may remain stationary; they never regress. Rebellious spirits are 'punished' only in the sense that they do not go forward. They may have to begin their new incarnate lives under exactly the same conditions as before— which were, anyway, the most appropriate conditions for their advancement."*

—Which spirits must do this?

▲ *"The ones who fail to fulfill their tasks or have wasted the learning experiences afforded by their physical existence."*

179. Have all the beings that live on any given planet arrived at the same level of perfection?

▲ *"No. The situation is similar to the one on Earth. Some spirits are more advanced, others less."*

180. When a spirit passes from one planet to the next, does it retain its intelligence?

▲ *"Yes. Intelligence is never lost. But the spirit might not have the same means of expressing it. This depends on both its level of advancement and the capabilities of the body it takes."*[1]

181. Do beings on other planets have bodies like ours?

....

1 *See questions 367-370 on the influence of the body over the spirit's ability to manifest its faculties.*

▲ *"Without question they have bodies, because a spirit needs some material envelope that allows it to act on matter. This envelope, though, can be more or less material depending on the level of spiritual progress of the different planets. In the house of God there are many mansions, and many differing levels among those mansions. Some know this while on Earth; others have no conception of it."*

182. Is any exact knowledge of the physical and spiritual state of the different planets possible?

▲ *"We spirits can only reply according to your present degree of advancement. In other words, we can't reveal such things indiscriminately. Many people are not at a stage that would allow them to understand such revelations; they would find them confusing."*

Discussion: As a spirit advances, the physical body it inhabits becomes less and less coarse. This body no longer moves heavily on the ground. Its needs are less gross. And on more advanced planets, beings no longer need to kill other beings for food. A spirit incarnated on such a planet enjoys a greater degree of freedom, and it has powers of perception unknown to us: it sees in actuality what we see only in thought.

The purity of a spirit is reflected in the moral excellence of the being in which it is incarnated. In such a being bodily desires and appetites are weaker. Self-centeredness gives way to feelings of fellowship. Consequently, on planets more advanced than Earth, wars are unknown. No one thinks of doing harm to anyone else, and so there is no motive for hatred or conflict. The beings on these planets intuit their future; and since they have clear consciences, their attitude toward death connotes no fear. For them, death is simply a process of transformation.

The life span on the different planets appears to be proportional to each planet's degree of physical and moral advancement—a perfectly reasonable arrangement. The less material the body, the less prone it is to the physical vulnerabilities that eventually disorganize it. The purer the spirit, the less subject it is to passions that undermine and destroy it. This correspondence between moral progress and physical qualities proves the excellence of Providential law in providing ways to reduce suffering.

183. On entering a new life on another planet, does the spirit always have to go through a new infancy?

▲ *"Infancy is a necessary stage of life on all planets, but in many of them it is not as inhibiting (for the spirit) as it is on yours."*

184. Can a spirit choose the planet it will live on?

▲ *"Not always. But it can request a particular one, and if the spirit has earned it, the request might be granted. The access spirits have to the various planets differs according to their level of progress."*

—If a spirit doesn't make a request, what determines the planet on which it will be reincarnated?

▲ *"Its degree of progress."*

185. Is the physical and moral state of the thinking beings on each planet always the same?

▲ *"No. Like the beings that live on them, planets are subject to the law of progress. All of them began, like yours, in an unadvanced state. But Earth, too, will undergo a transformation similar to theirs. When its inhabitants as a whole choose goodness, it will become a terrestrial paradise."*

Discussion: The peoples now on Earth will gradually disappear, succeeded by others whose members will be increasingly more evolved. This is an altogether natural process. Our current peoples have themselves succeeded other, less developed ones.

186. Do planets exist on which spirits no longer need material bodies and have no envelope except the perispirit?

▲ *"Yes. This envelope becomes so ethereal that you wouldn't be able to perceive it. This is the state of the fully purified spirits."*

—Isn't there, then, a clear line of demarcation between beings in their later incarnations and pure spirits?

▲ *"No such demarcation line exists. Gradually, the difference between these two orders grows less and less. They blend into one another as the darkness melts into the dawn."*

187. Is the substance of the perispirit the same on all planets?

▲ *"No, it is more or less ethereal. On going from one planet to another, a spirit takes on the matter appropriate to each planet, changing its envelope with lightning quickness."*

188. Do pure spirits live on special worlds, or are they in universal space without being attached to any particular one?

▲ *"The pure spirits live on certain worlds. But they aren't confined to them as humans are confined to Earth. To a much greater extent than others, they have the power of going everywhere."*[2]

Progressive Transmigrations

189. Does the spirit enjoy the full range of its faculties as soon as it is formed?

▲ *"No. Spirits, like human beings, have their infancy. Early on, their life is*

....

2 Translator's Note: *The following footnote is presented for historical reasons as it reflects the views (and hopes) of the mid-1800s. Unless we take it to mean spiritual forms of life, we must embrace the conclusions of modern space science that there is no Earth-like physical life on these planets.*

"According to the spirits, Earth is one of the least advanced planets in terms of physical and ethical development of its inhabitants. Mars is said to be even less developed, while Jupiter is considered to be greatly superior to Earth in every respect. The sun is uninhabited by incarnate beings, but it does serve as a meeting place for spirits of the higher orders, who send out waves of thought from it toward the planets of the solar system. These spirits guide the planets through the agency of less elevated spirits, transmitting directives to them by means of the cosmic principle. Physically, our sun appears to be a focus of energy; in nature and function, other suns seem to be identical to ours.

The size of planets and their distance from the sun have no necessary relation to their level of advancement. Thus Venus is said to be more advanced than the larger Earth, and Saturn less advanced than the more distant Jupiter.

Several spirits who were well-known persons on Earth have claimed to be reincarnated on Jupiter. Indeed it has been a matter of surprise that people who do not seem to have earned it, are sometimes admitted onto this seemingly more advanced world. But there should be nothing surprising in this. Consider, first, that some of these spirits may have been sent to live on Earth to fulfill a mission, though not a salient one in our eyes. Second, between their lives here and those on Jupiter, spirits may have led intermediate lives in which they advanced. Third, spiritual orders represented on Jupiter may be as numerous as on Earth, and there may be a great deal of difference between the various degrees, just as there is here. It is, then, no more logical to assume that a spirit is on a level with the most advanced beings of Jupiter simply because it lives there than it is to suppose that an ignoramus and a philosopher are on the same level because they live in the same town. The lifespan is also as varied on other planets as it is on Earth, though no comparable age standards can be established for them. A person who died some years ago was summoned at an assembly and claimed that he had been incarnated for six months on a planet unknown to us. Asked about his age on the planet, he answered, "That is a point I can't decide. In the first place, we don't count time in the same way you do, and in the second, our way of life is different from yours. We develop much more rapidly here so that, while apparently only six Earth-months have passed since I came here, I already have the mental ability of an adult person on Earth."

A great many similar replies have been given by spirits, and there is nothing impossible about them. After all, numerous animals on Earth reach their full maturity within a few months. Why couldn't it be similar with intelligent beings on other spheres? The level of development of a thirty year old on Earth may be only a sort of infancy on more advanced planets, where an individual soul can expect to make far more progress in the course of a lifetime. In reality, people who view our present selves as being in every way the normal type in Creation are simply shortsighted. It is a strange narrowing of God's creative possibilities to suppose that our way of life is the only one."

mostly instinctual, with little consciousness of themselves or their acts. Their minds develop only little by little."

190. What is the soul like when it is first incarnated?

▲ *"It is in a state comparable to an infant's. Its intelligence is only beginning to unfold. It is, so to speak, just trying out material life."*

191. Are the souls of our primitive peoples in a state of infancy?

▲ *"Relatively. But they've already achieved a certain amount of development, since they have emotions."*

—Are you saying that emotions are a sign of development?

▲ *"Development, yes; but not perfection. Emotions indicate activity and self-consciousness. In the truly primitive soul, intelligence exists only in a state of potentiality."*

Discussion: Considered in its entirety, the life of a spirit goes through successive phases resembling those that mark the lifetime of human beings. The spirit also passes gradually from the initial state to infancy, and arrives, after a number of stages, at adulthood—the time at which it reaches perfection. There are differences, however. The spirit is not subject to sickness or decline, like the human being. A spirit's life, while it has a beginning, will have no end. A spirit needs, from our point of view, an immense length of time to pass from spiritual infancy to spiritual adulthood, i.e., the stage at which its progress is complete. The spirit progresses through its experiences on many different worlds—not just one. Its existence comprises a series of incarnate lives, each of which affords it an opportunity to progress. Its many lives resemble the life of a person, which is composed of a series of days, in each of which one acquires new experience and knowledge. But just as there are unprofitable days in a human life, there are also incarnate lives in the existence of a spirit that are unrewarding because the spirit did not manage them well.

192. By leading perfect lives on Earth, can we skip the intervening steps of the ascent toward perfection and arrive at the state of pure spirits?

▲ *"No. What you imagine to be perfection on Earth is very far from it. There are qualities entirely unknown and presently incomprehensible to you. You may be as perfect as it is possible for an earthly nature to be. But you are still at a great remove from true and absolute perfection. The situation is similar to that of a precocious child who still has to pass through youth to reach adulthood. Or that of a sick person who has to go through convalescence before finally getting well. Furthermore, a spirit has to advance in knowledge as well as moral qualities. If it advances in one direction, it has to advance equally in the other. But certainly the more an individual advances in the present life, the shorter and less distressing his or her trials will be in future ones."*

—Can we assure ourselves at least that, after the present life, our future ones will be less bitter?

▲ *"Yes, without question. You can limit the length and the difficulties of the road. The only person who stays at the same point is the one who doesn't care to advance."*

193. Can someone in a new life descend to a point lower than one he or she has already reached?

▲ *"Socially, yes. But not spiritually."*

194. Can the soul of a good person, in a new incarnation, animate the body of a scoundrel?

▲ *"No. A spirit cannot go back."*

—Can the soul of a bad person become the soul of a good one?

▲ *"Yes, if the person has made efforts to change. In these cases, the new incarnation is a reward for attempts at amendment."*

Discussion: Spirits always move upward on the ladder to perfection; they never regress. In the hierarchy of existence, they raise themselves gradually. And although in the course of their different incarnate lives they may lose social rank, as spirits they never descend from the one at which they have arrived. Thus the soul of someone who has been at the pinnacle of earthly power may, in a later incarnation, animate the humblest day-laborer, and vice-versa. The elevation of ranks among human beings is sometimes in inverse ratio to that of their moral state. Herod was a king; Jesus, a carpenter.

195. Wouldn't the realization that advancement is inevitable lead some people to continue doing wrong in their current lives? After all, they can always rationalize that they will improve at a later time.

▲ *"A person capable of making that kind of calculation doesn't really believe in anything, and wouldn't be restrained to any greater extent by a fear of eternal punishment—which the person's reason would reject anyway. An imperfect spirit, it is true, might reason along the lines you suggest, but only during an incarnate life. Once free of its material body, the spirit begins to think very differently. Soon it understands the great mistake it has made, an insight that causes it to carry the opposite attitude into the next incarnation.*

This is the way progress comes about and the reason some of you on Earth are more advanced than others: some have experience that others don't, though everyone will eventually acquire all necessary experience. Each spirit, of course, can speed up or slow down its own advancement indefinitely. If this kind of rational perspective had been given to people, skepticism would not be so widespread today."

Discussion: A person in an undesirable position wants to change that position as soon as possible. Thus, someone who is convinced that the trials of present life result from his or her own imperfections will want to ensure that the next lifetime will be less painful. This conviction will be much more effective in drawing such a person away from the wrong road than the questionable threat of eternal flames.

196. Since spirits can only be made better by undergoing the trials of incarnate life, can we say that the material life is a sort of filter through which spirits are required to pass in order to remove impurities as they reach perfection?

▲ *"Yes, this is the case. Under the trials of incarnate life they improve by avoiding wrong-doing and doing good. But many successive incarnations are needed to succeed, and these will be longer or shorter depending on a spirit's own efforts to reach its goal."*

—Does the body influence the spirit to speed its progress, or does the spirit influence the body?

▲ *"Your spirit is everything. Your body is a garment that rots—nothing more."*

Discussion: We might think of spiritual purification in terms of the juice of the grape. The juice contains the essence we call spirit or alcohol. This substance is tainted, however, by the presence of various foreign substances that change its nature. It can be brought to a state of purity only after going through several distillations, each of which clears away part of its impurities. The still represents the physical body into which the spirit enters to be purified. The foreign substances represent the imperfections from which the spirit is gradually freed as it evolves toward perfection.

Children After Death

197. Is the spirit of a child who dies in infancy as advanced as that of an adult?

▲ *"Sometimes much more so. The spirit, especially if it has already made considerable progress, may have lived longer and acquired more experience in previous lives."*

—The spirit of a child may, then, be more advanced than that of its father?

▲ *"This is not uncommon. Don't you often see cases of this superiority on Earth?"*

198. A child who has died in infancy has had no chance to do wrong. Does its spirit belong to the higher orders of the spirit hierarchy?

▲ *"If an infant has no opportunity to do wrong, it has none to do good either; and God will not exonerate its spirit from the trials it must undergo. If such a spirit belongs to a high degree, this isn't because it died as a child but because it achieved that degree during previous lives."*

199. Why is life so often cut short in childhood?

▲ *"A brief lifespan in a child may be, for the incarnated spirit, the completion of a previous life that was interrupted before its appointed end. Also, a child's early death is often a trial of purification for its parents."*

—What becomes of the spirit of a child who dies in infancy?

▲ *"It begins a new life."*

Discussion: Let us suppose a person has only one life, and that, after this life ends, his or her future state is fixed for eternity. If this were so, what standard of merit could God use that would justify giving eternal happiness to humans who die at an early age? And by what standard could a person dying so young be excused from the frequently painful conditions of progress imposed on everyone else? Such an arrangement is irreconcilable with God's justice. On the other hand, reincarnation assures that the most absolute justice is accorded equally to everyone, without exception or favor. We are all responsible for our own progress. Each of us must merit happiness through right action and bear the consequences of wrong-doing.

It is also irrational to consider childhood a state of innocence. Unfortunately, we sometimes see children who, before their environment can have had any appreciable influence on them, exhibit the most undesirable behaviors imaginable. From birth and despite the excellent examples set by their parents, these children reveal a range of emotional and psychological predispositions that lead them to lie, cheat, steal, and even commit murder. The law regards them as having acted without knowledge and absolves them. The law is right: they act instinctively rather than deliberately. But where do the instinctual differences one sees in same-age children, who have been brought up under the same conditions and subjected to the same influences, come from? And how do we explain a child's tendency toward wrong-doing when it becomes obvious that the child's experiences and education could not have produced such tendency? The answer is to be found in the spirit's lack of advancement. The person who exhibits these characteristics does so because his or her spirit has made relatively less progress than others. Since this is the case, the individual suffers as the result of wrong-doing in previous lives, not because of any particular wrong-doing as a child in the present life. Providential law acts in the same way for each spirit, and the justice of God reaches all equally.

Gender in Spirits

200. Do spirits have gender?

▲ *"Not as you understand it. Gender, in your sense, depends on the body's organization. Love and sympathy do exist among spirits, but they are founded on similarity of feelings and attitudes."*

201. Can a spirit who has animated the body of a man in one life animate the body of a woman in a new one, and vice-versa?

▲ *"Yes, the same spirits animate men and women."*

202. Do spirits prefer to be incarnated as men or women?

▲ *"Spirits are indifferent about the matter. Decisions about gender are based on the trials a spirit must undergo."*

Discussion: Spirits incarnate themselves as men or women but have no gender themselves. Since they are required to develop in every direction, changes in gender, just like changes in social position, furnish them with special trials and duties, and the opportunity to acquire new experience. A spirit who has always incarnated as a man would only know about the experiences of a man.

Family Relationships

203. Do parents transmit a part of their souls to their children, or do they only give them biological life to which souls will later add the moral and intellectual faculties?

▲ *"Since the soul is indivisible, the parents are responsible only for giving biological life. A stupid father may have bright children, and vice-versa."*

204. Do our family ties extend beyond our present lives?

▲ *"They must. The succession of incarnations establishes relationships among spirits that date from previous lives. These relationships are often the basis for the instant likes and dislikes you develop for people that you've seemingly met for the first time."*

205. The doctrine of reincarnation, some people argue, destroys family ties because it carries relationships back to periods prior to our present existence.

▲ *"It doesn't destroy them. On the contrary, the conviction that current relationships are based on previous attachments strengthens ties between family members. It also makes decent conduct toward others even more imperative, since your neighbor or your employee may be the incarnated spirit of someone who was bound to you in another life by kinship and love."*

—Nonetheless, it diminishes the importance many people attach to their ancestry. After all, we may have had for a father a spirit who has belonged to a different race or social position.

▲ *"True. But this kind of importance is based mostly on pride. What most people honor in their ancestors is title, rank, and fortune. The same person who would be humiliated to have an honest shoemaker for a grandfather will boast that he or she is descended from some corrupt lord or lady. But whatever people say or do, they can't prevent things from going on according to the Divine ordering. God hasn't regulated the laws of nature to satisfy the demands of human vanity."*

206. If there isn't an actual line of ancestry among spirits successively incarnated in the same family, is it pointless to honor the memory of one's ancestors?

▲ *"Certainly not. You ought to be glad to belong to a family in which elevated spirits have been incarnated. Besides, while spirits don't proceed from one another, their love for individuals related to them by family ties is real. Often they incarnate themselves in a particular family because they have been influenced by pre-existing feelings of friendship and compatibility. But you can be certain that the spirits of your ancestors are not gratified when you honor their memory out of feelings of pride. Their merits might have been great, but they can only help you by inspiring you to follow the good examples they set. It is only your emulation of their good qualities that makes your remembrance of them pleasing and worthwhile in their eyes."*

Physical and Psychological Likeness

207. Children inherit physical characteristics from their parents. Do they also inherit psychological ones?

▲ *"No, because they have different souls or spirits. The body proceeds from the body. But the spirit doesn't proceed from any other spirit. Between descendants of the same family, a blood relationship is the only link."*

—What causes the psychological resemblance that sometimes exists between parents and children?

▲ *"Spirits who share the same attitudes and tendencies are drawn to each other."*

208. Do the spirits of parents influence the spirit of their child after its birth?

▲ *"They have a very great influence. As we have already told you, spirits must assist one another's progress. The parents have the mission of developing, through education, the spirits of their children. This is their appointed task, and they can't fail to complete it without being held accountable."*

209. Why do good parents often give birth to children who are inclined to wrongdoing? In other words, how is it that the good qualities of the parents don't always attract a good spirit to animate their child?

▲ *"A less advanced spirit may ask to have good parents, hoping their advice will help it change its ways. God often grants such requests."*

210. Can parents attract an advanced spirit into the body of their child through prayers and intentions?

▲ *"No, but they can improve the spirit of the child they've brought into the world. It is given to them for that purpose, and they are expected to help it advance. A difficult child is often sent as a trial to the parents."*

211. What causes the same character traits to appear in siblings and especially in twins?

▲ *"Affinity—the attraction of two spirits who have the same viewpoints and are happy to be together."*

212. In Siamese twins, whose bodies are joined and who share some organs, are there two spirits—that is to say, two souls?

▲ *"Yes, but their resemblance to one another often makes it seem to you as if there were only one."*

213. Since the spirits who incarnate as twins are brought together by affinity, why do we sometimes see twins who dislike each other?

▲ *"It isn't a rule that only empathetic spirits are incarnated as twins. Spirits who are unfriendly to each other may choose to work out their differences together in the physical realm."*

214. How should we interpret stories of children fighting in their mother's womb?

▲ *"As a figure of speech. It is one way of figuratively expressing the deeply rooted animosity these children have toward each other. It is also another way to acknowledge that animosity dates from before their birth. We notice that you seldom make sufficient allowance for the figurative and poetic element in certain statements."*

215. Why do the different peoples of the Earth have distinctive characters?

▲ *"Spirits constitute different communities that are formed by their similar tendencies and stage of evolution. Each people of Earth is a great community which is formed by the assembly of like-minded spirits. The tendency of these spirits to congregate, in turn, produces the resemblances that constitute the distinctive character of a people. After all, would good and benevolent spirits want to incarnate among the ruthless? No; the same principle of affinity that attracts spirits to particular families attracts families to particular nations. They go to the region on Earth, to the people where they will feel most in harmony."*

216. Does a newly reincarnated spirit retain any traces of the psychological character it had in its previous life?

▲ *"Yes, it might. But as a spirit improves, it changes. Consider, in this regard, that its social position may change greatly over successive lives. If a spirit who has been a nobleman in one life becomes a manual worker in another, its tastes will be entirely different. You would be hard put to recognize the two as the same being. Yet in the successive lives of a spirit, which retains its individuality from life to life, certain likenesses of character may appear. The changes in education and social custom that attend each new incarnate life will, nonetheless, modify the spirit's character until, growing gradually better, it is totally transformed. Through trials of purification and its own efforts, an individual who was proud and insensitive will become loving and humble."*

217. Does an individual in its different incarnations, retain any traces of the physical character of its previous lives?

▲ *"The body is destroyed; the new has no connection with the old one. Still, the spirit is reflected in the body. The body is only matter but, since it is modeled on the qualities of the spirit, the spirit impresses on it a certain character. You see this most particularly in the face and especially in the eyes, which have been accurately described as the mirrors of the soul. In other words, the face reflects the animating spirit more than does the rest of the body. This is so true that the sight of a very ugly face can actually give pleasure if it forms part of the envelope of a good, wise, and humane spirit. On the other hand, the very handsome faces of some persons often fail to create the positive response you would expect; these faces might even be displeasing. Moreover, while it may seem at first that only a well-made body could be the envelope of a good spirit, you run into very decent and quite superior people every day who have some physical handicap. Thus, although physical similarities among a spirit's successive incarnate bodies are not marked, similarities in taste and tendency can produce what is commonly called a family resemblance."*

Discussion: The body, which clothes the soul in its new incarnation, may have no connection with the one the soul has just left, since the two may belong to different races. It would be a mistake, then, to conclude that resemblance between individuals, which may only be the result of chance, indicates a succession of lives in the existence of the same spirit. Nonetheless, the qualities of a spirit often modify the organs that serve to reveal them and will impress a distinctive stamp on the face and even on an individual's general manner. This is the reason that we sometimes find an expression of nobility and dignity marking the humblest envelope, while the fine clothes of a wealthy person often fail to cover the wearer's poorly developed character. Some persons, who have risen from the lowest social ranks, adopt the habits and manners of the higher ranks without effort and seem only to have returned to their native element. Others, despite the advantages of birth and education, always seem to be out of place in refined society. How can we explain these facts unless we see them as a reflection of what the spirit has been in its previous lives?

Innate Ideas

218. Do people retain any traces of the views they held and the knowledge they gained during prior lives?

▲ *"They have a vague memory of them. It is these unconscious memories that are responsible for what you call innate ideas."*

—Isn't the theory of innate ideas simply nonsense?

▲ *"No. The knowledge gained in past lives isn't lost. A spirit, when freed from matter, always retains what it has learned. It may, during incarnation, partially and temporarily forget its knowledge. But a latent intuition of it helps the spirit in its progress. If not for this intuition, a spirit would have to begin its education all over again. Instead, with each new life, a spirit starts its development at the point at which it had arrived at the end of its preceding life."*

— If this is the case, isn't there a very close connection between two successive lives?

▲ *"The connection isn't always as close as you might think. The conditions of the two lives are often very different; and in the interval between them, the spirit may have made considerable progress."*

219. There are some people who seem to grasp certain subjects like mathematics

and languages intuitively and without study. Where do such extraordinary talents come from?

▲ *"These gifts are the result of progress previously made by the soul, though it has no present consciousness of this progress. Where could those intuitions come from otherwise? The body changes; the spirit in its individuality does not change, although it changes its garments often."*

220. In going from one incarnation to the next, can we lose certain intellectual faculties—for instance, the taste for an art?

▲ *"Yes, if you have used it poorly. Moreover, an intellectual faculty can remain dormant during an entire lifetime because the spirit wishes to exercise another, quite different faculty. But the original faculty still exists and will come into play again in a later life."*

221. Do we owe to memory the intuition of God's existence and the presentiment of a future life, both of which are universal notions?

▲ *"Yes, to what you have preserved of what you knew when you were spirits. But your pride often stifles this memory."*

— Is the same quality of memory responsible for certain beliefs, found among every people, that are analogous to principles of the Spiritist Doctrine?

▲ *"This body of principles is as old as the world, and it is found everywhere—which proves it to be true. The incarnate spirit preserves the intuition of its spiritual state and possesses an instinctive consciousness of the invisible world. But this intuition is often distorted by prejudice and corrupted by superstitions that arise from spiritual unawareness."*

MANY LIVES: ADDITIONAL CONSIDERATIONS

222. "The doctrine of reincarnation," people sometimes object, "is not new; it is simply a revival of the old doctrine of Pythagoras."[1] We have never claimed that the Spiritist Doctrine is a modern idea but that, since communication between spirits and humans occurs according to natural law, it must have existed from the beginning of human history. Traces of it, we have always tried to demonstrate, can be found in humankind's earliest records. Nor did Pythagoras originate the idea of metempsychosis.[2] He borrowed it from the philosophers of India and Egypt where, from time immemorial, it was the general belief of both commoners and the most eminent thinkers.

How did the idea come to the ancients? Was it through revelation or intuition?

We don't know. But no idea could have so traversed the historical

....

1 Translator's note: Pythagoras (c.580-500 BC), Greek philosopher and mathematician. Around him, inspired by his teaching, gathered a group strongly religious in nature, devoted to the reformation of political, moral and social life. He is also credited with the theory of the functional significance of numbers in the objective world and in music. Pythagoras left no writings, so all that is known of his doctrines comes from his disciples; it has been suggested that some of the views generally attributed to him may actually have been advanced by them. In this paragraph, Allan Kardec refers to Pythagoras's belief in the notion of metempsychosis.

....

2 Translator's Note: Metempsychosis: the ancient doctrine, still accepted today by certain branches of Hinduism and Buddhism, by which a soul (spirit) may enter another human body or that of an animal according to its deeds in a previous life. The word derives from the Greek meta_(over) and empsychoum (to put a soul into).

eras and held such sway over humanity's greatest minds without some rational basis. The antiquity of the doctrine is an argument in its favor, not an objection. Still, we cannot forget an important distinction between the ancient doctrine of metempsychosis and the modern one of reincarnation: spirits who profess the latter absolutely reject the idea that a human soul can pass into an animal, and vice-versa.

The spirits, therefore, presently assert a doctrine that is inconceivably old and that still inspires a vast number of minds. They have, however, stripped it of the encrustations of age-old superstitions and presented it under a more rational aspect—one more consistent with evolutionary laws and more in harmony with God's designs. In this regard, it is noteworthy that this book is not the first instance in which the spirits have made this assertion. Numerous communications along the same lines were received in many countries before the book's publication, and their number has greatly increased since.

It might be asked here why all the spirits' statements on reincarnation do not agree. We will return to this question elsewhere. For the moment, we would like to examine the matter from another point of view, one irrespective of the spirits' declarations. For the sake of argument, we will put their statements aside for a time and imagine the spirits never made them. We will even suppose that the very existence of spirits has never been revealed. Now, placing ourselves momentarily on neutral ground and admitting the hypotheses that many earthly lives and one earthly life are alike possible, let us see which of the two is more in keeping with reason.

Some people reject the idea of reincarnation simply because they dislike it. They declare that their present existence has been enough for them, that they have no desire to begin another. But God does not consult our desires and opinions in regulating the universe. Either the law of reincarnation exists, or it does not. If it does, we must submit to it no matter how displeasing we presently find it, for God will not request our permission to apply it. A sick person cannot say, "I've suffered enough today; I don't choose to suffer tomorrow." No matter how unwilling that person is, the laws of nature require that he or she endure suffering— tomorrow and perhaps day after day—until the illness is cured. Likewise, if people are destined to reincarnate, they will eventually do so, despite rebelling (like children refusing to go to school) against necessity. Such objections seem too childish to deserve serious examination. But by way of reassurance, we should say that the law of reincarnation is by no means as terrible as it might appear. It teaches that the conditions of individuals' next existences depend on themselves and that they will be happy or unhappy according to their present deeds. They may even, by their actions in this life, raise themselves above the need for further purification on the earthly plane.

We take it for granted that we are addressing here people who believe in some sort of after-life and who do not anticipate either annihilation or, what amounts to the same thing, the merging of their individual souls in a Universal Whole, like droplets of rain falling on a vast ocean. If you do believe in an after-life, you also believe that it will not be the same for everyone. Otherwise, doing good and living with integrity on Earth would make no sense. After all, if the same thing is going to happen to everybody, why shouldn't we satisfy all our appetites and desires and "bid the world go hang"? Thus, we assume that you believe that the after life will be more or less happy depending on what you do in your present life, and that you aspire to as much happiness in the after-life as possible, especially if you believe that you will be there for all eternity. Let us also assume that you don't think of yourself as belonging to Earth's spiritual elite and therefore as entitled to perfect happiness in the after-life. Consequently, if you look honestly at the matter, you have to admit that some people are better than yourself and deserve a higher place— although this admission doesn't, of course, class you among the irredeemable.

Place yourself for a moment, then, in the condition in which, according to your own reckoning, your spiritual life entitles you to be. Suppose, in that case, that someone comes to you and says, "You suffer, you aren't as happy as you could be. At the same time, you see other people enjoying an unalloyed happiness. Would you like to exchange your position for theirs?" "There's no question of it," you would reply. "What do I have to do?" "Something very simple," comes the answer, "you only have to begin again what you have done badly and try to do it better." Would you hesitate one moment to accept the offer, even if it meant you had to live through several lifetimes of trial?

We might take an even more commonplace illustration. Suppose someone comes to a poor person and says, "Here is an immense fortune. It is yours on one condition: you must work hard for one minute." In response to such an offer, the laziest individual would say, without missing a beat, "I am ready to work for one minute, for two minutes, for an hour, for a whole day! What is a day's work compared to ease and plenty for the rest of my life?" The analogy with reincarnation could not be more apt. How long does an incarnate life last compared to eternity? Less than a minute, less than a second.

Sometimes people also argue that "God, who is sovereignly good, would not require humans to begin a series of sorrows and tribulations all over again." But is it kinder, really, to condemn a person to perpetual suffering because of a few moments of error than to give that person a way of repairing his or her faults?

To illustrate this idea, suppose that two manufacturers had workers who eventually hoped to become partners of their employers. The workers, though, made such bad use of their allotted time that they deserved to be fired. One of the manufacturers, in fact, dismissed his workers. Despite the appeals, one worker, who couldn't find another job, died in poverty. The second manufacturer, on the other hand, said to her workers "You've wasted a day and done your work badly. You need to make some restitution for the loss. Because of that, I'll let you start over again. Try to do well. If you do, I'll keep you on; and you can still work for the promotion I promised you."

Do we need to ask which manufacturer was more humane? Would God be less just and compassionate than a human being? The idea that our fate is decided forever by a few years of trial on Earth, during which we cannot achieve perfection in any case, fills the mind with dread. The contrary idea consoles us. It leaves us hope. Consequently, without pronouncing for or against reincarnation, or accepting the hypothesis of many lives over that of one life, we can assert that, if the matter were left up to us, no one would choose to take on the irrevocable sentence that comes with the "one life" doctrine. A philosopher once said that "if God did not exist, it would be necessary to invent him."[3] The same might be said of reincarnation. But, as we have already remarked, God does not ask our permission or consult our preferences in establishing the providential order.

With which hypothesis, then, does the balance of probabilities lie?

We can consider the matter from still another point of view, again omitting any statements of spirits and examining the question solely as a matter of philosophical inquiry. Consider that, if the law of reincarnation does not exist, we have only one incarnate life. If our present material life is our only one, the soul of each individual must have been created at the same time as his or her body. We might, of course, assume that the soul existed prior to the body. But in that case we would have to ask what the soul's condition was beforehand. If it did have a prior existence, what was it like? Was it aware of itself? If not, its state must have been equivalent to non-existence. Finally, if the soul in this pre-incarnate state had anything like individuality, that individuality must have been either progressive or stationary. In any case, we must ask how evolved the soul was at the point of its incarnation.

As we have said, it is possible to assume either that the soul comes into existence at the same time as the body or that it exists prior to the body. Both positions lead us to ask the following:

1.   Why do souls reveal so many talents independent of education?

....
3 *Translator's Note: A* bon mot *of the French philosopher, Voltaire (1694-1778).*

2. Why do some young children display extraordinary aptitudes for certain arts and sciences, while many of us display none either as children or adults?

3. Where do some individuals come by innate or intuitive ideas that others lack?

4. How is it that some children are inclined to good, others to wrongdoing, some to kindness, others to selfishness, often despite the conditions into which they were born?

5. Why are some people, quite apart from their education, morally richer than others?

6. Why are some born in the wilderness while others live in the most technologically advanced societies? If we take, say, a Hottentot[4] baby and bring her up in the most renowned schools, can we make her a Laplace or Newton?

What philosophy or theological system can resolve these questions? Either the souls of human beings are equal at their birth, or they are not. But if they are equal, why do discrepancies exist? Can it simply be a matter of different physical organization in the body and brain?   The latter hypothesis is monstrous: it makes of the human being a mere machine. If it were true, no one would be responsible for any individual action, since any wrong-doing could rightly be attributed to physiological defects. If, on the other hand, souls are created unequal, God must have made them so. Yet, if this were true, why is this innate superiority accorded to some and not others? And would such partiality be consistent with God's justice and love for us?

If you admit the possibility that we have all lived numerous lives, all these questions are answered. According to this hypothesis, humans bring with them, at birth, intuitions of the knowledge they have previously acquired, and will be more or less advanced in their earthly lives depending on the number of their prior lives and on how far along they have come on the road to perfection. The situation is similar to a meeting where everyone's age is different. The extent of development for each individual at the meeting will, on the whole, correspond to the number of years he or she has already lived. Put in terms of the hypothesis of many lives, the number of years is to the life of the body as the number of existences is to the life of the soul. Now, take the analogy a step further. Imagine that a thousand individuals of all ages have been simultaneously brought together. A veil has been thrown over their pasts, however; and you, unaware of that past, imagine them all to have been born on the same day. Naturally, you will wonder why some individuals are tall and

....

4 Translator's Note: Hottentot: a people of southern Africa believed to be related to the Bantu and Bushmen.

others short, why some are wrinkled while others have smooth skins, why some are knowledgeable whereas others seem uninformed. But remove the obscuring veil, discover the truth about their various ages, and all the differences become explicable.

A just God could not create souls more or less perfect. But if we accept the idea that we have all led many lives, there is nothing in the differences in quality we see around us that is inconsistent with the most rigorous standard of fairness, because these differences are rooted not in the present but in the past.

This argument is not based on any pre-conceived system or on a wild guess. We start from a fact that is obvious—the inequality of natural aptitudes and of intellectual and moral development—and we find no current theory that can account for it. We offer another theory that is at once simple, natural, and rational. Is it reasonable to prefer a theory that does not explain a fact to one that does?

In regard to question six above, one may reply that the Hottentot is of an inferior race. In such a case, we beg to inquire whether she is not a human being. Since she is, why has God refused her and her whole race the privileges granted to Caucasians? The Spiritist Doctrine does not admit the existence of different classes of human beings. Instead, it argues that spirits living on Earth are in different stages of development and are all equally capable of attaining the same progress. Does not this view of the human race seem more compassionate and in agreement with a loving God?

We have been considering the soul in regard to its past and present. If we consider it also in regard to the future, we encounter difficulties that modern thinkers find equally inexplicable:

1. If our future destiny is determined solely by our present life, what will be the respective positions in that future of educated and uneducated persons? Will they be on the same level, or will there be a difference in their degree of happiness?

2. Will the person who has spent a lifetime working on personal transformation and intellectual growth be placed on the same level with someone who has been unable to advance—not through any personal fault but because he or she has had neither the time nor the opportunity?

3. Can someone who has unknowingly done wrong be justly punished for that wrong-doing, though it has not been the result of his or her own choice?

4. While we try to raise the level of humanity's knowledge, raise its moral standards, and spread the benefits of civilization, millions die every year in complete ignorance of these efforts. What will their fates be? Will they be treated as irredeemable? And, if not, have they

earned the right to be placed in the same category as those who have progressed?

5. What will be the fate of children who die before they can act wrongly or rightly? Should they be placed among the supremely happy? If so, what have they done to deserve such a favor? And why should they, any more than others, be exempt from further undergoing the trials of life on Earth?

Which of our two hypotheses can better solve these problems? Undoubtedly, if we admit the fact that we have had many lives, our answers will conform to the idea of Divine justice. According to this justice, what we are unable to do in one life we can do in another. Thus, no one is exempt from the action of the law of progress; everyone is rewarded progressively, depending on his or her own efforts. At the same time, no one is excluded from eventually achieving eternal happiness, no matter what obstacles he or she has to encounter on the road.

The questions arising from this subject could be greatly multiplied. Even so, existential and moral problems that can be solved only by appeal to the hypothesis of many lives are innumerable. We have restricted our inquiry here to problems that are very general in nature.

There are critics who object to reincarnation on a more particular premise. "No matter what the arguments in its favor," they say, "the doctrine of reincarnation is not accepted by the Church. To accept it would be to participate in the overthrow of religion."

We do not intend to answer this objection here. It is enough, for the present, to have shown the eminently ethical and rational character of reincarnation. We confidently maintain, however, that a doctrine that is both ethical and rational in nature cannot be antagonistic to a religion that attributes to the Divine Being perfect goodness and the highest reason. In our turn, we may ask what would have happened to the Church if it had continued to oppose the overwhelming evidence of science, if it had excommunicated everyone who did not believe in the six days of creation or the sun's movement around the Earth? If it had insisted on professing these ideas as articles of belief, it would, eventually, have lost all authority and credit among civilized people. But the Church is not so backward. Whenever any matter of evidence has been established, the Church has wisely sided with the evidence. If it is proved, then, that the facts of human life are irreconcilable with a particular belief about God's justice and that various points of Christian belief can only be explained by appeal to reincarnation, the Church will certainly acknowledge that the antagonism in the two views is, as in the scientific cases, only apparent— the result of linguistic misinterpretation. Moreover, as we will show elsewhere, religion has no more to fear from reincarnation than it had from the discovery of the motion of the Earth and the periods of geologic formation, though both at first appeared to contradict the Bible. Indeed, the principle of reincarnation is implied by many passages in the Bible, including the Gospels:

"As they were coming down the mountain [after the transfiguration] Jesus instructed them, 'Don't tell anyone what you have seen, until the Son of Man has been raised from the dead.' The disciples asked him, 'Why then do the teachers of the law say that Elijah must come first?' Jesus replied, 'To be sure, Elijah comes and will restore all things. But I tell you, Elijah has already come, and they did not recognize him, but have done to him everything they wished. In the same way the Son of Man is going to suffer at their hands.' Then the disciples understood that he was talking to them about John the Baptist."[5]

Since Christ declares in this passage that John the Baptist was Elijah, it follows that the spirit or soul of Elijah must have been reincarnated in the body of John the Baptist.

Whether we accept the idea of reincarnation or not, we must undergo it if it really exists. The central points we want to establish here are these: (1) the teaching of the spirits who proclaim reincarnation is eminently Christian; (2) reincarnation is founded on the doctrine of the immortality of the soul; (3) it is further based on the doctrines of future rewards and sorrows, the justice of God, and human free will; (4) it is compatible with the moral doctrine of Christ. It cannot, therefore, be anti-religious.

None of the arguments for reincarnation above, as we have noted, depend on statements made by spirits—and deliberately so, since in the minds of many, spirit statements lack authority. If we and many others have adopted reincarnation, it is not simply because spirits have proclaimed it, but because it seems eminently rational and because it solves problems that are insoluble by the opposite hypothesis. Had it been suggested to us by a mere mortal, we would have accepted it with equal confidence and promptly renounced our old opinion—for when an opinion has been shown to be wrong, we have more to lose than gain by persisting in it. And, even though proclaimed by spirits, we would reject the doctrine of reincarnation if it had appeared contrary to reason—as, indeed, we have rejected many other ideas the spirits have proclaimed. (We know by experience that we can no more blindly accept ideas advanced by spirits than we can those suggested by humans.) The supreme rationality of reincarnation is, in our minds, its greatest merit. It has been confirmed by positive facts that have removed any doubt as to its possibility. And when these facts are as widely appreciated as the ones that have taught us the truth about the formation and rotation of the

....

5 Translator's Note: Matthew, 17:9-11.

Earth, opposition will vanish.

The doctrine of reincarnation is the only one that explains what, in its absence, is inexplicable. It at once offers consolation and strictly conforms to the most rigorous stand of justice. It is an anchor of safety given to humanity by a merciful God. Jesus Himself makes the truth of this last assertion explicit. In John 3:3-5, He says, replying to Nicodemus: "I tell you the truth; no one can see the kingdom of God unless he is born again." And when Nicodemus asks, "How can a man be born when he is old. Surely he cannot enter a second time in his mother's womb to be born!" Jesus replies, "I tell you the truth, no one can enter the kingdom of God unless he is born of water and the Spirit. Flesh gives birth to flesh, but the Spirit gives birth to spirit. You should not be surprised at my saying, You must be born again."[6]

....

6 See question 1010 on the resurrection of the body.

CHAPTER X

SPIRIT LIFE

Free Spirits [1]

223. Is the soul reincarnated immediately after it separates from the body?

▲ *"Sometimes, but more commonly the time between incarnations is relatively long. On very advanced planets, reincarnation takes place in relatively shorter times, since material life there is less dense and heavy than on Earth. On such planets the spirit, even while incarnate, retains the use of nearly all its spirit abilities."*

224. What happens to the soul between incarnations?

▲ *"It becomes a free transient spirit and aspires to a new destiny. It is in a state of hopefulness and waiting."*

—How long are these intervals?

▲ *"For some, a few hours; for others, thousands of years. Strictly speaking, there are no fixed limits to the time spent in the spirit-world. Still, while reincarnation can be postponed almost indefinitely, the spirit's stay is never perpetual. Sooner or later, it starts a new life."*

—Does the length of time between incarnations depend on the will of the spirit, or is it imposed as part of the purification process?

▲ *"It depends on the spirit's free will. Spirits, remember, act with full awareness. For some, the length of time may be an imposition for correction purposes. Others may freely choose to lengthen this period in order to pursue certain courses of learning."*

·····························

1 *Translator's Note: The term* free spirits *is used here to refer to those intelligences who are not incarnated in a physical body. They are, so to speak, free from the limitations imposed by matter.*

225. Is the fact that some spirits spend more time in the spirit-world before taking up a new life necessarily a sign that they belong to the lower spirit orders?

▲ *"No. Such spirits are from every order. As we've already said, incarnation is a transitional state. In their normal state, spirits are disengaged from matter."*

226. Are all free spirits in a transient state?

▲ *"Those who will be reincarnated are. However, the spirits who have reached perfection are not between physical lives. Their state is more permanent."*

Discussion: Because of their qualities, spirits differ in their degrees of advancement. As they go through their experiences, they may find themselves in one of three stages: (1) incarnated, that is to say, united to a material body; (2) disengaged from a material body and waiting for a new incarnation; (3) pure or perfect spirits who no longer need incarnation.

227. How are free spirits instructed?   Their learning process can hardly resemble ours.

▲ *"They study their past and look for means of raising themselves to a higher degree. They observe everything that is going on in the regions they visit. They listen to the lectures of accomplished beings and to the advice of wiser spirits. In this way they acquire new ideas."*

228. Do spirits retain any human feeling?

▲ *"On leaving the body, spirits of the higher orders also leave behind humanity's darker passions; they retain only the love of goodness. Less advanced spirits, on the other hand, retain their earthly imperfections. Otherwise, they would be of the highest order themselves."*

229. Why don't spirits, on departing Earth, leave their negative traits behind, since they can see how disastrous their consequences were?

▲ *"Do you think that persons who are, for instance, extremely jealous will lose this fault the moment they die? After death, each spirit is immersed in a field of mental images; images that carry the imprint of former traits. This is especially true for those with strongly marked feelings and appetites. They are not by any means free of the influence of matter. Occasionally, however, they have glimpses of the truth, which show them the right path."*

230. Do spirits progress in the spirit-world?

▲ *"They can make great advances, depending on their efforts and how much they want to improve. It is in the material life, though, that they put the new ideas they've acquired into practice."*

231. Are transient spirits happy or unhappy?

▲ *"When they retain earthly feelings and desires, they suffer. They are happy depending on how dematerialized they have become. As they go about their lives in the spirit-world, spirits see what they need in order to become happier; and the insight inspires them to find ways of filling those needs. But spirits are not always permitted to reincarnate when they want—in which case, the lengthening of their stay in the spirit-world becomes a form of correction."*

232. Can spirits in the spirit-world go to all the other planets?

▲ *"It depends on how advanced they are. When a spirit leaves the body, there is no guarantee that it will completely disengage from the material environment of the planet. Unless it has raised itself to a higher level while incarnate, it is still attuned to that planet. Of course, progressive ascent is something every spirit should constantly strive for; otherwise, perfection would be unattainable. A spirit can, however, go to more advanced planets, even though it will find itself a stranger there. It can, so to speak, only get a glimpse of those planets. But these glimpses frequently spark in the spirit a desire to progress; it wants to become worthy of living there and experiencing the joys it sees."*

233. Do pure spirits ever go to less advanced planets?

▲ *"Very frequently. If they did not, those planets would be left to themselves, without guides to direct them."*

Transitional Worlds

234. Are there places that serve as resting-places for free spirits?

▲ *"Yes. These places are way stations, graduated according to the nature of the spirits who go to them. Spirits find the conditions there that will help them restore their energies."*

—Can the spirits on these transitional places leave when they want?

▲ *"Yes, they can go to any region they need to. They are like birds of passage that land on an island to rest, recover strength, and push on to their final destination."*

235. Do spirits progress while on transitional worlds?

▲ *"Certainly. The spirits who gather there do so with a view toward instruction and receiving permission to enter higher regions."*

236. Given their special nature, are these worlds permanently destined to be the dwelling places of free spirits?

▲ *"No, their role in the cosmos is temporary."*

—Do incarnate beings live on them also?"

▲ *"No, their surface is barren. To live on them one must have no material wants or needs."*

—Is this sterility permanent, and does it result from anything special in the nature of their environment?

▲ *"No, their sterility is temporary as well."*

— Are they devoid of the beauties of nature?

▲ *"The beauties of space are enough. They reveal the inexhaustible richness of creation no less admirably than earthly beauty."*

—Since the state of these planets is temporary, will the Earth, at some future date, fall into this category?

▲ *"It has already."*

—When?

▲ *"During its formation."*

Discussion: Nothing in nature is useless: everything has a purpose, a destination. There is no void. Every portion of space is inhabited. Thus, even during the long evolutionary stages that preceded humanity's appearance on Earth and before the earliest formation of organized beings, there was no absence of life here. Beings without human wants or sensations found a welcome refuge. Even in its embryonic state, God ordained that Earth should be useful. Who dares say, then, that only one among the innumerable planets circulating in space—one so small it would be lost in a crowd—has the exclusive privilege of being inhabited? What, in that case, would be the purpose of the others? Would God have created them simply to delight us? The absurdity of the idea is incompatible with the wisdom that appears everywhere in God's work. This notion becomes still more unacceptable when we reflect on the countless celestial bodies we are unable to see. On the other hand, it is a grand and sublime idea that forming planets, although unfit to sustain organic life, may nonetheless be peopled with living beings for whom the conditions are quite appropriate. It is an idea that might clear up more than one mystery.

Perceptions, Sensations, and Suffering of Spirits

237. Does the soul, when it has returned to the spirit-world, have the same perceptions it had in earthly life?

▲ *"Yes—and others it did not have in that life, because its body veiled them. Intelligence, for instance, is an attribute of the spirit; but it operates more freely when the flesh does not impede it."*

238. Are the perceptions and knowledge of spirits unlimited?   In short, do they know everything?

▲ *"The closer to perfection they come, the more they know. Spirits of the higher orders possess a wide range of knowledge; those of the lower orders are in a state of relative unawareness."*

239. Do spirits understand the First Cause of all things?

▲ *"Again, it depends on how advanced and purified they are. Less advanced spirits know no more than humans."*

240. Do spirits perceive time as we do?

▲ *"No, and this is why you do not always understand us when you ask for dates and epochs."*

Discussion: The life of spirits is exterior to the idea of time as we perceive it. The sense of duration in time does not exist for them. Years, which seem so long to us, appear to them as so many instants lapsing into Eternity, just as a rugged terrain appears smooth when seen from far above.

241. Do spirits have a truer, more precise view of the present than we do?

▲ *"A spirit's view, compared to yours, is pretty much what eyesight is in comparison to blindness. We see what you do not see; therefore, we judge differently from you. A spirit's ability, however, is related to the extent of its progress."*

242. How do spirits acquire knowledge of the past? Is this knowledge without limits for them?

▲ *"When we spirits turn our attention to the past, we see it as though it were the present—exactly as you do when you recall something that may have struck you with particular vividness. There is one difference. Just as our view is no longer obscured by the material veil that dulls your mental abilities, we also remember things that are now inaccessible to your memory. But spirits do not know everything pertaining to their creation."*

243. Do spirits foresee the future?

▲ *"The more they have progressed, the better they are able to see it. The future appears to them to be like the present. Very often, they know it only partially. But even when they foresee it more clearly, they are not always allowed to reveal it.*

After death, the soul sees and embraces all its past lives at a glance. But it cannot see what is in store for it. This knowledge is only possessed by souls who, after a long succession of lives, have achieved oneness with God."

—Do pure spirits have complete knowledge of the future?

▲ *"'Complete'? No. God alone knows it."*

244. Do spirits see God?

▲ *"Seeing and understanding God is reserved only for spirits of the highest order. Spirits of the lower orders feel and perceive God indirectly."*

—When a spirit of a lower degree says that such and such a thing is permitted or forbidden to it by God, how does it know that God has really issued this command?

▲ *"It does not see God, but it feels the sovereignty of God. When something is not to be done or said, the spirit has a kind of intuition, an invisible warning, that commands it to hold back. Aren't you, too, sometimes conscious of a secret impression telling you to do or say something? It is the same with us, only the impression is much stronger. The essence of free spirits, as you can appreciate, is more receptive than yours; and we are better at intuiting Divine warnings."*

—Does God transmit directives to each spirit directly or through the intermediary of other spirits?

▲ *"Directives do not come directly from God, unless a spirit has made itself worthy of such communication. God transmits orders through spirits of high degree."*

245. Is spirit-sight localized, like the sight of incarnate beings?

▲ *"No, it exists within the spirit."*

246. Do spirits need light in order to see?

▲ *"To see, they have no need of exterior light. For them, there is no darkness except what they might have to experience as an expiation."*

247. Do spirits need to travel in order to see two different points? Can they, for instance, see two hemispheres of the world at the same time?

▲ *"Spirits transport themselves from point to point with the speed of thought and can virtually see everywhere at the same time. A spirit's thought can radiate at the same moment to many different points. But this ability, you should understand, depends on its purity. The less pure the spirit is, the narrower is its range of sight. Only higher spirits can take in a whole at a single glance."*

Discussion: Vision is a property inherent in the nature of spirits. It permeates their whole being—like light that shines through every part of a lantern. It is a universal insight, extending to everything and embracing time, space, and objects simultaneously. Darkness or material obstacles do not exist in its presence. We need only think for a moment to see that this must be the case. In a human being, sight is produced by the play of light on our eyes; without light, a person can only be in darkness. But vision is an attribute of the spirit, independent of an exterior agent. Consequently, spirit-sight is independent of light.

248. Do spirits see things as distinctly as we do?

▲ *"More distinctly. Their sight penetrates what yours cannot. Nothing obscures it."*

249. Are spirits aware of sounds?

▲ *"Yes. They hear sounds that are inaudible to you."*

—Does hearing exist within the spirit's being, like sight?

▲ *"All of a spirit's senses form part of its being. Once clothed in a material body, its perceptions reach it only through the channel of the body's sensory organs. But restored to freedom, the perceptions of a spirit are no longer localized."*

250. Since its senses are part of a spirit's very being, can a spirit deactivate or shield itself from the senses?

▲ *"A spirit sees and hears only what it chooses to see and hear. You must take this statement, however, only in a general sense and mainly as descriptive of spirits of the higher orders. At certain times, spirits of a lower hierarchy may be compelled to see or hear if it is useful to their advancement."*

251. Are spirits affected by music?

▲ *"Do you mean the music of Earth? What is that compared to the music of the celestial spheres? Nothing on Earth can give you any idea of that harmony. One is to the other as a savage howl is to the loveliest melody. Still, spirits of the lower orders may take pleasure in hearing your music because they are unable to appreciate anything more sublime. Given the sensitivity of their perceptions, music has inexhaustible charms for spirits. We mean, of course, celestial music. The spiritual imagination can conceive of nothing more exquisitely beautiful."*

252. Are spirits moved by natural beauty?

▲ *"Not necessarily. The beauties of nature vary largely according to each planet. Spirits are aware of them to the extent that they are able to appreciate and understand them. But, for highly advanced spirits, the perfection of the whole transcends any local expression of natural beauty."*

253. Do spirits experience our physical needs and sufferings?

▲ *"They know them because they have undergone them. But since they are spirits, they do not experience them materially, as you do."*

254. Do spirits feel fatigue and need rest?

▲ *"Not as you understand it. They have no bodies whose strength needs to be restored and thus do not need your kind of rest. Still, to the extent that it is not in a state of constant activity, a spirit does rest, though not materially. Its action is completely mental, and so is its rest. In other words, there are moments when its thought becomes less active and no longer directed toward a special object. This constitutes a state of repose that has nothing to do with the rest of the body. The fatigue of spirits, we should add, is also proportional to their advancement. More evolved spirits have less need of rest."*

255. When a spirit says that it suffers, what is the nature of the suffering?

▲ *"Mental anguish, which may cause far more pain than any physical suffering."*

256. Why, then, do spirits sometimes complain that they suffer from cold or heat?

▲ *"These are sensations caused by the recollection of sufferings they went through on Earth. Sometimes these imagined sufferings are as painful as if they were real. But complaints of cold and heat are often only metaphors for expressing the situation in which spirits find themselves. When they remember their earthly bodies, they experience the same sort of effects they knew on Earth. Take off your robe and for a few moments you will feel as if it is still on your shoulders. It is that kind of after-effect."*

Theoretical Explanation of the Nature of Sensation in Spirits

257. The body is the seat of physical pain. Our organism is, if not the primary cause, the more immediate source of pain sensations. A spirit becomes aware of pain but that awareness is an effect (not the cause) of the pain. Indeed, while the memory of pain may be wrenching, a spirit is not, so to speak, physically affected. A spirit cannot be affected by cold or heat—it can neither freeze nor burn. The way the spirit experiences pain is similar to what some people go through on Earth: sometimes the mere memory, or even the expectation, of pain can be very hurtful and, in some extreme situations, cause a person's death. A case in point would be a patient who has recently undergone limb amputation and who still has the sensation of pain in the lost limb. Yet it is obvious that neither the amputated limb nor the point of amputation can be the real cause of this feeling. It is solely a mental event; the impression of formerly experienced pain is retained in and reproduced by the patient's brain. The suffering of spirits, it may be inferred, must be of similar nature.

In the following summary we discuss the role that the spiritual body plays in phenomena of a spiritual nature. Our discussion will shed some light on a variety of phenomena, such as spirit-sightings, the state of the spirit at the moment of death, and the fact that so many newly free spirits still believe themselves to be incarnate. Our account also provides a rationale for the stunning images presented by those who committed suicide, who had a violent death, or who overindulged themselves in earthly pleasures.

The perispirit, or spiritual body, is the link that unites the spirit and the material body. Drawn from the Cosmic Principle,[2] it shares essential properties with matter and electromagnetism. It is made of a subtle form of matter and is responsible for modeling the organic life, though not the intellectual one which has its seat in the spirit. The perispirit is the agent through which the sensations of the physical organs are registered by consciousness. When the body is destroyed, however, the sensations in the perispirit are no longer localized, which explains why a spirit doesn't usually say that it suffers in the head or the feet or any other particular area. Moreover, in the spirit-world, the spiritual body experiences sensations in ways quite different from those it knew on Earth. Freed from the body, a spirit may suffer; but this suffering is not like bodily suffering. Nor is it always of an exclusively mental nature (like remorse, for example). We have seen spirits, in fact, walk through flames without experiencing any painful effects, so we know that extreme temperatures make no impression upon them. The pain they feel, therefore, is not a physical pain in the true sense of the term. It is, rather, an undefined feeling that spirits experience within themselves and that they are not always able to explain, precisely because it is generalized and not produced by an external agent. At base, it is a mental feeling rather than a material sensation. Nonetheless, as our next example shows, a spirit's suffering is sometimes more than mental impressions.

Observation has revealed that the spiritual body, or perispirit, disengages itself slowly from the body at death. During the first few moments, a spirit does not clearly understand its situation and thinks of itself as living rather than dead. It sees its body beside it and knows the body is its own but does not understand that it is separated from the body. This state of confusion continues as long as the slightest connection between the body and the perispirit remains. An individual who had committed suicide said to us, "No, I am not dead," and added, "and yet I feel the worms devouring my body." Now, the worms were certainly not devouring its perispirit, still less the spirit itself. But through a sort of psychic resonance it received the sensation of what was going on in the discarded corpse. It was the sight of the decaying body that produced the illusion of decay; and it was this that the spirit mistook for its own reality. Memory, then, did not produce the sensation of suffering here but the perception of something actually taking place.

....

2 *Translator's Note: Cosmic Principle: see chapter 2, especially question 27 and its footnote.*

From these facts, we can deduce the following. During life, the physiological systems receive stimuli from the external environment and
transmit them to the spirit through the intermediary of the spiritual body,
which closely interacts with the central nervous system. The body, once
dead, no longer feels these stimuli, since neither the spirit nor the
perispirit remains in it. But the perispirit, when disengaged from the
body, still experiences sensations, though limited and no longer identified
with specific organs. Consider, though—and this is a vital point—that the
perispirit is no more than an agent for the transmission of physical stimuli to the spirit. If it could exist independently of the spirit, the spiritual
body would no more be able to feel sensation than the material body does
when it is dead. Moreover, the spirit, if it had no perispirit, would be
impervious to sensations of a material nature—as are, in fact, completely
purified spirits. We know that the more advanced a spiritual being is, the
more ethereal its spiritual body becomes. Indeed, the spiritual body
grows lighter and lucent as the identification with matter dies down.

But, it can be argued, the perispirit transmits agreeable as well as
unpleasant sensations to the spirit. If the purified spirit is impervious to
painful sensations, it must also be denied pleasurable ones. This would be
true if we were talking about the influence of matter as it is known to us.
The sound of our instruments, the odor of our flowers, produce no
impression on spirits of the highest orders. Yet these spirits experience
very vivid sensations, of a charm indescribable to us and of which we can
have no idea. In relation to the sensations known to the higher spirits, we
are similar to people who are born blind and who have never experienced
light. We know these sensations exist. But we cannot explain their nature
or the way they are produced. All we can say is that we know that spirits
possess perception, sensation, hearing, sight, as attributes of their whole
being. However, we know nothing of the process by which their senses
operate; and the spirits can give us no further explanation because our
language is woefully inadequate to express a higher level of ideas. Their
problem is not very different from our having to convey modern notions
of science, art, and philosophy through an underdeveloped tribal dialect.

In saying that spirits are impervious to earthly sensations, we are
speaking of spirits of a very high order, whose refined envelopes are quite
different from ours. Spirits whose perispirits are of denser quality perceive our sounds and odors; unlike human beings, though, their sensitivity is not localized. They feel molecular vibrations throughout their whole
being; these impressions are then translated into perceptions internally.
They hear the sound of our voices and understand us through the transmission of thought rather than speech. Indeed, it is this aspect that supports the contention that the more purified the spirit the more refined the
perceptions. As for sight, this faculty is independent of our light. The faculty of vision is an essential attribute of the soul, for whom darkness has

no existence. Here again, its potential is a function of the spirit's purification. The spirit, therefore, possesses within itself all the sensorial faculties, though during incarnate life these are deadened by the heaviness of our physical bodies. In the spirit-world, by contrast, these faculties become more and more vivid as the spiritual envelope becomes progressively more etherealized.

The spiritual envelope, or perispirit, which is drawn from the atmosphere in which the spirit finds itself, varies depending on the nature of the different planets. In passing from one planet to another, spirits adjust their envelopes as we change our garments when we pass from summer to winter or travel from the North Pole to the Equator. When higher intelligences visit us, they assume a denser envelope compatible with our environment. Their perceptions are therefore produced in the same way as the perceptions of spirits of our world. However, no matter whether they belong to high or low orders, spirits hear and feel only what they choose.[3] Lacking sensorial organs, they can, so to speak, turn their perception on and off at will. There is only one thing they are compelled to hear—the advice of the wise. Furthermore, the faculty of sight is always operating in spirits; yet, depending on their rank, they are able to make themselves invisible to one another. (Spirits of a higher order can go unnoticed by those of a lower one; the opposite situation is impossible.) Finally, while always dim and confused in the first moments after death, the sight of a spirit becomes clearer as it is freed from the body. Then it acquires not only clarity of perception but also the power of seeing through material obstacles. The degree to which a spirit's vision extends through space and time depends of course entirely on its advancement.

"Your theory" some will say, "is anything but encouraging. We thought that once freed from our bodies, the instrument of our sufferings, we would no longer suffer. Now you tell us that we will still suffer in the other life. And though we will not experience it in the same way as here, suffering is nonetheless distressing, whatever its nature. It isn't a pleasant outlook by any means." Sad to say, this is true. We may still have to suffer in the spirit-world, but we may also choose to suffer no more, if we so desire and work for it.

Our present sufferings are sometimes independent of us. But just as often they are the consequence of our own free will. If we trace them back to their source, we find a great number are due to events we might have thwarted. We owe many of our ills and infirmities to our excesses and ambitions—in a word, to the indulgence of our various feelings and appetites. The person who lives soberly in all respects, who avoids excess, who is simple in taste and modest in desire, would escape most of the struggles of human life. This is also true for the spirit-life, in which suf-

....

3 Translator's Note: See question 250 for a qualification of this point.

fering always results from the way the spirit lived on Earth. In that life, the spirit will no longer suffer, say, from gout or rheumatism. But its wrong-doings here will cause it to experience other sufferings there no less distressful. Such distress results from the links that exist between spirit and matter. Thus, the more detached a spirit is from matter, with its desires and indulgences, the fewer painful sensations it will experience. All of us should so act in this world, then, to free ourselves as much as possible from this influence. We possess free will, and consequently, the power of choosing to do or not to do. We can, if we like, conquer our instincts and appetites and rid ourselves of hatred, envy, jealousy, and pride. We are capable of throwing off the yoke of selfishness and purifying our souls by cultivating our own highest feelings. We can, moreover, do good and live with compassion while giving the things of this world only their just importance. In this way we can, even in our present incarnate circumstances, affect our own transformation and achieve deliverance from the influence of matter. Then the memory of physical sufferings in life will not be distressful or create unpleasant impressions. Those sufferings will have affected the body only and left no traces on our souls. The calmness of a good conscience will exempt us from them and we will enjoy a pure sense of happiness.

We have questioned many thousands of spirits belonging to every class. We have studied them at every period of their spirit-life, following them step by step from the moment of their deaths, with a view toward discovering the changes that take place in their ideas and feelings. This examination has invariably shown us that, on the one hand, the sufferings of spirits are the direct result of earthly misconduct, for which they have to endure the consequences; and on the other, that their new existence is, for those who have followed the right road, a source of ineffable happiness. The spirits who suffer do so because they have willed it (through their actions) and have only themselves to thank for it—in the other world, as in this one.

Choice of Trials

258. Before incarnating, does a spirit foresee what will happen to it in its new life?

▲ *"Yes, the spirit plans the kind of trials it will undergo. It has full use of its free will."*

—Doesn't God impose the trials of life as a chastisement?

▲ *"Nothing happens without the permission of God, who has established all the laws that govern the universe. But in giving a spirit free choice, God makes the spirit entirely responsible for its own acts and for all their consequences. Nothing stands in the way of its future; the right road is as freely open to it as the wrong one. But even if it goes wrong, the consoling fact remains that not all is lost, that the goodness of God will allow it to begin again the task it has done badly. Moreover, try not to confuse what derives from God's will and what comes from human will. If a natural danger (for example, a hurricane) threatens you, you have not created that danger. Environmental phenomena are part of the laws of Nature. As a spirit, you might have voluntarily elected to expose yourself to this kind of danger, because you have seen it as a valuable learning experience. Ultimately, however, it's the Divine will which determines whether or not the chosen trial comes to pass."*

259. If the spirit chooses the kind of trials it will undergo, have we foreseen and chosen all the difficulties we experience in our earthly life?

▲ *"This is not the case. You cannot choose and foresee all the things that will happen to you in this life in all their detail. You do choose the general nature of the trials you will be subjected to. The details of the trials result from the general situation you have chosen and, often, from your own actions once in the situation.*

"For instance, if a spirit chooses to be born among dishonest people, it knows beforehand the kinds of temptations it will be exposed to, but not each individual action it will take. Those actions are the effect of its free will. A spirit knows that, in choosing a particular road, it will have such and such a struggle to undergo. It knows, therefore, the nature of the ups and downs it will meet in life. It does not know the form under which these will present themselves, since they spring from circumstances and the force of things. It is only the leading events of its new life, the ones that will exercise a determining effect on its fate, that the spirit foresees. Think of it like this. If you enter a road full of ruts, you know you must walk very carefully or run the risk of stumbling. Maybe, if you are sufficiently on your guard, you won't stumble at all. But if, while you are strolling down a street, a tile falls on your head, don't suppose that, as the common saying goes, 'it was written.'"

260. Why would a spirit choose to be born among people who are leading a crooked life?

▲ *"It must be sent into the conditions that furnish the elements of the trial it has asked for. There has to be a correspondence between the imperfections it desires to be free of and the social surroundings into which it is called to live. For example, if a spirit needs to struggle against the tendency to steal, it may choose to live among people inclined to thievery."*

—If there was no evil on Earth, then spirits could not find the necessary conditions for certain kinds of trials.

▲ *"If that was the case on Earth, there would be no reason to complain. Imagine the worlds of higher order, where evil no longer exists and goodness is dominant. Try to bring about such a state of things as soon as possible on your Earth."*

261. Must the spirit, in the course of its earthly journeys, undergo every sort of temptation? Must it encounter all the circumstances that excite pride, jealousy, greed, sensuality, etc.?

▲ *"Certainly not. As you know, many spirits have taken, from the beginning, a road that has spared them from having to undergo many of these trials. It is true, too, that spirits who have allowed themselves to be drawn into a certain road are exposed to all the dangers of that road. A spirit, for instance, may ask for riches, and its request may be granted. What it does from that point depends on its character. It may become greedy or giving, selfish or generous. It may make an excellent use of its wealth or waste it foolishly. But this does not mean that it must experience every corrupting desire that can come with wealth."*

262. A spirit, at its origin, is simple, ignorant, and without experience. How can it choose a life intelligently, and how can it be responsible for that choice?

▲ *"God supplies what the spirit lacks, outlining the road it must take as you would guide an infant by the hand. But God allows the spirit, as its free will develops, to become the master of its choices. It is then that the spirit may lose its way and take the wrong path, refusing to listen to the advice of good spirits who try to instruct it. This is the true 'fall of man.'"*

—When a spirit possesses free will, does its choice of an earthly life depend on its volition alone, or does God sometimes impose a life as a means of purification?

▲ *"God, who can afford to wait, never rushes the work of purification. Nonetheless, an existence may be imposed on a spirit when, through unawareness or stubbornness, it fails to realize what is in its own best interest. In these cases, Providence sees that a particular kind of life would serve the spirit's advancement and at the same time furnish the conditions of purification."*

263. Do spirits choose their next life immediately after death?

▲ *"No. For many, the ability to choose is impaired by the misconception that their unhappy state is eternal. As we told you, these impressions are in themselves a method of expiation."*

264. What motivates a spirit's choice of trials?

▲ *"It chooses those trials that will help rid itself of faults and speed up its progress. Thus, some may impose on themselves a life of poverty and privation. Others might want to test their powers of resistance to the temptations of wealth and power—much more dangerous because of the possible abuses and cravings these temptations may develop in them. Still others might want to strengthen their good resolutions by having to struggle against the influences of a vicious environment."*

265. If some spirits select this kind of environment as a trial of their goodness, don't others make the same choice out of a desire to live in surroundings compatible with their tastes—surroundings, in other words, where they can give free rein to their appetites?

▲ *"Undoubtedly such cases occur, but only among spirits with an imperfectly developed moral sense. Even in these instances, however, the particular lifestyle chosen will bring about important lessons to the spirit. Sooner or later, the spirit comes to understand that indulging its lower instincts leads to unwelcome consequences. Sometimes, the consequences are felt for so long that they seem eternal. In other words, a spirit will remain in this situation until it understands the seriousness of its predicament and demands, on its own, to be allowed to repair itself by undergoing more beneficial experiences."*

266. Wouldn't a spirit naturally choose the easiest trials?

▲ *"It might seem so from your point of view but not necessarily from the spirit's. When it is freed from matter and all illusions end, it thinks differently."*

Discussion: While on Earth and subject to the influence of worldly ideas, humans see only the painful aspect of the trials they experience. As a result, it appears natural to us that in the spirit-world a spirit would choose only trials that are filled with material advantages. But when a spirit returns to spirit-life, it can compare those coarse and fleeting pleasures with the unchanging happiness it occasionally glimpses there, and it will realize that this greater joy can be had only by achieving mastery of the lessons afforded by earthly life. It may, therefore, choose the hardest trials, the most painful existence, hoping to reach the happier state faster—just as a sick man often chooses the bitterest medicine if he believes it will speed up his cure. The person who aspires to immortalize his or her name by discovering an unknown country does not seek the most flowery road but the one most likely to lead to that country. And he or she will brave the dangers of this road for the sake of the glory that will follow success.

The doctrine of free choice in the planning of our lives and trials no longer seems extraordinary if we consider that spirits, when free of matter, look at things differently than us. They see the ends to which their trials are intended to work—ends far more important to them than the fleeting pleasures of earthly life. After each life, they see the steps they have already taken and realize what qualities they still lack. Then they willingly submit to the difficulties of incarnate life, asking to undergo trials that will help them advance. There is nothing surprising, then, about a spirit choosing a hard or painful life. It knows that it cannot, in its present state of imperfection, enjoy the perfect happiness it desires. But it sees glimpses of that happiness and seeks ways to improve itself, which is the only means it has to reach its goal.

Don't we witness, every day, examples of similar choices? Consider, for instance, the person who works constantly so that he or she can eventually live comfortably and securely; or the soldier who volunteers for a dangerous mission; or the entrepreneur who risks everything in the interests of science or personal fortune. Humans voluntarily undergo hardships that, if they last them out, will result in honor or profit. We will put up with nearly anything for gain or glory. Aren't all the competitive exams we submit to, in advancing our careers, trials of this kind? A person who wants a high position in science or art or industry has to go through all the lower degrees that lead to that position and that constitute so many trials. Human life is modeled after spirit-life, presenting the same difficulties only on a smaller scale. On Earth, we often choose the hardest conditions as a way of reaching the highest ends. Why should a disincarnated spirit, who sees much farther than when it is incarnated, not choose an arduous or painful existence if the result is eternal bliss? People who say that because spirits can choose their own lives they will demand to be princes and millionaires, are like the blind—they "see" only what they can touch.

A spirit is like a traveller who, in the depths of a fog-bound valley, can make out neither the length nor the sides of the road. Once on top of the hill, however, and with the fog cleared away, the traveller can take in both the road along which he or she has come and the distance still left. The point to reach and the obstacles still to be overcome are clear, and it is possible for the traveller to make plans that will assure a successful completion of the journey. While incarnated, the spirit is like the traveller at the foot of the hill; when freed of earthly troubles, it is like the traveller who has reached the summit. The aim of the traveller is to obtain rest after the fatigue of his or her journey. The aim of the spirit is to attain to perfect happiness after its hardships and trials.

Spirits say that between physical lives they seek, study, and observe in order to make wise choices. The same thing is true of us. We often spend years preparing for a professional career. And if we fail in the one we chose, we train for another. Each career we undertake constitutes a phase, a period, in our lives. A large part of every day, too, is spent in deciding on and preparing for what we will do the next

day. For a spirit, different incarnate lives are so many transitional phases, periods, days, within its normal spirit-life.

267. Can a spirit choose its next incarnate life while still in an incarnate state?

▲ *"Depending on its motives, its desires can exercise a certain amount of
influence. But on returning to spirit-life, it often judges things very differently. Only as a spirit can it make the actual choice. Nonetheless, during
material life, it can personally determine the choice, since it has occasional
moments when it is detached from matter."*

—Many humans want earthly power and riches. But surely they don't want
purifications or trials.

▲ *"Undoubtedly. In these cases, a materialistic instinct drives the person to
seek power and wealth in hope of enjoying all their pleasures. From a spiritual perspective, however, the spirit could only desire them in order to master the desires and challenges that power and riches pose."*

268. Must a spirit constantly undergo trials until it reaches the state of perfect
purity?

▲ *"Yes. But they are different from the trials you know. You see trials in the
hardships of earthly existence. When a spirit accomplishes a certain degree
of progress, it no longer has to undergo experiences of that nature.
Nonetheless, it has to perform the tasks required to continue its progress—
for instance, aiding others to work out their own improvement. There is
nothing painful in any of these duties."*

269. Can a spirit make a mistake about the value of the trial it chooses?

▲ *"It might choose one that exceeds its strength—in which case, it will fail. Or
it may choose a trial from which it will learn nothing—as when it decides,
for instance, to lead an idle and useless life. But in such cases, it sees, on
returning to the spirit-world, that nothing has been gained; and then it asks
to make up for lost time."*

270. Why do some people select one career rather than another?

▲ *"You can answer this question yourselves. Aren't career preferences dependent on what we have told you about the choice of trials and the progress you
have made in prior lives?"*

271. As a spirit studies the various conditions of incarnate life that will help it
progress, why would it ever consider, for example, being born among cannibals?

▲ *"The spirits who have accomplished some progress are obviously not reincarnated as cannibals. As a rule, those who choose such experience are at
that level or even lower."*

Discussion: Cannibals, we know, are not at the lowest degree of spiri-
               tual development. In fact, there are planets on which we
               find brutality and ferocity to an extent unknown on Earth.

For such spirits to be reincarnated among our cannibals is a step forward for them—as it would be for a cannibal to become part of a civilized community here. If these spirits currently aim no higher, it is because their limitations prevent them from understanding higher degrees of progress. Spirits advance only gradually; they cannot clear the distance between barbarity and civilization at a single bound. This is one of the reasons reincarnation exists and why it really reflects the justice of God. After all, what would happen to the millions of human beings who die every day in the most backward conditions imaginable if God did not give them the means to arrive at higher states? And why would God refuse them the favor granted to everyone else?

272. Can spirits from less advanced planets than Earth, or from our own more backward peoples (cannibals, for instance), be born among more advanced peoples?

▲ *"Yes. These spirits, trying to reach a degree still too far above them, sometimes do come to Earth. But they have instincts and habits that clash with the convictions and habits of the societies they enter, so they feel completely out of place."*

Discussion: Often spirits of this kind present us with the sad sight of violent natures in the midst of civilization. To return to their original milieu would not be a descent for them but a resumption of their natural ethical station. They might even gain by such a return.

273. Can a more advanced individual be reincarnated, as a means of purification, among a less advanced people?

▲ *"Yes. This would depend on the kind of purification needed. A good spirit sometimes chooses an influential existence among a backward people in order to hasten its progress. In this instance the reincarnation is a mission."*

Relationships in the Spirit–Realm

274. Do the different degrees of advancement establish a hierarchy of powers among spirits? In other words, do subordination and authority exist among them?

▲ *"Yes. The authority of spirits over one another is very great. Their power results from their moral ascendancy. Their influence over the lower ones is, so to speak, irresistible."*

—Can the less advanced spirits exempt themselves from this authority?

▲ *"As we have said, the authority is irresistible."*

275. Do the power and consideration an individual enjoys on Earth give him or her ascendancy once in the spirit-world?

▲ *"No. In the spirit-world the humble are exalted and the proud are abased. Read the Psalms."*

—In what sense should we understand "exalting" and "abasing"?

▲ *"Spirits belong to different orders because of their moral merit. Accordingly, a person who once held the highest rank on Earth might find him or herself in the lowest rank in the spirit-world, while the maid or chauffeur of this person may be in the highest. Haven't we made this clear? Jesus says that 'Whoever exalts himself will be humbled, and whoever humbles himself will be exalted.'"*[4]

276. When someone who has been important on Earth finds him or herself in an inferior place in the spirit-world, is this change of position a cause of humiliation?

▲ *"Often very much so—especially if the person has been haughty and envious."*

277. After dying in battle, will a soldier who meets his general in the spirit-world still acknowledge him as a superior?

▲ *"Titles are nothing. Moral superiority is everything."*

278. Do spirits of different orders mix together in the other life?[5]

▲ *"They see each other, but they are separated. According to their mutual likes and dislikes, they approach or shun each other—just as you do. The spirit-life is one of varied conditions and relationships, and the earthly life is only a vague reflection of it. Spirits of the same order are drawn together by a sort of affinity and form groups or families united by a common aim—the good ones by the desire to do good, the bad by the desire to do wrong. They gather together because of the similarity of their activities and by the wish to be among those they resemble."*

Discussion: The spirit-world is like a great city where individuals of all ranks and conditions see and meet each other but do not necessarily socialize. As in a city, circles are formed by similarities in tastes, and good and bad spirits share the same space without having to interact.

279. Are all spirits equally approachable to each other?

▲ *"The good go everywhere, as they must in order to influence wrong-doers. But the regions the good spirits inhabit are forbidden to those of lower degrees because of the disturbing nature of the latter's thoughts and desires."*

....

4 *Translator's Note: Matthew 23:12.*

....

5 *Translator's Note: See Chapter 6, starting with question 100, for a discussion of the different orders of spirits.*

280. What are relations like between good and vile spirits?

▲ *"The good ones try to combat the tendencies of the others and help raise them to a higher degree. For good spirits, this interaction is a mission."*

281. Why do less advanced spirits take pleasure in encouraging us to do wrong?

▲ *"Jealousy. They haven't earned a place among the good and want to prevent other, inexperienced spirits from enjoying happiness, too. They are driven to make others suffer what they suffer themselves. You see the same emotion at work among humans."*

282. How do spirits communicate with each other?

▲ *"Spirits need only see each other to communicate their ideas. Their 'language' is more meaningful than yours as their thoughts are reflected in themselves. In addition, the Cosmic Principle acts as a medium that conducts their thoughts through the universe, much like air conducts sounds. By means of the Cosmic Principle, spirits can send their thoughts across different worlds."*

283. Can spirits hide their thoughts or conceal themselves from each other?

▲ *"No, with them everything is open—most especially so with those who are very advanced. They may withdraw from, but they are always visible to, each other. This is not an absolute rule, however. The higher spirits are perfectly capable of making themselves invisible to the lower ones, if they find it useful to do so."*

284. How can spirits, who have no bodies, establish individuality?   And how is this individuality distinguishable from other spiritual beings?

▲ *"Their individuality is established by their perispirit, or spiritual body. Just as the body does among you, the perispirit makes a separate personality of each spirit, distinct from all others."*

285. Do spirits who have lived together on Earth recognize each other?   For instance, do sons recognize theirs fathers, and friends their friends?

▲ "Yes—from generation to generation."

—How do people who were acquainted on Earth recognize each other in the spirit-world?

▲ *"We see our past lives, which we can read as if they were books. When we see the points of linkage with our friends and enemies, we also acquire awareness of their complete journey from life to death."*

286. Does the soul see, immediately after death, the relations and friends who have returned to the spirit-world before it?

▲ *"Immediately is not always the right word. As we have said, the soul requires time to regain self-awareness and shake off the influence of matter."*

287. How is the soul received when it returns to the spirit-world?

▲ *"The good are received as dearly beloved brothers and sisters whose return has been eagerly awaited. Wrong-doers are treated with indifference."*

288. How do spirits of the lower orders feel at the sight of a like-minded spirit when it arrives?

▲ *"They are pleased at seeing another who resembles them and who, like them, is deprived of any spiritual joy. On Earth, a band of scoundrels rejoices on meeting another scoundrel. It is the same here."*

289. Do our relatives and friends come to meet us when we are leaving Earth?

▲ *"Yes, they will come to meet a spirit they love. They greet you as if you had come back from a journey and congratulate you on your escape from the dangers of the road. They also aid you in freeing yourself from the bonds of the flesh. But to be met in this way by loved ones is a favor granted only to the upright soul. The soul of the wrong-doer is left alone or taken in by spirits like itself."*

290. Are relatives and friends always reunited after death?

▲ *"It depends on how evolved they are and the paths they have to follow. If one is further advanced and progresses more rapidly than the other, the two cannot remain together. They may see each other occasionally, but they can only be reunited for good when the one behind catches up or when both reach the state of perfection. Moreover, a spirit is sometimes deprived of the sight of its relatives and friends as a means of correction."*

Affinity of Spirits; Eternal Halves

291. Do spirits have special personal attachments among themselves that go beyond the general feeling that comes from affinity?

▲ *"Yes—just as humans do. But the link between spirits is stronger when the body is absent because it is no longer affected by physical passions."*

292. Can spirits feel hatred for each other?

▲ *"Hatred exists only among spirits of the lower orders. They are also the ones who sow enmity and dissension among humanity."*

293. Do those who have been enemies on Earth remain enemies in the spirit-world?

▲ *"No. They often see that their earthly hatred was stupid and caused by something foolish. Only imperfect spirits retain the animosities of earthly life—and, as they gradually become purified, they will rid themselves of these feelings. Spirits whose anger has been roused by some mere material interest on Earth forget their dissension as soon as they are in the spirit-world. Since the cause of their dissension no longer exists, they may greet each other with pleasure, as if no hostility had ever existed between them."*

Discussion: Just as two school fellows who, on reaching the age of rea-
              son, realize the silliness of their childhood quarrels and no
              longer hold grudges against each other.

294. Does the memory of earthly wrongs done to one another create obstacles
among spirits?

▲ *"Yes, it may keep them apart."*

295. How do those we have wronged feel about us after death?

▲ *"If they are good, they accept your regrets and forgive you. If not, they might
resent you and even seek revenge. God may allow this to happen as a warning."*

296. Can the personal affections of spirits change?

▲ *"No. Spirits cannot be mistaken in each other. The mask behind which the
devious hide on Earth does not exist in the spirit-world. The affections of
spirits—when these feelings are genuine—are unchangeable, a source of
supreme happiness."*

297. Does the affection that two spirits have felt for each other on Earth continue
in the spirit-world?

▲ *"Yes, if that affection was founded on feelings of empathy. If its source was
physical, however, it ends. Affections are more solid and lasting among spirits than among humans because they are not subject to material interests or
personal pride."*

298. Is it true that souls are predestined to be united and that each of us has a spiritual counterpart somewhere in the universe—another half, so to speak, with
whom we will one day reunite?

▲ *"No. There is no such thing as a special, predetermined union between two
souls. Union exists among all spirits depending on their degree of perfection.
The greater the perfection, the more united they are. It is the harmony among
them that produces the complete and perfect happiness at which they eventually arrive. Discord, on the contrary, produces all the ills of human life."*

299. How, then, should we understand the term "other half," which spirits sometimes use to indicate other spirits for whom they have a special liking?

▲ *"The expression is incorrect. If one spirit were half of another, it would, if
separated from the other, be incomplete."*

300. When two perfectly attuned spirits are reunited in the spirit-world, are they
reunited for all eternity, or can they separate and unite with other spirits?

▲ *"Spirits in the state of perfection are united among themselves. When a spirit passes to a higher degree it will develop affinity with other spirits, but it
will continue its affection for those it has left behind."*

301. Do two completely attuned spirits complete each other, or does their attune-

ment result from having a similar character?

▲ *"Attunement arises from the perfect agreement of their tendencies and instincts. If one were necessary to complete the other, they would have no individuality."*

302. Does similarity of thought and feeling alone constitute perfect attunement among spirits, or does it also require the same degree of intellectual development?

▲ *"It results from equality in the degree of elevation."*

303. Can spirits who are not now well attuned become so in the future?

▲ *"Yes. All spirits will achieve this state in time. Consider the case of two spirits who were once together. One may have advanced more rapidly than the other. But the latter will eventually reach the point where it can be with the more advanced one. Their reunion will take place all the sooner if the more advanced one fails in its trials and remains stationary."*

—Can two spirits who are currently well attuned with each other stop being so?

▲ *"Certainly, if one of them, lacking energy, lags behind while the other advances."*

Discussion: The theory of "twin-souls" (or "other-halves") is simply a metaphorical representation of the union of two spirits who share many common aspirations and a mutual affection; it should not be taken literally. Spirits who use the expression are not of the higher orders and have a narrower range of view. Consequently, they try to express their meaning by using terms familiar to them from their earthly lives. The idea that two souls were created for each other, and will be reunited and eternally integrated with each other at some indefinite period, is completely incorrect.

Memory of Incarnate Lives

304. Does a spirit remember its incarnate lives?

▲ *"Yes. Having lived many times as a human being, it remembers what it has been and often smiles at its own past foolishness."*

Discussion: As an adult smiles at the "follies" of youth and childhood.

305. Does the memory of an incarnate life present itself to a spirit completely and spontaneously, as soon as death occurs?

▲ *"No. Depending on how much attention the spirit focuses on it, the memory comes back slowly—just as an object gradually becomes visible to you out of a thick fog."*

306. Does the spirit remember all the details of a previous life? Does it take in the

whole of it at a single glance?

▲ *"It remembers a previous life more or less distinctly and in detail, depending on the influence specific events have exercised. There are many things, of course, that it will consider unimportant and won't even try to remember."*

—And if it chose to remember those "unimportant" things, could it?

▲ *"It can recall the most minute details of every incident of the life, even its thoughts. But unless this serves a useful purpose, the spirit won't bother with it."*

— Does a spirit realize the purpose of its earthly life?

▲ *"Certainly it will see and understand better than it did while incarnate. It realizes that, to be able to eventually reach the divine realm, it needs to undergo purification and that with each incarnation it leaves some of its imperfections behind."*

307. How does a previous life present itself to a spirit's memory? Is it through a determined effort of the imagination, or is it more like a moving picture revealed before its eyes?

▲ *"In both ways. The actions it is interested in remembering will appear as though taking place in the present. The others it will see more or less dimly or entirely forget. Also, the more advanced a spirit is, the less importance it will attach to material things. This is why, when you evoke a spirit who has recently left the Earth, you find that it has difficulty remembering the names of certain acquaintances or other seemingly important details. It no longer concerns itself with them, and their names quickly fade from its memory. But you always find that it perfectly remembers the events and names that have molded its intellectual and moral progress."*

308. Does a spirit remember the lives previous to the one it has just left?

▲ *"Its entire past is spread out before it like so many trips undertaken by a traveler. But, as we have told you, it does not remember all its past actions with absolute clarity—only the ones that have influenced its present state. Its earliest lives, which can be regarded as comprising its spirit-infancy, are lost in vagueness and disappear in the night of oblivion."*

309. How does a spirit view the body it has just left?

▲ *"As an uncomfortable garment that has hindered it and that it is happy to get rid of."*

—How does it feel on seeing the body decay?

▲ *"Almost always, indifferent. The body is something it no longer cares about."*

310. After a time, does a spirit recognize its mortal remains or objects it once owned?

▲ *"Sometimes. It depends on the importance it attaches to earthly things."*

311. Is a spirit's interest aroused by the attitude of its loved ones toward its former belongings? Is it happy to see the respect they pay them?

▲ *"A spirit is always pleased when its loved ones remember it kindly. It knows, too, that particular objects will serve them as fond mementos. But it is their thoughts that really attract it, not the objects."*

312. Do spirits remember the sufferings they endured in their last incarnate life?

▲ *"Frequently. And the memory makes them value all the more vividly the happiness they now enjoy as spirits."*

313. Does a spirit who has been happy on Earth regret leaving the enjoyments it knew here?

▲ *"Only less advanced spirits have regrets. Spirits of the higher orders find the happiness of Eternity immeasurably preferable to the temporary pleasures they found on Earth."*

Discussion: Here again the attitude of evolved spirits is similar to adults who show trivial regard for the simpler delights of their infancy.

314. Does a spirit regret leaving important work unfinished when death interrupts that work?

▲ *"No. As a spirit, such a person realizes that others are destined to complete the work. Rather than experience regret, the spirit will try to act on the minds of other people, influencing them to complete what it began. If on Earth the person's aim was to be useful to the human race, this aim does not change in the spirit-world."*

315. When someone has left behind works of art or literature, does the spirit of that person take the same interest in them as when living?

▲ *"It judges them from another point of view. It may even disapprove of things it admired in life."*

316. Does a spirit still take an interest in the progress of arts and sciences on Earth?

▲ *"This depends on its degree of elevation and the mission it has to undertake. What appears magnificent to you often is very insignificant to spirits. If they do take an interest in something, it is only as a scholar who becomes interested in the work of a student. They appreciate anything that nurtures the progress of incarnate spirits."*

317. Do spirits have any feelings toward their native lands after death?

▲ *"Spirits of the higher orders find that their country is the universe. Their only preference, in regard to Earth, is for the place where they find individuals with whom they felt the greatest affection."*

Discussion: Depending on their moral and intellectual development, spirits see situations and things in infinitely varied ways.

Spirits of the higher orders rarely come to Earth. What we do here is so paltry compared to the grandeurs of Infinity that they have very little interest in our affairs—unless, of course, they have been sent here to help us progress. Spirits of the intermediate orders visit Earth more frequently, but they still judge its affairs from a higher point of view than they did while incarnate. The ones from the lower orders are plentiful here. They make up a large portion of the invisible population and retain much the same ideas, tastes, and tendencies they had while alive. They mix in with our gatherings, occupations, and pastimes—playing the parts that could be expected from their character. No longer able to satisfy their material appetites, they love to watch others overindulge theirs and try to excite those appetites by any means possible. Nonetheless, some are inclined to watch in order to acquire knowledge and advance.

318. Do spirits change their ideas in the spirit-world?

▲ *"Very considerably. To the extent that a spirit is free from matter, its ideas can undergo great changes. It might retain the same ideas for a long period. But gradually the influence of matter diminishes, and it sees things more clearly. At that point it begins looking for ways to progress."*

319. Since spirits have already lived in the spirit-world before being incarnated, why do they feel surprise on re-entering that world?

▲ *"The feeling is only momentary and results from the bewilderment that follows their waking. As the memory of the past comes back to them and earthly impressions fade, they re-establish their roots in the spiritual life."*[6]

Funeral Services, Memorials

320. Are spirits affected by the memory of loved ones on Earth?

▲ *"Much more so than you can imagine. If they are happy in the spirit world, the thoughts of their loved ones make them happier. If they are unhappy, such thoughts bring consolation."*

321. In some countries a special day is set aside for the remembrance of the dead. Are spirits drawn toward their living friends on that day, and do they make it a point to meet the ones who go to pray beside their graves?

▲ *"Spirits answer the call of fond memories on this day as they do on any other."*

....

6 *Translator's Note: See questions 163-165 for a complementary discussion of the state of the soul after death.*

—Do they go specially to their burial-places on this day?

▲ *"They go to the cemeteries in great numbers, attracted by the thoughts of their earthly relations. But each spirit goes solely for its own friends, not for the crowds of visitors."*

—What form do they take when they come to these places, and how would they look if they could make themselves visible to us?

▲ *"They would take the form and appearance they had during their lifetimes."*

322. Do the spirits of people who have been forgotten go to the cemeteries despite the fact that no one visits their graves. Do they grieve because no one remembers them?

▲ *"What is Earth to them? They are only linked to it by the heart. If no one on Earth feels affection for a spirit, nothing remains to attach it to your planet. The whole universe is before it."*

323. Is a spirit more pleased when its friends visit its grave, or when they offer prayers for it in their homes?

▲ *"A visit to the grave is a sign, a way of showing a spirit that it has not been forgotten. A prayer, as we have said, sanctifies the memory. As long as it comes from the heart, the place where the prayer is offered doesn't matter."*

324. When statues are erected to deceased persons and buildings are named after them, are the spirits of those persons present at the dedication? And are they pleased with these kinds of ceremonies?

▲ *"If they are able, spirits often attend them. But they attach more importance to how they are remembered than to the honors."*

325. Why do some persons want to be buried in one place rather than another? Do their spirits go there more willingly after death? And does a spirit's interest in matters so mundane indicate its lack of progress?

▲ *"The desire is prompted by a spirit's affection for certain places. And yes, it signals a certain lack of spiritual development. To an elevated spirit, one spot on Earth is very much like any other. After all, it knows that it will be reunited with its loved ones, whether they are buried far apart or not."*

—Does it serve any purpose to bury all the members of the same family together in one cemetery?

▲ *"This kind of reunion doesn't matter to spirits, although it does help humans recall their loved ones and relieve their grief."*

326. When the soul has returned to spirit-life, is it pleased by the honors paid to its mortal remains?

▲ *"When a spirit reaches a certain degree of advancement, it comes to see the uselessness of honors and is indifferent to them. But many spirits, when they first return to the spirit-world, take great pleasure in the honors people pay them. Others, to be sure, are disturbed to find they have been forgotten; but these spirits are still holding on to some of the false ideas they had in their earthly lives."*

327. Do spirits ever attend their own funerals?

▲ *"Very often. But in cases where they are still in the state of bewilderment that follows death, they do not understand what is going on."*

—Are they flattered when large numbers of persons attend their funerals?

▲ *"More or less. It depends on the feelings that brought those people together."*

328. Is a spirit ever present at meetings of its heirs?

▲ *"Almost always. Providence offers such occasions as learning experiences and for the spirit to reassess its views. The spirit is able then to determine what the declarations of affection and devotion it heard during life were really worth. And often its disappointment on seeing greedy friends and relatives fight over its former property is very great. As for greedy heirs—they will answer for their actions in due time."*

329. Should the respect that human beings have traditionally and universally shown the dead be attributed to an intuitive belief in a future state?

▲ *"Yes. Without such a belief, your respect would have no object or meaning."*

CHAPTER XI

RETURN TO THE BODY

Preludes to Return

330. Do spirits foresee the time of their next incarnation?

▲ *"They have presentiments of it in the same way a blind person feels heat when approaching fire. They know they will be reincarnated, just as you know that you will die, but without knowing when the change will occur."[1]*

—Reincarnation, then, is a requirement of spirit-life, as death is a requirement of the incarnate life?

▲ *"Certainly."*

331. Do all spirits concern themselves with their approaching incarnation?

▲ *"Some never give it a thought and—strange as it may seem—know nothing about it. In some cases, they are left in uncertainty about their future as a form of admonition and correction."*

332. Can a spirit speed up or delay the moment of reincarnation?

▲ *"A strong desire on the spirit's part can hasten it. And if it shrinks from the trial—spirits being no braver or more decisive than humans—it can put off the process for a while. But there is a price to pay. The spirit suffers from it, just as patients suffer when they refuse to take the medicine that will cure them."*

333. Suppose a spirit finds itself reasonably happy in the spiritual realm and it is, say, at an average level of development with no immediate desire to better itself. Could it prolong its stay indefinitely?

---

1 *See question 166 for a discussion on reincarnation.*

▲ *"No, not indefinitely. Sooner or later, every spirit feels the need to move ahead. All spirits have to ascend. It is their destiny."*

334. Is the union of a given soul with a given body predetermined, or is the body chosen only at the last moment?

▲ *"Each spirit selects its own trials and requests to be reincarnated. The spirit who is to animate a given body, however, is always assigned beforehand. And God, all seeing and all knowing, has foreseen and foreknown that a particular soul will be united with a particular body."*

335. Is the spirit allowed to choose the body it will enter, or does it only choose the kind of life that will provide its trial?

▲ *"It may choose a body too, since the imperfections of a given body are also trials that will help it advance—if, in fact, it succeeds in overcoming the obstacles the body places before it. The choice doesn't always depend on the spirit, but it is often allowed to request a particular body."*

—Can a spirit, at the last moment, refuse to enter the body it has chosen?

▲ *"It might. But, depending on circumstances, it may aggravate its plight and make matters worse than the trial it sought to avoid."*

336. Is it possible that a child about to be born will not find a spirit willing to incarnate in it?

▲ *"God provides for all possibilities. Every viable fetus has a spirit connected to it. Nothing is ever created without a design."*

337. Is the union of a given spirit with a body ever imposed?

▲ *"Yes—when the consciousness is still too unadvanced to choose wisely. If the circumstances of a child's birth and the position it will have in the world represent an experience the spirit needs to undergo, it may be compelled to accept a particular body."*

338. If several spirits ask to incarnate in the same body, how is the choice made among them?

▲ *"Many may ask, but Divine Providence decides what is best. But, as we have already said, the spirit is chosen before the union with the body."*

339. Is the moment of incarnation accompanied by confusion similar to the one that follows human death?[2]

▲ *"Yes, but the confusion is greater and lasts much longer. At death, the spirit is set free; at birth, it re-enters the rehabilitation colony."*

340. Does a spirit see the moment of reincarnation as a solemn one—as something serious and important to it?

▲ *"It is like an ocean voyager who sets sail on a dangerous journey, not know-*

····························

2 *Translator's Note: See questions 163-165 on the state of the spirit following physical death.*

ing whether he will reach his destination or die by drowning."

Discussion: The traveler, beginning a perilous ocean voyage, knows the
                risks he has to face but has no advance knowledge of
                whether he will survive the adventure. The same thing
                happens with the spirit. It knows the nature of the trials it
                must face; it doesn't know whether it will succeed or fail.
                Just as the death of the body sets it free, reincarnation, for
                the spirit, signifies a form of confinement—or rather, of
                exile. The spirit leaves the spirit-world for the incarnate
                one in the same frame of mind that we leave the incarnate
                world. The spirit knows that it will be reincarnated, just as
                a person on Earth knows he or she will die. But, just like the
                person, it only becomes aware of the change at the moment
                it occurs. At this moment, a state of confusion possesses the
                spirit, as it does a dying person, and lasts until the new life
                is fully established. The beginning of reincarnation is, for
                the spirit, a period of apprehension.

341. Before incarnation, is the spirit's uncertainty about the outcome of the trials
in its new life a source of anxiety?

▲ *"Yes, very great anxiety, since those trials (depending on how well they are
borne) will either accelerate or delay its progress."*

342. When a spirit returns to the spirit-world, friends come to receive it.[3] Are spirit-friends also present at the moment of reincarnation when it leaves the spirit-
world?

▲ *"If the spirit belongs to a rank in which affection reigns, spirits who love it
will remain with it to the last moment, encouraging it and often even following it into the new life."*

343. Sometimes in our dreams we see beings who show us affection but whose
faces we don't recognize. Are these the spirit-friends who have followed us into
incarnate life?

▲ *"Yes, in many cases. They come to visit you in the same manner as someone
visits a student in a boarding school."*

Union of Spirit and Body; Abortion

344. When does the spirit unite with the body?

▲ *"The union begins at conception; it is complete only with birth. From the
moment of conception, the spirit assigned to animate a given body is united
with that body by the perispirit, which brings spirit and body closer and closer as the moment of birth approaches. When that moment arrives, the infant's*

....

3 *Translator's Note: This point is discussed in question 160; also in questions 291-
303.*

cry announces that it is now among the living.

345. Is the union between the spirit and the body final from the moment of conception? Could the spirit, during the early stages of union, suddenly refuse to animate the body?

▲ *"The union is definitive in one sense: no other spirit can replace the one who has been chosen to inhabit that particular body. But, since the link that holds the two together is weak at first, it is easily broken and may be severed if the spirit wills it—that is, if it draws back from the trial. In that case, the child dies."*

346. What happens to the spirit if the body it has chosen dies before birth?

▲ *"It chooses another body."*

—What is the purpose of still-births?

▲ *"Most often, deaths of this kind result from imperfections in the matter."*

347. Can a spirit benefit in any way from an incarnation in which the body dies a few days after birth?

▲ *"In this case, the new being's self-awareness is not very developed and its death has little importance for the spirit's progress. As we have told you, such deaths are often intended as a trial for the parents."*

348. Does a spirit know beforehand that the body it chooses has no chance of living?

▲ *"Sometimes. But if it chooses a body for this reason, it may be doing so to avoid the trial of a life on Earth."*

349. If, for some reason, a spirit fails to accomplish the goals of a proposed incarnation, does it immediately reincarnate?

▲ *"Not always immediately unless a decision has been made previously for such a spirit to reincarnate right away. Under normal conditions, the spirit requires time to make a new choice."*

350. When a spirit is definitively united to an infant body and can no longer refuse the union, does it sometimes regret the choice it has made?

▲ *"If you mean to ask whether, as an adult, the spirit may complain about its life and wish things were otherwise, the answer is yes. But if you mean to ask whether, as a spirit, it regrets the choice it has made to reincarnate, we answer: no. Once incarnate, the spirit does not remember making a choice and, for that reason, cannot regret having made it. But it may find the burden too heavy and beyond its strength. In extreme situations the spirit may even think of giving the incarnate life up."*

351. During the time between conception and birth, does a spirit have the use of all its faculties?

▲ *"To some degree. It depends on the stage of gestation at which the physical* body has arrived. As yet, the spirit still has not fully incarnated in the new body; it is only attached to it. From the moment of conception, however, a change takes place in the spirit, a state of confusion signaling that the time has come for it to enter a new life. This condition becomes more and more pronounced until the time of birth. Between the two periods—that is, while its new body is in the womb—the spirit's state is similar to that of a sleeping person. As the moment of birth approaches, its thoughts and ideas fade away; so do memories of the past, of which it will no longer be conscious once incarnated. Once it returns to the spirit-world, though, this memory will come back to it little by little."

352. At the moment of birth, does the spirit have all its faculties intact?

▲ "No. They return gradually with the growth of the body's organs. Life in a body is a new existence for the spirit, and it has to learn how to use all this new body's instruments. But with the maturing of the faculties, the spirit's ideas do come back to it little by little—just as they do to a person who wakes up out of deep sleep and finds that she is in an entirely different place from the one she was in before she fell asleep."

353. Since the union of the spirit and the body is not complete and definitive until birth has taken place, can we consider the fetus as having a soul?

▲ "The animating spirit exists, as it were, outside the fetus. At this point, the incarnation is only in process. It is still coming about. The fetus is linked to the spirit, then; but, strictly speaking, it has no soul."

354. What is the nature of life in the womb?

▲ "It is akin to vegetative—that is, unconscious—functioning, though it already has a biological life. Union with the spirit at birth adds a spiritual life."

355. Medical science has shown us that the bodies of some infants are so constituted that the infants cannot survive outside the womb. If so, why are these children produced?

▲ "This often happens. God permits the births of such infants as a trial, either for the parents or the animating spirit."

356. Among still-born children, are there some who were never intended for the incarnation of a spirit?

▲ "Yes. Some of these children never had a spirit assigned to them. Medical science could have done nothing for them. In such a case, the experience is intended as a trial for the parents."

—Can an infant of this kind come to its full term?

▲ "Yes, sometimes. But it does not live."

—Every child that survives birth, then, has a spirit incarnated in it?

▲ *"What would the child be if that weren't true? It would not be a human being."*

357. What are the consequences of abortion for a spirit?

▲ *"It is a life that is null and must be restarted."*

358. Is induced abortion a crime, no matter at what stage of gestation it is induced?

▲ *"Every transgression of God's laws is a crime. The mother, or anyone else, who takes the life of an unborn child is committing a crime. Why? Because an abortion prevents the soul from undergoing the trial of which the destroyed body was to have been the instrument."*

359. In cases where the birth of the child would endanger the life of the mother, is it a crime to sacrifice the child to save the mother?

▲ *"No. It is better to save the mother."*

360. Is it rational to treat the fetus with the same respect as the body of a baby that died around the time of birth?

▲ *"In the one, as in the other, recognize the will and the handiwork of God. These are always to be respected. One is not less deserving than another. The designs of Providence sometimes are beyond our comprehension."*

Moral and Intellectual Qualities

361. Where do good and bad human qualities come from?

▲ *"From the spirit who is incarnated in the person. The purer the spirit is, the more inclined to goodness a person will be."*

—It would seem that a good person is the incarnation of a good spirit, and a cruel person of a bad spirit.

▲ *"Yes. But you should say 'of an imperfect spirit.' Otherwise, it will seem that there are spirits who will always be bad—'devils,' as you call them."*[4]

362. What is the character of individuals in whom sly and foolish spirits are incarnated?

▲ *"They are irresponsible, deceitful, and sometimes mischievous."*

363. Do spirits have any feelings or appetites that we don't?

▲ *"No. If they had, they would communicate them to you."*

364. Is it only one spirit that gives a person both moral and intellectual qualities?

▲ *"Certainly it is the same! You do not have two spirits in you."*

....

4 *Translator's Note: The progression of spirits is discussed in Chapter 5.*

365. Why are some people of high intelligence, which obviously indicates advancement, also morally corrupt?

▲ *"Because the spirit incarnated in such a person has undeveloped ethical principles. In addition, the person tends to give in to the influence of other, even less evolved, spirits. The upward progress of a spirit is accomplished only slowly, and such progress does not take place simultaneously in all directions. During one lifetime a spirit may advance intellectually, during another morally."*

366. Some people believe that our various intellectual and moral qualities are the products of many different spirits incarnated in one person, with each spirit having some special faculty. How should we view this theory?

▲ *"Its absurdity becomes clear the moment you give it serious thought. Each spirit is destined to possess all possible aptitudes. But, in order to progress, it must possess one sole and unitary will. If a person were an amalgam of different spirits, a unitary will would not be possible. And the spirit would possess no individuality since, at the death of the body, all the spirits would fly off in different directions, like birds escaping from a cage. Humans often complain of not understanding certain things, and yet how clever you are in multiplying difficulties—even though the simplest and most natural explanations are right before you! This view is just another instance of the way you often mistake effects for causes. It is similar to the pagan view of God. The pagans believed in the existence of as many gods as there were observed phenomena in the universe. But, even among them, the more sensible ones saw in those phenomena only a variety of effects having for their cause the same God."*

Discussion: Concerning this subject, the physical and spiritual realms offer us several comparisons. For instance, in previous eras, when our attention was focused exclusively on the physical appearance of natural phenomena, we believed in the existence of many kinds of matter. Today, we understand that all these phenomena, varied as they might appear, are actually the result of changes in a single elementary form of matter. Likewise, the range of human abilities is a manifestation of one cause—the incarnated spirit within—not of several spirits. You can compare the human being to a pipe organ: it produces many different kinds of sounds using the same air. (In other words, there are not as many different kinds of air as there are sounds.) Furthermore, according to the theory of several spirits to each person, when someone acquires or loses an aptitude or tendency, it is the result of a corresponding number of spirits coming and going. But this would mean that the spirit lacks individuality and, consequently, responsibility. Fortunately, the manifestations of spirits who have demonstrated their personality and identity have conclusively disproved the theory.

Influence of the Body

367. When the spirit joins the body, does it become identical with its matter?

▲ *"Matter is only the envelope of the spirit, just as clothing is the envelope of the body. A spirit, in uniting itself with a body, retains its spiritual qualities."*

368. Does a spirit have full and free exercise of its faculties after union with the body?

▲ *"The use of faculties depends on the organs that serve them as instruments. The heaviness of matter, certainly, weakens their use and effectiveness."*

—Apparently the material envelope obstructs the free manifestation of a spirit's faculties, just as the opacity of ground glass obstructs the emission of light?

▲ *"Yes. The body is a highly opaque obstacle."*

Discussion: The influence that the body exercises on a spirit might also be compared to that of muddy water, which impedes the movements of objects thrown into it.

369. During its incarnation, does the full exercise of a spirit's faculties depend on the development of its bodily organs?

▲ *"These organs are the soul's instruments for manifesting its faculties. The manifestation, therefore, depends on the development and perfection of the organs. You can compare it to the perfection of a piece of manual work, which relies on the good condition of the tools the worker uses."*

370. Can we conclude that, because of the influence of the body's organs, a connection exists between the development of the brain and the development of moral and intellectual qualities?

▲ *"Do not confound cause and effect. A spirit always possesses the qualities that properly belong to it. But, remember, the organs do not produce the qualities; the qualities stimulate the development of the organs."*

—According to this view, the diversity of aptitudes shown by each person depends solely on the qualities of the person's spirit?

▲ *"To say that it does so 'solely' is not entirely correct. The qualities of the spirit undoubtedly are the basis for those aptitudes. But you must allow for the influence of matter, which limits all humans, more or less, in the exercise of the faculties inherent to their souls."*

Discussion: An incarnate spirit brings with it certain inherent predispositions. If we say that each of these predispositions corresponds to a section of the brain, we are arguing that their full development is an effect, not a cause. Indeed if human faculties result only from the operation of physiological systems, humans are no more than machines, lacking free will and responsibility for their actions. Moreover, if this theory were true, we would have to admit that the greatest geniuses—scientists, poets, artists—exist only because nature has, by chance, endowed them with an exceptional organic structure. Similarly, the stupidest man could become a Newton, a Virgil, or a Raphael,[5] had he been provided a brain with certain characteristics. The idea becomes still more absurd when we try using it to explain moral qualities. According to this theory, if nature had given Saint Vincent de Paul a different kind of brain, he might have been a scoundrel; and the greatest scoundrel alive, with the right type of brain, might turn into a Saint Vincent de Paul! If, however, we admit that our organic capabilities are an effect and not a cause, that they develop through use—as muscles develop through exercise—we arrive at a far more rational theory. Consider an analogy equally conclusive and commonplace. Certain signs indicate to us that a person is an alcoholic. Now, is it the signs that make this person an alcoholic, or is it the alcoholism that produces the signs?

The development of predispositions, we may safely assert, is modeled by the spirit's faculties.

Mental Handicaps

371. Is there any truth to the belief that the souls of the mentally handicapped are inferior to those of people who have normal mental ability?

▲ *"No. They have human souls that are often more intelligent than you suppose—souls that suffer acutely from their inability to make themselves understood, just as the mute suffer from their inability to speak."*

372. What purpose does Providence have in creating the mentally handicapped?

▲ *"They could be incarnations of spirits undergoing correction. They suffer from their physical constraints and the difficulty in expressing themselves*

....

5 *Translator's Note: Sir Isaac Newton (1642-1727) mathematician and natural philosopher who established the foundations of modern physics; Virgil (70-19 B.C.) great Latin poet, author of masterpiece poem* **Aeneid**; *Raphael Sanzio (1483-1520) Italian master painter of the Renaissance period. In this paragraph Allan Kardec also refers to St. Vincent de Paul, whose life and achievements are summarized in the Biographical Appendix at the end of this book.*

through impaired organs."

—Then it is not correct to say that the organs don't influence our faculties?

▲ *"We have never said that organs have no influence. They influence your faculties greatly; they just don't produce them. A skillful musician will not make good music with a bad instrument, but that will not make him or her a bad player."*

Discussion: We must distinguish here between normal and pathological states. In the normal state, the mind overcomes the obstacle of matter. But there are cases in which matter creates a resistance so powerful that the manifestations of the spirit are impaired or changed. This is the case with mental retardation and mental diseases. These are pathological cases in which the soul can't fully express itself. Human law, accordingly, exempts such persons from responsibility for their actions.

373. What good can come from the existence of the mentally handicapped, who cannot do either good or evil and therefore cannot progress?

▲ *"This kind of life could be a consequence of the extreme abuse of certain abilities. It may constitute a pause in the spirit's development."*

-The body of a mentally handicapped person may, then, contain a spirit that has animated a genius in a previous life?

▲ *"Yes, high intelligence sometimes becomes a curse when it is abused."*

Discussion: Intellectual superiority is not always accompanied by superiority of moral values. The greatest genius may need much purification. A person of intellect who abuses his or her gift will face a future life of an inferior nature—in itself a great cause of suffering for the spirit. The obstacles to the expression of its gifts are like chains that curtail the movements of an athlete. Therefore, retardation may be considered a brain impairment, a physical handicap as a limitation of the limbs, and blindness as a deficiency of the visual organs.

374. In the spirit-state, are mentally handicapped persons conscious of their condition?

▲ *"Yes, very often. They realize that the chains that limit them are a trial and a form of purification."*

375. When a person is mentally ill, what is the state of his or her spirit?

▲ *"A free spirit receives impressions directly. When incarnate, though, the spirit is in an altogether different condition, since it can only operate through the use of bodily organs. If some of these organs are injured, its actions are blocked. With the loss of the eyes, it becomes blind; with the loss of hearing, deaf, etc. Suppose, then, that the brain, which presides over intelligence and the will, is partially or entirely weakened or altered in its function. A spirit with such an impaired organ will experience a profound sense of dysfunction."*

—It is always the body, and not the spirit, that is disorganized?

▲ *"Yes. But do not forget that, just as a spirit acts on matter, matter to a certain extent acts on spirit. So a spirit may find itself, for a time, affected by the damaged organ and under the influence of distorted impressions. If the physical life is long, the impressions may exert a sort of conditioning influence on a spirit. But it will recover all its faculties when the material impressions wear out."*

376. Why does mental illness sometimes lead to suicide?

▲ *"The spirit suffers from physical constraints, from the inability to act freely. Consequently, it sometimes sees death as a way to break its chains."*

377. After death, is the spirit of a mentally ill person still affected by this state?

▲ *"It may be, for some time afterwards—at least, until it is completely freed from matter. It is like waking from a deep sleep. It takes some time to reconnect with reality."*

378. How does a mental disease affect a spirit after its death?

▲ *"As a resonance, an echo of its former life. This is, naturally, a burden to the spirit, who needs a certain amount of time to recover its intellectual abilities after the period of dormancy caused by its disease. As a result, the spirit's condition persists for a while, depending on how long it suffered from the disease in its incarnate life. As a general rule, a spirit, when freed from the body, still feels for a time the impression of the links that united it with the body."*

Infancy

379. Is the spirit who animates the body of a child as advanced as the spirit of an adult?

▲ *"It may be more so if, before the reincarnation, it had progressed farther than the adult. Actually, only the underdevelopment of the child's organs prevents the spirit from fully manifesting its qualities."*

380. Does a spirit think as a child or as an adult during infancy of the body?

▲ *"Because the brain is underdeveloped during infancy, the spirit cannot show the reasoning capacity of an adult. Its intellectual range remains narrow until the infant grows older and its reason evolves. Furthermore, the perturbation the spirit experiences during the process of incarnating does not immediately stop at birth; it ends only gradually, as the body's organs mature."*

Discussion: One observation of human life confirms the truth of the
                preceding reply: the dreams of childhood do not have the
                same character as those of adults. The subject matter of
                such dreams is almost always immature—an indication of
                what the spirit's thoughts are like during the early stages
                of physical development.

381. When a child dies, does its spirit immediately regain the full extent of its faculties?

▲ *"It should, since it is free of its fleshly envelope. But in reality the spirit
regains its former clarity of thought only when the separation is complete—
that is to say, when there is no longer any connection between the spirit and
body."*

382. During childhood, does the incarnate spirit suffer from the constraints its underdeveloped body imposes on it?

▲ *"No, childhood is a necessary stage, a part of the plan of Providence. It is a
time of rest for the spirit."*

383. Why must a spirit go through infancy?

▲ *"The purpose of incarnation is to improve the spirit. A spirit is more impressionable during childhood, when the impressions it receives more easily mold
its personality, and therefore promote its progress. To that end everyone
entrusted with the education of a child should contribute."*

384. Why are an infant's first sounds always cries?

▲ *"In order to attract the mother's attention and get the care it needs. It is the
baby's means of communication. If an infant only made sounds of pleasure,
the people around it wouldn't much bother about its wants. In these arrangements, you have to admire the wisdom of Providence."*

385. Why does the character of young people change, especially as they go through adolescence. Is it the spirit that changes?

▲ *"The spirit, as it regains self-awareness, reveals itself as it was before incarnation. You have no idea of the secrets hidden under the seeming innocence
of children. You do not know what they are, what they have been, or what
they will be. Still, you love and cherish them as part of yourselves—to such
a degree that the love of a mother for her children is said to be the greatest
love one being can have for another. Why do even strangers feel affection
and goodwill toward a child? Do you know the origin of that feeling? No?
Then we will explain it. Children are beings God sends into new lives. God
gives them all the external appearance of innocence, so that even misdeeds of
the worst possible nature are concealed in the unconscious memory. The
apparent innocence does not mean, then, superiority. Innocence is merely the*

image of what they ought to be. If they are not, the responsibility is theirs alone.

"*But it is not only for themselves that God gives the appearance of innocence to children. It is also for the sake of their parents, whose love is so necessary to them in their fragility. This love would greatly diminish if parents believed their children were harsh or angry by nature. Viewing them as good and gentle, however, they give them all their affection, and surround them with the most minute and delicate care. But when, after fifteen or twenty years, children no longer need this protection and assistance, their real characters begin to emerge. The person who is really good remains good, though even then his or her character reveals many traits and nuances that were hidden earlier. You see that God's ways are always for the best; and for the pure of heart, they are easily explained. But understand this well: the spirit of a newborn may have come from a place where it has acquired habits totally different from yours. How would it be possible for this new being—with feelings, inclinations, and tastes entirely opposed to yours—to adjust to your sphere of life if it did not pass through the sieve of infancy, as Providence has determined? Through the sifting process of infancy, the diverse spirits who people the universe develop common and harmonious ways of self-expression in the worlds they are called to inhabit. You, too, after dying and reincarnating, may find yourself in a sort of infancy, in the midst of a new community. In your new non-earthly existence you will be unaware of the habits, manners, and relations of a realm that is new to you, and you will find it difficult to express yourself in a language you are not used to—a language livelier than your thought is today.*[6]

"*There is still another purpose in childhood. Spirits only enter incarnate life in order to improve, to grow. The tender nature of the young makes them more pliable, more open to the advice of individuals whose experience can aid their progress. In this way tendencies toward wrong-doing are re-directed and faulty characters are gradually reformed. God entrusts this moral modeling to the parents as a duty, as a sacred mission of which they will have to give a solemn account. So you see, childhood is not only useful, necessary, indispensable, but the natural result of the laws of God.*"

Affinities and Antipathies

386. Could two spirits, who have already known and loved each other, meet again and recognize each other in another incarnate life?

▲ "*They could not recognize each other, but they might be mutually attracted. The attraction that results from the ties of a former life often brings about the most intimate and affectionate unions in a subsequent lifetime. It often happens in your world that two persons are drawn together by circumstances*

....

6 *Translator's Note: See question 319 on the spirit's immediate impressions upon returning to the spirit world.*

that appear to be merely fortuitous but are due really to the unconscious attraction of two spirits seeking each other out."

—Would it not be good for them to recognize each other?

▲ *"Not always; the memory of past lives would have more disadvantages than you suppose. After death they will recognize each another, and then they will remember the periods they spent together."[7]*

387. Is the feeling of spontaneous affinity always the result of prior acquaintance?

▲ *"No. Two spirits who have affinity may naturally gravitate to each other, without prior acquaintance, as incarnate beings."*

388. Are the apparently chance meetings that sometimes take place between two persons really due to prior ties of affection?

▲ *"There are, among thinking beings, orders of relationship of which you are presently unaware. Magnetism[8] is the pilot of the science that will enable you to understand them at a future period."*

389. What causes the instinctive aversion we sometimes feel for people we meet for the first time?

▲ *"The latent aversion of two spirits who recognize each other and divine each other's nature, without the need for words."*

390. Is instinctive antipathy always a sign of a lower nature on the part of one or both the parties who feel it?

▲ *"Spirits do not necessarily have bad natures because they are not well attuned. The antipathy may spring from a dissimilarity in their way of thinking. But as the spirits evolve, these differences fade away and aversions disappear."*

391. Does the hostility of two persons begin with the better or the worse one?

▲ *"It may begin simultaneously on the part of both. But, in that case, its causes and effects are different. A wrong-doing, misguided spirit feels hostile toward anyone who can see into its inner nature. When it meets such a per-*

....

7 See question 392 on forgetfulness of the past.

....

8 Translator's Note: Magnetism, as employed here, refers primarily to the broad notion prevalent at the time that there are forces that attract individuals to one another and to particular circumstances of life. Allan Kardec proposed the word magnetism, as an extension of the nascent field of science that studied the properties of magnets. This notion is similar to the principle of synchronicity that C.G. Jung proposed almost a century later (Synchronicity, 1952) according to which events and thoughts are connected in other ways than only cause and effect. This theory was supported by Arthur Koestler's concept of a "fundamental unity of all things" presented in The Roots of Coincidence (1972). Synchronicity also found support in Ilya Prigogine's theory about chaos and order in the Universe for which he won the 1977 Nobel Prize for Chemistry. The enlightened spirits that dictated the Doctrine stated correctly that there is a deeper order of relationship among thinking beings (consciousness) and matter.

son for the first time, it unconsciously anticipates that person's disapproval. Its aversion then changes into hatred or jealousy and inspires it with a desire to do that person harm. A good spirit, on the other hand, feels discomfort and the need to keep a certain distance, knowing it will be met with contempt because of the differences in feelings and attitudes. But strong in its own superiority, it will neither hate nor feel jealousy toward the other. It will feel compassion for the person."

Forgetfulness of the Past

392. Why can't the incarnate spirit remember its past?

▲ *"As human beings you cannot, and may not, know everything. God, being wise, has determined so. Without the veil that hides certain things from you, you would be dazzled, as if you had suddenly passed from darkness to light. Through the forgetfulness of the past, you are more fully your essential selves."*

393. How can we be held responsible for our deeds, and rid ourselves of our faults, if we do not remember them? How can we gain by experiences acquired in lives we have forgotten? We might understand that the trials of life are a lesson to us if we could only recall the wrongs that have brought those trials about. But if we forget our former lives, each new life must be like the first one, so that all the work must begin again. How can we reconcile this with God's justice?

▲ *"With each new life a spirit becomes more discerning and more capable of distinguishing between good and bad. What would happen to free choice, however, if the spirit remembered all its past? When a spirit re-enters its original life (that is, the spirit-life), its whole past unrolls before it, revealing the wrongs it committed, the causes of its sufferings, and what it could have done to prevent its faults. It then understands the justice of the situation it is in and seeks out a new life that will help it repair the mistakes of the life it has just left. It asks for a new trial similar to the one in which it failed or which it considers likely to aid its progress. And it requests that its superiors in the spirit-world help it to succeed in the new trial. It knows that the spirit who will guide it in the new life will give it an intuition of its past faults and so assist in curing them. These intuitions come like a natural, deeply felt desire to resist certain impulses. You may attribute your resistance to the teaching you have received from your parents, but it is in reality the voice of your conscience. It is an echo of your past, warning you not to fall back into the faults of your previous lives. The person who undergoes the trials of the incarnate life with fortitude and resists its temptations consequently rises in the hierarchy of spirits when he or she returns to the spirit-world."*

Discussion: While we don't have an exact memory of what we have been and done in the past, we do have, during our present incarnate life, an intuition of our previous lives. This intu-

ition takes the form both of instinctive tendencies and conscience. In other words, the intuition of the past gives rise
to an intent to avoid committing the same mistakes again.

394. On planets more advanced than ours, where beings are not prey to our physical wants and infirmities, do they understand that they are better off than we are?
Happiness, after all, is usually relative. Since planets even better than ours have
not reached perfection, the inhabitants must have their own troubles and annoyances—like the rich person on Earth who doesn't go through the physical privations of the poor but nonetheless experiences difficulties that embitter life. What
we are asking is this—Do the inhabitants of those planets consider themselves to
be just as unhappy, according to their own standard of happiness, as we consider
ourselves to be according to ours, especially since they don't remember their past
lives either?

▲ *"There are worlds where the inhabitants have a clear recollection of their past
existences and do appreciate the happiness they enjoy. However, there are
other worlds where the inhabitants, though living in better conditions than
you do, are subject to disappointments and suffering, and do not appreciate
their happiness. Why? Because they don't remember a life in which there
was greater unhappiness. Although they show limited appreciation for their
state while incarnate, they will value it more justly as spirits."*

Discussion: Our forgetfulness of our past lives, especially the painful
                ones, offers a striking example of the wisdom and good-
                ness of God. Only on the most advanced worlds, where the
                memory of painful lives will be no more than the shadowy
                memory of a bad dream, will we be able to recover the
                memory of our past in its entirety. By contrast, in worlds
                such as ours, the memory of past miseries would only
                magnify our present hardships. Such considerations lead
                us to conclude that whatever has been created by God is
                for the best. It is not up to us to find fault with God's works
                or decide the way the universe should be governed.

                The memory of former personalities during our present
                lives would bring with it many serious disadvantages. In
                some cases, it would cause us to be cruelly humiliated. In
                others, it might inflate us with pride and vanity. In all
                cases, it would hinder the action of our free will. God gives
                us just what is necessary and sufficient for our better-
                ment—i.e., the voice of conscience and our instinctive ten-
                dencies—and keeps from us anything detrimental.
                Moreover, if we could remember our own former person-
                alities and actions, we would also remember those of other
                people, and that kind of knowledge could have a disas-
                trous influence on our social relations. Since we don't

always have reason to be proud of our past, it is obviously better that a veil has been thrown over it. These facts are in perfect agreement with the statements of spirits concerning life on more advanced planets. On those planets, where virtue reigns, there is nothing painful in past memories, and so their inhabitants remember their preceding lives as we remember today what we did yesterday. Their sojourns on less advanced planets are no more to them, as we have said, than the memory of an unpleasant dream.

395. Can we receive revelations about our former lives?

▲ *"Not in all cases. Many, however, know who they have been and what they have done. If they were allowed to speak openly, they would make curious revelations about the past."*

396. Some people believe they have a vague memory of an unknown past, which comes to them like the fugitive image of a dream. Is this belief only an illusion?

▲ *"It is sometimes real; but, just as often, it is an illusion. You should guard against it, since it may simply be the effect of an excited imagination."*

397. In incarnate lives more developed than ours, is the memory of earlier lives more exact?

▲ *"Yes. The less material a body is, the more clearly the incarnate spirit remembers past lives. The memory of the past is always clearer for those in more advanced realms."*

398. If our instinctive tendencies are a reflection of the past, can someone study those tendencies and discover the mistakes he or she has made?

▲ *"Undoubtedly, up to a certain point. But this person would also have to consider the improvement in his or her spirit and the resolutions to improve made in the spirit-world. Such a person's present life may be much better than the preceding one."*

—Could it be worse? That is to say, could someone make a mistake in one life he or she did not make in a preceding one?

▲ *"This depends on the degree of advancement. Incapable of resisting temptation, this person might be drawn into committing new errors. But such errors do not indicate a backwards movement for the spirit. Remember, a spirit may advance or remain stationary, but it can never go back."*

399. The difficulties of the incarnate life are at once trials in which we purify ourselves of past faults and a series of lessons for the future. From the nature of those difficulties, can we conclude anything definite about the character of our preceding life?

▲ *"Frequently you can, because the nature of the trials always corresponds to previous faults. But it would be unwise to think of this as an absolute rule. The instinctive tendencies offer a better indication, since the trials a spirit undergoes concern the future as much as the past."*

Discussion: When a spirit reaches the end of its term in the spirit-
world, it chooses the trials that, in its next incarnation, will
speed up its progress. In other words, it requests the kind
of life that will help it advance. The trials of the new life
always correspond to the faults of which the spirit must
cleanse itself. If it succeeds in this struggle, it rises in rank;
if it fails, it will have to try again. A spirit always possesses free will. While in the spirit-world it uses its free will to
plan the kind of life it wants to experience on Earth. Once
here, it uses free will to decide what to do and to choose
between right and wrong.

In the incarnate life, the spirit temporarily forgets its former lives, as if they were hidden from it by a veil. It retains
its free will, however, since to deny humans that quality
would be to reduce them to machines. Still, some occasionally have a vague consciousness of their former lives
which, under certain circumstances, may actually be
revealed. But this occurs only as a result of a decision of
higher spirits, who make the revelation spontaneously and
always for some useful end—never to gratify idle curiosity. Nor can a spirit's future lives be revealed during its
incarnate life, since the quality of these lives will depend
on the manner in which it lives its present one and on its
own personal choices.

The temporary forgetfulness of mistakes is no obstacle
to a spirit's improvement. The knowledge it had of them as
a free spirit, and its own desire to overcome them, guide it
intuitively, inspiring it to resist the tendency toward
wrong-doing while incarnate. This inspiration is the voice
of conscience, which the good spirits reinforce if the person
is only willing to listen to their advice. Although a person
does not know exactly what acts he or she committed in a
former life, a sense of previous faults and character is usually discernible. We need only study ourselves to know
what the self has been—not by what it is at the moment,
but by its tendencies.

The difficulties of the incarnate life act both to redeem
us of past errors and to make us better in the future, provided that we bear them with fortitude and without complaint. The nature of the difficulties and trials we must
undergo may also enlighten us as to what we have been
and done, just as we infer the crimes of which a convict has

been guilty from the penalty the law inflicts on him. Thus, the individual who has erred through pride may be humiliated and placed in an inferior position. The self-indulgent and greedy person may find poverty. The hard-hearted one may be treated severely. The tyrant may know subordination. The bad son may meet with the ingratitude of children. The idle may be subjected to hard work. Just so do our earthly trials unfold.

CHAPTER

XII

THE LIBERATION OF THE SOUL

Sleep and Dreams

400. Does an incarnate spirit really want to be in the body?

▲ *"Does a captive want to stay confined? An incarnate spirit always desires to be free; and the coarser its body, the greater its desire."*

401. Does the soul rest, as the body does, during sleep?

▲ *"No. The spirit is never inactive. The bonds connecting it to the body loosen during sleep. And since the body doesn't require its presence in that state, the spirit is relatively free to move about and seek the company of other spirits."*

402. How can we verify that the spirit is liberated during sleep?

▲ *"Through dreams. While its body sleeps, the spirit enjoys other faculties it is unaware of in the waking state. Its abilities expand markedly. It can communicate with other spirits, either on Earth or on other planes. It remembers the past and sometimes foresees the future. Thus, you often say: 'I had a strange dream, a frightful one, which seemed very real.' But this is a misconception on your part. The dream may be a recollection of places and things you saw in the past or a foresight of what will happen later in your life, or even in a future life.*

"Human beings unfortunately know little of the most ordinary phenomena of their lives. You like to think you are wise, but the most trivial things overwhelm you. You are unable to answer the questions asked by all children: 'What do we do during sleep? What are dreams?'

"Sleep causes a partial liberation of the soul from the body. When you sleep, your spirit is, for a time, in the same condition that you will confront after death.

"*Individuals who have an active dream life are likely to be liberated from matter almost immediately at death. During their dreams they often seek the company of more advanced spirits, converse with them and receive their advice. They may even begin projects in the spirit-world that they will find either under way or complete after death. Consequently, you must realize how preposterous it is to be afraid of dying because, according to St. Paul, 'you die every day.'*[1]

"*All we have said here refers to spirits who have already attained reasonable progress. During sleep the common mass of spirits seek the lower spheres, to which they are attracted by old affections or their own primitive inclinations; and once there they indulge in every sensual pleasure. On these visits they also receive vile suggestions, often baser than they conceive of when awake.*

"*The eight hours of camarederie one spends with like-minded souls during sleep time often give rise, upon wakening, to closer relationships on Earth. Conversely, the activities that take place during sleep may also help to explain the undeniable dislike that one may sometimes feel toward certain people. When this happens, one knows in the heart that the cause is the difference in the levels of consciousness. Sleep helps, too, to explain the indifference of some people toward personal relationships on Earth, as they find enough emotional sustenance in their spiritual friendships. To sum up, the sleep state has a stronger influence on one's life than one can imagine.*

"*Through sleep, incarnate spirits are always in touch with the spiritual plane. This is why evolved spirits don't hesitate to incarnate among you. Whenever they come to your planet, God allows them, as a way of offsetting their close contact with earthly energies, to replenish themselves in the sources of higher good. Sleep is a door God opens for them; through it, they enter the spirit-world and commune with their friends. Thus they patiently wait for the final liberation that will return them to their proper places. Sleep is also a time of leisure when they can relax before returning to their tasks. In short, sleep has more influence on your life than you realize.*

"*As for remembered dreams, they are the recollection of what your spirit experienced during sleep. Notice, however, that you don't always have dreams with true spiritual activity. What this means, primarily, is that your soul doesn't always attain the full liberation that its development permits. Frequently, you may only remember the confusion that accompanies your departure from or return to the body. These memories are all mixed up with vague recollections of what you did or what occupied your thoughts in your waking state. How else can you explain the bizarre dreams that the simplest but also the wisest people experience? In addition, unprincipled spirits may*

----

1 *Translator's Note: 1 Corinthians 15:31*

use the dream state to torment weak and vacillating souls.

"You will experience, finally, the development of another kind of dream. Although it is as ancient as your ordinary ones, little is known about it. This is the kind of dream that came to Joan of Arc, Jacob, the Jewish prophets[2], and some Hindu seers. It is the recollection of the soul's experiences while completely liberated from the body—the recollection of that other life we have just mentioned. But be careful to distinguish between these two kinds of dreams. Otherwise, you risk falling into contradictions and errors that might hurt your understanding."

Discussion: Dreams are a product of the freeing of the soul, which becomes more energetic as the activities of daily life are suspended. In the dream state the soul enjoys an all-penetrating clairvoyance which extends to far away and unknown places, and even other realms of life. This state of freedom may also produce the recollection of events from present and prior lives. However, many times we are struck by a fantastical jumble of incoherent images. These images result from the mixing up in the memory of extravagant scenes observed in other domains and the lively impressions of incidents of our earthly lives.

The incoherence of dreams can be explained still further by limitations in our ability to remember them clearly. The situation is somewhat similar to that of a story from which sentences and parts of sentences have been accidentally deleted. Place the deleted parts of those sentences back into the story at random and you will find that all intelligible meaning has been lost.

403. Why don't we always recall our dreams?

▲ *"In what you call sleep, only the body rests. The spirit is always in motion. During sleep, it recovers part of its freedom and contacts those closest to it, on this or other realms. But the body's matter is heavy and it is difficult for the spirit, on waking, to retain the impressions it received during sleep, since these did not come through its physical organs."*

....

2 *Translator's Note: Examples of such dreams among Biblical figures abound; see, e.g., Genesis 37:5-6 (Joseph's dreams) and 1 Kings 3:5-15 (Solomon). Jacob's dream is related in Genesis 31:10-13. In this paragraph the spiritual instructors also refer to Joan of Arc (1412-1431), the French peasant girl who through dreams and clairvoyance led the French forces in battles against the English. She was canonized by Pope Benedictus XV in 1920.*

404. What do you think of the differing systems of interpreting dreams?[3]

▲ *"Dreams don't have the significance certain psychics and other interpreters give them. Does it make sense, really, to believe that a certain kind of dream can signify a particular event? In fact, dreams may present images that are real only for the spirit. In this sense, they are true. More often than not, they have no direct connection with what is going on in the spirit's physical life.*

"As we said before, dreams can, with God's permission, predict the future or give a vision of something that is happening at a distant place to which the spirit has traveled. You probably know of many instances in which people have appeared in dreams to relatives and friends to warn them about things that are going to happen to them. Now, what are these apparitions except the souls or spirits of persons who have come to communicate with loved ones? When you are fully convinced that what you saw during those moments actually occurred, isn't this a proof that the event wasn't simply a figment of your imagination—especially when the event had never crossed your mind while you were awake?"

405. Often we see things in dreams that appear to be predictions but that don't come to pass. How do you explain that?

▲ *"Such predictions may come to pass for the spirit alone, though not in the flesh. This means that sometimes the spirit sees and experiences what it wants because it goes looking for it. But you mustn't forget that during sleep the spirit is always under a certain degree of material influence; consequently, it is never completely free of earthly ideas. Worries during the waking period may project the desired or feared realities onto what appears in the dream. This, indeed, is 'a figment of the imagination.' When the mind is extremely absorbed with any idea, it tends to associate everything it sees with that idea."*

406. At times, in a dream, we see incarnate people who are well known to us doing things we know absolutely that they hadn't considered doing. Isn't this the result of pure imagination?

▲ *"'Absolutely hadn't considered doing,' you say? How do you know? Their spirits may come to visit yours, and yours may visit theirs. But, in your waking state, you may not be aware of their ideas. However, be careful because you frequently link people you know with events taking place in unrelated contexts or in others' lives."*

....

3 Translator's Note: The knowledge of and interest in the area of dreams has expanded greatly in recent years. The modern era of sleep and dream research started in 1953 with the first studies of eye movement during sleep. Presently, research work extends across the areas of Physiology, Psychology, and Medicine. The value of dreams in understanding human physiology, behavior, and health is gaining increased recognition. The kind of dreams Allan Kardec refers to here involve conscious activity on the part of the spirit. Such dreams belong to the category of psychic dreams according to the categorization of the new research.

407. Is it necessary that the body be completely asleep before the soul is liberated?

▲ *"No. The spirit recovers its freedom as soon as the body's senses become lethargic. It seizes every opportunity to liberate itself that the body offers. As soon as the body's vital energy level decreases, the spirit separates from it. The more languid the body is, the freer the spirit."*

Discussion: This explains why, in a state of drowsiness or twilight sleep, we frequently see the same type of images we see in dreams.

408. At times we seem to hear words pronounced distinctly within ourselves. Yet these words have no connection to anything we are thinking about. Where do they come from?

▲ *"Yes, you will hear entire sentences, especially when your senses begin to get sluggish. Sometimes you hear the faint echo of the words of a spirit who wishes to communicate with you."*

409. Often, in a state of twilight sleep and with our eyes closed, we see distinct images—figures we can make out in the minutest detail. Is this a real visual effect or imagination?

▲ *"When the body becomes lethargic, the spirit tries to liberate itself. When it does, its vision expands. If the body sank any deeper into sleep, these figures would become part of a dream."*

410. Sometimes, when we are drowsy or asleep, we have ideas that amaze us but that disappear from waking memory, despite our best efforts to recall them. Where do these ideas come from?

▲ *"From the liberated spirit's use of its extended abilities. Also, they may be advice given by other spirits."*

—What is the purpose of such ideas and advice, since we cannot recollect or benefit from them?

▲ *"These ideas belong more to the spirit-world than to the physical one. Generally, you forget them when in the body, but as a spirit you remember and will recall them at the appropriate time. They will then seem to you to have come from the inspiration of the moment."*

411. Does an incarnate spirit, when liberated from matter and acting as a spirit, know when its death will occur?

▲ *"It may get a glimpse of the point in time, sometimes quite clearly. This is what gives some individuals an intuition of death and may even allow them to foresee the time of their death with perfect accuracy."*

412. Can the activity of the spirit during sleep cause fatigue in the body?

▲ *"Yes, because the spirit is attached to the body in the same way as a captive balloon is fastened to a post. Just as the movements of the balloon shake and put a strain on the post, the activity of the spirit reacts on the body and may cause it to feel tired."*

Out of Body Visits Between the Living

413. The fact that the soul is liberated during sleep suggests that one lives two lives simultaneously: the life of the body, and the less conspicuous life of the soul. Is this perspective correct?

▲ *"In its liberated state (that is, sleep), the life of the soul takes priority over the life of the body. Strictly speaking, though, this doesn't constitute two lives but two phases of a single existence, since a human being cannot live double lives."*

414. Can acquaintances visit each other during sleep?

▲ *"Certainly. Many people who, in daily life, believe they don't know certain persons often meet and talk with them during sleep. Conceivably, you could even have friends in another country without being aware of it. And it's very common during sleep for you to visit friends, relatives, and people you know who can be of help to you. You pay such visits practically every night."*

415. Why do these nightly meetings happen if we don't remember them?

▲ *"The intuition of them generally remains with you when you are awake. Often you will have certain ideas that seem spontaneous to you—ideas you don't really know how to account for. These meetings could be the origin of such ideas."*

416. Can we willingly bring about such spirit-visits? For instance, can we say before going to sleep: "Tonight I will meet such and such person in spirit and will speak with it about this or that subject?"

▲ *"Here is what happens. You fall asleep and gain access to the spirit-realm. As a spirit, liberated from the limitations of matter, you may pay little attention to the affairs of your earthly life or the plans you laid out while awake. But note that our statement applies primarily to individuals with a certain degree of elevation. Other spirits will spend their spirit-lives in very different ways. They may unleash their feelings and appetites, or remain inactive. Consequently, a spirit may very well visit the people it planned to see while in the incarnate state. But please understand—the mere fact that such a plan was contemplated doesn't necessarily imply that it will be carried out."*

417. Can a number of incarnate spirits, during sleep, assemble together?

▲ *"They definitely can. The ties of friendship, old and new, often bring together spirits who are happy to be in each other's company."*

Discussion: The term "old" here must be understood as referring to ties of friendship from previous lives. We bring back with us, on awakening, an intuition of the ideas we have received at such meetings, though we remain unaware of their source.

418. Someone believes that a close friend has died, though the friend is still alive. Could this person meet that friend as a spirit and discover the truth? And could an intuition of that fact be retained on awakening?

▲ *"As a spirit you could certainly see a friend and know about his or her condition. Moreover, if such knowledge will not interfere with your appointed experiences you will likely awaken with a clear sense of his or her true situation."*

Telepathy

419. A discovery simultaneously occurs to several different people. Where does the idea actually come from?

▲ *"As we have already said, spirits communicate with each other during sleep. On waking, the mind will remember what it has learned but will forget the source. The waking person then supposes that he or she has originated the idea. Thus, several people may discover the same thing at the same time. When you say that an idea is 'in the air,' you use a figure of speech that is much closer to the truth than you realize. Everyone unconsciously helps to spread it."*

Discussion: Likewise, although we are not aware of it, our spirit frequently shares with other spirits the worries we have in our waking state.

420. Can spirits communicate among themselves while the bodies are awake?

▲ *"A spirit is not confined to its body like a jack in the box. It radiates in all directions. It can communicate with other minds even when its body is awake, although it is difficult to do so."*

421. How can two perfectly awake people often have the same idea at the same time?

▲ *"Two highly attuned minds may communicate with each other while in an awakened state."*

Discussion: The communion between two individuals well attuned to each other allows them to communicate without the use of spoken language. We say that they communicate by telepathy—the language of spirits.[4]

∙∙∙∙∙∙∙∙∙∙∙∙∙∙∙∙∙∙∙∙∙∙∙∙∙∙∙∙

4 *Translator's Note: See Chapter 10, especially question 282 for a discussion of communication between spirits.*

Apparent Deaths, Catalepsy[5]

422. People in a cataleptic state generally see and hear what is going on around them, but they can communicate none of it. Do they receive their impressions through their eyes and ears?

▲ *"No. The spirit receives the impressions. It remains in a state of awareness, though it lacks the power of self-expression."*

—Why is this so?

▲ *"The body's condition prevents it. Such an unusual physical state also proves that humans consist of something besides the body—here, the body is not functional, yet the spirit acts."*

423. Can a spirit in a state of catalepsy separate itself entirely from its body (so that the body appears dead) and afterwards come back and animate it?

▲ *"In catalepsy, the body is not dead; it continues to function, at least partially. As in the case of the chrysalis, its vitality is latent, not extinguished. But remember that as long as a spirit is connected to the body, there is life. It is only when the ties that bind the two break, as the result of actual death, that the separation is really complete. From this point onward, the spirit will never again return to that body. Thus, when a person who is apparently dead comes to life again, you can safely say that the process of death was not consummated."*

424. Is it possible to interfere with the process of dying and strengthen ties that are on the verge of breaking down? In other words, can we, with timely help, restore life to a person who would have died otherwise?

▲ *"Yes, definitely. You have proof of it every day in magnetic (spiritual) healing, which frequently provides a powerful active element in such cases.[6] This kind of healing restores to the body vital energy that is necessary to its functioning."*

Discussion: Lethargy and catalepsy are believed to proceed from the same cause, i.e., the temporary loss of consciousness and power of motion due to a still unexplained physiological condition. They differ in this respect: in lethargy, the sup-

....

5 *Translator's Note: Catalepsy: a condition in which consciousness and feeling are suddenly and temporarily lost, and the muscles become rigid; it may occur in epilepsy, schizophrenia, and can be induced by hypnosis.*

....

6 *Translator's Note: Magnetic Healing: therapy based on the principle that human beings possess energies (vital force) that can be directed to another person by effect of will. This concept is found at the base of such methods as psychic healing, faith healing, and therapeutic touch. This class of procedures has gained greater scientific recognition since the extensive hospital research conducted by Dolores Kruger, Ph.D. and published in* The Therapeutic Touch, *Prentice Hall, 1979.*

pression of vital force is generalized. In catalepsy, the suppression may be localized, though it may affect an extensive portion of the body. In both cases there is intellectual activity, which prevents these states from being confused with death. Lethargy is usually spontaneous but may be induced.[7]

Spontaneous and Induced Trance

425. Is there any connection between spontaneous trance and dreaming?

▲ *"In a spontaneous trance, the independence of the soul is greater and its perceptions are sharper than during the dream state—which is, in fact, only an undeveloped form of this type of trance. While in the trance state, the spirit has complete self-control and is entirely free from the influence of matter. Its body is in a cataleptic-like state and no longer receptive to external impressions. This phenomenon occurs most often during sleep because the spirit is able, temporarily, to leave its body, which remains at rest.*

"In a particular type of spontaneous trance, commonly referred to as somnambulic,[8] the spirit of the trance subject, worried about some problem, commands its body to perform certain actions. The use of the body in this manner is reminiscent of the way spirits use tables or other material objects to produce physical manifestations, or use the hand of a sensitive to transmit written messages. In dreams, by contrast, the body operates at a minimal level. Its ability to send information to, and receive impressions from, the spirit is greatly reduced. Further complicating the situation, dreams are also affected by the spontaneous emergence of random images from the unconscious.

"It is easy to understand, therefore, why a spirit would have no recollection at all in cases of trance and why a large number of dreams seem incoherent. However, some of the apparent incoherence may be explained by an incomplete recollection of resolutions made by the spirit or of events that have taken place in a remote past."

·····················

7 *Translator's note: These definitions reflect the state of medical knowledge in the mid 1850s. Modern definitions do not address the issue of localization of the symptoms.*

·····················

8 *Translator's note: In recent times this category of phenomena has not been observed with enough frequency to deserve mention in modern parapsychological research. Its complexity, and the risks associated with it, may have directed the research interest toward other areas of paranormality. The same may have occurred with the subjects who, endowed with a broad sensitivity, preferred to focus their energy on the development of other faculties.*

426. Is there a relation between a spontaneous and an induced trance?

▲ *"They are the same thing, except that one is provoked."*

427. What is the nature of what some call hypnotic (or mesmeric) force?

▲ *"Some have called it 'animal or electric magnetism'.⁹ Whatever you call it, this force is ultimately a transformation of the Cosmic Principle."*

428. What gives some trance subjects the power of clairvoyance?

▲ *"We have told you: when in trance, it is the soul who sees."*

429. How can a trance subject see through opaque objects?

▲ *"The only reason that objects appear opaque to you is the coarseness and density of your perceptions. As we previously told you, matter is not an obstacle for a spirit, who can easily see and pass right through it. In trance a subject often tells you that she sees through her forehead, her knee, etc. But because you are plunged into matter, you can't understand that she can see without eyes. She herself, influenced by earthly ideas, believes she needs her eyes. However, if left by herself, she would quickly realize that the seat of her vision is not localized in any specific part of her body or, better yet, that she sees independent of her body."*

430. Since the clairvoyance of a trance subject is that of the spirit, why can't she see everything, and why does she make so many mistakes?

▲ *"In the first place, average spirits don't see and understand everything. Remember, they still share your misconceptions and predispositions. Furthermore, as long as they remain attached to the material world, they cannot make use of all their capabilities. God has given the gift of trance to the human species for a serious and useful purpose, not to inform you about matters you are not prepared to know. This is why trance subjects are often unable to give flawless information."*

······························

9 *Translator's note: Magnetism: related to properties of "animal magnetism" a system of healing proposed by Franz Anton Mesmer (1733-1815) in* De Planetarium Influxu *(1766). According to Mesmer, we are immersed in a fluid (Cosmic Principle) that is universal and continuous through which celestial bodies, the earth, and animated bodies mutually influence each other. This influence manifests itself in the human body through properties analogous to those of the magnet: it can be communicated, changed, destroyed, and reinforced. The early magnetizers used it for healing and for the production of a class of phenomena they called somnambulism. Under magnetically induced trance, somnambulists were able to produce a variety of paranormal phenomena such as thought reading, and clairvoyance. This field evolved into what is known today as Hypnotism through the work of James Braid who in 1841 presented his scientific discovery in an address before the British Medical Association. The official recognition of Hypnotism by the British Medical Association as a genuine pain-relieving therapy came in 1893. For a more extended discussion of Cosmic Principle see question 27 and its footnote.*

431. What is the source of a trance subject's innate ideas. How can he speak accurately about things he ignores in his waking state and that are often above his intellectual capacity?

▲ *"A trance subject may have more knowledge than you give him credit for.*[10] *This knowledge remains latent, however, because his body is too imperfect for him to remember all he knows as a spirit. To sum up, a trance subject is just like the rest of you—a spirit who has been incarnated with a purpose. The trance state simply shakes the spirit out of the lethargy of incarnation.*

"We have frequently told you that all of us have had many lives. The immersion in a new physical life causes a spirit to forget, temporarily, the knowledge it had previously acquired. While in trance, however, the spirit may be able to access this knowledge, though not always completely. At this point, it cannot tell where the knowledge comes from or how it came to have it. Once the trance is over, the spirit's recollections fade from its consciousness, and it re-enters the oblivion of incarnate life."

Discussion: Experience shows us that trance subjects also receive communications from other spirits, who tell them what they should say and provide them with information they do not know. Aid of this kind is seen frequently in medical examinations.[11] The spirit of the trance subject diagnoses the illness, while another spirit indicates a way to treat it. This cooperative effort is often evident to observers. It is revealed especially by such expressions on the part of the trance subject as "I'm told to say," "I'm forbidden to say," etc. In the latter case, it is always inappropriate to persist in trying to extract information the trance subject refuses to disclose. By doing so, we open the way to unprincipled spirits, who will babble about anything, regardless of the truth.

································

10 *Translator's Note: In hypnotic trance subjects have shown a remarkable capacity to remember previous knowledge and experiences. Several research works have been published on the subject; among the most remarkable is B. Weiss,* Many Lives, Many Masters, *Simon & Schuster, 1988, and Ian Stevenson,* Twenty Cases Suggestive of Reincarnation, *Charlottesville, Virginia: University Press. Virginia, 1974.*

································

11 *Translator's Note: The best known case in modern history is Edgar Cayce (1877-1945). By putting himself in a light trance condition Cayce could diagnose ailments and prescribe remedies. In forty-three years of healing he accumulated records of over 14,000 cases. He dedicated himself unselfishly to healing the sick and became known in the United States as "The Sleeping Prophet." For a more detailed account of his gifts and work, see T. Sugrue,* There is a River: The Story of Edgar Cayce, *Dell, 1972.*

432. How do you explain the remote viewing ability of some trance subjects?

▲ *"Doesn't the soul go to distant places in the dream state? It does the same thing in a trance."*

433. Does the extent of the trance subject's clairvoyance depend on the physical body or on the nature of the spirit incarnated in it?

▲ *"On both. But there are physical organizations that allow the spirit to liberate itself from matter in a relatively easier manner."*

434. Are the abilities of the trance subject identical to those of the spirit in the spirit-world?

▲ *"They are the same—up to a certain point. Above all, you have to take into account the dulling influence of the physical body."*

435. Can trance subjects see other spirits?

▲ *"It depends on the nature and extent of their abilities. Most of them see other spirits perfectly well. But they don't always recognize them right away as spirits, mistaking them instead for incarnate beings—a mistake made especially by those who are unfamiliar with the findings and methods of the Spiritist Doctrine. Understanding nothing about the essence of spirits, they are surprised to see them in human form and assume they are living persons."*

Discussion: The same effect is produced among spirits who, after death, suppose that they are still alive. They notice no difference in the environment or in the bodies of the spirits they meet and therefore conclude they are still incarnate.

436. When trance subjects see things at a distance, does their sight come through the agency of the body or the soul?

▲ *"How can you ask such a question? It is the soul that sees, not the body."*

437. Since it is the soul that travels to distant places, why does the trance subject's physical body nonetheless feel the heat or cold that is present in those places?

▲ *"The body and soul are still attached to each other, and it is this connective link that transmits sensations. When two people in two different cities communicate with each other by electrical means, it is the electricity that makes their communication possible.[12] They can communicate as if they were standing right next to each other."*

438. Is the trance subject's condition after death influenced by the use he or she made of this ability?

▲ *"Definitely. And to a considerable extent. The same holds true with the good or bad use of all the abilities God has given you."*

....

12 Translator's Note: The answer refers to telegraphy, although it could apply in modern times to telephony and telecommunications in general.

Ecstatic Trance

439. How do you define ecstatic trance? How does it differ from other forms of trance?

▲ *"Ecstatic trance is a more refined form of trance. The soul of an ecstatic subject is far more independent."*[13]

440. Does the soul of someone in an ecstatic trance really enter the higher realms?

▲ *"Yes, the spirit sees those realms, realizes the happiness of their inhabitants, and wishes to remain there. But there are realms that are inaccessible to spirits who are not sufficiently purified."*

441. Ecstatic trance subjects, elated with transcendental life, frequently express a desire to leave the physical world. Is this desire genuine? Wouldn't the instinct for self-preservation prevail?

▲ *"It depends on the spirit's advancement. If you realize that your future condition is going to be better than your present one, you will naturally try to loosen your physical bonds."*

442. If the trance subject were left alone, could his or her soul leave the body?

▲ *"Yes, the subject might die. This is why it's necessary to call the person back, appealing to everything that might hold it in this world and stressing especially the fact that the disruption of the physical bond at this point would prevent a return to the higher realms it longs for."*

443. Sometimes an ecstatic subject claims to see things that are obviously the product of an imagination colored by earthly beliefs and prejudices. Can't we conclude, then, that not everything he sees is real?

▲ *"What the person sees is a reality. However, the manner he or she chooses to describe it and the meanings they infer from it are personal. This reality may be expressed in a language that has developed out of a personal context or that reflects socially conditioned ideas and prejudices that may allow hearers to better understand the communication. Here is where the subject is especially liable to make mistakes."*

444. How reliable are the revelations of an ecstatic subject?

▲ *"Not very. The process is prone to mistakes, especially when attempts are*

....

13 *Translator's Note: By means of this type of trance the individual goes into a state of ecstasy, the body slips into deep passivity, the subject's extra sensorial perceptions are greatly expanded, and may allow access to higher realms. The phenomenon of religious ecstasy is well documented and found in most religions. Scholars propose that there are several levels of ecstatic trance, from a purely physical suspension of sensorial awareness to a truly spiritual connection with the Divine Mind. The Roman Catholic church has documented an impressive number of cases, most famous of which are the stigmata ecstatics. These while in trance develop the stigmas of Jesus in their own bodies. St. Francis of Assisi was a stigmatic, as were St. Catherine of Siena, St. Rita of Cassia, and more recently, Padre Pio.*

made to probe what, for human beings, are mysteries beyond their compre-
hension. In this case, the subject's imagination often takes over, or he or she
may become the sport of deceiving spirits, who are always ready to take
advantage of misguided human enthusiasm."

445. What is the value of ecstasy and trance phenomena? Should we view them
as a kind of initiation into a future life?

▲ *"In these states, the subject may receive glimpses of the past and future. If*
you study such phenomena carefully, you will find the solutions to many
mysteries that are impenetrable to reason."

446. Can trance phenomena be reconciled with a materialistic vision?

▲ *"The individual who studies them honestly, without preconceived ideas,*
could be neither a materialist nor an atheist."

Second Sight (Clairvoyance)

447. Is there any connection between second sight and the phenomena of dreaming and trance?

▲ *"They are all the same thing. What you call second sight is a state in which*
the spirit is partially free, although the body is not asleep. Second sight is the
sight of the soul."

448. Is second sight a permanent ability?

▲ *"Second sight is permanent, though you may not always be able to exercise*
it at will. However, on less material worlds, spirits free themselves from mat-
ter more easily and enter into telepathic communication with each other nat-
urally. On these spheres, second sight is a permanent faculty; the spirits'
visual capacity is similar to the state of expanded perception of your trance
subjects. Their more ethereal nature considerably facilitates their communi-
cation with you."

449. Does second sight always occur spontaneously?

▲ *"In general, yes. But the will often plays an important part in producing it.*
Take fortune-tellers, for instance—some of them really have this gift and use
it whenever they want."

450. Can second sight be developed by exercise?

▲ *"Yes, effort always leads to progress; and as the veil is lifted, the nature of*
things will become more transparent."

—Does this gift depend on the individual's physical organization?

▲ *"Physical organization undoubtedly has a great deal to do with it, since there*
are organizations that are incompatible with it."

451. Why does second sight seem to run in certain families?

▲ *"Just like a physical ability, it is inherited and can be developed through practice and discipline."*

452. Is it true that circumstances can develop second sight?

▲ *"An illness, the approach of danger, any great commotion, may unleash it. In such situations, the body is in a condition that allows the spirit to see what it cannot through the use of ordinary vision."*

Discussion: Times of crisis, great calamities, powerful emotions, and every event that overly excites the mind may all induce second sight. Providence has given us this gift as a means of escaping threatened danger. Many groups that have been subjected to persecution in the past have offered innumerable instances of its action.

453. Is everyone who is gifted with second sight aware of it?

▲ *"Not always. For many people, it is perfectly natural and they think anyone should be able to do it with enough motivation."*

454. Does a form of second sight explain the ability of people who, though not endowed with superior intelligence, seem to have sharper judgment than others?

▲ *"Their souls have greater powers of perception. Their judgment is less clouded by the veils of matter."*

—Can this gift be used to obtain knowledge of the future in some cases?

▲ *"Yes, it can. It can also produce premonitions, depending on the extent of the gift."*

Trance, Ecstasy and Second Sight: A Summary

455. The phenomenon of natural trance occurs spontaneously and is independent of any known external cause. It is also true that in susceptible subjects the identical state can be artificially induced through hypnosis. But whereas the fact of natural trance is indisputable and (despite the remarkable character of the phenomenon) widely acknowledged as a reality, many people regard artificial trance as unbelievable simply because it is induced. Charlatans abuse it, detractors charge repeatedly. We grant that this is true, and it is all the more reason for placing the subject in the hands of competent investigators. In fact, scientists are increasingly accepting both natural and induced trance states as serious areas of investigation, even though they are doing so by many side roads rather than entering through the main gate. We suspect then that, as induced trance is granted full recognition, the quacks will be discredited.

    The trance state is far more than a matter of psychic phenomenon to the Spiritist Doctrine. To us, it projects a light on the subject of psychology and allows for a more objective study of the soul. As we know, one of the characteristics of the soul is to see without dependence on the eyes. To those who object to trances on the grounds that the trance subject doesn't always physically see what he or she is told to see, we would answer that the means of sight are different and therefore the effects must be different, too. To require identical effects from different instruments is an unreasonable demand. The soul has its own properties, just as the eyes have theirs, and we should judge the effects of those properties on their merits rather than by analogy.

The clairvoyance that is characteristic of both induced and natural trances originates from a single cause. It is an attribute of the soul, an ability inherent in the spiritual being who exists within each of us. Clairvoyance, then, has no limits except those assigned to the soul itself; and trance subjects see wherever their souls go, regardless of distance. They do not, in any case, report their observations from the point where their bodies are located—as if looking through a telescope—but from the place where their souls are actually present. This is the reason the subject's body remains throughout in a subdued state, seemingly deprived of sensation; it must wait until the soul returns to it. This partial separation of soul and body constitutes an abnormal state that can last for a considerable period, though not indefinitely. Consequently, the body experiences fatigue after a time, especially when the soul engages in some difficult pursuit.

Soul-vision or spirit-vision is not circumscribed, it has no specific location, and trance subjects cannot accordingly pinpoint any specific organ of sight. They see because they see, ignorant of why or how. For them, as for spirits, sight has no special focus; and if asked about the matter, they will refer to that part of the body where the most vital activity seems to be occurring—often in the brain, but sometimes in the epigastric area[14] or in whatever organ seems to provide the strongest link between the spirit and the body.

The scope of clairvoyance in trance is limited, since the spirit's own knowledge and abilities are limited—even when it is completely free—by its level of progress. Once connected to matter, these restrictions naturally become even more pronounced—which is one reason that the clairvoyant trance state is neither common nor very dependable and why it is all the less reliable when its natural purposes are diverted and it becomes the object of curiosity and useless experiments.

Trance subjects enter into a state of relative freedom that enables them to communicate more easily with other incarnate or disincarnate spirits.

....

14 *Translator's note: Referring to the epigastrium, the upper central region of the abdomen.*

This communication takes place through contacting the radiant energy of their spiritual bodies, so their thoughts are transmitted as if through an electric wire. Trance subjects, therefore, do not need to express their thoughts through speech. They perceive thought—a fact that renders them impressionable and highly subject to the spiritual atmosphere around them. One result of this susceptible condition is that a large gathering, especially one where scoffers and curiosity seekers are present, can interfere substantially with their faculties. Indeed, an intimately familiar environment alone can fully call forth their gifts. The presence of ill-intentioned or unfriendly people has the same constricting effect on them as the hand has on a sensitive plant, whose leaves fold together when touched.

While in trance, subjects often report seeing their spirit and their body simultaneously. Trance subjects, however, do not always understand this condition. Nor do they always realize the duality, which often leads them to speak of themselves as if a second person were present.

Trance subjects often reveal a knowledge beyond their educational level and even beyond their apparent intellectual capacity. We can explain this by remembering that, while a spirit acquires increased knowledge and experience in each of its incarnate lives, it partially forgets them during reincarnation. But as soon as it finds itself free from the body—either by death or trance—it remembers what it once knew. Consequently, the intellectual and scientific ignorance of trance subjects in their waking state is often at variance with the knowledge they demonstrate during trance. Depending on the circumstances of the trance and the suggested objective, they may draw knowledge from their own experiences, from their relative clairvoyance of things presently occurring, or from advice received from other spirits. However, the quality of their remarks is in great measure dependent on their advancement. Thus, whether spontaneous or induced, the trance state provides undeniable proof of the existence and independence of the soul by disclosing the sublime wonder of its liberation from the body. It is a gift of Providence through which God opens up for us the book of our own destinies.

When trance subjects describe what is occurring at a distance, they do indeed see those things and events—but without the use of the physical eyes.[15] Moreover, they are aware of being transported to, and see themselves at, the place they are describing. Something of themselves is really present there; and that something can only be the soul or spirit. By

....

15 *Translator's Note: Extensive research evidence is found in the following: R. Targ and H. Puthoff, Mind Reach, 1977; and C.T. Tart, "A Psychophysiological Study of the Out-of-the-Body Experiences in a Selected Subject,"* Journal of the American Society for Psychical Research, *1968, 62.3.*

this means God has placed before our very eyes the simplest and most obvious means to study the nature of our spiritual existence—even as we lose ourselves in abstractions and unintelligible metaphysical subtleties.

Turning to ecstatic trance, we find in it the state in which the soul's independence from the body is most clearly revealed—becoming, so to speak, palpable. In dreaming and induced trance states, the spirit wanders about the earthly realm. In an ecstatic trance state, it penetrates into an unknown world, that of illuminated spirits. There it communicates with those spirits, being careful however not to exceed certain limits, since to cross over completely would amount to severing the bonds connecting it with matter and bringing about the death of its body. In this world, the spirit is immersed in bright and radiant surroundings, enraptured by harmonies unknown on earth, and overcome by a bliss that defies description. In short, it enjoys a foretaste of celestial ecstasy and may be said to have placed one foot on the threshold of Eternity.

In the ecstatic trance state, the prostration of the physical body is almost complete. The body no longer possesses anything beyond organic life. The soul is held by a single thread, which would rupture forever with only a small effort. In such a state, all earthly thoughts disappear, replaced by perceptions that constitute the very essence of the immaterial being. Absorbed completely in this sublime contemplation, the soul views earthly life as only a temporary stay. The successes and misfortunes of the material world, its gross joys and afflictions, appear as so many trifling incidents on a journey, the end of which the soul feels lucky to glimpse.

In ecstatic and other trance states the individual may have similar experiences, but the insights will vary with the person's level of awareness. The more enlightened the individuals, the more their spirits understand and perceive. Frequently, however, the ecstatic shows more excitement than actual awareness and, as a result, her revelations are often a mixture of truths and errors, veering from sublime ideas to ridiculous fancies. This excitement, when not properly controlled, may become a weakness since it opens the way for unevolved intelligences to interfere. Surely, this is a potential problem, but it does not discredit the phenomenon. It is our responsibility to evaluate each case on its own merits and apply our best judgment in analyzing each assertion made.

When the liberation of the soul occurs in the waking state, it produces the phenomenon of second sight or double vision. Individuals with this faculty can see, hear, and feel beyond the limits of human perception. They break through the barriers of ordinary sight as if the latter were a mirage, perceiving things and events as far as the action of their souls extend. At the moment second sight occurs, the physical state of the subject changes perceptibly. The whole countenance reflects a kind of exalted state. The eyes become vacant (the person stares blankly) and the perception has little to do with the surrounding setting.

People endowed with second sight consider their gift to be as natural as ordinary sight. They regard it as an attribute of their being and are not aware of its exceptional character. Generally, they tend to forget their passing clairvoyance; and the memory of their revelations becomes more and more vague until, dream-like, it disappears. The gift of second sight varies from a confused sensation to a clear and distinct perception of things present or at a distance. In its early stages, it gives the person a kind of inner certainty, a spiritual insight, about certain actions. When more refined, it produces presentiments. When highly developed, it allows the person to view events that have already occurred or are about to occur.

Natural and induced trances, ecstatic trance, and second sight are varieties of experience that spring from one and the same cause. They are, like dreams, natural phenomena and have existed throughout the ages. History shows they have been known, and often abused, from remotest antiquity. More importantly, they furnish explanations for innumerable facts that our superstitious prejudices have led us to believe are supernatural.

XIII

SPIRITUAL INTERVENTION IN THE INCARNATE WORLD

Probing Human Thoughts

456. Do spirits see everything we do?

▲ *"They can if they choose, since they are constantly around you. But, practically speaking, a spirit sees only the things that interest it."*

457. Can spirits see our most secret thoughts?

▲ *"You cannot conceal your thoughts or actions from them. Often they see what you would rather hide from yourselves."*

—Apparently, then, it's easier to keep something hidden from a person who is alive than to hide it from that person after his or her death?

▲ *"Yes. Just when you imagine you have hidden yourselves from every eye, there is often a crowd of spirits around you, watching you."*

458. What do such spirits think of us when they observe us?

▲ *"It depends on the quality of the spirits themselves. Frivolous ones enjoy the little annoyances they cause you and laugh at your outbursts of impatience. More serious spirits pity your imperfections and try to help you rid yourselves of them."*

Influencing Thoughts and Actions

459. Do spirits influence our thoughts and actions?

▲ *"To a greater extent than you suppose they can have a significant influence on both."*

460. Do all our thoughts originate with us or do some come from spirits?

▲ *"Your soul is a spirit who thinks. However, you must have noticed that many differing thoughts on the same subject will frequently come to mind at the same time. In these cases, some of the thoughts are your own; but some are ours, too. This holding of two opposed ideas, incidentally, is the cause of some of your self-questioning."*

461. How can we distinguish between our own thoughts and the ones suggested to us?"

▲ *"Your own thoughts generally occur to you first. The thoughts and options suggested to you appear as a subtle voice in your mind. But the distinction doesn't serve much practical purpose, and usually it is better not to make it. Without it, your judgment isn't compromised. When you decide to follow the right road, you do so more spontaneously; and if you take the wrong one, your responsibility is more definite."*

462. Do people of high intelligence and genius always draw their ideas from their own minds?

▲ *"Frequently. But when they don't find the required ideas within, they often make an unconscious appeal for inspiration—an invocation produced without a full awareness of what they are doing. Then, if the persons involved are capable of understanding and worthy of receiving the suggestions, the spirits will propose them."*

Discussion: If God had found it useful for us to distinguish clearly between our own and suggested thoughts, we would have the means for doing so, just as we have the means for distinguishing between day and night. When Providence leaves a matter in a state of vagueness, it is for our own good.

463. It is sometimes said that our first thoughts are the best. Is this true?

▲ *"They may be good or bad, depending on the nature of the person. In any case, always listen to good inspirations."*

464. How can we tell whether a suggested thought comes from a good spirit or from an unenlightened one?

▲ *"Study its quality. Good spirits give only good advice. It is for you to distinguish between the good and bad."*

465. Why do unenlightened spirits incite us to do wrong?

▲ *"To make you suffer as they do."*

—Does this lessen their sufferings?

▲ *"No. They act out of jealousy."*

—What kind of sufferings do they want to make us experience?

▲ *"The ones that are common to their own less evolved order, which is far removed from God."*

466. Why does God allow these spirits to tempt us?

▲ *"They are the instruments through which your faith and constancy in doing good are tested. As a spirit, you must advance in the knowledge of the Infinite. For this to happen, you must pass through the trials and experiences associated with the human condition in order to bring forth your latent goodness.*

"When harmful influences act on you, it is because your instinctual desires have attracted them to you. They are always there, ready to help you fulfill your darkest desires. But they can only push you in the direction of wrong-doing when you yourself give way to those impulses. The mission of good spirits, on the other hand, is to lead you into the right road. For instance, if you are bent on committing murder, you will have around you a swarm of harmful spirits who will keep that inclination alive. But other spirits will also surround and try to influence you to refrain. These spirits seek to restore the balance. The decision as to how you will act is left up to you."

Discussion: In this way God leaves the choice of the road we will follow, and the opposing influences we will yield to, to our own consciences.

467. Can we free ourselves from the influence of spirits who tempt us to do wrong?

▲ *"Yes. They can only attach themselves to people whose thoughts and inclinations attract them."*

468. Do spirits renounce their attempts to influence us when we counter their suggestions with our own good resolutions?

▲ *"What else can they do? When they find they cannot succeed in their aims, they give up. But, like the cat watching for the mouse, they are always on the alert for a favorable moment, a period of weakness."*

469. How can we neutralize the influence of these spirits?

▲ *"Do only what is right and put all your trust in God. By doing so, you repel and deny them power over you. Be careful not to listen to the suggestions of anyone who inspires bad thoughts in you, causes trouble between yourself and others, or arouses your instinctual passions. Distrust especially the spirit who flatters your pride—it is attacking you at your weakest point. This is why Jesus tells us to say, in the Lord's Prayer, 'keep us clear of temptation, and save us from evil.'"*[1]

....

1 *Translator's Note: Luke 11:2.*

470. Have the spirits who tempt us and try to test our resolve received a mission to do this? And if they have, are they responsible for accomplishing such a mission?

▲ *"No spirit ever receives a mission to do wrong. It does wrong of its own free will. And it also suffers the consequences of its actions. God never commands a spirit to tempt—or absolves you from the responsibility of repelling temptation."*

471. Sometimes we feel a vague anxiety and uneasiness, or else an inward satisfaction, and cannot identify a cause for either. Are these feelings simply a result of physiological conditions?

▲ *"Almost always they are an effect of the ideas you unconsciously receive from spirits, whether you are awake or asleep."*

472. When spirits want to excite wrong-doing in us, do they merely take advantage of our circumstances? Can they manipulate situations that favor their intentions?

▲ *"They take advantage of any favorable circumstance they find. But they also bring events about and will urge you toward the object of your desires without your ever being aware of it. For instance, someone picks up a roll of banknotes in the street. Now, the spirits have not brought the money to this particular spot. But they may have suggested to the person the idea of going that way. And, when the person finds the money, they may suggest the idea of keeping it, even while others are encouraging him or her to restore it to its rightful owner. This is the way all temptations work."*

Controlling Influences

473. Can a spirit temporarily take over an animate body and act in the place of the spirit rightfully incarnated in it?

▲ *"A spirit does not enter a body as you enter a house. It might, however, associate itself with a person with similar defects and qualities, and the two of them may act together. But one always acts of one's own free will. No other spirit can take the place of one who is incarnated in a given body. A spirit is indivisibly united with its body until the hour Providence has decreed the body must die."*

474. If there is no such thing as "possession" in the ordinary sense of the term—that is to say, the cohabitation of two spirits in the same body—is it possible for an incarnate spirit to find itself so influenced by a another that its will is paralyzed?

▲ *"Yes. It is this domination that actually constitutes what you call possession. But it happens only when the subject, by its own free will or weakness of character, agrees to it. We should add that people often confuse possession with cases of epilepsy or madness—cases that require the help of a doctor rather than a clergyman."*

Discussion: The word possession, as it is commonly understood, presupposes the existence of demons—i.e., a category of essentially evil beings—and the fusing of one of these beings with a human soul. But since demons do not exist and since two spirits cannot inhabit the same body simultaneously, there is no such thing as "possession." The word should only be used to indicate a state of mental subjugation.

475. Can a soul drive away these disturbing presences through its own actions and thus free itself of their influence?

▲ *"You can always shake off a burden if you are determined enough to do it. "*

476. Can the fascination exercised by this kind of spirit be so complete that the subjugated person is unaware of it? And, in this case, couldn't a third person intervene and put an end to it? Would you tell us, in any event, how we might stop this kind of influence?

▲ *"The will power of an upright person may be useful in attracting the cooperation of good spirits. The more upright someone is, the more power he or she possesses both to drive away wrong-doing spirits and draw good ones nearer. Still, even the best person is powerless in cases where the subjugated individuals refuse to participate in efforts to liberate themselves. There are men and women, unfortunately, who take pleasure in a state of dependence, especially one that panders to their lower appetites. But in no case can someone with an impure heart exercise a liberating influence. The more advanced spirits shun that person, and the less evolved ones feel no respect in his or her presence."*

477. Do formulas of exorcism have any power over ill-intentioned spirits?

▲ *"No. These spirits laugh at anyone trying to influence them by these means and simply go on about their business."*

478. In some cases, even well-meaning individuals fall victim to negative influences. What is the best means of getting rid of the spirits trying to control them?

▲ *"Wear down their patience; pay no attention to their suggestions; show them they are wasting their time. When they see they can't do anything, they will go away."*

479. Is prayer effective in ending negative spirit influence?

▲ *"Prayer is always a successful means of getting help. But remember that muttering certain words is not enough. God helps those who help themselves—but not those who limit their action to asking for help. People in such a situation must do everything they can to rid themselves of the imperfections that are attracting these spirits."*

480. What should we think of the "casting out of devils" spoken of in the Gospels?

▲ *"What do you mean by the word 'devil'? If you mean a less advanced spirit who subjugates a human being, this much is evident: when its influence is destroyed, the spirit will be driven away. You are dealing here, however, with a matter of language. If you attribute a problem to a devil, you will say— when you have resolved it— that you have driven the devil out. Statements like this can be true or false, depending on the meaning you attribute to certain words. The most serious truths appear absurd when you only focus on the form in which they are presented, or when you take allegory as fact. Learn this principle well—it has universal application."*

Mass Hysteria[2]

481. Do spirits play a part in the phenomena exhibited in cases of mass hysteria?

▲ *"Yes, a very important one—as does hypnotic suggestion which, whether human beings or spirits use it, is the original source of the phenomena. Unscrupulous people, unfortunately, often exaggerate the effects. In doing so, they leave hypnotic suggestion open to ridicule."*

—What is the nature of the spirits who help produce phenomena of this kind?

▲ *"Never very advanced. Do you think spirits of a high order would waste their time in this way?"*

482. How can a whole population be suddenly thrown into a state of mass hysteria and crisis?

▲ *"Through mutual affinities. As you well know, under certain conditions the mental disposition of some people may affect the will of others. You know enough about the effects of hypnotic power to realize this. And you also can presume the part certain spirits may play because of affinity."*

Discussion: Among the strange peculiarities found in hysterics, several are identical to those found in induced trance: physical insensibility, thought reading, sympathetic transmission of

....

2 *Translator's Note: "Convulsionnaires" is the word used in the original French text. According to* Le Petit Robert, *one of the most respected dictionaries of the French language, the word is linked to a movement of fanatic Jansenists who were prey to bouts of hysteria on the tomb of the Deacon Paris at the Saint-Medard Cemetery, Paris, in 1732. Jansenism   was a movement founded by Cornelius Jansen, based on the notions of "divine grace" and "predestination." It denied free will and maintained that human nature is corrupt and that Christ died for the elect and not for all men.   In France, Jansenists were considered morally austere and fanatic. (For more on this see two articles by Allan Kardec in the October 1859 and November 1859 issues of* Revue Spirite.) *Other instances that could perhaps be catalogued as cases of mass hysteria include the Salem Witch Trials in 1692, the response to "War of Worlds" in 1938, the Red Scare in 1950, and the Jonestown mass suicide in 1978.*

sensations, etc. Therefore, it is not unreasonable to say that these people are in a waking trance, and unwittingly and unconsciously influencing each other.

483. What causes the physical insensibility sometimes seen in hysterics—and in other people, too—when they are subjected to extreme physical pain?

▲ *"In some instances it is simply the effect of a powerful feeling, which acts on the nervous system in the same way as do some drugs. In others, mental excitement deadens the sensitivity of the organism. Life seems to retire from the body and concentrate itself in the spirit. Haven't you noticed that, when the mind is intensely occupied with a matter, the body doesn't feel or see or hear?"*

Discussion: In certain cases of excruciating suffering, people who are extremely devoted to some cause often demonstrate a calmness and coolness that can only be explained by saying that their sensory apparatus has been neutralized by a sort of psychic anesthesia. We know that, in the heat of battle, a soldier often receives a severe wound without being aware of it, whereas under ordinary circumstances he might find a simple scratch extremely painful.

In cases of collective hysteria, the causes are mainly physical and only secondarily of a spiritual nature. In this context, an interesting question is why the intervention of police authorities brings the phenomenon to a stop. Simply stated, their intervention nullifies the predisposition of certain individuals to slip into hysteric behavior. However, this form of intervention is powerless when the phenomenon is induced by spirits.

Bonds of Affection Between Spirits and People

484. Do spirits develop special bonds with certain people?

▲ *"Good spirits empathize with everyone who is good or wants to improve. Inferior spirits, on the other hand, prefer wrong-doers or people who have tendencies in that direction. In either case it is the affinity of feelings that gives rise to special ties between spirits and people."*

485. Are the bonds of affection between spirits and people exclusively spiritual?

▲ *"True affection has nothing base or sensual in it. But a spirit's attachment to a living person is not always a matter of true affection. It may, sometimes, be inspired by the remembrance of earthly passions."*

486. Do spirits take an interest in our misfortunes and our prosperity? And are the ones who wish us well upset when we undergo the ills of life?

▲ *"Good spirits do you all the good they can. They rejoice with you in all your joys, and they mourn over the afflictions you do not bear with forbearance, since these afflictions then produce no beneficial result. In such cases the person is like the sick man who rejects treatment."*

487. Which causes the most pain to our spirit friends—our physical sufferings or our moral failings?

▲ *"They grieve most of all over your self-centeredness and callousness toward others, which are the root causes of all your troubles. They smile at your imaginary sorrows, the ones born of pride and desire; and they rejoice when you brave the tribulations that will shorten your term of trial."*

Discussion: Our spirit friends know that our incarnate life is only transitory and that the tribulations we experience here are the means by which we will reach a happier state. Consequently, they are more troubled by our moral imperfections, which keep us back, than by our temporary physical ills. Spirits attach as little importance to misfortunes that affect only our earthly aspirations as we do to a brief moment of regret. They regard such misfortune as the passing crisis that will restore the sick person to health. They grieve with us in our sufferings, as we grieve with our friends in theirs. But they judge the events of our lives from a different perspective. While less advanced spirits try to discourage us in order to impede our advancement, good ones seek to inspire us with the courage that will allow us to turn our trials into future gains.

488. Do relatives and friends who have entered the spirit-world before us feel more affection for us than spirits who are strangers?

▲ *"Undoubtedly they do. And, depending on their power, they often assist you."*

—Do they value the affection we still hold for them?

▲ *"Very much so, but they may forget those who forget them."*

Guardian Angels, Mentors, and Guides

489. Are there spirits who associate themselves with a particular individual and protect and help that person?

▲ *"Yes. You call them spirit guides or guardian angels."*

490. What does the expression 'guardian angel' mean?

▲ *"A spirit guide of high degree."*

491. What is the mission of spirit guides?

▲ *"They stand in relation to you as parents toward their children. They lead the objects of their protection into the right road, aid them with good advice, console them in their afflictions, and keep up their courage as they undergo the trials of earthly life."*

492. Is a spirit guide assigned to an individual from birth?

▲ *"From birth to death. And guides will often extend their protection into the spirit-life after death—even through several successive incarnate lives. These lives, of course, are only very short phases in a spirit's entire existence."*

493. Is the mission of a spirit guide voluntary, or is it a duty?

▲ *"Your spirit guide, who has accepted the task, is obligated to watch over you. But a spirit can choose a ward among beings with whom it feels an affinity. In some cases, then, this office is a pleasure; in others a duty."*

—Does a spirit, in becoming attached to a particular person, refrain from protecting other individuals?

▲ *"No. But it does so less exclusively."*

494. Is the spirit guide indissolubly bound to the person it guards?

▲ *"No, it may quit its position in order to fulfill various missions. In that case, the ward is placed in the charge of another spirit."*

495. Will a spirit guide sometimes abandon its ward if the ward refuses to follow its advice?

▲ *"It will withdraw if it sees that its advice is useless and that the person continues to hold stubbornly to negative influences. But the spirit does not abandon the person entirely and continues trying to make itself heard. So, you see, it is not the spirit guide who leaves the person, but the person who closes his or her ears to the guide. As soon as you call it back, the spirit guide will return to you.*

"If there is a single doctrine that, through its charm and beauty, should win over the incredulous, it is this one of spirit guides, guardian angels. What an enormous consolation it is to think that you always have near you beings superior to yourself who will advise you, sustain you, and aid you in climbing the steep ascent of self-improvement; beings, moreover, whose friendship is truer and more devoted than the most intimate union Earth can offer. Those beings have been placed near you following God's directives and are there out of their love of God. They fulfill a noble but difficult mission. Wherever you are, they are also—in prison, in places of entertainment, in your loneliness, in your sickness. Nothing ever separates you from them— these friends whom you cannot see but whose gentle persuasions you feel and whose wise instructions you hear in the innermost recesses of your heart.

"If you realized fully the truth of this doctrine, it would very often aid you in your moments of need and save you from harmful influences. After death,

you will learn how often your guardian angel sought to help you. It will say to you 'I urged you to take a certain road, and yet you would not follow my leading. I showed you the void opening before you, and yet you persisted in throwing yourself into it. I caused your conscience to hear the voice of truth, and yet you followed the wrong advice. Why?' Try, then, to establish between yourselves and your guides the affection and intimacy that exists between tried and loving friends. Share your fears with them, and listen closely. Do not think of hiding anything from them—they are the eyes of God, and you cannot deceive them. Think of the future, and try to advance on the upward road. If you do, your trials will be shorter, your existence happier. Take courage! Cast off your prejudices and mental reservations, enter on the new road that opens before you, and persevere. You have guides; follow them. Your goal cannot fail you, for it is God you move toward.

"To those who think it impossible that spirits of high degree would bind themselves to so difficult a task, requiring so much patience, we reply that God has not given us tasks above our strengths. Nor has God abandoned you on Earth without friends and support. To us distance is nothing. We can communicate with you from many millions of miles away, from any sphere on which we find ourselves. We possess faculties you cannot imagine. Every guardian angel has a ward and watches over that ward as a parent watches over a child, rejoicing when he or she follows the right road and mourning when advice is rejected.

"Don't be afraid of tiring us with your questions. On the contrary, always stay in contact with us—you will be stronger and happier for it. It is this ability to communicate with your guardian angel that makes you extra-sensorial beings and that one day will drive disbelief in us from your world.

"You have received instruction; instruct in your turn. You have talents; raise up your fellow human beings. You do not know how great the work is that you perform. It is the work of Christ—the work God has given you. Why has God supplied you with intelligence and knowledge if not to share them with your fellows, to help them advance on their road to eternal happiness?"

(St. Louis and St. Augustine)

Discussion: The doctrine of guardian angels watching over their wards, even given the distance that separates the orbs of the universe, has in it nothing that should surprise us. It is as natural as it is grand and sublime.

On Earth, we see how parents watch over their children, though great distances may separate them, helping them through encouragements and good advice in their letters. We should not judge it any more surprising, then, that spirits should guide us, taking us under their protection as we move from one dimension of life to another.

To them the vast distances separating the spheres of spirit-life are less than the distance that separates continents on Earth for us. They also have at their disposal the Cosmic Principle that binds together everything in the universe and makes all the realms part and parcel of each other. This is the universal vehicle for transmitting thought, just as for us the air is the vehicle for transmitting sound.

496. If a spirit abandons a ward, can it do the ward harm afterwards?

▲ *"Good spirits never harm anyone. If you distance yourself from your guide, spirits of ill-nature may gain access to you. It is unjust then to blame your guides for misfortunes when they are of your own doing."*

497. How can a spirit guide allow its ward to succumb to the influence of ill-intentioned spirits?

▲ *"Such spirits may band together in an attempt to counteract the efforts of the guide. But it is the ward, by his or her attitude, who determines which of the two influences ultimately prevails. If the guide realizes that its advice is being repeatedly ignored, it might temporarily withdraw to help someone else more receptive. But the guide always stands ready to return to its ward."*

498. Does a spirit guide allow a ward to wander into wrong paths because it cannot cope with the malevolent spirits who may be influencing the ward?

▲ *"No. It's not they can't; they choose not to. The guide knows that the ward will become wiser and better through these self-inflicted trials. The guide will continue to assist him or her by mentally suggesting the best course to follow, though unfortunately the ward doesn't always listen. Recall that the power of ill-intentioned spirits over you stems only from your own weakness, carelessness, and self-centeredness. In short, their strength results from your lack of resolve in resisting their suggestions."*

499. Is the spirit guide constantly with the ward? Are there no circumstances under which the guide, without abandoning him or her, may lose sight of a ward?

▲ *"There are some conditions under which the presence of the spirit guide is not necessary to the ward."*

500. Does a time arrive when a spirit no longer needs a guardian angel?

▲ *"Yes, just as a time arrives when the student no longer needs the teacher. Eventually, the spirit will advance to the point where it becomes self-guided. But this does not happen on Earth."*

501. Why is the influence of spirits on us hidden? And why isn't their protection readily apparent to us?

▲ *"If you counted heavily on their support, you would not be acting on your own accord and your spirit would not progress. In order to advance you need to acquire experience, often at your own expense. You need to exercise your powers; otherwise, you will be like a child who is never allowed to walk by itself. The influence of the spirits who desire your welfare is always regulated in such a way as to leave you your free will. Without having responsibility for your actions, you will not advance on the road that leads to God. If you do not anticipate help, you will put forth maximum effort. Your guide, however, watches over you and calls you from time to time to warn you of dangers ahead."*

502. When the spirit guide succeeds in leading a ward onto the right road, does the action benefit the guide in any way?

▲ *"It is an admirable work and will be a source of joy for the spirit as well as a credit of love. The spirit rejoices when its care is crowned by success and triumphs, as a teacher exalts in the success of a pupil."*

—Is the spirit guide held responsible if the ward does not succeed?

▲ *"No, since it has done everything it deemed appropriate."*

503. Does the spirit guide feel regret when a ward takes the wrong road? Doesn't such a sight disturb its own peace?

▲ *"It grieves at the ward's errors and feels a good deal of pity. But it isn't anguished as earthly parents would be, because it knows that there is a remedy for these mistakes and that what is not done today will be done tomorrow."*

504. Can we ever know the name of our guardian angel?

▲ *"What value is there in knowing names you would not recognize? Do you suppose there are no spirits but the ones you know about personally?"*

—But how can we call on a guardian angel without knowing a specific name?

▲ *"Use any name you like—that of any superior spirit for whom you have an affinity or feel veneration. Your spirit guardian will answer the appeal. All good spirits are friends and assist each other."*

505. Are the spirit guardians who take well-known names always the persons who bore those names?

▲ *"No, but they are spirits who have a close affinity with those persons and who therefore take a name that will inspire confidence in you. When you aren't able to perform a duty in person, you send someone in your place, who acts in your name."*

506. When we are in the spirit-life, will we recognize our spirit guardian?

▲ *"Yes. It is often a spirit you knew before incarnating."*

507. Do all spirit guardians belong to the higher classes of spirits, or can they be found among those of average advancement, too? Can a parent, for example, become the spirit guardian of a child?

▲ *"A parent might, but guardianship presupposes a certain degree of eleva-*

tion, and, in addition, a power or virtue granted by God. A parent who watches over a child may, accordingly, be assisted by a more advanced spirit."

508. Can spirits who have left Earth under favorable conditions become spiritual guardians of loved ones left behind?

▲ *"Their power is more or less limited by their position. They do not always have full liberty to act."*

509. Do primitive people and those of a debased nature have spirit guardians and, if so, are those spirits equal in order to those of more advanced individuals?

▲ *"Every human being has a spirit guardian. But the quality of supervision is always in proportion to the task. You do not use a professor of philosophy to instruct a child who is just learning how to read. Likewise, a guardian spirit's advancement is always related to that of the person it protects. And while you yourself have a spirit of higher degree who watches over you, you may, in turn, become the guide of an individual who is less advanced. The progress you help the spirit make will contribute to your own. In any case, God does not ask anything of a spirit that is inconsistent with its nature or beyond the degree at which it has arrived."*

510. Consider a father who had been watching over his child from the spirit world, but who now has to reincarnate. Can he continue to perform this task in the physical realm?

▲ *"The task, in that case, becomes more difficult. But the parent may ask someone qualified for help in carrying it out. Spirits, however, do not undertake missions they cannot pursue to the end. An incarnate spirit, especially on planes where life is excessively material, is too much bound by the body to devote itself entirely to another spirit—that is to say, to personally watch over the other's needs. For this reason, spirit guardians who are not advanced enough for the work of guardianship on their own will receive assistance from higher-ranking spirits. Then, if anything should go wrong, another spirit will be on hand to occupy that spirit guardian's place."*

511. In addition to the spirit guardian, is there also a bad spirit attached to each individual—a spirit who will incite the person to wrong-doing and consequently provide needed opportunities for the struggle between good and bad?

▲ *"'Attached' is not really the right word. It is very true that wrong-doing spirits try to lure you off the right road when they have an opportunity. But when one of them associates itself with an individual, it does so of its own accord, hoping for a willing listener. In this case, the person will receive suggestions and ideas from both his guide and the bad spirit. This is how the so-called struggle between good and evil spirits takes place. The victory will go to the one whose influence the person voluntarily embraces."*

512. Can we have several spirit guardians?

▲ *"You always have around you a number of empathetic spirits from various ranks who have taken an affectionate interest in you. Depending on your inclinations you may also have others who will incite you to take the wrong path."*

513. Do caring spirits assist an individual because it is their mission?

▲ *"In some cases they may have a temporary mission. But, in general, they are drawn to an individual because of intellectual or emotional affinities."*

—Empathetic spirits may, then, be either good or bad?

▲ *"Yes, you are surrounded by spirits who have an affinity with you, no matter what your character is like."*

514. Are "familial spirits" the same as friendly spirits and spirit guardians?

▲ *"There are many gradations in guardianship and affinity. Give them any names you like. But 'familial spirit' is used to indicate a general friend of the family."*

Discussion: From the above explanations and our observation of the nature of spirits who associate themselves with human beings we draw the following conclusions:

• The spirit guide, also guardian angel, is one whose mission is to follow each person throughout his or her incarnate life and to help that person progress. The spirit's degree of advancement is always much superior to that of the person helped.

• A familial spirit is one who associates itself with certain persons and is useful to them within the frequently narrow limits of its power. Familial spirits are generally well intentioned, though sometimes unevolved and trivial. They busy themselves with the everyday details of human life and act only by the order or with the permission of spirit guardians.

• Empathetic spirits are those drawn to us by personal affection and similarity of tastes and inclinations. The length of their relationship with us almost always depends on circumstances.

• Wrong-doing spirits are those who approach individuals for the purpose of harming or misleading them. They always act on their own initiative and do not come as the result of a mission. Their tenacity depends on the access an individual accords them. Consequently, we are always free to listen to or repel the suggestions of these spirits.

515. There are people who exercise a sort of charismatic charm over certain individuals whom they may either inspire to take the right road or lead astray. How do you explain this situation?

▲ *"Some persons do possess this power. Where the influence is used for wrong, one can assume the action of ill-intentioned spirits assisting the charismatic individual. Providence allows this to happen in order to test the affected person's resolve."*

516. Could a spirit guide incarnate itself in order to accompany us more closely in our earthly life?

▲ *"That sometimes happens. But more often they will entrust this mission to a trustworthy person on Earth."*

517. Are there spirits who associate themselves with a family in order to watch over and aid them?

▲ *"Some spirits may take such a task. But do not attribute familial or ethnic pride to spirit guardians."*

518. Since spirits are attracted by affinity, are they also attracted to groups of persons who are working for some specific cause?

▲ *"Spirits prefer places where they mingle with peers. They are more comfortable among such persons and more certain of being heeded. We live in a world of relationships. All humans attract influences to themselves based on their inclinations and do so both as individuals and as members of collective wholes—that is, as a society, a city, a country. Spirits of varying degrees assist social groups depending on their character and objectives. Since imperfect spirits withdraw from advanced ones, the ethical progress of societies, like that of individuals, tends to keep away negative influences and attract good ones. These spirits kindle and keep alive the sense of ethical integrity in a people, just as others may sow degrading passions."*

519. Do societies, cities, and countries have their special spirit guardians?

▲ *"Yes. They constitute collective individualities who are pursuing a common goal and who require a higher direction."*

520. Are the spirit guardians of a whole people more advanced than the ones attached to individuals?

▲ *"As in the case of individuals, their advancement is always in proportion to the degree of the people they serve."*

521. Can certain spirits advance the progress of the arts by protecting the individuals who cultivate them?

▲ *"There are those who assist certain individuals when called upon. But the guides must consider them worth helping. They can do nothing for people who imagine themselves to be something they are not. They cannot make the blind see or the deaf hear."*

Discussion: The ancients converted these special spirit guides into
                deities. The fabled Muses were nothing but allegoric per-
                sonifications of the spiritual guides of arts and sciences,
                just as the Roman *lares* and *penates*[3] were personifications of
                the spiritual guides of the family circle. Among the mod-
                erns, the arts, various industries, cities, countries, all have
                protecting patrons, i.e., spirit guardians of a high order,
                though they go by names different from the ones adopted
                in the ancient world.

                Just as each person is attended by a sympathetic spirit,
                every group attracts spirits who are attuned to the feelings
                and attitudes that characterize that group. In short, simi-
                larity of thought attracts spirits to a group. And spirits sur-
                round, influence, and assist a group to the extent that they
                share the predominant moral and intellectual views of the
                individuals in it.

                Among the countries of the world, habits, manners, the
                dominant characteristics of the people, and, above all, the
                laws (in which a country finds its character reflected) exer-
                cise a powerful attraction for spirits. Countries that strive
                to uphold high standards among their citizens counteract
                the influence of unethical spirits. Wherever the laws sanc-
                tion injustice and inhumanity, however, good spirits are in
                the minority and a mass of unscrupulous ones flock in,
                attracted by these conditions. These spirits keep the people
                immersed in false ideas and paralyze good influences,
                which at best are only partial and lost in the crowd of bad
                ones—rare wheat in the midst of tares. By studying the
                characteristics of various countries, or of any human
                grouping, it is easy to get an idea of the invisible popula-
                tion that partakes of their lives and actions.

Presentiments

522. Is a presentiment always a warning from a spirit guardian?

▲ *"Prior to incarnation, a spirit is aware of the principal events of its coming
life—that is to say, of the kind of trials it is about to experience. When the
events are of an exceptional character, the spirit preserves vivid images*

....

3 *Translator's Notes:* Muses *refers to any of the nine Greek goddesses that protected the creative arts;* lares, *to the ancient Roman gods who protected the settle-
ment and resided wherever men cultivated the land;* penates, *to the ancient Roman
gods who protected the storeroom of the house.*

which are archived in its innermost consciousness. When the critical moment of the trial draws near, this image emerges as a presentiment. In surfacing, the image may also trigger an instinctual reaction, which you have called 'the voice of instinct.' In other circumstances a presentiment may be advice that you receive privately from a spirit who wishes you well."

523. Presentiments and the voice of instinct are always somewhat vague. What should we do when we are in a condition of uncertainty?

▲ *"When you are in doubt, call on your spirit guardian or ask God to send you a messenger."*

524. Do our spirit guides' warnings concern only our moral guidance? Do they sometimes give us presentiments about our other personal affairs?

▲ *"Their warnings come at every significant moment of your life. In every-thing you do, your spirit guides try to persuade you to take the best possible course. But you often close your ears to their friendly counsel and find your-selves in trouble through your own fault."*

Discussion: Our protecting spirits help us by their advice and by awak-ening the voice of conscience in us. But since we do not always attach enough importance to these hints, the spirits will also give us more direct warnings through the people around us. Any one of us will, on reflecting on the various circumstances of our lives, recognize that we have received advice on many occasions that, had we followed it, would have saved us a good many problems.

The Events of Human Life

525. Do spirits exercise an influence over the events of our lives?

▲ *"Certainly they do. They give you advice."*

—Do they exercise this influence in any way other than the thoughts they suggest to us? In other words, do they directly interfere in the course of earthly events?

▲ *"Yes, but their actions never overstep the laws of nature."*

Discussion: We imagine, incorrectly, that spirits only reveal themselves through extraordinary phenomena. We would like them to help us by performing miracles, and accordingly we imag-ine them as always carrying a sort of magic wand. But this is not the case. In reality, their help comes through natural means and their intervention usually occurs without our being aware of it. For instance, they will deliberately bring about the meeting of two individuals who seem to have run into each other by chance. Or they will suggest to someone the idea of going in a particular direction. They will call our attention to some special point in order to bring about a favorable result. In this way, we suppose ourselves to be following only our own impulses and thus preserve our freedom of will.

526. Since spirits can act on matter, can they bring about the incidents that will insure that a given event will happen? For example, a man is destined to die in a certain way and at a certain time. He climbs a ladder, the ladder breaks, and he is killed. Did spirits cause the ladder to break as a way of fulfilling this man's destiny?

▲ *"It is true that spirits can act on matter. But they use this power for carrying out the laws of nature, not debasing them by causing some unforeseen, supernatural event to occur. In the case you have just mentioned, the ladder breaks because it is rotten or not strong enough to hold the man's weight. But since the man was destined to die in this way, the idea of climbing the ladder might occur to him as if spontaneously. Thus, when the ladder collapses under his weight, his death will have taken place naturally, without any miraculous intervention."*

527. Here is another example—one in which the ordinary conditions of matter appear insufficient to account for the event. A woman is destined to be killed by lightning. She is overtaken by a storm and finds shelter under a tree. Lightning strikes the tree, it falls, and the woman is killed. Have the spirits caused the lightning to strike the tree and kill this person?

▲ *"The explanation is exactly the same as the previous one. The lightning strikes the tree at a particular moment without any breach of the laws of nature. But the lightning did not strike the tree because the woman happened to be under it. The woman was unconsciously attracted to take shelter under a tree where lightning was about to strike. The tree would have been struck whether the woman was under it or not."*

528. An enraged person shoots at someone, narrowly missing the person. Has some friendly spirit turned the bullet aside?

▲ *"If it were not the destiny of the individual to be hit, a friendly spirit would suggest getting out of the bullet's path or would find a way of interfering with the assailant's aim. These are the only options, since the bullet, once fired, must follow the line of its trajectory."*

529. What are we to think of magic bullets that, in certain legends, infallibly hit their target?

▲ *"They are purely imaginary. Human beings delight in the marvelous; the marvels of nature do not content you."*

— Can the spirits who inspire us in important decisions of our lives be thwarted by other spirits who want our lives to go in a different direction?

▲ *"What the Divine Mind has designed will take place. Time changes and difficulties will not happen outside of the Divine Plan."*

530. Are there petty and scornful spirits who cause the various small difficulties that ruin our projects and upset our plans? In short, do such spirits bring on the minor troubles of human life?

▲ *"They may take pleasure in annoying you; but this serves as a test of your self-control. If they see that they have not succeeded in upsetting you, they tire of the game. You do them a wrong and an injustice, however, when you blame them for all your small failures. Most such failures result from your own heedlessness. If your dishes break, look to your own awkwardness, not to the influence of spirits."*

—Do spirits who cause these minor annoyances act from a sense of personal animosity? Or do they seek the first person who comes in handy as a means of satisfying a general malice?

▲ *"They act from both motives. In some cases, they are enemies you have made during your present life. In others, they are enemies from a past life who have followed you into this one. Some, though, act without a fixed motive."*

531. In the case of those who have harmed us on Earth, does their animosity disappear when they return to the spirit-world?

▲ *"In many instances spirits realize the injustice of their actions and regret the wrong they have done. But there are cases, too, in which they remain hostile and continue to hound you. This is permitted as a continuation of your trial."*

—Can we end this kind of persecution? And if so, how?

▲ *"Often you can do it by praying for them, returning good for their wrongdoing, and gradually making them see that their actions are mistaken. In all cases, if you can show that you have the patience to rise above their antagonism, they will stop attacking you, since they have nothing to gain by continuing."*

Discussion: Experience shows that certain spirits pursue revenge through more than one lifetime. This is to say that, sooner or later, we will have to take responsibility for the harm we do to others.

532. Can spirits prevent misfortunes from happening to their protégés?

▲ *"Only to a certain extent. Misfortunes may serve a Divine purpose. But spirits can help you endure your sufferings with fortitude, and in this way ease them.*

"Realize, too, that you are responsible to a great extent for averting misfortune or at least lessening it. When you make use of the mental abilities God has given you, you enable friendly spirits to give you their most effective help—that is, to suggest their most useful ideas. But, remember, spirits only help those who help themselves—a truth implied in the words, 'Seek,

and you will find; knock and it will be opened to you.'[4]

   "In addition, you should recognize that some misfortunes are not always what they appear to be. The good that a misfortune will bring about is often greater than the apparent trouble. You aren't always aware of this fact, though, because you think too much about the present moment and your own immediate satisfaction."

533. Can spirits help us obtain material means and notoriety if we ask them?

▲ *"They will sometimes help make it possible—as a lesson to you. But just as often, they refuse, as you refuse to meet the demands of a spoiled child."*

—Is it good or wrong-doing spirits who help with these favors?

▲ *"Both. The quality of both the request and the favor depends on the motivation behind them. Still more often than not these gifts come from spirits who do not have your best interest at heart and find the material pleasures of wealth an easy way to undermine you."*

534. At times fate seems to place obstacles in the way of our plans. Is this always due to the influence of spirits?

▲ *"Spirits will occasionally set up obstacles for you but usually your own bad judgment is to blame. Position and character play a large part in your successes and failures. And if you persist in following a path that is not right for you, you have clearly become your own worst enemy. Do not, then, attribute setbacks to spirits when they result from your own stubbornness and mistakes."*

535. When anything fortunate happens to us, should we thank our spirit guardian for it?

▲ *"First, thank God, without whose permission nothing takes place; next, thank the good spirits who are God's agents in such matters."*

—What happens if we do not thank them?

▲ *"The same thing that happens to all the ungrateful."*

—In that case, why are there people who never pray and never give thanks, but still manage to succeed in everything they do?

▲ *"Wait and see. The undeserving owe a great debt for their temporary prosperity. The more they have received, the more they will have to account for."*

Production of Natural Phenomena

....

4 *Translator's Note: Matthew 7:7*

536. Are the major natural catastrophes due to random causes, or do all of them serve a providential purpose?

▲ *"There is a reason for everything. Nothing takes place without the permission of God."*

—Do these phenomena always serve a purpose related to human life?

▲ *"Sometimes they relate directly to you. But usually they occur as a means of re-establishing a state of equilibrium and harmony among physical forces."*

—The will of God is, we fully admit, the primary cause of these and all other phenomena. But since we know that spirits, as agents of the Divine will, act on matter, we would like to know whether some of them influence the elements— whether they can agitate, calm, or direct them.

▲ *"It could not be otherwise. God does not act directly on matter and, for this reason, has placed devoted agents on every step of the ladder of the worlds."*

537. Ancient mythology is based on ideas that the Spiritist Doctrine embraces as well, but there is this difference: the ancients regarded spirits as divinities and represented them as having special attributes. Some of their gods and goddesses had power over the winds, others over lightning; others again presided over vegetation, etc. Does this belief have any foundation in reality?

▲ *"It is totally baseless."*

—Could there be spirits who live in Earth's interior and preside over the development of its geological phenomena?

▲ *"Spirits do not literally live in Earth's interior. But they can influence natural phenomena. One day the causes of all these phenomena will be clear to you, and you will understand them better."*

538. Do the spirits who preside over natural phenomena form a special order in the spirit-world? Are they separate beings, or have they lived physical lives like us?

▲ *"No. They, too, will reincarnate on Earth and may have already done so."*

—Do these spirits belong to the higher or lower degrees in the spirit-hierarchy?

▲ *"It depends on what their positions require of them. Some give orders, others carry them out. The ones who actually perform the material functions always belong to less advanced orders."*

539. Are certain natural phenomena—storms, for example—the work of a single spirit or a group of spirits?

▲ *"A team of spirits may directly influence such a phenomenon."*

540. Do these spirits act freely, with knowledge and intention; or instinctively, from an unreasoning impulse?

▲ *"Some act in one way, some in the other. You might compare their activity to the trillions of marine polyps that build up coral reefs in the ocean. Can anyone believe there is no providential intention in this transformative process, that it is not a vital part of the planet's general harmony? Yet, simply by providing for their own material wants and without any awareness that they are God's instruments, animals of the lowest degree accomplish this feat. In the same way, even the least advanced spirits are useful to the general whole. In the time before they acquire full consciousness of their action and free will, they are assigned to take part in the development of the various departments of nature, to produce phenomena of which they are unwitting agents. They begin by carrying out the orders of their superiors. Subsequently, with the evolution of their intelligence, they come to take responsibility for tasks themselves. In similar fashion, they will come one day to direct developments in the spiritual realm. In this manner everything in nature is linked together, from the most primitive atom to the archangel—who, incidentally, also began existence as an atom. It is an admirable law of harmony, which your mind is still too narrow to grasp in all its complexity."*

In Time of War

541. In a battle, do spirits help and support each side?

▲ *"Yes. And they uphold the courage of each side."*

Discussion: The ancients represented gods as taking part in battles alongside humans. These gods were nothing more than allegorical representations of spirits.

542. In war, right can only be on one side. How can spirits, then, support the wrong side?

▲ *"As you know very well, there are spirits who pursue conflict and destruction exclusively. For them, war is war. They don't care whether the cause is just or unjust."*

543. Can spirits influence a general in planning a campaign?

▲ *"Undoubtedly spirits may use their influence to this end, just as they can influence all human ideas and plans."*

544. Could hostile spirits suggest poor strategies that will cause a general to be defeated?

▲ *"Yes. But the general does have free will, doesn't he? If he is incapable of distinguishing between a good idea and a bad one, he must, in the end, pay the consequences. In this case, he would be more fit to obey than command."*

545. Is a general ever guided by second-sight—an intuitive perception that shows him the result of his strategy beforehand?

▲ *"In the case of a military genius, this kind of intuition—inspiration, as it is called—will give him a sort of inner certainty. This intuition may also come from spirits' suggestions."*

546. In the heat of battle, what becomes of the spirits of soldiers who are killed?

Do they continue to take an interest in the struggle after death?

▲ *"Some do; others withdraw."*

Discussion: As in all other cases of violent death, the spirit of a soldier who is killed in battle experiences bewilderment during the first few moments. The spirit does not realize that its body is dead and still believes itself to be taking part in the action. Only gradually does the reality of the situation set in.

547. Do the spirits of those who fought against each other in life still regard each other as enemies after death? Are they still enraged with each other?

▲ *"Under these circumstances, a spirit is rarely calm. For a brief time, it may still be roused up against the enemy and might even pursue him. But as the spirit regains awareness, it sees that its animosity no longer serves any purpose. Depending on its character, however, it may retain traces of hostility for a time."*

—Is it still aware of the din of battle?

▲ *"Yes, perfectly."*

548. While a spirit is coolly watching a battle, does it witness the separation of the souls from the bodies of fallen combatants? How does this phenomenon affect it?

▲ *"Very few deaths are completely instantaneous. In most cases, the spirit whose body has just been mortally wounded is not aware of the condition for some time. As it begins to realize its new situation, it tries to move about and extricate itself from the dead body. After a short time, the sight of its dead body becomes an accepted fact. With the release from the body, the spirit gradually starts to realize its new reality. For an uninvolved observer the process appears altogether natural—the physical body is lifeless, the seat of life is now in the spirit."*

Pacts with Spirits

549. Is it true that we can enter into pacts with evil spirits?

▲ *"No. There are no such pacts. But there is empathy between base human natures and vile spirits. Let us say, for example, that you want to harm your neighbor but don't know how to go about it. One solution, you decide, is to ask for help from some of the ill-meaning spirits who, like you, only want to do wrong and who, in return for the help they give you, expect you to help them with their own sorry schemes. Of course, your neighbor may be able to dispel this conspiracy by summoning spiritual help and through the use of his or her own willpower. But you should understand that the person who wants to do wrong calls up ill-meaning spirits by this desire alone. And if those spirits actually lend assistance, the person involved invariably finds*

*him or herself obliged to serve them as a repayment. What you call a 'pact,'
then, consists simply in the reciprocity of assistance in wrong-doing."*

Discussion: Subjection to wrong-doing spirits comes from yielding to
                the corrupting thoughts they suggest—not from "an agree-
                ment" between individuals and those spirits. The idea of a
                pact, as it is commonly understood, is a figurative repre-
                sentation of the affinity between similar incarnate and dis-
                carnate spirits.

550. How should we interpret the fantastic legends of persons who sell their souls
to Satan in order to obtain certain favors?

▲ *"Every fable contains a teaching and a moral. The mistake is to take fables
literally. The one you have just referred to is an allegory, and can be
explained as follows. People who call forth wrong-doing spirits to help them
achieve wealth, fame or any other favor, rebel against Providence. They abandon their own life-plan, seeking to avoid the learning experiences they were
to have undergone in the earthly life. They will, needless to say, reap the consequences of this rebellion in the future. We do not mean that their souls will
be condemned to misery forever. The fact remains, however, that, instead of
detaching themselves from matter, they have plunged deeper and deeper into
it. Consequently, in the spirit-world they will experience pain of conscience
until they have redressed their ill-fated choices through new trials that will,
more than likely, be even harder and more distressing than the ones they
rebelled against. But in the here-and-now, their self-indulgence brings these
individuals into a coalition with unprincipled spirits and creates between
them a tacit agreement that will, if unbroken, lead to their moral ruin.
Fortunately, if they have a firm determination to do so, it is always possible
for them to break away with the help of good spirits."*

Occult Powers, Charms

551. Can an ill-natured person, who can command the help of a wrong-doing spirit, cause harm to his or her neighbor?

▲ *"No, God would not permit it."*

552. What should we think about the belief in the power of some persons to cast
spells over others?

▲ *"Certain people possess a very strong suggestive power. If their own natures
are bad, they may well use this power for injurious ends, in which case they
may be seconded by other ill-meaning spirits. But let us caution you: do not
believe in any pretended magical power. It exists only in the imagination of
the superstitious, who are unaware of nature's true laws. The 'facts' that
have been produced to prove the existence of this pretended power actually*

derive from imperfectly observed and, above all, imperfectly understood natural causes."

553. Some people claim to be able to control the wills of spirits through formulas and ritual acts. What is the effect of these practices?

▲ *"Those who claim so in good faith lack real knowledge and expose themselves to ridicule. On the other hand, if they are knowingly making a false claim, they are rogues and deserve to be held accountable for their misrepresentations. All such formulas are mere hokum. There is no 'sacramental word,' no cabalistic sign, no talisman, that has any power over spirits. Spirits are attracted by thoughts, not meaningless sounds or material objects."*

—Haven't spirits sometimes dictated cabalistic formulas?

▲ *"Yes. There are spirits who will give you strange signs and words and prescribe certain acts, and with these you may be able to perform what you call 'conjurations.' But you can be quite sure that these spirits are simply having fun at your expense. They amuse themselves with your credulity."*

554. Isn't it possible that someone's confidence in a talisman will attract a spirit? In this case, after all, the person's thought is the real agent of action whereas the talisman acts only as a sign that helps concentrate and direct the thought.

▲ *"This is quite possible. But the kind of spirit attracted in this way will depend very much on the purity of intention and the loftiness of attitude of the person attracting it. And it is rare that someone who is naive enough to believe in the power of a talisman is not motivated by material gain rather than spiritual progress. In any event, these practices suggest a pettiness of character and a weakness of mind that naturally open the door to imperfect and mocking spirits."*

555. What meaning should we give to the term "sorcerer"?

▲ *"When they are honest, those whom people call sorcerers or shamans are persons gifted with exceptional abilities—for example, healing power or clairvoyance. When they use these powers to do things you do not understand, you conclude that they have supernatural powers. Many of your learned scholars have passed for sorcerers in the eyes of the unenlightened."*

Discussion: The Spiritist Doctrine and the study of magnetism[5] have given us the keys to a whole class of phenomena around which superstitious minds have woven fantastic theories.

....

5 *Translator's note: Magnetism: Here it refers to the human power to induce a hypnotic state. This force was believed to be at the base of mesmeric phenomena, precursor of modern hypnotism. Nineteenth-Century scientific opinions about the cause of the phenomena ranged from 'the existence of an animal emanation or nerveforce' (J.P.F. Deluze) to 'mental suggestion' (Abbe Faria). Interestingly enough, the modern notion of 'energy fields' may bring scientific acceptance to the concept of sharing and transfer of energy between living beings.*

The knowledge resulting from the convergence of these two areas explains the true mechanisms and causes of such phenomena, explanations that are the best safeguard against credulity. This knowledge separates what is possible within the laws of nature from all that stems from popular myth.

556. Do some persons really have the gift of healing by the laying on of hands?

▲ *"Again, the power to heal depends on the healer's purity of intention and desire to do good—in which case, good spirits will come to the healer's aid. But be on your guard. People who are too credulous, too enthusiastic, tend to find the marvelous in the simplest and most natural occurrences. And in instances like healing, they will exaggerate the facts. You should also be wary, in listening to these healing testimonials, of people who have something to gain by working on the credulity of others."*

Blessings and Curses

557. Do blessings and curses actually draw down good and evil on the people who receive them?

▲ *"God does not listen to curses. Nonetheless, the person who utters a curse is guilty before Divine Justice. But since on Earth you are continuously subject to two opposing influences, good and evil, a curse may have a momentary influence, though this does not occur outside of the Divine Plan. In fact, this influence is allowed to occur as a further trial for the person who is the curse's object. Curses are usually bestowed on wrong-doers and blessings on the good. But neither blessings nor curses can ever turn aside Justice. Blessings are more likely to take effect when the person leads an upright life, curses when a person lives a wicked life."*

OCCUPATIONS AND MISSIONS OF SPIRITS

558. Spirits strive for self-improvement. Do they do anything else?

▲ *"As trusted workers, they execute the will of God and so contribute to the universal harmony. Life in the spiritual realm is a continuing occupation. But because spirits have no physical bodies to grow tired and no wants to satisfy, that life is not the arduous undertaking it is on Earth."*

559. Do imperfect spirits also have a useful role in the universe?

▲ *"All spirits have duties to perform. Just like the designing architect, the humblest bricklayer has a part to play in the construction of a building."*[1]

560. Does each spirit have specific responsibilities?

▲ *"As Ecclesiastes says, 'for everything there is a season and a time.'*[2] *Spirits are fulfilling their destinies in the world today as they have fulfilled them in other times and as they will continue to do in the future. Each spirit must acquire knowledge and experience by living and operating in the many different realms in the universe."*

561. Is the work spirits do permanent for each of them, and are particular kinds of work exclusive to certain spirit orders?

▲ *"Spirits attain knowledge and ability through an evolutionary process. No one receives knowledge without effort. This is the Divine program."*

· ·

1 See question 540 on the role of less advanced spirits in the production of natural phenomena.

· ·

2 Translator's Note: Ecclesiastes 3:1.

Discussion: Likewise, no human being ever becomes expert in a field
                without first acquiring a thorough knowledge of all its
                details and operations.

562. Are the spirits of the higher orders, who have acquired all possible knowledge, in a state of absolute rest; or do they also have occupations?

▲ *"Do you expect these spirits to remain idle throughout Eternity? That would be everlasting torture!"*

—What is the nature of their work?

▲ *"They interpret and communicate God's will throughout the universe and ensure that it is carried out."*

563. Are the occupations of spirits carried on without interruption?

▲ *"If you consider the fact that they live by thought and that their thinking is always active, then, yes—their occupations are continuous. But don't make the mistake of comparing spirit activities with human ones. Because of their commitment to serving others, they find their work a source of delight."*

—This is true for good spirits. Is it the same for less evolved ones?

▲ *"These spirits have occupations suitable to their nature. Would you give tasks intended for a knowledgeable and experienced person to an unseasoned beginner?"*

564. Are there idle spirits who do no useful work?

▲ *"Yes. But the situation depends on their level of awareness, and the idleness is always temporary. There are spirits, just as there are human beings, who live for themselves. Eventually, though, they feel the need for activity and find their happiness in becoming useful. We refer here, it is important to note, only to spirits who have self awareness, which is not the case of spirits in the initial stages of evolution."*

565. Do spirits analyze our works of art? Do these works interest them?

▲ *"They examine everything that might lead to spiritual improvement."*

566. Does a spirit who excelled in a particular area while incarnate—a painter or an architect, for example—continue to show a special interest in that area in the spirit-world?

▲ *"Ultimately, the spirit is interested in everything that enables it to help foster the advancement of humankind. Besides, if a spirit had one particular interest in one incarnation, it might have had many others in previous ones. A pure, well-rounded spirit must go through a variety of experiences so that it is hard to pinpoint its particular area of expertise. You should consider, too, that a field that is seen as sublime on Earth may seem like child's play in the higher spiritual planes; in these planes, there are areas of knowledge that are so advanced they have no counterpart in your realm. Thus, generally speak-*

ing, advanced spirits will interest themselves in any activity that promotes human progress."

—This is the case with more advanced spirits. Is it the same with the more ordinary spirits of Earth?

▲ *"No, their interests are more similar to yours because their outlook is narrow."*

567. Do spirits take part in our activities and pastimes?

▲ *"The less advanced ones do. They are around you and, depending on their natures, often play an active role in influencing your pursuits. They excite or moderate your desires and enthusiasms and in this way push you into different life experiences."*

Discussion: Spirits pay attention to things on Earth as their degree of perfection leads them. More advanced spirits are concerned only with matters that will assist human evolution; less advanced ones interest themselves in things that are still connected to their recent material memories and ideas.

568. Do spirits who have missions accomplish them while incarnate or as free spirits?

▲ *"Both situations may occur."*

569. What kinds of missions would free spirits have?

▲ *"They are so varied that it would be impossible to describe them, and the human mind would not understand many of them. Spirits execute the plan of God. It is impossible for humans to comprehend all of God's designs."*

Discussion: Whether incarnate or not, spirits on missions always have goodness as their aim. They are in charge of helping humankind progress, preparing the way for forthcoming events, and watching over their occurrence. Some spirits have specific missions: assisting the sick, the dying, and the afflicted. Others act as guardian angels, guiding their wards by mentally conveying good thoughts. There are as many missions as there are matters to be overseen in the physical as well as the spiritual realm. In the end, the spirit advances according to the manner in which it has fulfilled its mission.

570. Are spirits always conscious of the missions they are to carry out?

▲ *"No. Some spirits are blind instruments. Others know their objectives very well."*

571. Do only elevated spirits carry out missions?

▲ *"The importance of a mission is related to the capacity and evolution of a spirit. On Earth, a military courier may deliver important information. By doing so, he or she fulfills a special mission. But it is not a mission a general would ever think of undertaking."*

572. Is a mission imposed on a spirit, or does it choose the mission freely?

▲ *"The spirit requests the mission and is happy when it is granted."*

—Do several spirits ever ask for the same mission?

▲ *"Yes. There are frequently several candidates. Not all of them, of course, can be accepted."*

573. What would be the mission of an incarnate spirit?

▲ *"To instruct and help human beings in their progress, and to improve their institutions directly and materially. These missions are more or less general and important: the farmer fulfills a mission no less significant than the ruler's or the scholar's. Everything in nature is interconnected. Moreover, at the same time the spirit is evolving through the incarnation process, it cooperates in the fulfillment of God's plan. Each one of you has a mission on this planet since all of you can be useful for something."*

574. What is the mission of the intentionally idle on Earth?

▲ *"These people are to be pitied for their poor judgment. They will one day account for their time. Usually they start experiencing the results of their unwise lifestyle in this very life by the disgust and boredom they feel."*

—Since these people were given a choice, why did they prefer a lifestyle that could benefit no one?

▲ *"Among spirits, just as among humans, there are some who reject a life of usefulness and work. God allows this to happen, knowing that the spirits will eventually understand the burden of their uselessness and will be the first to ask for an opportunity to make up for lost time. It may also happen that a spirit chooses a more useful life but, once incarnate, strays from it under the influence of indolent beings. As a result, it feels incapable of being useful."*

575. The common occupations seem to be more in the nature of day-to-day tasks than missions. As we understand the word, mission refers to something more inclusive and less personal. Given this point of view, how can we recognize a person who has a mission on Earth?

▲ *"You can identify individuals who have missions by the greatness of their acts and the progress toward which they lead humanity."*

576. Are people with important missions assigned the mission before birth, and are they consciously aware of it in life?

▲ *"Sometimes they are aware, though often they ignore it. Once on Earth, they will have a vague sense that they are intended to do something. Gradually their missions will become clear to them, as the proper circumstances arise.*

God will lead them toward the necessary ways and means that will allow them to carry their missions out."

577. Are a person's good works always determined by a previously established mission, or can there be unplanned missions?

▲ *"Not all human works result from previously established missions. Sometimes you may be the instrument that a spirit uses to perform a task it considers particularly useful. You become partners in the mission. For example, a spirit sees the need to write a book that it would have written on its own if incarnate. Accordingly, it looks for a willing writer likely to understand its thoughts and ideas, mentally suggests the plan of the book, and helps the writer produce it. The writer might not have come to Earth with the mission of writing the book but ends up doing it anyway. The same thing happens with certain works of art, discoveries, and inventions. We should also mention that, during sleep, a person may visit with its spirit partner, and together they will decide on how their mutual tasks will be executed."*

578. Can a spirit fail in its mission through its own fault?

▲ *"Yes, but this is unlikely among those of higher orders."*

—What happens in that case?

▲ *"The spirit will have to start the mission all over again. It may also have the additional burden, in a new incarnation, of repairing any wrongs it may have done."*

579. How can God, who assigns all missions, give one to a spirit who might fail?

▲ *"God is fully aware of a spirit's potential for carrying out a given mission. A critical mission is only entrusted to a spirit qualified to fulfill it. You should remember that God, unlike you, has knowledge of the future."*

580. Does the spirit who is assigned a mission experience the same apprehension as the spirit who undertakes a trial of purification?

▲ *"No. The former spirit has the confidence that comes from prior accomplishment."*

581. Among those individuals of superior knowledge who impact human progress, some impart wrong ideas and misconceived notions to us. In what light should we regard these persons?

▲ *"As people who have fooled themselves, who have not lived up to the task they were supposed to carry out. Nonetheless, always take circumstances into account. People of great ability necessarily speak to their own time. A teaching that seems incorrect or foolish in a later era may have been quite sufficient for the era that first heard it."*

582. Can parenthood be considered a mission?

▲ *"Absolutely. It is a major responsibility that is more important to the parents' future than they might suppose. God places a child under the care of parents so that they can help it become a good person. To start with, a child has a fragile and delicate constitution just so that it will better assimilate the good qualities the parents are to nurture in him or her. Unfortunately, some people pay more attention to the trees in their backyards than to their children. They would rather look after their apples and pears than watch over their children's characters. But when a child fails in life as a result of this kind of neglect, the parents are held responsible. The sufferings of that child will fall on them, too—a penalty for not doing what they should have to help the child progress."*

583. When a child takes the wrong road despite the dedication of good parents, are they still held responsible?

▲ *"No. As a matter of fact, the more vicious the disposition of the child the greater is the parents' merit for turning the child away from wrong."*

—If a child, despite neglect and bad examples on the part of the parents, develops in a positive direction, do the parents have any credit for it?

▲ *"God is fair."*

584. Often a military commander or a conqueror becomes blinded by his personal motives and will do anything to attain his objectives, even to the point of bringing about widespread calamity. How should we understand the mission of such persons?

▲ *"Although his actions are unjustified, war calamities may become a means for the fulfillment of higher plans. Sometimes, paradoxically, they serve to accelerate a people's progress."*

—Will this kind of person gain from any beneficial results that the calamities might create?

▲ *"Each of you is rewarded for your good works and for the uprightness of your intentions."*

Discussion: The occupations of incarnate spirits reflect their physical condition. In the spirit-world, however, spirits have occupations that are suited to their degree of advancement. Some visit other planes where they study and prepare themselves for new incarnations. Others, more evolved, occupy themselves with the progress of humankind— directing events, inspiring uplifting thoughts, and helping capable individuals further human knowledge and growth. Others have the specific task of watching over individuals, families, social groups, cities, and countries: these are the guardian angels, protecting spirits, and familiar spirits. Other spirits help maintain the natural order. Less advanced spirits, who constitute the great mass, involve themselves in our trivial occupations and pastimes.

Imperfect spirits eagerly await the opportunity to advance, and this waiting is often a source of anguish. Often their desire to do harm is a reaction to the frustration of not yet enjoying the happiness of more advanced spirits.

CHAPTER

XV

THE THREE KINGDOMS

The Mineral and Plant Kingdoms

585. Some scientists divide the natural world into three kingdoms: the mineral, the vegetable, and the animal (some naturalists would add a fourth, the human). Others divide it into two classes—organic and inorganic. Which is preferable?

▲ *"They are equally good. As to which is more appropriate, it all depends on your point of view. If you look at nature in its material aspect, there are only organic and inorganic existences. Considered from a philosophical standpoint there are evidently four classes."*

Discussion: These four classes are distinguished by well-marked characteristics, although at their extremes they merge into each other. Inert matter, which constitutes the mineral kingdom, possesses only mechanical force. Plants, composed of matter, are endowed with vitality. Animals, composed of matter and endowed with vitality, also have instinctive intelligence, which, though limited in scope, gives them awareness of their existence and individuality. Human beings, who possess everything that is found in plants and animals, rise above both because of their special intelligence, which gives them an awareness of the future, the perception of non-material things, and the knowledge of God.

586. Are plants conscious of their existence?

▲ *"No, they have only organic life and do not think."*

587. Do plants feel sensations? Do they suffer when they are mutilated?

▲ *"Plants receive physical impressions; they do not feel pain."*

588. Is the force that attracts plants toward each other independent of will?

▲ *"Yes, since they do not think and, accordingly, have no will."*

589. Some plants—for example, the mimosa[1] and the Venus fly trap—move in ways that indicate great sensitiveness and, in some cases, a sort of will. The Venus fly trap seizes the fly that lights on it, sucks out its juices, and even seems to set a snare in order to kill it. But do these plants really think or have a will of their own? Are they an intermediate category between the vegetable and animal kingdoms?

▲ *"Everything in nature is differentiated, but transitional stages link all beings together. Plants do not think and consequently have no will. But neither does the oyster that opens its shell think, nor any of the other zoophytes.[2] They have only a blind natural instinct."*

Discussion: The human organism furnishes similar examples of movements that take place without our willing them—e.g., the activity of our digestive and circulatory organs. For instance, the pylorus[3] closes itself on contact with certain substances, as if to refuse them passage. It is the same in the plant kingdom with the sensitive plant, the movements of which do not necessarily imply thought on the part of the plant, much less will.

590. Do plants, like animals, have an instinct for self-preservation, i.e., a sort of impulse to seek what is useful and avoid what is harmful?

▲ *"You can call it instinct, if you like. It depends on your definition of the word. When you see two particles bond in a chemical reaction, it is because they suit one another. There is a chemical affinity between them.[4] But you do not call that instinct."*

591. Are plants more perfect in nature on more advanced worlds, as other beings are?

▲ *"Everything on those planets is more perfect. Still, on these worlds plants are always plants, animals always animals, humans always humans."*

∙∙∙∙∙∙∙∙∙∙∙∙∙∙∙∙∙∙∙∙∙∙∙∙∙∙∙∙∙

1 *Translator's Note:* Mimosa pudica: *Also called the sensitive plant, the mimosa is a small, tropical shrub native to Brazil. It has fernlike leaves that quickly fold together if touched and then slowly resume their original form.*

∙∙∙∙∙∙∙∙∙∙∙∙∙∙∙∙∙∙∙∙∙∙∙∙∙∙∙∙∙

2 *Translator's Note: A zoophyte is an invertebrate animal such as a sea anemone or sponge that remains attached to a surface and superficially resembles a plant.*

∙∙∙∙∙∙∙∙∙∙∙∙∙∙∙∙∙∙∙∙∙∙∙∙∙∙∙∙∙

3 *Translator's Note: The pylorus is the opening from the stomach into the duodenum, controlled by a strong sphincter muscle.*

∙∙∙∙∙∙∙∙∙∙∙∙∙∙∙∙∙∙∙∙∙∙∙∙∙∙∙∙∙

4 *Translator's Note: Chemical affinity: the force by which atoms are held together in chemical compounds.*

Animal and Human Domains

592. When we compare the intelligence of humans and animals, it is difficult at times to draw a clear line of separation between them. In several well-known respects, some animals are notoriously superior to humans. Can we ever distinguish between them with any precision?

▲ *"Your scientists are still far apart on this issue. Some of them regard the human simply as a type of animal; others are equally sure that the animal has human qualities, with a difference of degree only. They are all wrong. Humans are beings apart, capable of sinking very low or rising very high. Physically, they are like the animals, though less well provided for: nature has given animals everything they need, while humans, using their intelligence, must see to their own needs. Like animals, too, humans have bodies that are subject to destruction. But unlike an animal, a human has a spirit with a destiny, and humans alone, among beings in the material world, are aware of that destiny. That is why it is so painful to see humans debase themselves and fall below the level of animals. You must learn to elevate your nature. Recognize that in possessing the knowledge of the existence of God, you are superior to all other creatures on Earth."*

593. Do animals act only from instinct?

▲ *"This, again, is mere theory. It is very true that instinct predominates in most animals. But some of them act with an apparent will of their own. This is a type of intelligence, even if its range is narrow."*

Discussion: No one who has ever observed animals will deny that some of them possess, in addition to instinct, the ability to perform complex behaviors in a manner that indicates intention and an awareness of their circumstances. This is intelligence of a sort.

The operation of this intelligence, however, is bound up almost wholly with self-preservation and the satisfaction of physical needs. The skills of animals, admirable as we find some of them, are not progressive. Animal behavior is set within constant, repeating patterns, and their activities cannot change. A young bird, isolated from the rest of its species, will build its nest in exactly the same way as its parents, without ever having been taught by them. Some animals are, we know, capable of being trained. But their mental development, if we can so describe it, falls within very narrow limits. It is almost entirely the result of human action producing reflexive behaviors in beings that lack true learning capacity. Furthermore, since this training is artificial, it is temporary and purely individual. Once the animal is left alone, it disappears; and the animal reverts to its natural state.

594. Do animals have a language?

▲ *"If you mean a language formed by syllables and words, no. But if you mean a method of communication among themselves, yes. They say much more to each other than you imagine. But this 'language' is limited, like their ideas, to their bodily wants."*

—Some animals lack the ability to produce sounds. Does an animal of this kind lack language?

▲ *"They understand each other by other means. You communicate in other ways than through speech, don't you? And what about persons who are mute? They communicate, do they not? Well, just like you, animals live their lives in relationship to each other. As a result, they have their own means of imparting information and expressing sensations. The privilege of language is by no means exclusive to humans. Do you really think that fish, for instance, have no communicative bond? Still, the language of animals is instinctive, limited to the scope of their wants and perceptions. Yours, on the other hand, is perfectible; it lends itself to all the ideas of which your intelligence makes you capable."*

Discussion: It is evident that fish, swimming upstream in schools, must at some level have a common realization of their situation and must exchange information that allows them to behave in a way that assures the welfare of the school. Their vision may be acute enough for them to signal each other. Or water itself may act as a medium for transmitting vibrations that are emitted from their bodies. But whatever the case, they have some means of communicating, as do all animals that make no audible sound but act in concert. It should not seem so strange, then, that spirits can communicate among themselves without having recourse to speech.[5]

595. Do animals act on their free will?

▲ *"They are not the mere machines you suppose them to be. But their freedom of action is limited to their needs and cannot be compared to human freedom. They are inferior to humans precisely because their freedom is restricted to the acts of their material life."*

596. Certain animals have the ability to imitate human speech. Why is this ability found among birds rather than, for instance, among apes? Apes resemble us far more, anatomically.

....

5 *See question 282 on communication among spirits.*

▲ *"This results, in some bird species, from the structure of the vocal chords, aided by the mimetic instinct. These birds imitate human speech, just as the ape imitates your gestures."*

597. Since animals have an intelligence that gives them a degree of free action, do they have a principle independent of matter?

▲ *"Yes. And it survives their bodies."*

—Is this principle a soul, like a human soul?

▲ *"Call it a 'soul' if you like. It depends on what you mean by the word. Still, it is inferior to the human soul. There is as great a difference between the 'soul' of an animal and that of a human being as there is between the soul of a human being and God."*

598. After death does the 'soul' of an animal keep its individuality and its self-consciousness?

▲ *"It preserves its individuality but not an awareness of its identity."*

599. Can the 'soul' of an animal choose to be incarnated in one kind of animal rather than another?

▲ *"No. It does not possess free will."*

600. Given that the 'soul' of the animal survives its body, is it in a transient state after death, like the human soul?

▲ *"It is in a sense because it is not united to a body. But its state does not compare with a spirit's. The spirit is a being who thinks, has self-consciousness, acts of its own free will. In the case of an animal, the 'soul' is classed, after its death, by the spirits charged with that work. It is almost immediately reincarnated and does not have the opportunity to connect with other beings."*

601. Do animals follow a law of progress like humans?

▲ *"Yes. This is why on more evolved planets, where humans are further advanced, the animals are, too. They also have a more developed means of communication. But even on these planets they are always inferior to humans and subject to them. They are, on such planets, intelligent attendants."*

Discussion: There is nothing unreasonable in this last statement. Suppose that our most intelligent animals—e.g., the dog, the elephant, the horse—had bodies designed for manual labor. Under human direction, they could do almost anything.

602. Do animals progress, like human beings, through their wills, or through the force of events?

▲ *"Through the force of events. This is why there are no trials of purification for them."*

603. Do animals on more evolved planets have a knowledge of God?

▲ *"No. The human is a god for them, just as spirits were formerly gods for you."*

604. So even advanced animals on more evolved planets are always inferior to humans. But God, it seems, has created here beings that are condemned to a state of perpetual inferiority. Isn't this arrangement contrary to the unity of design and progress evident in God's other work?

▲ *"Everything in nature is linked together by a sequential chain. As yet, you cannot grasp these connections, and thus ideas arise from them that seem contradictory to you. Occasionally you might catch a glimmering of the truth by an effort of intelligence. But until you have fully developed your intellectual abilities, and freed yourself from self-centeredness and unawareness, you will not actually be able to see God's work clearly but only through a narrow and distorting lens. God, you should realize, cannot be self-contradictory. Everything in nature is harmonized by the operation of general laws that do not deviate from the sublime wisdom of the Divine."*

—Intelligence, then, is a common property and the point of contact between human and animal souls?

▲ *"Yes. But animal intelligence is concerned only with material life. Human intelligence gives your life a moral basis."*

605. When we think of all the points of contact between humans and animals, we might conclude that we actually have two souls: an animal and a spiritual one. Without the spiritual soul, we would continue to live, but we would only have animal life. (In other words, animals are like us, minus the spiritual soul.) Our good and bad instincts, then, may primarily reflect the predominance of one kind of soul over the other. Is this a correct view?

▲ *"No. Human beings have only one soul. But the body has instincts, and accordingly your species alone has a double nature—one animal, the other spiritual. Through the body you participate in the instinctual life of the animals; through the soul you participate in the non-material life of spirits."*

—Thus, besides our own imperfections, of which we must rid ourselves, we also have to struggle, as spirits, against the influence of matter?

▲ *"Yes, the less advanced a spirit is, the tighter the bonds are that unite it with matter. This is inevitable. The human being has a single soul; and the souls of animals and humans are distinct, so that the one soul cannot give life to a body created for the other. But, remember. If you do not have an animal 'soul' per se, you do have a body; and the body often drags you down to the animal level. It, like the animal, is endowed with vitality and instincts geared to the pursuit of its immediate needs."*

Discussion: A spirit, in incarnating in a human body, brings to that body the intellectual and moral essence that makes it superior to the animals. But the dual nature of humans—animal and spiritual—is the source of two complex categories of drives: those having their source in the animal nature, and those proceeding from the spirit itself. The less evolved the spirit, the greater will be its identification with the physical body, the instrument through which it satisfies its passions. However, as the spirit becomes purified it gradually sheds that identification, gradually frees itself, and rises towards its true destination.

606. Where does the intelligent principle that makes up the animals' particular kind of soul come from?

▲ *"From the universal intelligent element."*

—Then human and animal intelligence come from the same principle?

▲ *"Yes, but in the human it is far more developed."*

607. You have said that the human soul, at its origin, is in a state similar to the infant's, that its intelligence is only beginning to unfold.[6] Where does the soul complete this earliest phase of its career?

▲ *"In a series of lives prior to the period of human development."*

—Do you mean that the soul was once the intelligent principle of less advanced species?

▲ *"As we have said, everything in nature is linked together and tends toward unity. It is in these less evolved beings that the intelligent principle is developed, gradually individualized, and made ready for the human realm. And it is through its subjection to this preparatory process—which is akin to germination—that the principle undergoes a transformation and becomes spirit. At the transforming moment each spirit begins its period as part of humanity, having a sense of the future, the power to distinguish between right and wrong, and responsibility for its individual acts. The development is similar to your own human one: after infancy comes childhood, then youth, adolescence, and finally adulthood.*

"Is this beginning in any form demeaning to you? Is the greatest genius humiliated by having been a shapeless fetus in his or her mother's womb? Actually, if anything ought to humiliate the genius, it is how insignificant humans are in the scale of being and how powerless any human is to plumb the depths and wisdom of Divine designs and laws. Recognize the greatness of God in this admirable harmony. It connects everything in nature. To think that God could have made anything without a purpose and created intelligent beings without a future is an affront to God's all-embracing goodness."

—Does the human phase of the spirit begin on our Earth?

....

6 *The spirit-instructors made this statement in the answer to question 190.*

▲ *"Earth is not the point where the spirit first incarnates as a human being. In general, the human period begins on less developed planets. This is not, however, an absolute rule, and in certain special conditions a spirit may start on Earth from the outset. But, again, such situations are the exception rather than the rule."*

608. After death, does the spirit have any awareness of its existences prior to its human period?

▲ *"No. Its life as spirit did not start on Earth. Actually, it can hardly recall its earliest human lives, just as you no longer remember your earliest days as an infant, still less your existence in the womb. This is why spirits tell you that they do not know how they began."*[7]

609. Once a spirit enters on its human period does it retain any traces of what it has previously been—that is to say, of where it was during its pre-human period?

▲ *"It depends on the distance that separates the two periods and the progress the spirit has made. For a few generations there might be a reflex of the primitive state, because nothing in nature ever takes place through an abrupt transition. There are always links that unite the extremities in the chain of beings or events. But as free will develops, these traces disappear. The reason that the first steps toward progress are so slow in the first place is that the will plays no part. But as the spirit arrives at greater self-awareness, the pace of progress picks up."*

610. Are the spirits who say that humans are beings apart from the rest of creation wrong?

▲ *"No, but the question is not adequately developed. There are things that can only be known at their appointed time. In reality, the human is a being apart—you have qualities that distinguish you from all others, and you have a separate destiny. The human species is the one that has been chosen for the incarnation of beings who are capable of knowing God."*[8]

Metempsychosis

611. Is the common origin of the intelligent principle of living beings a vindication of the doctrine of metempsychosis?[9]

....

7 *The spirits' limited knowledge of their own origin is discussed in question 78.*

....

8 *Translators' Note: The evolution of animal forms on earth, as determined by Darwin, follows a parallel principle at the spiritual level. The "rudimentary intelligent principle" of the animal will inhabit forms successively more developed until it has gathered all the elements to enter the stage of human "spirit." Starting with the most rudimentary human experiences, it will gradually, and over millennia, reach the level of the civilized person, continuing from there into the infinite.*

....

9 *Translator's Note. Metempsychosis - see definition in question 222.*

▲ *"Two things can have the same origin but not resemble each other later on; a tree—with its leaves, flowers, and fruit—is unrecognizable in the nucleus of a seed. From the moment the intelligent principle becomes developed enough to become a spirit and enter on its human phase, it no longer has any connection with its primitive state. It no more has the 'soul' of a beast than a tree has the soul of a seed. Of the animal only the body remains, and the biological instincts including the instinct of self-preservation. You cannot say, therefore, that a particular person is the incarnation of such and such an animal. As it is commonly understood, the doctrine of metempsychosis is untrue."*

612. Can a spirit that has animated a human body be incarnated in an animal?

▲ *"No. This kind of incarnation would be a retrograde movement, and a spirit never goes backward in its development. The river does not flow back to its source."*[10]

613. But even though the doctrine of metempsychosis is wrong, couldn't it result from an intuitive memory of the different phases of human existence?

▲ *"Many beliefs, including metempsychosis, share in this memory. But, as with many of their intuitive ideas, humans have perverted this one."*

Discussion: If we take metempsychosis to mean the progress of the soul from a lower to a higher state (i.e., to indicate spiritual transformation), the doctrine is true. It becomes false the moment we assume that it refers to an animal soul transmigrating directly into a human being and vice versa. This idea implies a retrograde movement on the part of the human, an impossibility. Also, the fact that different species cannot intermix genetically indicates that they belong to orders of beings that cannot be assimilated—a fact that reflects a difference in the "sparks" that animate them. For if one spirit could animate both human and animal, we would naturally expect the identity established between the two to reveal itself through sexual reproduction. More importantly, reincarnation as now taught by spirits is founded on the upward movement of nature and on the progress of humans within their own species. This detracts not one jot from our dignity: we are demeaned only when we make corrupt use of the abilities God gave us to help us advance. Still, the antiquity and universality of the doctrine of metempsychosis, along with the large number of eminent people who have professed it, proves

....

10 *The answer to question 118 reiterates this point.*

that the principle of reincarnation has its roots in nature itself. This fact, far from diminishing the likelihood of truth in reincarnation, must be regarded as constituting a strong argument in its favor.

The point at which spirits begin their existence is one of those issues that refers back to the origin of things and the hidden designs of God. As human beings we will never understand these matters completely. But we do often hypothesize about them, devising in explanation theoretical systems that may or may not approach the truth. Like us, spirits, who are far from knowing everything themselves, have their own individual opinions, which may agree more or less with reality.

Spirits, then, do not think alike when it comes to the links between the human and animal species. According to some, a spirit arrives at the human period only after having developed (as a spirit) and become individualized through incarnation in the different kingdoms of creation. According to others, the human spirit always belonged to the human race, without passing upward through the orders of the animal kingdom. The former hypothesis has the advantage of establishing a greater purpose for the animals who form the links of the chain that will end with thinking beings. The latter theory puts more emphasis on a special separate status for the human race;[11] it can be summarized as follows:

One animal species does not evolve, in a spiritual sense, from another. Accordingly, the "soul" of the oyster will never evolve into more complex organisms (species), be they a fish, bird, quadruped, or human. Each species is a

....

11 *Translator's Note: The wording of this section is somewhat difficult. The reader should keep in mind that the discussion that follows examines one theory of origin that was possibly popular at the time. The many theories about the origin of life are just that, theories—attempts at explaining reality—, since God alone has the final word. The theme of the origin of life is still controversial today, more than one hundred fifty years after Darwin's Theory of Evolution. In America, the number of believers in Creationism, based on the facts of the Bible, is still significant. It is interesting to notice that Alfred Russel Wallace, co-author with Charles Darwin of the modern biological principle of natural selection, was a proponent of the idea that a spiritual element intervened in human evolution. In between the two extremes of the spectrum—natural evolution and creationism—there is the Theistic evolution theory, according to which natural evolution has indeed taken place, but under the guidance of God, not simply as the result of natural forces. The Spiritist conception reflects many of the foundation notions that support the Theistic theory. The Spiritist theory of the origin of life is presented in Allan Kardec's* Genesis.

distinct type, both physically and 'spiritually'. Each individual in a species draws from the universal source the extent of intelligent principle that corresponds to the nature of its organic structure and its role in the natural world. When an animal dies this quantum of intelligent principle returns to its source.

Further, the theory maintains that, while human beings clearly constitute a link in the physical chain of living beings, from a spiritual perspective there is no connection whatsoever between humans and animals. Humans, and humans alone, possess a spirit, the divine spark that animals lack and that gives humans a moral and an intellectual sense. The spirit is the essential element, it pre-exists the physical body and maintain its individuality after death.

According to this theory, the same model would be reproduced in more advanced worlds. There, animals would continue to belong to distinct (fixed) species and have as their purpose to serve incarnated spiritual beings (see question 188). Those animal species would have no relationship with the ones that inhabit our Earth.

In conclusion, it is fair to ask, what is the origin of the spirit? What is its starting point? Is it really formed by the individualizing of the intelligent principle? This is a mystery we presently cannot penetrate. As we have indicated, we can do no more than spin theories. What is certain, what reason and experience both indicate, is the survival of each spirit and the persistence of its individuality. Equally certain is its progression, as well as the fact its happiness depends on its advancing on the path of good. As for the nature of the relationship between the human and animal realms, we repeat that this is, so to speak, truly known only by God, like many other matters that currently add little to our advancement and that we foolishly persist in trying to discover.

PART III
ETHICAL AND MORAL LAWS

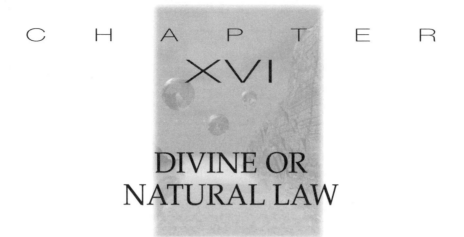

CHAPTER XVI

DIVINE OR
NATURAL LAW

The Characteristics of Natural Law

614. What does the term "natural law" mean?

▲ *"The law of nature is the law of God. It is the only rule that ensures human happiness, since it reveals what you as human beings should and should not do, and since you only suffer when you disobey it."*

615. Is this law eternal?

▲ *"It is as eternal and unchangeable as God."*

616. Can God have given us laws in one era and then revoked them in another?

▲ *"God cannot be mistaken. Humanity has to change its laws periodically because the latter are flawed. But the laws of God are perfect. The harmony that regulates both the material and spiritual realms is based on laws established from all eternity."*

617. What areas of life do the Divine laws cover? Do they refer to anything beyond our moral actions?

▲ *"All the laws of nature are Divine laws. The scientific researcher studies the laws of nature in the physical realm; the righteous person studies the laws of moral living and strives to follow them."*

—Can we, as humans, master both these aspects of natural law?

▲ *"Yes, but a single lifetime is not enough to do it."*

Discussion: If we consider only the distance that separates civilized from barbaric people, we must acknowledge that the few years of the human life span are inadequate for the creation of a perfect being: there is simply too much knowledge to be acquired. This inadequacy becomes even more apparent when, as happens with many individuals, the life span is cut short. Concerning Divine laws, we find that they are of two kinds. Some regulate the movements and relations of matter. These are the physical laws, and their study is the domain of physical science. Other laws concern human relationships—to the self, to God, and to others. These are the moral laws, and they govern both the life of the soul and our conduct and attitude toward others.

618. Are the Divine laws identical everywhere?

▲ *"Reason tells you that they must be adapted to the special needs of the various planets and attuned to the progress of the beings who live on each one."*

The Knowledge of Natural Laws

619. Has God given us the means of knowing the law?

▲ *"All of you may know it, but not all of you will understand it. The ones who understand it best are those who strive to live right, and make their study their reason for being. One day, however, everyone will comprehend the law: that is the destiny toward which progress is inevitably leading you."*

Discussion: In light of this principle, the justice of the various incarnations each of us must undergo is plain: with each new lifetime, our intelligence is more developed and we can more clearly discern what is good and what is bad. On the other hand, if each person had to accomplish everything in a single lifetime, what would be the fate of the many millions of human beings who die every day in the darkness of ignorance, who have not had the opportunity of an education?[1]

620. Does a spirit understand the law of God more clearly before or after an incarnation?

▲ *"Its understanding depends on how evolved it is. After being united with a body, it will preserve an intuitive memory of the law. But the strength of physical drives may lead a person to ignore them."*

621. Where is the law of God written?

▲ *"In the conscience."*

—Since we carry the law of God in our consciences, why was it necessary to reveal it to us?

....

1 *See questions 171 to 222 for an overview of central aspects of reincarnation.*

▲ *"You had forgotten or misunderstood it. God then willed that it should be recalled to your memory."*

622. Has God given the revelation of the law to some individuals as a mission?

▲ *"In every era this mission has been entrusted to particular persons—that is to say, to spirits of higher degree who have incarnated themselves for the purpose of furthering human progress."*

623. But there have been many, isn't it true, who have professed to instruct humanity but have sometimes made mistakes in their reasoning and have, as a result, led us astray?

▲ *"Some individuals, lacking true inspiration from the Supreme Source but full of ambition, have claimed for themselves a mission they never received; and undoubtedly these persons have led many of you into delusion. Still, many were men and women of genius, and great truths can often be found mixed with their flawed teachings."*

624. What are the characteristics of the true prophet?

▲ *"The true prophet is upright and inspired by God. He or she may be recognized by both word and deed. God does not use the mouth of a liar to teach the truth."*

625. What is the most perfect example that God has offered to us as a guide and model?

▲ *"Jesus."*

Discussion: Jesus is the God-given model of moral perfection toward which we should all strive. Animated by the Divine Spirit, Jesus was the purest being who has ever appeared on Earth; and the doctrine He taught is, accordingly, the purest expression of the Divine law. Others who have professed to instruct humanity in the law of God have, by contrast, sometimes led it into error. The reason is not hard to discover. The latter have been swayed by ideas and feelings of a too earthly nature and have confused laws that regulate the life of the soul with those that govern the life of the body. Many pretended revealers, moreover, have announced as Divine laws what were only human ones, which they devised to serve their own interests and to assure their domination over others.

626. Did Jesus alone reveal the Divine laws that have been shown to us? Did we have no other way of knowing about them before His time except through intuition?

▲ *"As we have said, these laws are evident everywhere. All the teachers who have ever meditated on wisdom have been able to grasp and communicate them from the remotest times. Through their teachings these wise men and women prepared the ground for the sowing of the seed. The Divine laws, you see, are written in the book of nature; they can be read by anyone who searches after them. In every epoch, consequently, you will find upright individuals who have proclaimed the highest moral principles. For this reason, too, these principles are found in the moral codes of every people, although in an incomplete state and often tainted by ignorance and superstition."*

627. Since the true laws of God have been taught by Jesus, what is the purpose of the teachings the spirits have given us? Do they have anything more to teach us?

▲ *"Jesus often spoke allegorically, conveying His teachings in parables that were appropriate to the time and place in which he lived. Now, however, the time has come for their true meaning to be made intelligible to everyone. It is necessary to explain and develop the Divine laws because so few understand them and still fewer practice them. Our mission is to help you understand and feel them in all their sublimity, by presenting them in a way that is clear to reason. Hopefully, our mission will encourage the self-centered to change, and transform those who hide flawed characters behind masks of goodness and religiousness. We are invited to help prepare the reign of good announced by Jesus; to furnish the explanations that will make it impossible to interpret the law of God according to self-interest or otherwise distort the meaning of what is wholly a law of love and compassion."*

628. Why hasn't the truth always been placed within everyone's reach?

▲ *"Each thing can only happen in its own time. Truth is like light: you must become accustomed to it gradually or it will only dazzle you. Never before has humanity received communications as full and instructive as the ones you are receiving at present. In ancient times there were, as you know, individuals who possessed knowledge they believed sacred and who kept it a mystery from those they considered unworthy. But you can well understand, from what you know of the laws governing the phenomena of spirit-communication, that they received only a few fragmentary truths, scattered through a mass of teachings that were generally symbolic and often wrongly interpreted. Nonetheless, there is no early philosophical system, no tradition, no religion, that you should neglect to study. All of them contain the germs of great truths. They may seem at times to contradict each other—they have been distorted, after all, by various and baseless accretions. But, with the help of the key the Spiritist Doctrine gives you, they can be easily reconciled. Through the Spiritist Doctrine, you now have access to a class of facts that previously seemed contrary to reason but that is being irrefutably demonstrated with every passing day. Do not fail, then, to make the older systems a subject of study. They are rich in lessons and may contribute greatly to your education."*

Good and Bad

629. How would you define the moral law?

▲ *"The moral law is the rule for proper action, that is to say, for distinguishing practically between the good and the bad. It is founded on the observance of the law of God. You act rightly when you take the good of everyone as your aim and rule for action. To the extent that you do so, you obey the law of God."*

630. How can we distinguish between good and bad?

▲ *"Good is anything that conforms to the law of God; bad is anything that departs from it. To do right is to conform to the law of God; to do wrong is to break it."*

631. Do we have it in our power to distinguish between good and bad?

▲ *"Yes, you do when you believe in God and desire to do what is right. God has given you intelligence in order to discriminate between the two."*

632. Since we are subject to error, can't we be mistaken in our appreciation of good and bad and believe that we are doing right when we are doing wrong?

▲ *"Jesus said: 'So always treat others as you would like them to treat you.'[2] The whole of the ethical law is contained in that commandment. Make it your rule of action, and you will never go wrong."*

633. The rule of "do to others what you would have them do to you," which is a rule of reciprocity, cannot be applied to conduct toward oneself. Does the natural law provide a safe rule of conduct here?

▲ *"When you eat too much, it hurts you. In that discomfort, you find the limit of what you require in the way of food. Exceed the limit, and you suffer the consequences. It is the same with everything else. Natural law traces out for you the limits of your needs: to overstep those needs is to bring unwelcome effects on yourself. Pay attention, then, to the voice in you that says 'Enough!' and you will avoid most of the problems you usually blame on nature."*

634. Why does the bad—I use the word here in its ethical sense—exist in the nature of things? Couldn't God have created the human species in more favorable conditions?

▲ *"We have explained that a spirit is created as a simple and ignorant being.[3] Eventually God allows the spirit the freedom to choose its own road. If it takes the wrong one, so much the worse—its journey toward perfection will*

....

2 *Translator's Note: Matthew 7:12 - The golden rule.*

....

3 *See question 115 for a more in-depth treatment of the issue of spirit creation and question 199 for additional perspectives on life trials and evolution.*

be longer. Consider that, without mountains, you would never realize the possibility of ascending and descending; without rocks, you would never understand that there are such things as hardness. Well, spirits have to acquire experience in the same way; and in order to acquire it they must come to know both the good and the bad. This is the reason why spirits must experience life in physical form."

635. Different social positions create different wants for people. Doesn't this violate the idea that the natural law is uniform?

▲ *"Diversity in positions is natural and in accord with evolution. It does not invalidate the unity of natural law, which applies to everything."*

Discussion: The conditions of human existence vary according to times and places. With this variation comes different wants, which in turn brings about the rise of corresponding social needs. Since this diversity is in the order of things, it must also be in agreement with the law of God. God's law, however, is not diverse; it is based on a principle of unity. God leaves it to our reason to distinguish between necessary and frivolous wants.

636. Are the good and the bad absolutes for everyone?

▲ *"The law of God is the same for all, whereas the bad exists primarily in one's intentions. Good is always good, and bad always bad, no matter what someone's position in life may be. The only difference between one person and the next is their degree of individual responsibility."*

637. When a cannibal eats human flesh, should we consider him or her guilty for doing so?

▲ *"We have said that the essence of wrong-doing is in the will. A person is more or less guilty depending on the level of the understanding."*

Discussion: Circumstances modify the consequences of good and bad thoughts and acts. A person may do things that are highly objectionable, but his or her responsibility depends on the means he or she has for distinguishing between right and wrong. As a result, an enlightened individual who commits a minor violation has less excuse for it, in God's sight, than a savage who gives way to cannibalistic impulses.

638. Harm sometimes seems to be the result of the force of things. For instance, circumstances may be such that material destruction, or even taking someone's life, is necessary. Are cases like these violations of God's law?

▲ *"Wrong is still wrong, even when it becomes necessary. But the need for acts of this kind diminishes as the soul progresses. The soul's responsibility for its actions is always proportional to the progress and comprehension it has of the implications of its actions."*

639. We often do wrong because of the circumstances someone may have forced on us. Where does the greater fault lie in these cases?

▲ *"With the one who caused your wrong-doing. If you are led into the wrong path because someone has placed you in an impossible position, you are less accountable for it than the person who led you. Individuals always suffer the consequences of their wrong-doing—not only for the wrongs they have personally committed but also for the ones they have caused others to commit."*

640. If we profit by someone else's wrong-doing, even though we took no part in it ourselves, are we as accountable as if we had been involved?

▲ *"Yes. To take advantage of a crime is to take part in it. You might shrink from doing the actual deed. But if you knowingly benefit from it, you are equally as guilty as the person who did it; and you only prove that you would have done it yourself if you had had the chance."*

641. Is it as bad to desire to do wrong as it is to do it?

▲ *"That depends on the specific case. If you voluntarily resist the desire to do wrong, especially when there is a good possibility of fulfilling that desire, you are acting with integrity. But if your only reason for not doing something wrong is the lack of opportunity, you are as guilty as if you have done it."*

642. In ensuring our future happiness, is it enough simply not to have done anything wrong?

▲ *"No. You must do good, and to the utmost of your ability. Each of you is responsible, both for all the wrong you have done and all the good you have failed to do."*

643. Are there people who, because of their circumstances, cannot do good?

▲ *"There is no one who cannot do some good, though the very selfish find it otherwise. The mere fact that you exist in relationship with other beings makes it possible. Every day of your lives provides you with numerous opportunities. Remember that doing good is not a passive activity, restricted to giving to charity. It means being as useful as you can be whenever and wherever your help is needed."*

644. Isn't it true that the situation in which a person lives has a good deal to do with leading that person into vice and crime?

▲ *"Yes. But that situation is itself, oftentimes, part of the trial the spirit has chosen while in the state of freedom. It selected those 'temptations' in order to gain the merit of resisting them."*

645. When someone is plunged into an atmosphere of vice, doesn't the impulse to do wrong become almost irresistible?

▲ *"It may be strong, but it is not irresistible. Even in an environment of this kind, filled with every kind of enticement, you will sometimes find people of great integrity. The spirits of these people have acquired the strength to*

*resist temptation; and while they are testing that strength, they fulfill an
important mission by exercising a positive influence on the people around
them."*

646. Does the merit earned by a good action depend on the conditions under
which the action was performed? In other words, are there different degrees of
merit in doing right?

▲ *"The merit corresponds to the difficulty involved. There is very little merit
in doing right that requires no self-denial and effort. The poor person who
shares a last crumb of bread has greater merit in God's eyes than the rich one
who gives away what he or she doesn't need in the first place. Jesus makes
this clear in the parable of the widow's mite."*[5]

The Divisions of Natural Law

647. Is the whole of God's law contained in the 'love thy neighbor' principle?

▲ *"That rule contains all the duties humans owe to one another. But it has various applications; and unless these are made evident, people will continue to
neglect them as they do today. Besides, natural law embraces all the circumstances of life, and the rule you are referring to addresses only one part
of it. People need precise directions. General precepts are too vague; they
leave too many doors open to individual interpretation."*

648. What do you think of the division of natural law into parts—that is, the laws
of worship, work, reproduction, preservation, society, equality, liberty, and, finally, the law of justice, love and compassion?

▲ *"It was Moses who divided the law of God into ten parts; and the Ten
Commandments can, in fact, be made to cover all the circumstances of life.
You can, of course, devise your own system; but it will have no more value
than any other classification scheme. Incidentally, the last law you mention
is the most important. The law of justice, love and compassion includes all
the others; and when humanity observes this law, it advances more rapidly
in the spiritual life."*

· ·

*5 Translator's Note: Mark 12:42-44. "But a poor widow came and put in two very
small copper coins, worth only a fraction of a penny. Calling his disciples to him,
Jesus said, "I tell you the truth, this poor widow has put more in the treasury than
all the others. They all gave out of their wealth; but she, out of her poverty, put in
everything—all she had to live on."*

XVII

THE LAW OF WORSHIP

The Purpose of Worship

649. What is the purpose of worship?

▲ *"To worship is to raise your thoughts toward God. As you worship, you draw your soul closer to the Source of Life."*

650. Is worship the result of an inborn feeling, or is it something handed down to us by education?

▲ *"Like the belief in Deity, worship is the result of an inborn feeling. Because humanity is keenly aware of its own frailty, it bows before the Being who can protect it."*

651. Was there ever a people that completely lacked this inborn feeling?

▲ *"No. There never was a nation of pure atheists. The vast majority feel that there is a Supreme Being over them."*[1]

652. Does worship have its source in natural law?

▲ *"Worship is part of the natural law because it is the result of an innate human feeling. This explains why worship is found, in different forms, throughout the world."*

....

1 *Translator's Note: The book was written in the mid-1800s and therefore before the Communist Revolution of 1917 which abolished the practice of religion in the newly formed Soviet Union, thus setting the pattern for succeeding Communist governments in religious matters. By 2000, Communism had collapsed in most of Eastern Europe and Asia, and worship again flourished.*

External Acts of Worship

653. Are external acts —i.e.,ritual ceremonies—essential to worship?

▲ *"True worship is in the heart."*

— Are external acts of worship useful?

▲ *"Yes. If they are not just for public display, they set a good example. But people who worship for the sake of appearances do more harm than good, especially if their apparent spirituality is contradicted by their conduct."*

654. Is there a form of worship God prefers?

▲ *"As we said, worship should come from the heart, with sincerity and a genuine desire to do what is good and avoid the bad. This is a large improvement over merely revering God with rituals that don't in themselves make anyone better. You are all brothers and sisters, children of God, and you're all invited to celebrate and honor the law, whatever the form by which you know and experience God's presence.*

"Do not indulge in hypocrisy. If your worship is not genuine and is out of line with your normal character, you are setting a bad example. If you claim to love God but are self-centered, envious, unkind, unforgiving, and greedy, you are religious with your lips—not with your heart. God, who sees all things, would tell you that your conscience will eventually hold you accountable for your actions. The more you know, the greater your responsibility. If a blind person bumps into you, you are likely to forgive; you will be less understanding if it is a person who sees.

"To ask whether any form of worship is more acceptable than another is like asking whether God has any preference for prayers in a particular language. What you should remember is that the hymns addressed to the Supreme Being will only reach their goal if they are truly heartfelt."

655. Is it wrong to observe the external rites of a religion only out of respect for people we associate with, although their belief is different from ours?

▲ *"As in other cases, it all depends on your intention. If you are being genuinely considerate of the beliefs of others, you are doing no wrong. You are doing much better, in fact, than ridiculing those beliefs, which would be really uncharitable. However, if you attend such rituals with hidden agendas, then you are being highly disrespectful toward God and your associates. There is no merit in pretending to humble oneself before God only to gain the approval of others."*

656. Is it better to worship in a group or alone?

▲ *"When people who share similar thoughts and feelings worship together, they are more easily joined by good spirits. But that does not mean that individual worship is less acceptable; you can surely worship God in your own inner sanctuary."*

About Contemplation

657. Do people who give themselves up to a life of contemplation, who do nothing wrong and think only of God, have any special merit?

▲ *"No. If they do nothing bad, they do no good either. The failure to do good is, in itself, bad. It's important to think about God, but that is not all there is to life. You have all been given tasks to perform in your lives. If you give life entirely to meditation and contemplation, you have no merit. You would be living only for yourself. What good would that do humanity? Again, God has endowed you with a conscience that will hold you accountable for the good you have failed to do."*

Prayer

658. Is prayer meaningful to God?

▲ *"Yes, if it comes from the heart. It is the thought behind the prayer that counts. A heartfelt prayer is more meaningful than one you simply read from a book, no matter how elaborate the prayer book is. So when you pray, don't do it just with your lips but with your whole being. Prayer is meaningful if it is offered with conviction, love, and candor. If you are vain and self-centered, your prayers are going to be shallow unless they actually lead you to consider a humbler attitude."*

659. What is the true essence of prayer?

▲ *"Prayer is an act of worship. To pray is to think of and to draw yourself closer to God. As you commune with the Source of Life keep in mind three things: praising, asking, and thanksgiving."*

660. Can prayer make a person better?

▲ *"A heartfelt prayer not only gives you more strength to withstand life's various trials, but it also puts you in closer contact with good spirits who are eager to help you. A heartful prayer is an unfailing means of obaining spiritual assistance."*

—There are people who pray a great deal; yet they often seem unfriendly, envious, harsh, intolerant, even vicious. How can this be?

▲ *"It is not how much you pray, but how you do it. If all you care about is how lengthy your prayers are, you are shutting your eyes to your own imperfections as you pray. For some people, prayer is just a chore, a pastime, not a period of looking inward. Prayer, in such cases, is ineffective; it is the way you pray that counts."*

661. Is there any use in asking God to forgive our faults?

▲ *"God can see the good and bad regardless of how ostentatious your prayers are. You will be forgiven based on the change in your behavior, not on your choice of words. Good deeds are the best prayers."*

662. Is there any use in praying for others?

▲ *"If you wish to do good and pray, you will attract compassionate spirits who share your inner intention. Together you can have a positive influence on the persons you are praying for."*

Discussion: Together, mind and will provide us with an inner power that goes far beyond the physical realm. To pray for others is to exercise our will. If we are ardent and sincere, we will be joined by compassionate spirits who will come to the rescue of the persons for whom we are praying. They do this by suggesting to these persons good thoughts and by granting them the strength they need. But, here again, we need more than lip-service.

663. As we pray for ourselves, can we prevent our trials from taking place or change their nature?

▲ *"Your experiences are part of a general plan, and there are some trials that you are better off going through. In all cases, the courage you display while undergoing your troubles does not go unnoticed. With prayer, you gather strength from the good spirits who come to you. You can also develop a more positive outlook toward your problems. Unaffected prayer is never useless; the very comfort it provides is a benefit by itself. The saying `Heaven helps those who help themselves' couldn't be truer. Technically, God has instruments to intervene in your favor. Consider, however, that what appears to be a tragedy from the perspective of the physical realm may be a blessing in the context of the general order of the universe. Besides, many of your sorrows are self-inflicted; they could be the result of your own shortsightedness. Nonetheless, your requests are granted more frequently than you suppose. When a solution is not produced right away, you are often too quick to discount the value of prayer, but help usually comes so naturally that it seems to be the result of the ordinary course of things. What is even more common is for Providence to suggest to your mind a better way to deal with your difficulties."*

664. Is it useful to pray for the dead, especially those that we suppose are suffering? How can our prayers help them? Can prayer overturn Divine justice?

▲ *"Prayer cannot overturn the natural law, but it is a great source of comfort for the spirit you are praying for. To this spirit, your prayers show that you care, that it is not suffering alone. Moreover, your interest could also encourage the afflicted spirit to seriously reconsider its attitude; such intro-*

spection might, by itself, shorten its sorrows. And if there is a genuine desire to overcome the situation, the good spirits will be in a better position to provide guidance, comfort, and hope. As Jesus prayed for the `lost ones,'[2] you should not neglect to remember those who might be in greatest need of your prayers."

665. Some people are against prayers for the dead because this practice is not prescribed by the gospels. What should we think of this view?

▲ *"Christ said 'Love one another.'[3] This is a principle you should all strive to live by. In reality, natural law must follow its course; but your prayers on behalf of a suffering spirit are accepted by God as a display of love and affection that always brings relief and consolation to the sufferer. Moreover, the afflicted spirit will be ready to be helped once it makes a genuine commitment to change its character and starts assuming responsibility for its misdeeds. Then, the spirit will be comforted to know that a kind heart is interceding on its behalf. Further, your prayers will produce in it feelings of gratitude and affection. Both you and the suffering spirit will then have observed the law of love and union that pervades the universe. Love and oneness are the aim of a spirit's education."[4]*

666. Can we pray to spirits?

▲ *"You can pray to them in their role of messengers and helpers of the Divine Being. But their ability to act on your request depends on their advancement and God's permission. As such, prayers you address to them will be attended to if granted by God."*

Polytheism

667. If the belief in many gods is baseless, why is it one of the most ancient and widespread human beliefs?

▲ *"For humanity, the concept of one God is the result of intellectual development. In their early stages, humans could not conceive of a formless, immaterial Being who could act on matter. Therefore, they attributed to this Being a physical nature, with a form and face. Not only that, but they accorded Divine status to everything that seemed to be the result of a superhuman intelligence. Whatever early humans could not understand was assigned to a power in the supernatural realm. Given the great number of these misun-*

....

2 *Translator's Note: Luke 15:6. "Rejoice with me; I have found my lost sheep."*

....

3 *Translator's Note: John 13:34. "A new command I give you: Love one another. As I have loved you, so you must love one another."*

....

4 *Reply given by M.Monod, a Protestant minister of Paris, who passed away in 1856. The preceding reply to question 664 was dictated by the spirit St. Louis.*

derstandings, there arose in people's minds numerous divine powers to account for them. In all ages, though, there have been enlightened persons who have understood the impossibility of a universe simultaneously governed by a multitude of equal powers. That is part of how the notion of a single God came about."

668. Phenomena attesting to the action of spirits have occurred and been known since the most ancient times. Could these phenomena have led to belief in many gods?

▲ *"Men and women applied the term 'god' to anything that surpassed human power. For them it was natural to see spirits as gods. In some cases, even persons were made into gods. All that was needed was for an individual, while alive, to distinguish him or herself from all others by dint of actions, intelligence, or a perceived occult power. Then, after death, he or she would be worshiped as a god."*

Discussion: The word "god" had a wide range of meanings among the ancients. It did not, as in our day, represent the Supreme Intelligence but was a generic term applied to all beings who appeared to stand outside the pale of ordinary humanity. Thus, immaterial beings who revealed themselves through paranormal phenomena—as these occurrences are called today—were called gods, just as today we call them spirits. It is, one might say, simply a matter of words. The crucial difference is that, while the ancients were led by their leaders into believing that the so-called gods merited sumptuous temples and shrines, we realize today that spirits are simply beings like ourselves, more or less advanced, but lacking a physical envelope. A careful study of the attributes of the pagan gods shows that they precisely fit our present-day definition of "spirit." Each had an incorporeal body, as well as responsibilities in both the physical and the non-physical realm.

The existence of spirits is acknowledged in different ways by different peoples. In all phases of human history, spirit-manifestations have been observed, though they have been diversely interpreted and often abused under the veil of mystery. Many religions have regarded them as miracles; skeptics have looked on them as hocus-pocus. At present, thanks to a more serious study of the subject carried on in the broad daylight of scientific investigation, the doctrine of spirit-presence and spirit-action, stripped of the superstitious fancies that have obscured it for ages, reveals to us one of the most sublime and important principles of nature.

Sacrifices

669. The custom of offering human sacrifices dates from remotest antiquity. How could people have been led to believe that such an atrocity could be pleasing to God?

▲ *"First of all, not all ancient peoples conceived of God as the source of all goodness. Among primitive societies, matter ruled over spirit. In the moral sense, these peoples were not yet mature. That is why they so often gave themselves up to brutal instincts.*

"Second, the inhabitants of the primitive world considered a living being much more valuable in the sight of the gods than a lifeless object. The natural implication was to immolate on their altars first animals, and, later, men and women. To them, the value of a sacrifice was proportional to the importance of the offering. Even in your present day, when you are about to buy someone a gift, it is not uncommon to spend an amount that will express the esteem in which you hold that person. It was only natural for primitive peoples to do the same in regard to their gods."

— You are saying that the sacrifice of animals preceded that of human beings?

▲ *"Undoubtedly this was the case."*

— According to this explanation, the custom of sacrificing human beings did not originate in mere cruelty. Is that right?

▲ *"Yes. This custom was based on a false idea of what would be acceptable to God. (A good example is the story of Abraham and the sacrifice of his son, Isaac.[5]) In later times, humans have debased this idea still further by immolating their enemies, the objects of their own personal animosity. But the Source of Life would never have demanded sacrifices of any kind, either of animals or human beings. God cannot be honored by useless destruction."*

670. Have human sacrifices, when offered with a truly religious intention, ever been pleasing to God?

▲ *"No, never. But Providence always weighs the intention behind every action. If, in their ignorance, the ancients truly believed that they were performing a laudable deed by immolating their fellow beings, God would have accepted their intentions, though never the deed itself. As the human race*

································

5 *Translator's Note: "Isaac was the firstborn of Abraham, then 100 years old, and Sarah. God came to Abraham and instructed him to go to the land of Moriah, where he was to offer his son in sacrifice. When Abraham got to the altar, ready for the sacrifice, God stopped him and told him that since he had not withheld his son, God would make his offspring as numerous as the stars in the sky and they would populate the earth." Gen 22:1-18.*

worked through its own progress, it naturally came to realize this grave mis-conception and to abhor the idea of sacrifices. However dense the veil of materiality that shrouded the souls of ancient peoples, their free will even then gave them a glimmering perception of their true spiritual origin and destiny. Many of them intuitively understood the atrocities involved in sac-rifice but indulged in them anyway to satisfy their own passions."

671. In human history, we are all aware that entire nations have set out to exter-minate each other because of their religious differences and because, by so doing, they believed they would make themselves acceptable to God. Behind this atti-tude we find a motivation similar to the one that led to the sacrifice of human beings. What do you think of "religious wars"?

▲ *"Such wars are seconded by spirits of the lower orders, and the individuals who wage them are in direct opposition to the Divine precept that we should love others as ourselves. All peoples worship the same God, regardless of names. It is senseless, then, to wage war on the basis of religious differences or of a presumed moral superiority.*

   "Furthermore, not all peoples were touched by the words of the Christ in the same way, so one shouldn't expect all to believe in Him. But could any-thing be more paradoxical than to try to impose His peaceful message by fire and the sword? Truly, Jesus's message should be made available to all; but his teachings must be spread only through persuasion and gentleness, never by violence and bloodshed. Nowadays, for instance, many of your fellows do not believe in certain spirit-teachings. How could you expect them to accept your statements if your very actions negate them?"

672. Was the offering of the fruits of the earth more acceptable in the sight of God than the sacrificing of animals?

▲ *"Evidently God must have found it more agreeable to be worshiped by the offering of the fruits of the earth than by the blood of victims. But we have already answered your question in telling you that God weighs the intention and places little importance on the outward fact. A heartfelt prayer is a hun-dredfold more agreeable to God than all the offerings you could possibly make. We repeat: the intention is everything; the act, nothing."*

673. Couldn't these offerings be made more agreeable to God by dedicating them to the relief of the poor? Wouldn't it be truly spiritual to commit to the poor the first-fruits of all that God has given us?

▲ *"God always blesses those who do good; to help the poor and afflicted is the best way of honoring the Divine. We do not mean to say that God disap-proves of the way you pray, but a great deal of the money spent in your rit-uals could be more usefully employed. The Source of Life loves simplicity in everything. A person who attaches more importance to appearances than to what goes on in the heart has a narrow perspective of reality. How, then, can we conceive of a Supreme Being who assigns more importance to form than to substance?"*

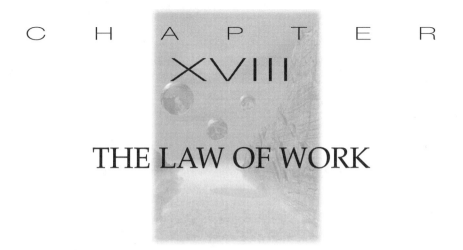

XVIII

THE LAW OF WORK

The Necessity for Work

674. Is work a requirement of the law of nature?

▲ *"Work is a law of nature, which is proved by the fact that it is necessary for survival and that the maintenance of civilization requires that you perform it. Through work, you provide for both your needs and your enjoyments."*

675. Should we understand that "work"only defines material occupations?

▲ *"No; the spirit works, just as the body does. Every sort of useful occupation is work."*

676. Why do we have to work?

▲ *"Because of your physical nature, and because through work you develop your intelligence. Without work, you would remain children intellectually. This is why God has arranged it so that you owe your food, your safety, and your well-being entirely to your labor and activity."*

677. Why does nature provide for all the needs of animals?

▲ *"Everything in nature is in a constant state of activity. Animals, too, have their tasks, but their 'work' is limited to the furthering of their own preservation. Unlike human beings, whose work is aimed at both self-preservation and intellectual development, animals do not intentionally work to promote progress. Unknowingly, however, animals fulfill their share in the divine plan. Humans often don't realize the extent of animals' contribution to the work of nature."*

678. Are the inhabitants of realms more evolved than Earth subject to the same need to work?

▲ *"The nature of work is always related to the needs it supplies. The less material those needs are, the less material is the work. But do not suppose that the inhabitants of those realms are inactive and useless. Idleness would be a torture to them rather than an enjoyment."*

679. Are the rich exempt from the law of work?

▲ *"From material work perhaps, but not from the obligation of becoming useful, according to their means, and of developing their own intelligence and that of others, which is work in itself. If God has given you enough wealth to assure your earthly existence and you do not have to win your bread by the sweat of your brow, your duty to make yourself useful to others is all the greater. Given much, you have a greater amount of time for doing good."*

680. Aren't there some people who are incapable of working at anything whatever and whose existence is entirely useless?

▲ *"God is just and disapproves only of someone who is voluntarily useless. Such a person lives on the labor of others. God wills, however, that each of you make yourselves useful according to your abilities."*[1]

681. Does the law of nature require that children care for their parents?

▲ *"It does, just as it requires that parents work for their children. For this reason, God has placed in you the seed of filial and parental love. Through this love, the members of a family are led to help each other—a duty that, in the present state of your society, you too often lose sight of."*[2]

The Limits of Work

682. Since rest is always required after work, is it also a law of nature?

▲ *"Rest restores strength to the body. And it is necessary in order to give a little more freedom to the mind, enabling it to raise itself above matter."*

683. What is the limit of work?

▲ *"The limit of your strength. But God gives you liberty to decide on this point individually."*

684. What should we think about people who misuse their authority, overworking those under them?

▲ *"They commit one of the worst mistakes. If you exercise authority over oth-*

....

1 *See question 643, for an extended discussion on this issue.*

....

2 *See question 205 on family ties.*

ers, you are answerable for any abuses of your responsibility. Such abuses are against the divine law."[3]

685. Do we have a right to retire in old age?

▲ *"Yes, you are only obliged to work according to your strength."*

—What resources should there be for the elderly who need to support themselves but cannot do so?

▲ *"The strong should assist the weak. Where family help is unavailable, society should take its place. Such is the law of love and charity."*

Discussion: To say that it is necessary to work is not to make a complete statement of the subject. The worker must also be able to find work, and this is not always possible. Unfortunately, when work is not available, deprivation soon follows. This is an evil for which economists are constantly seeking a remedy in the balance of production and consumption. But this balance, supposing it to be attainable, will always be subject to fluctuations, and during the intervals the worker must live. This brings us to an element that has not been considered enough: education. We speak here not only of the education of the mind but also of the character and of habit, education itself being the totality of acquired habits. Every day, large numbers of people enter society who have no principles and nothing with which to curb their instincts. This being so, we can hardly wonder at the disastrous consequences that follow in their wake. Once properly educated, however, these individuals will bring into their daily lives habits of order, an ability to plan for themselves and their dependents, and a degree of respect for the rights of others, that will allow them to endure periods of difficulty with greater ease. Laxness and the inability to plan for the future can only be understood and cured through sound instruction. Universal education is, then, the starting point for and the essential element of our social well-being, the one pledge of security for all of us.

....

3 See question 273 on the possible consequences of this kind of abuse.

C H A P T E R

XIX

LAW OF REPRODUCTION

The Population of the Earth

686. Is the reproduction of living beings a law of nature?

▲ *"Evidently it is. Without reproduction, the material world would come to a very speedy end."*

687. If the world's population keeps growing at its current rate, will the planet eventually become too crowded?

▲ *"No, Divine wisdom will always provide for and maintain equilibrium in this matter. God permits nothing useless to happen. But from your present perspective you see only a corner of the universal panorama. The harmony among its various parts is imperceptible to you."*

The Evolution of Races

688. At the moment there are races on Earth whose numbers seem to be quickly dwindling. Will they eventually disappear?

▲ *"Yes. Others will take their place, just as others will take yours some day."*

689. Are the people now on Earth a new creation or the descendants of more primitive humans?

▲ *"They are the same spirits, who have come back to improve themselves through new physical experiences.[1] They are still, of course, very far from*

....

1 *Translator's Note: According to United Nations population studies (1995), the world population has grown from approximately 310 million in the year 1000, to 2520 million in 1950, 6000 million in 1999, and is expected to reach 9300 million in 2050. Therefore, this assertion must be taken in the context that the population of souls pursuing their evolutionary journey on Earth has grown over time. This is consistent with the discussion in question 687.*

perfection. But modern peoples, although still developing steadily, will have their own period of decline; they, too, will finally disappear. In the very long term, they will be replaced by other, more evolved races who will be descendants of the present peoples, exactly as civilized people of your time are descended from the rough-hewn primitives of old."

690. From a strictly physical point of view, are the bodies of the people within a race a special creation or have they evolved from the bodies of primitive races?

▲ *"The origin of races is hidden in the night of time. But since all races belong to one great human family, whatever their primitive roots may have been, they have been able to mix and produce new types."*

691. Again from a purely physical point of view, what is the dominant characteristic of primitive races?

▲ *"The development of brute force at the expense of intellectual power. Today the opposite is happening. People act through their intelligence rather than through their physical strength; and because of it, they accomplish much more than they once did. They have learned to take advantage of natural forces, which animals cannot do."*

692. Is the scientific improvement of vegetable and animal species contrary to the law of nature? Would we be more in accord with that law if we let them follow their normal course?

▲ *"The duty of every conscious being is to help, in every way possible, to further progress. Perfection is the aim of everything in nature and making improvements that lead toward it is assisting in the working out of Divine intentions. Human beings are instruments for accomplishing these higher ends."*

—Unfortunately, in our efforts to make these improvements, we are generally motivated by self-interest and often don't have any other goal in mind than increasing our personal gain. Does this diminish the value of our action?

▲ *"Even if your motivations leave you with no merit, the fact remains that the work of progress gets done. You can add to the value of your work, though, by inspiring yourself through a noble motive. In making these improvements, you develop your intelligence, which is the greatest benefit from your effort."*

Obstacles to Reproduction

693. Are human laws and customs that interfere with reproduction contrary to the laws of nature?

▲ *"Anything that limits the operations of nature is contrary to the general law."*

—But there are many animal and vegetable species that would be harmful to other species and would rapidly become a danger to us if their reproduction was not curbed. Are we wrong to control it?

▲ *"Out of all the living beings on Earth, God has given you the power of thought and action. You should use it for the general good, and never abuse it. This power gives you the ability to regulate the reproduction of other species according to your needs. But you should not limit that reproductive capacity without some good reason. Consider this difference. Your intelligent action is a counterbalance established by God to help restore the equilibrium of natural forces. Again, you are distinguished here from the animals, because you act in full awareness. Animals also contribute to maintaining the equilibrium, but they act unconsciously—through an instinct for destruction that drives them, for instance, to kill prey. This instinct is valuable to them because it ensures their survival; but it also prevents the numbers of the animals and vegetables they feed on from becoming too large and thus becoming a source of danger."*

694. What about the use of birth control methods in order to more freely enjoy sensuality?

▲ *"It demonstrates the dominance of the body over the spirit and how steeped we are in the physical nature."*

Marriage and Celibacy

695. Is marriage—that is to say, the permanent union of two people—contrary to the law of nature?

▲ *"It represents a more evolved stage in human development."*

696. What effect would the abolition of marriage have on human society?

▲ *"It would mean a return to the life of the animals."*

Discussion: In the natural state, the union of the sexes is random and entails no responsibility. Marriage is one of the first signs that a social structure has developed. While conditions vary, marriage can be found among all peoples, establishing a principle of cooperation and mutual commitment between partners. The abolition of marriage would, we can be certain, return humanity to its infancy and would even place us below certain animals whose instincts lead to a lifetime bond to a single partner.

697. Is the idea that a civil marriage cannot be dissolved found in the law of nature, or is it a human law?

▲ *"A human law, altogether contrary to the law of nature. But humans change their laws at will. Only natural laws are unchangeable."*

698. Do people who choose celibacy have any particular merit in God's sight?

▲ *"No. People who choose to stay single from selfish motives fail to perform their share of duties in the social order."*

699. Don't some people, though, decide to stay celibate in order to devote themselves entirely to the service of humanity?

▲ *"That is a very different thing. Recall that we said 'from selfish motives.' Every sort of personal sacrifice has merit when it is made toward a good end. In these cases, the greater the sacrifice, the greater that person's worth."*

Discussion: God cannot be self-contradictory and find evil in one of the natural laws. Thus celibacy—which is contrary to the law of reproduction—cannot, *per se*, be a virtue. However, there is much merit in celibacy when it results from a genuine intention to forego the joys of parenthood in order to work for the common good. Every sacrifice of personal gain for the good of others is a step on the path of spiritual progress.

Polygamy

700. Numerically, men and women are almost equal. Does this also give us some idea of the way human beings ought to be numerically grouped in marriage?

▲ *"Yes. Every arrangement in nature has a specific purpose. "*

701. Which conforms better to the law of nature, polygamy or monogamy?

▲ *"Polygamy is a human institution, and the abolition of it in a society signals an era of social progress. Marriage, according to the Divine design, should be based on the affection of the men and women who enter into it. But in polygamy there can be no real affection. There is only sensuality."*

Discussion: If polygamy actually corresponded to the law of nature, it should be possible to establish it everywhere. In fact, the rough numerical equality of the sexes makes this impossible. Polygamy has to be regarded, then, as simply a custom, adapted to the needs of certain peoples but destined to disappear as their societies progress.

THE LAW OF
PRESERVATION

The Instinct for Self-Preservation

702. Is self-preservation a principle of the natural law?

▲ *"Definitely. All living beings possess the instinct of self-preservation, whatever the extent of their intellectual development. In some, it is purely instinctive; in others, it is subordinate to the reasoning capacity."*

703. Why did God grant this instinct to living beings?

▲ *"All beings are necessary to the working out of the designs of Providence. And to fulfill those plans, they must have a will to live. This desire is essential to their continued evolution. It is instinctive to them, without their being consciously aware of it."*

The Means of Self-Preservation

704. When humans were given the will to live, did God also provide us with the means of survival?

▲ *"Yes, and if you do not find such means, it is because you lack initiative. God wouldn't instill the will to live in you without furnishing you with the means to survive. This is why Earth has been engineered to produce whatever its inhabitants require."*

705. Why, then, doesn't Earth produce enough to supply everything humans require?

▲ *"Mother Nature is a wonderful mother. But human beings neglect her, are ungrateful to her, and often blame her for the results of their own incompetence or imprudence. Earth does, in fact, provide you with everything that is essential; but you make excessive demands. What you need, really, is to learn how to be satisfied. An Arab in the desert can always find the means to survive, because he doesn't create artificial needs. But when you waste half the resources you use simply to satisfy whims, you shouldn't be surprised at shortages. Why don't you take responsibility and regret not having provided for hard times? Actually, it is not Nature that lacks foresight, but you who neglect your own best interest."*

706. Should we understand that only products from the soil are considered to be the fruits of the earth?

▲ *"The soil is the primary source from which all resources derive, since these resources are, on the whole, only transformations of the products of the soil. This is why you must consider as fruits of the earth everything you enjoy in this world."*

707. Some people invariably lack the means of subsistence, even when surrounded by abundance. How do you explain this?

▲ *"The first reason is the selfishness of those who control the means; the second is often the needy's own negligence and lack of effort. The Bible tells you, 'Seek and you will find'.[1] Seeking, however, does not mean that it is enough just to look to the land. You must work the land with energy and persistence. Don't let yourself be discouraged by the obstacles you encounter, either. Often these are nothing but the means to put your forbearance, your patience, and your determination to the test."[2]*

Discussion: Wherever humanity multiplies its needs, it also multiplies the sources of labor and the means of survival. But there is still a great deal to be accomplished; and when humanity does eventually reach its total productive capacity, nobody will be able to complain that they lack essentials, unless it is through their own negligence. Unfortunately, many people live their lives in ways Nature never intended. Everybody, it is true, has a place under the sun. But there is a condition: each of us must be content with our own space and avoid coveting someone else's. And we must learn not to hold Nature accountable for the faults of the social system (which can be very ambitious and self-interested).

However, we would have to be blind in this regard not to recognize the progress that the more evolved societies have made. Thanks to the admirable efforts of both phil-

....

1   *Translator's Note: Matthew 7:7.*

....

2   *See question 534 for a complementary answer related to the handling of personal challenges.*

anthropists and scientists who have worked unceasingly to improve our material lot, and despite constant increases in the size of the population, shortages in production have for the most part decreased. And our situation, even at its most disastrous, cannot be compared to that of the not-so-distant past. Public health—an element essential to our security and welfare—was unknown to our predecessors; today, it is the object of enlightened attention. Among us, the miserable and suffering can more often find protection. Science is everywhere put into action, contributing to an increase in the general well-being. Should we say, then, that we have reached perfection? Certainly not! But what has been done provides us with a good idea of what can be done with persistence—if, that is, we are sensible enough to seek for happiness in positive and serious things instead of in fantasies that cause us to stand still instead of improve.

708. Aren't there conditions in which the means of survival have nothing to do with human will, where shortages of the most essential things result from circumstances?

▲ *"There are frequently difficult tests that you must undergo and that you know beforehand you will be subjected to. Your merit lies in your fortitude (that is, where your intelligence doesn't provide you with some way of escape). If you have to face death, let us say, you must accept it with courage and faith, and avoid complaining. How much better it is to realize that in death the time of your real freedom has come and that rebelling against your end may cause you to destroy the value of resignation."*

709. In very critical times some people are forced to sacrifice their fellow human beings in order to keep from starving. Do they commit a crime? And if so, is the crime lessened by the need to survive that was created by the self-preservation instinct?

▲ *"We answered this before when we said that there is great merit in forbearance and courage before all trials. Any violence against human life is considered a crime, and in the case of homicide, has grave consequences."*

710. On planets where bodies are more perfect, do the beings still need food?

▲ *"Yes, but their nourishment is relative to their nature. Their 'foods' would not be very substantial to you, with your gross stomachs; likewise, they could not digest your foods."*

Enjoying The Fruits of the Earth

711. Is it an inherent human right to enjoy the fruits of the Earth?

▲ *"This right proceeds solely from the need to preserve life. God would not impose a duty without giving you the means to execute it."*

712. Why did God make material possessions attractive?

▲ *"In order to encourage you to fulfill your missions and also to test your power of temperance."*

—What is the purpose of 'temptation'?

▲ *"To develop your reason, which will protect you from abuses."*

Discussion: If the only incitement to exploit the fruits of the Earth was their usefulness, human indifference could have jeopardized the harmony of the universe. God, however, allows us to receive pleasure from our use, thus luring us to carry out the designs of Providence. But, through these pleasures, we are tested both in our discernment and in our strength to refrain from abusing them.

713. Does Nature establish limits to such pleasures?

▲ *"Yes, limits are set by your real needs. You are the primary victim of your own overindulgence."*

714. What about the person who is always looking to increase his or her pleasures through all kinds of abuses?

▲ *"An unfortunate being who should be deplored, not envied. Such a person is on a ruinous path."*

—Do you mean physical or spiritual ruin?

▲ *"Both."*

Discussion: People who engage in abuse—of drugs, sex, food, etc.—in order to maximize pleasure for pleasure's sake place themselves below the animal level, since even animals know how to observe limits in satisfying their needs. Such individuals renounce their reasoning faculty, which God gave us to guide our actions; and the more abuses they indulge in, the more control they forteit over their spiritual nature. The result of these abuses is disease, decadence, and finally early death—all consequences of violating the Law.

Needs and Wants

715. How can we know the limits of our needs?

▲ *"The sensible person knows them through intuition. There are many others who learn them only by hard experience."*

716. Can't we say that the limits of human needs are established by our bodily structure?

▲ *"Yes, but human beings are insatiable. Nature has set your proper limits, as you rightly observe, by giving you a particular kind of body. But your vices change your constitution and create artificial needs for you."*

717. We all know of people who live extravagantly, overconsuming when others don't even have the bare essentials. How are we to view them?

▲ *"They ignore the law and will be held accountable for the hardship they may cause others."*

Discussion: The dividing line between the essential and the superfluous is not at all absolute. Modern life has created needs that were non-existent in earlier eras. The spirits who dictated these teachings didn't want us to deny ourselves every modern comfort. But everything is relative, and common sense must place everything in its proper order. Civilization develops the moral sense and, simultaneously, those altruistic feelings that lead us to lean on and support each other. Hence, individuals who live at the expense of others, exploiting the advantages of progress for their own exclusive benefit, have nothing but the veneer of civilization. They are similar to those whose religious devotion is limited to public acts of faith.

Self-Imposed Suffering

718. Does the law of self-preservation require us to provide for our bodily needs?

▲ *"Yes, since work would be impossible without energy and health."*

719. Are we to be blamed for seeking comfort?

▲ *"The desire for comfort is part of human nature. Abuses are, however, condemned because they go against the law of self-preservation. The pursuit of material comfort is not contrary to the laws of life, except when it comes at the expense of someone else or when it unduly compromises your physical and psychological health."*

720. Do self-inflicted hardships, endured for the purpose of spiritual purification, confer any special merit?

▲ *"Do good to others and your value will be greater."*

—Is there any kind of self-imposed hardship that carries spiritual value?

▲ *"Yes, those in which you abstain from frivolous pleasures. When you do so you raise yourself above matter and elevate your soul. There is also merit in resisting a temptation that would lead you to abuse, and in depriving yourself of essentials in order to give to the needy. If, however, your self-sacrifice is merely for show, your actions are devoid of value."*

721. The ascetic life of sacrifice has been practiced throughout the ages and among many different people. Does it have any merits from any point of view?

▲ *"Ask if anyone else benefited and you will have your answer. If nobody benefited except the person who sacrificed, and the sacrifice prevented him or her from doing good, it was self-centered, regardless of the guise under which it was performed. According to Christian love, the true sacrifice is to endure hardships for the sake of others."*

722. Is abstaining from certain foods, as some peoples do, a rational idea?

▲ *"Anything you eat that does not do harm to your health is permitted. The leaders of these people in ancient times prohibited certain foods because it served a useful end; and, in order to give more credibility to their laws, they presented them as coming from God."*

723. Is eating meat contrary to natural law?

▲ *"In your physical constitution, flesh nourishes flesh. The laws of preservation impose on you the duty of maintaining your energy and health in order to carry out the work that is expected of you. You should, however, eat according to the demands of your body."*

724. Does abstaining from animal and other foods have any merit as a purification?

▲ *"Yes, if you deprive yourself in order to help others. God cannot accept self-denial unless it is for a serious and useful purpose. This is why we say that those who deprive themselves merely for appearance's sake are being hypocritical."*[3]

725. What about mutilating the body or the bodies of animals as a means of purification?

▲ *"Why do you ask a question like this? Here is a good rule: in judging the value of an act, always try to discover if it is useful. If it is useless and harmful, it cannot have any value. You should know that only the actions that elevate the soul carry real merit. By practicing the Divine law, instead of violating it, you will be able to raise yourself above the dense conditions of Earth."*

726. If our trials on Earth place us on a higher level, depending on how we endure

---

3 *Question 720 reiterates this point.*

them, can we be elevated by trials we voluntarily create for ourselves?

▲ *"The only hardships that place you on a higher level are the natural ones, because they serve the Divine plan. Voluntary ones serve no purpose unless they are endured for the good of others. Do you really believe that people like bonzes and fakirs and the fanatics of certain sects advance on their path because they shorten their lives by enduring superhuman trials?[4] Why don't they work for the benefit of their fellow human beings instead? If they would visit the needy, console the despairing, work for the sick, and undergo self-denial in order to alleviate the burdens of suffering, their lives would be really useful and pleasing to God. Any voluntary suffering undergone with only self in mind must be considered as mere selfishness. It is only when someone suffers for the welfare of others that he or she practices love and follows the teachings of Christ."*

727. If we are not to create voluntary suffering, which is useless, shouldn't we take measures to protect ourselves from the hardships that we anticipate will pose a threat to us?

▲ *"The self-preservation instinct was given to all beings as a defense against danger and suffering. Chastise your spirit, not your body. Torment your pride and suppress your self-centeredness, which is like a snake devouring your heart. In this way, you will progress more than through self-imposed ordeals, which are outdated for this day and age anyway."*

---

4 *Translator's Note: Bonzes are Buddhist monks especially associated with China and Japan; fakirs are Muslim or Hindu religious ascetics, most of them mendicant monks.*

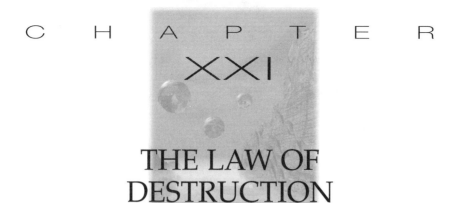

CHAPTER XXI

THE LAW OF DESTRUCTION

Necessary Destruction

728. Is destruction a law of Nature?

▲ *"Destruction gives way to renewal and regeneration. What you call destruction is nothing but a transformation that allows for renewal and transformation on Earth."*

—Can we say, then, that the destructive instinct was given to living beings as a means of working out the designs of Providence?

▲ *"Providence uses all beings as instruments for attaining its purpose. On Earth the nourishment of some living beings depends on the destruction of others. This serves two objectives: to maintain balance in the population of a species and to transform matter. But what dies, you must understand, is merely the physical envelope—which, in the human realm, is only an accessory to the spirit. The spirit, the essential thinking principle, is indestructible. It maintains the human body and through the transformations of matter the spirit accomplishes its progress."*

729. If destruction is necessary for transformation, why does Nature instill species with the self-preservation instinct?

▲ *"This is to prevent premature destruction, which would impede the development of the intelligent principle. This is also why God gave the instinct to live and to reproduce to each being."*

730. Since death will lead us to a better life and liberate us from the evils of the world, it is something we should desire more than fear. Why does each of us, then, feel such instinctive horror and apprehension when facing it?

▲ *"We have already told you. Humans must seek to prolong their lives in order to fulfill their tasks. It was for this reason that God gave you the instinct of self-preservation, which sustains you during your trials. Without it you would frequently fall into despair. But the secret voice that makes you reject death also tells you that you can do something to improve your lot. Every brush with death is a call for you to spend your time more usefully. But the ungrateful, instead of thanking God for this warning, bless their lucky star that they have escaped."*

731. Why, along with the means of preservation, did Nature simultaneously place the means of destruction in our path?

▲ *"The medicine comes with the sickness. As we previously told you, destruction is designed to establish balance, to maintain an equilibrium in nature."*

732. Is the need for destruction the same on all planets?

▲ *"It exists in proportion to the materiality of each planet. As inhabitants reach more refined physical and spiritual states, it disappears. On more advanced planets, living conditions are quite different from yours."*

733. Will the need for destruction always exist among us on Earth?

▲ *"It will diminish as the spirit gains mastery over matter. This is why the horror at destruction grows with intellectual and moral development."*

734. In our present state do we have an unlimited right to destroy animals?

▲ *"This right is regulated by the requirements of your food supply and your safety. Beyond that you do violence to the general harmony, and abuse is never a right."*

735. What about destruction that surpasses the limits of the needs and safety of everyone—for instance, when the object is solely to destroy for the sake of sport, without any beneficial purpose?

▲ *"It is an indication of the predominance of humanity's physical nature over its spiritual one. Understand that all destruction beyond the limits of the necessary violates God's laws. Animals don't destroy except when they have need. Humans, who have free will, do so wantonly and will be held accountable for abusing the freedom they were given. In these cases, they surrender to their lower instincts."*

736. In regard to the taking of animal life, some people are scrupulous in the extreme. Do they have any special merit?

▲ *"Carrying a commendable feeling to an extreme often invites abuses that offset any merit the intention might have. These attitudes, more often than not, result from superstitious fear rather than true kindness."*

Natural Calamities

737. What is the purpose of Providence in allowing major natural calamities to occur?

▲ *"They bring about transformations that will speed along your progress. As we have told you, destruction (physical death) is necessary for the moral renewal of spirits who, in each new lifetime, reach a higher level of perfection. You have to look at the objectives in order to appreciate the results of these events. Don't judge them from your own personal point of view and call them calamities because they bring you losses. These adversities are frequently necessary to accelerate the development of a better order that otherwise might not come about for centuries."*[1]

738. Couldn't God use other means than disasters of this kind to improve us?

▲ *"Yes, and it happens everyday of your life through all the opportunities you have to gain awareness and goodness. But when you fail in these lessons and grow prideful you are called to the test. By having to bow your head, you become more aware of yourself and your circumstances."*

—But is it fair that good as well as wrong-doing people should die in a calamity?

▲ *"During life human beings have their bodies as the sole point of reference; after death they begin to think differently. As we have already told you, the life span of the body is very short; a century on your planet is only a flash compared to Eternity. Hardships, which for you may last months or years, are not ends in themselves: they are experiences that will serve you in the future. Keep in mind that the spiritual life is the real thing.*[2] *Spirits are the children of God and the object of Divine attention. Their physical bodies are nothing but the garments they wear in the world of matter.*

"Great calamities which bring about widespread death can be compared to an army during a war. The uniforms of the soldiers may become torn, tattered, or lost; but the commanding officer is more interested in the well-being of his soldiers than in their uniforms."

—But aren't the sufferers in such calamities still victims, despite everything?

▲ *"If you consider life for what it is—how insignificant it is before Infinity—you would attach less importance to it. If these victims endure their sufferings without recrimination, they will have a great compensation in another life."*

Discussion: Whether death occurs through a calamity or an ordinary

....

1 *Question 744 discusses a man-made calamity: wars.*

....

2 *See question 85 for additional perspectives on the value and purpose of life in the spiritual realm.*

cause, it cannot be avoided when the time comes. The only difference is that, in the case of the calamity, many people depart at the same time.

If we could raise our thoughts high enough to contemplate the human race as a whole, and to take in the whole of its destiny at a glance, the scourges that now seem so terrible would appear to us only as passing storms in the destiny of the planet.

739. Do such natural calamities, despite the problems they cause, have any useful purpose from a purely physical point of view?

▲ *"They sometimes modify conditions in certain areas. But generally it is future generations that will enjoy the resulting benefits."*

740. Aren't such calamities also moral trials for us, forcing us to strive harder to get what we need?

▲ *"Yes. Calamities are trials that give you an opportunity to exercise your intelligence, to demonstrate your patience and resignation to higher laws. At the same time they give you the chance to grow in abnegation, selflessness, and love for others."*

741. Can we avert calamities?

▲ *"Yes, in part. But not in the way generally believed. Many calamities are the consequence of human negligence. However, as you develop scientific knowledge and accumulate experience you will learn how to probe into their causes and will be able to prevent them.*

"Still, some of the hardships that beset you are of a collective nature and subject to the designs of Providence. To one degree or other, each affected person has something to learn from such experiences, and it is impossible to avoid them. The best course is to find refuge in resignation and acceptance of a higher purpose. But at times the suffering is made more biting by the indifference and callousness of fellow human beings."

Discussion: Among natural calamities that are independent of human will, we find plagues, famines, floods, and crop-destroying weather. But we have also found the means to neutralize or at least alleviate the effect of these disasters through scientific means—e.g., the improvement of agricultural processes, crop rotation and irrigation, and the study of health conditions. One wonders, consequently, what we will do for our material well-being once we learn to use all our intellectual resources and when, in our struggle for survival, we begin to incorporate a feeling of real Christian love toward each other.[3]

Wars

742. What causes human beings to wage wars?

▲ *"The dominance of the animal over the spiritual nature. In the primitive state, humans are only capable of respecting the rights of the strong; consequently, war is the normal condition. But as you progress, you will realize how to avoid the causes of war, and wars will become less frequent. And when a war does become unavoidable, you will at least wage it with a greater element of compassion than before."*[4]

743. Will war ever disappear from Earth?

▲ *"Yes. A time will come when all people will know the real meaning of justice and live with true fraternity. Then, in truth, they will all be brothers and sisters. "*

744. Why does Providence allow wars to take place?

▲ *"It helps you to appreciate freedom and to progress."*

—If war results in freedom, how can you explain the fact that war usually leads to the oppression of conquered peoples?

▲ *"Oppression is merely a temporary condition that forces a people to evolve faster."*

745. What about those people who stir up war for their own benefit?

▲ *"They bear an immense guilt and will require many lifetimes to redeem themselves. They must answer for every person who died as the result of their ambition."*

Murder

746. Is murder a crime under God's laws?

....

3 *See question 707 for a complementary discussion of the theme of solidarity and social progress.*

....

4 *Translator's Note: An example of greater compassion even in times of war is the Geneva Convention, a series of international treaties for the purpose of ameliorating the effects of war on soldiers and civilians.*

▲ *"Yes, a tremendous crime. A person who kills someone has cut short a life that was either a blessed project of redemption or a mission of love. Hence, the heinousness of the act."*

747. Are all murderers equally guilty?

▲ *"As we have told you, God's laws are just. The intention rather than the deed is the important consideration."*

748. Is murder in self-defense justifiable under God's laws?

▲ *"Only in cases of absolute necessity. If a means exists to save your own life while sparing the life of the aggressor, it should be employed."*

749. Are we held accountable for murders we commit in war?

▲ *"Not when you are forced to fight. But you remain accountable for any atrocities you commit. Likewise, any compassion you show will be rewarded."*

750. Who is guiltier under God's laws—someone who kills a parent or someone who kills an infant?

▲ *"Both are equally guilty. A crime is always a crime."*

751. Why does infanticide remain as a custom, even to the point where it is legally sanctioned among certain intellectually evolved people?[5]

▲ *"Intellectual development is not necessarily followed by ethical advancement. A very intelligent spirit may be evil. It may have acquired knowledge but failed to evolve morally. "*

Cruelty

752. Should we consider cruelty part of the instinct of destruction?

▲ *"It is the instinct of destruction at its worst. Destruction is sometimes necessary; cruelty never is. It is always the consequence of a mean nature."*

753. Why was brutality a dominant characteristic of primitive peoples?

▲ *"These peoples were still controlled by the brutishness of matter. They surrendered totally to their animal nature and single-mindedly focused on self-*

....

5 Translator's note: Infanticide, since the beginning of civilization, has often been interpreted as a primitive method of birth control and of ridding the group of its weaklings. In other, more advanced societies, it has been seen as a religious offering, especially of the firstborn. Up to the 19th Century, when this book was first published, firstborn sacrifice was common among many peoples in India; here the motive was the offering of one's most precious possession to the deities. Surprisingly in modern times, at the occasion of the United Nations Conference on Women (held in China in September 1995), it was reported in the American press that the practice of infanticide, albeit limited, still occurred in the Peoples Republic of China as part of the Communist government's population control policy.

preservation. This is what generally made them cruel. Furthermore, they were under the influence of equally primitive spirits. Over time, and through interaction with more evolved cultures, this characteristic receded."

754. Doesn't cruelty result from the lack of a moral sense?

▲ *"You should say that the moral sense is undeveloped, not that it is absent. It is latent in all people and will eventually transform them into good and compassionate beings. It exists in the most primitive individual, just as the principle of a scent exists in a flower bud that has not yet bloomed."*

Discussion: Human beings possess the entire range of intellectual and moral faculties, though often in a rudimentary or latent state. Whenever circumstances are relatively favorable, these will develop. When one faculty becomes dominant, development of another may lag behind. Excessive stimulation of the physical nature may, so to speak, stifle the development of the moral sense. By the same token, the growth of moral assets tends to weaken the influence of carnal appetites.

755. Why do we find cruel and unevolved beings living among relatively civilized people?

▲ *"A tree may be heavy with good fruit and still have a few pieces that are shriveled and rotting. Some people are like bad fruit; or, if you will, they are primitives who only appear civilized, wolves among the sheep. Some backward and imperfect spirits will incarnate among more evolved people because they hope the experience will help them progress. But when their trials become harsh, they may be overcome by their primitive natures."*

756. Will society someday be purged of wrong-doers?

▲ *"Humanity, as we have said, is evolving. And because such individuals are controlled by their instinctual nature and are misfits among more civilized people, they will gradually disappear, like chaff that separates from the seed during threshing. But first they must undergo other incarnations and acquire the experience that will give them a better understanding of good and bad. The process is similar to biological experiments designed to improve animals and plant life: the improvement takes hold only after many generations. These generations are similar to the different incarnate lives."*

Duels

757. Can a duel be considered a legitimate defense?[6]

....

6 *Translator's Note: Duel: A private fight between two persons, using deadly weapons. Dueling eventually became socially and legally unacceptable and has disappeared with the advent of modern society. Nonetheless, the discussion provides insights on the handling of conflicts in modern life.*

▲ *"No, it constitutes murder; it is a nonsensical custom, on a par with barbarism. When humanity attains a higher degree of moral progress, people will realize that the duel is as ridiculous as the wars in the past that were considered to be 'God's judgment'."*

758. How should we think of a duel when one of the combatants, aware of his incompetence, is sure he hasn't the slightest chance of winning?

▲ *"As a form of suicide."*

—And when the chances are equal, is it a murder or a suicide?

▲ *"Both."*

Discussion: In all duels, even ones where the chances are equal, the duelist is guilty—first, because he makes a cold and deliberate attempt against the life of a fellow being; second, because he jeopardizes his own life to no useful end.

759. What is the purpose of the so-called "point of honor" with reference to a duel?

▲ *"Pride and vanity, two of humanity's open sores."*

—Aren't there cases where a person's honor is truly at stake and a refusal would be an act of cowardice?

▲ *"This depends on custom and usage. Different countries and centuries have different sets of values. But when you become better and more ethically evolved, you will understand that the real point of honor lies on a higher plane and that a wrong cannot be righted by killing or by being killed."*

Discussion: There is more dignity and true honor in admitting guilt when we have made a mistake; in forgiving when we are in the right; and in all cases, in overlooking insults when others offer them.

Capital Punishment

760. Will capital punishment be abolished in the future?

▲ *"Capital punishment will unquestionably disappear, and this will signal a new stage of progress for humanity.[7] When you become more enlightened,*

·····························

7 Translator's Note: The application of the death penalty has decreased steadily in the last two hundred years. Social progress and concern about human rights have increasingly limited capital punishment to crimes considered heinous or treasonous. The abolition of the death penalty in all European states was decreed in 1983. At the start of the Twenty-first Century the death penalty has been abolished de jure or de facto by 111 nations (Amnesty International, 2002). In the U.S. there is still considerable debate as to whether it constitutes an appropriate punishment for the most atrocious crimes. Changes in the public sentiment toward executions have been a major force behind the movement.

capital punishment will be abolished from the Earth. You will no longer have the need to judge or be judged by others. But this time is still far off in the future."

Discussion: Social progress still leaves much to be desired. However, we would be unfair if we didn't recognize some progress in the restrictions imposed on capital punishment in more advanced civilizations and on the type of crimes for which it can be applied.

Consider the guarantees that justice now offers defendants and the compassion with which defendants are treated even when they are found guilty. Compare this with the practices of the not-so-distant past. It is a sign, we must acknowledge, that humanity is moving forward on the path of progress.

761. The law of preservation gives each of us the right to preserve his or her own life. Can't we apply this same right when it comes to eliminating a dangerous member of society?

▲ *"There are other means of preserving oneself from danger than legally killing another person. We must open, not close, the door of repentance to a criminal."*

762. It is possible to banish capital punishment in civilized societies. But wasn't it indispensable in earlier times?

▲ *"Indispensable is not quite the word. People always consider a thing necessary when they cannot find a better alternative. But, as they become more discerning, they gain a better understanding of justice and realize the abuses that were committed in its name."*

763. Are the restrictions imposed on capital punishment a reliable indication of social progress in our society?

▲ *"Can there be any doubt of it? Doesn't your spirit feel shocked when you read reports of the human massacres that were once carried out in the name of justice, and frequently to honor the Divinity? Or read of the tortures that people once underwent in order to extract confessions from them? Very well, if you had lived in those times, you would find all this natural and perhaps you would have engaged in it. This is why something that seems fair in one period can be considered barbaric in another. Only the Divine laws are eternal. Human laws change as humans themselves progress. And they will continue to change until human laws come to agree perfectly with Divine laws."*[8]

....

8 Translator's Note: *This point represents a synthesis of the ethical paradigm that guides the Spiritist philosophy. The true, fundamental code of human ethics is of a timeless nature. The social customs and norms, and the juridical codes of the nations, evolve continuously, gradually moving in the direction of the perfect ethical system. Though in every epoch a kind of ethical relativism seems to justify and endorse egotistic expressions of varied nature, the underlying movement of society points toward that ethical code. The central objective of the Spiritist Doctrine is to accelerate the ethical transformation of individuals and, consequently, of their societies.*

764. Jesus said: "All who draw the sword will die by the sword."[9] Don't these words represent a sanction of the principle of retaliation? Isn't the death imposed on a murderer an application of this penalty?

▲ *"Be careful! You misinterpret these words. The law asserts that you are individually responsible for your actions. But consider that God acts through Divine, not human, laws. All of you are subject to these laws at all times as you are disciplined by your own misdeeds—whether in this life or another. Anyone who causes another human being to suffer will eventually find him or herself undergoing a similar affliction. This is the meaning of Jesus's words. Didn't he also say: 'Love your enemies'?[10] And didn't He teach you to ask God's forgiveness for your own offenses, and say that you will be forgiven in the same proportion as you have forgiven others? Be sure that you understand the full meaning of these words."*

765. What about the death penalty imposed in God's name?

▲ *"This is to usurp the place of God in the dispensation of justice. People who act in such a way reveal how far they are from understanding God and how much they still have to undergo to cleanse their consciences. Capital punishment is a crime, no matter in whose name it is employed; and those who apply it will endure the appropriate consequences."*

....

9 *Translator's Note: Matthew 26:52.*

....

10 *Translator's Note: Matthew 5:44; Luke 6:35.*

CHAPTER XXII

THE SOCIAL LAW

Is Social Life Necessary?

766. Is social life natural to human beings?

▲ *"Without question. God has created you to live in society. If you look at all your gifts of expression, especially speech, it is evident that social interaction is an essential activity of life."*

767. Is absolute isolation contrary to the law of nature?

▲ *"Yes. Human beings look for communal life as if by instinct. And why? Because they are destined to evolve through helping and sharing with each other."*

768. Does this search for life in society derive only from personal need, or does it actually originate in the wider objectives of Providence?

▲ *"The aim of human life is evolution. It is only by interacting with each other that you benefit from your many different strengths. In isolation, your mental and physical faculties will degrade."*

Discussion: No person excels in all areas. In social life we complement each other and thus ensure our progress and well being. That's why human beings are driven to live in society, and not in isolation.

Ascetic Life

769. Very well, we accept the fact that, as a general principle, social life falls within the laws of nature. But since all human inclinations are also part of nature, why should a reclusive life—if it reflects someone's genuine desire—be subject to

reproach?

▲ *"Because it may be lived out of self-centeredness. There are people who find satisfaction in alcohol, too; but can we really approve of alcoholism? God cannot be pleased when a person lives in a manner that is not useful to others."*

770. What should we think of those people who choose to live as recluses as a means of escaping harmful influences?

▲ *"It is simply an expanded form of self-centeredness."*

—What if this reclusiveness is a self-imposed sacrifice, done for the sake of purification? Is there merit in it?

▲ *"The best form of purification consists in doing more good than evil. The recluse avoids one evil only to fall prey to another: that is, he or she openly spurns the practice of love and charity."*

771. What do you think of people who leave society in order to devote themselves to helping the unfortunate?

▲ *"They evolve spiritually by letting go of earthly attachments. In addition, they observe the law of work by dedicating themselves to service."*

—What about individuals who find in reclusiveness the peace of mind that will allow them to carry out certain tasks?

▲ *"This is not the reclusiveness of the self-centered. Such people work for society even in their isolation."*

772. Since ancient times, various religious orders have prescribed a vow of silence. What is your view of this vow?

▲ *"Before you pose this question, you should ask if the ability to speak is a natural one and, if so, why God gave it to you. God disapproves of the abuse of a faculty, not its use. Nonetheless, silence is useful. In the silence your spirit becomes freer and may communicate with us. But the vow of silence itself serves no purpose. The people who see this self-imposed hardship as an act of virtue may have good intentions. But they show their misunderstanding of the actual laws of life."*

Discussion: The vow of silence, as well as the vow of reclusiveness, deprives us of social interaction. Only social interaction, however, provides us with opportunities to do good and to fulfill the law of progress.

Family Ties

773. Why do the ties among animals and their offspring loosen when the young reach adulthood?

▲ *"Animals live the biological, not the moral life. The tenderness of the animal mother for her young is prompted by the instinct of preservation. As soon as the young are able to take care of themselves, her task is complete; nature asks nothing more of her once she has bred. This leaves her free to mate and breed again."*

774. Some people, noting this loosening of ties among animals, believe that human family ties may only be the result of culture, not natural law. Are they right?

▲ *"Humans and animals have different destinies. Why try to equate the two? Humans have needs beyond ordinary physical wants—for example, the drive to progress. Social interaction is necessary to evolution, and family ties are the basis for life in society. This is why social interaction is a natural law. God wants humans, by living together in society, to learn to love each other."*[1]

775. What effect would the loosening of family ties[2] have on society?

▲ *"It would mean more deeply-rooted selfishness and individualism."*

....

1 *See question 205 for more details on family ties.*

....

2 *Translator's Note: The assertion of the spirits has been extensively supported by the work of philosophers and social scientists such as Herbert Spencer, Marx, Engels, and John Dewey. The break-down of the family has had a wide impact on society. The assortment of social ills—teen pregnancy, inner-city gangs and poverty, poor single-mothers, drugs—observed in the 1990s in the United States seems to have been the consequence of the loosening of family ties and social liberation of the 1960-80s. The development of a strong "me-first" attitude among large groups of society comes in direct support of the spirits' assertion.*

XXIII

THE LAW OF PROGRESS

The Natural State

776. Are "natural state" and "natural law" the same thing?

▲ *"No. By natural state we mean the primitive, as opposed to the civilized state. The natural law is concerned with the life and progress of humankind."*[1]

Discussion: The "natural state" may be thought of as the infancy of humanity and the starting point for all its future moral and intellectual development. But human beings, who are perfectible and who carry within themselves the seed of their self-improvement, are not destined to live as children forever. Eventually they leave the natural state, which is only temporary, for progress and civilization. Natural law presides over the process of evolution of living forms; and the better humans understand and conform to its principles, the more they progress.

777. In the natural state humans have fewer needs and do not suffer the self-imposed demands that come with more advanced states. Based on this, some people have suggested that the natural state allows for the most complete form of happiness on Earth. Is there any truth in this view?

▲ *"It is shortsighted. It is almost the equivalent of saying that adults would be fulfilled with the kind of happiness children enjoy, a state that derives from the satisfaction of their basic needs. The natural state is quite unsuited to you."*

....

1 Translator's Note: Chapter 16 is devoted, in its entirety, to a more in-depth treatment of natural law.

778. Can humanity return to the natural state?

▲ *"No. Humanity progresses constantly and cannot go back to its infancy. It evolves by following a plan. The idea that it could revert to a more primitive condition is contrary to the law of progress."*

The March of Evolution

779. Do we as human beings find the drive to progress built into us, or is it the result of education?

▲ *"It is an internal impulse. But not everyone evolves at the same time or in the same manner. It is for this reason that, in society, the more advanced individuals are expected to aid the progress of those behind."*

780. Does moral progress always follow intellectual progress?

▲ *"This would be the normal sequence; however, it doesn't automatically follow sometimes."*[2]

—How does intellectual progress lead to moral progress?

▲ *"By making people more discerning and better at making choices. Also the development of the free will follows the development of the intelligence. With free will, one's responsibility for his or her own actions increases."*

—Some of the most intellectually advanced nations are among the most degenerate. How can we explain this?

▲ *"Complete progress is our final objective. But nations, like individuals, progress step by step. And until they acquire a higher moral sense, they may use their knowledge and resources in inappropriate ways. The moral consciousness and intellectual capacity will come into equilibrium only in the long-term."*[3]

781. Is it possible for us to stop the march of progress?

▲ *"No. But you can delay it."*

—What should we think about those individuals who try to stop the march of progress and set humanity back?

▲ *"They will have to account for their actions. Their efforts will not succeed, however. They will be swept away by the sheer force of progress."*

Discussion: Progress, an imperative of the human condition, allows for

....

2 *See questions 192 and 365 for additional comments on the simultaneity of intellectual and ethical progress.*

....

3 *See questions 365 and 751 for additional comments on the issue of ethical values and intellectual capability.*

no opposition. It is a living force. Bad human laws may block it for a while; they cannot suffocate it. Whenever such laws become totally incompatible with progress, they will be overthrown, along with all the individuals who tried to impose them. This will be the situation until humanity harmonizes its laws with Divine justice, which aims at the well-being of everyone, not just the strong.

782. Aren't there some people whose theories and actions are contrary to progress but who are, from their own perspective, acting in good faith—supposing, as they do, that they are helping progress along?

▲ *"Yes. This is a minor obstacle. It will not stop the march of progress."*

783. Does human evolution always proceed slowly?

▲ *"There is a slow and steady progress that results from the force of things. But when a people fails to progress at a reasonable pace, a major jolt—either physical or moral—may fall on them as a way of speeding their transformation."*

Discussion: Humanity cannot live in perpetual ignorance. It must arrive at the objective set for it by Providence. Enlightenment, we know, comes through the accumulated force of things. Ethical, like social, revolutions penetrate the ideas of a people little by little, germinating down through the centuries and then suddenly exploding, overturning the ideas and institutions of the past, which can no longer respond to new needs and aspirations.

We often do not see in these commotions anything more than the disorder and confusion that affect our material interests. But anyone who sees beyond his or her personal interests will admire the intentions of Providence, which turn even the most dreadful events into opportunities to create good. They are like the storm, the hurricane, that after the turmoil leaves behind a clean atmosphere.

784. The human capacity for wrong-doing is impressive. Doesn't it seem that we are going backwards instead of progressing, at least from the moral point of view?

▲ *"You are mistaken in this regard. If you look at the overall picture, you will see that progress is taking hold. Human beings are growing in their understanding of what wrong is and responding to it, day by day, by correcting their shortcomings. Sometimes, however, the forms of wrong must be extreme in order to make people recognize the need for goodness and personal change."*

785. What are the biggest obstacles to progress?

▲ *"Pride and selfishness. We refer here to moral progress only, since the intellectual kind goes on continuously. At first, you will notice, intellectual progress seems to increase obstacles. It excites ambition and the love of riches. Yet these spur the scientific researches that ultimately enlighten the spirit. Understand that all things in the spiritual and physical worlds are connected and that good can be brought out of bad. This paradoxical state of things will not go on indefinitely. It will change as humanity begins to understand that, beyond earthly pleasures, there is an infinitely more fulfilling and longer lasting happiness."*[4]

Discussion: There are two kinds of progress—intellectual and moral. These mutually support each other, though they do not necessarily march in tandem. Among civilized nations in this century, intellectual progress has been stimulated and supported to a degree unheard of in the past. At the same time our ethical progress has lagged behind. Yet if we compare the social customs of the last few centuries with those of today, we find it undeniable that real moral progress has taken place. There is no reason to suppose, then, that moral progress has stopped. It is altogether probable that there will be as great a difference in moral conduct between the nineteenth and twenty-fourth centuries as there has been between that of the fourteenth and the nineteenth. To doubt the continuity of moral progress is to believe either that humanity has reached the summit of perfection, which is absurd; or that it is not ethically perfectible, which experience has proven to be incorrect.

Nations in Decline

786. History has shown us many nations that, overwhelmed by some event of catastrophic proportions, have apparently regressed to a lawless state. Where is the progress in such cases?

▲ *"When your house is about to collapse around you, you raze it, and rebuild it to be stronger and more comfortable. Until the reconstruction is finished, though, there will be havoc, noise, and confusion in your house.*

"Consider another analogy. You are poor and live in a shack. Suddenly, you get rich. Right away you leave the shack and move into a mansion. Later on, some fellow, as poor as you were once, takes over your old shack and feels very happy because he did not have anywhere to stay before. Well, under-

······························
4 *See the section on Selfishness in Chapter 27.*

stand that the incarnate spirits in a strife-filled nation may no longer be the spirits that incarnated there during the nation's golden time. Those spirits have advanced and moved on to more perfect habitations. Others, less advanced, have now taken over their places—which they will eventually leave as well."

787. Aren't there peoples who resist progress?

▲ *"Yes. But in so doing they sow the seeds of their own physical extinction."*

—What would be the future destiny of the spirits that animate these peoples?

▲ *"They will continue on their own path to perfection, as do all the others, passing through various lives. Progress is a natural right granted to all."*

—Thus, the civilized people of today could have been primitives, cannibals?

▲ *"Long before you became what you are today, you yourself were one—more than once."*

788. Nations are collective individualities: just like individuals, they go through their periods of infancy, maturity, and gradual decline. Doesn't this truth, which is historically verifiable, lead us to suppose that the most advanced nations of this century will, like the ancient ones, have their decline and fall?

▲ *"Nations that are inspired solely by materialistic values, whose greatness is founded on military might and territorial conquest, grow and die because, very like the individual, they exhaust their strength.[5] Nations in which social laws do not favor the education of the mind and heart disintegrate because only knowledge dissipates darkness, and only love eliminates selfishness. Nations, like individuals, have to acknowledge the life of the soul; and ones in which the laws are in harmony with the everlasting laws of God will live, becoming beacons for others."*

789. Will progress one day create a single nation out of the many now on Earth?

▲ *"No, it would be impossible. The diversity of climates, human needs, customs, and cultures, prevents it. These factors cause the rise of nation-states, the laws of which are appropriate only to those particular areas and contexts. However, Christian love knows nothing of the limitations of geography and does not discriminate based on color or belief. One day, when the Divine laws have genuinely inspired the codes of law in every nation, love will reign among you, as well as among your nations. All will live in peace, since none will try to harm their neighbors or try to live at their expense."*

· ·

5 Translator's note: History has confirmed this assertion. At the time of the spirits' statement and for most of the latter half of the 19th century, France was a great military power and intellectual mecca of the world, and Britain had an awesome domination of the seas and was, along with France, one of the dominant colonial powers. Their power and international weight have, however, greatly diminished since World War II.

Discussion: Humanity progresses through the personal contributions of truth-seeking individuals who are engaged in their own inner-transformation. When individuals of this higher type are plentiful, they take the lead and draw the rest of the group upward. Also, from time to time, individuals of great genius and power will appear in order to push humanity forward. Such people are instruments of Providence; through them, humanity will progress more in a few years than it ordinarily would in the course of several centuries.

The progress of nations makes the justice of reincarnation all the more evident. Through the efforts of its best people, a nation will advance intellectually and ethically; and its people will be happier both in this world and the next. But during its slow passage to this point, often encompassing centuries, thousands of its people will have died every day. What has happened to them? Did their relative lack of advancement deprive them of the happiness reserved for those who came later? Was their happiness always proportionate to their initial state? Divine justice would not permit so obvious an injustice. Through reincarnation, everyone has equal rights to happiness: no one is excluded from progress. People who lived in a barbaric era return in a more civilized period. Consequently, everyone profits by the upward movement of Earth's various nations—a movement from which the single-life theory excludes them.

The theory of one single life faces another obstacle. According to it, the soul is created at the same time as the body. But since there are some people who are obviously more spiritually advanced than others, it would follow that God exercised favoritism at the time of their creation. Why this favoritism? Why would someone who has lived no longer than others, and maybe even for considerably less time, deserve to be given a more advanced soul?

Another obstacle to this theory derives from the following. A nation evolves—let us say, over a thousand-year period—from barbarity to civilization. The persons who constituted this nation from its birth could not live so long. Thus, at the end of the thousand years, no trace remains of them. In the interim the country has become civilized and prosperous. The question then arises: what or who has evolved to bring about this new status? Is it the individuals who were once the country's barbarians? Or are we dealing with newly created but much more advanced souls? The latter certainly creates a dilemma. If the soul is created at the time of birth, the souls of the more advanced inhabitants did not exist at the time of barbarity. Note the implication: if this view is true, we would have to conclude that efforts to encourage human progress have no meaningful effect, other than putting God in the business of creating ever more advanced souls.

Compare this theory of evolution with the one presented to us by the spirits. Souls arrive at the nation's civilized stage carrying with them the imprint of all their former progress. They come, attracted by a state of things that corresponds to their own individual state of evolution. What can we conclude from this situation? That the efforts toward particular improvements in a nation result in the attraction of spirits who have attained a certain degree of development themselves, here or elsewhere.

This is the key to human evolution. When the majority of Earth's population has achieved a higher moral state, the planet will become a magnet for good spirits. Further, more backward intelligences, having failed to attain the virtues of the advanced ones, will gradually gravitate to less evolved planets, where they will find more appropriate opportunities for progress and can better ready themselves to move up to higher spheres.

Yet another obstacle to the single-life theory is that all the work for social improvement benefits only present and future generations. The fruits of these improvements are null for all previous souls, who made the mistake of coming too soon and thus having to endure a barbaric environment. The doctrine set forth by the spirits demonstrates that the fruits of progress begun in earlier generations benefit all equally, since the worker who was there at the first difficult hour will return to continue his or her tasks in a much improved and more hospitable environment.[6]

....

6 *See Chapter 9 for a more extensive review of the arguments in support of reincarnation.*

Civilization

790. Is civilization an indication of progress or, as some philosophers assert, of human decadence?

▲ *"It is progress, although it is only partial—given that human beings do not pass from infancy to maturity instantaneously."*

—Is it sensible to denounce civilization?

▲ *"It would be more appropriate to deplore those who misuse the fruits of civilization. Civilization itself is part of the Divine plan for humanity."*

791. Will modern civilization eventually correct its flaws and eliminate all the wrongs it has brought about?

▲ *"Yes—when humanity has evolved ethically to the same point it has reached intellectually. But naturally the fruit cannot come before the flower."*

792. Why doesn't civilization immediately produce all the ethical good that it is capable of producing?

▲ *"Either because human beings are not ready to do it or because they are unwilling."*

—Isn't this because creating new needs in civilization also stimulates new appetites and passions?

▲ *"Absolutely. But, like a tree that requires time to produce sweet fruits, the spirit needs time to develop to its full potential."*

793. How can we recognize an evolved civilization?

▲ *"By the state of its ethical progress. The belief that progress resides entirely in technological and material developments is false. The presumption that you are more civilized because you have better houses and better food than others is just as preposterous. You will only earn the right to call yourselves truly civilized when your societies rid themselves of every base desire, when you have learned to live in fraternity, and when you allow yourselves to be guided by Christian love. Until then you will be merely bright people navigating through the initial stages of evolution."*

Discussion: Civilization is a gradual process. As a people evolve, they are faced with new challenges. But, notwithstanding their complexity, some of these problems are in and of themselves indicative of progress. As people embrace higher moral values, the social anomalies that may exist are gradually eliminated.

To be considered truly and completely civilized, a nation must have reached a point at which its members have reduced to a minimum their expressions of selfishness, greed, and pride. In such an environment, intellectual and moral rather than material interests will predominate. There will be equal opportunity for personal growth and a greater degree of mutual good will, good faith, and generosity. The social foundations will be less rooted in class and race prejudices, which are incompatible with the principle of "love thy neighbor." The laws will be the same for everyone, without exception, and true justice will be exercised. The weak will be given legal protection; the opinions and beliefs of every person will be respected; and the number of the poor and unfortunate will be at a minimum. Finally, all people of good will will be secure in the realization that their minimum needs will be met.

The Progress of Human Law

794. Are natural laws sufficient to regulate human societies?

▲ *"Yes, if the people understood them and were willing to live by them. However, societies have particular demands that make human legislation necessary."*

795. Why is there such instability in human laws?

▲ *"In earlier times the strongest ruled and made the laws to benefit themselves. As humanity comes to a better understanding of justice it will see that these laws need to be changed. As human laws grow closer to the true standard of justice—that is, as they become more equitable and parallel to natural laws—they will grow more stable."*

Discussion: The development of modern societies has created a new range of human needs and social responsibilities. As a result, their members have found it necessary to regulate both. Unfortunately, the fairness of the social system has often been compromised by personal biases and desires. As progress takes place, these flaws will gradually be written out of the codes of justice. This explains why human law is progressive while the natural law is immutable.

796. Are strict criminal laws a necessary fixture of our modern society?

▲ *"The less advanced a society, the greater the need for such laws. But, sad to say, your laws are geared more toward penalizing than preventing wrongs. Education alone can reform humanity, which will then no longer need severe laws."*

797. How can we be led to reform our laws?

▲ *"This will happen naturally, by the force of events and the influence of people of integrity who strive for social progress. Many laws have been reformed, and many more will be. Just wait!"*

The Contribution of the Spiritist Doctrine

798. Will the Spiritist Doctrine become a popular belief or will it continue to be accepted only by a few?

▲ *"Spiritist ideas will be broadly accepted. Moreover, they will establish the beginnings of a new age in human history. They belong to the natural order of things, and the time will come when the Spiritist philosophy will take its place among the branches of human knowledge. But there is a long way to go: the Doctrine still has to overcome many material interests. Undeniably, there are people who encourage opposition to it, either due to personal pride and/or for some purely material reason. In time, though, these individuals will become more and more isolated and will eventually accept the reality already embraced by so many or risk ridicule for their opinions."*

Discussion: Deeply held ideas change only gradually, becoming weaker with each new generation. Finally, they disappear, along with all their advocates, who will be replaced by other individuals with newer principles, just as in the case of political ideas. Let us take paganism as an example. No one today believes in the ideas related to the worship of Jupiter or the Persian Mithras. Still, for several centuries after the birth of Christianity, traces of paganism remained; it was only with the renewal of the generations that they were finally erased. These teachings will go through a similar process. Spiritism has made considerable inroads, but several generations will pass before it can pierce through the shields of incredulity. Nonetheless, the growth of belief in Spiritist ideas will expand faster than that of Christianity because these ideas are based on Christian ideals and it is Christianity itself that gives Christian Spiritism sustenance and paves the way for its expansion. While Christianity had to destroy old ideas in order to develop, the Spiritist Doctrine has only to build new ones.

799. How can the Spiritist Doctrine contribute to human evolution?

▲ *"It can help disprove the ideas of philosophical materialism and thus make human beings understand where their real interest lies. It can eliminate doubts about life after death, so that people can feel secure about their future. And it can be vital in eradicating the prejudices of religions, social classes, and races. The Doctrine will, ultimately, teach humanity the great lesson of brotherhood under which all men and women will eventually live in solidarity."*

800. Do we have any reason to fear that the Spiritist Doctrine will not be able to survive human indifference and the attachments we have to material things?

▲ *"To suppose that people can be transformed quickly is to reveal a very limited knowledge of human nature. Ideas, as we have said, evolve at a gradual pace. Many generations are sometimes needed to eliminate traces of some attitudes. But while the process is slow at best, part of the veil is lifted with each new generation. The Spiritist philosophy has come to provide you with a complete structure of ideas that will help lift the veil entirely. Meanwhile, if it helps only one person get rid of one negative quality, it will have done sufficient good since that person's next step will be much easier."*

801. Why haven't the spirits brought us these ideas before?

▲ *"You do not teach children what you teach adults. There is a time for all things. Some Spiritist ideas have been communicated before; but they were not understood or, worse, they were corrupted. Now, you have much greater understanding. The work helped prepare the ground to receive these new seeds."*

802. Since the Spiritist Doctrine is a significant step forward in our evolution, why don't the spirits speed it up by making their manifestations so evident that even the most incredulous will believe?

▲ *"You say you need miracles in order to believe. God surrounds you with miracles by the handful, and yet many of you deny God's very existence. Jesus himself performed a number of miracles, but still he did not convince his contemporaries. And don't you know people who will tell you that 'we would not believe, even if we saw'? No, it isn't through prodigies that you will arrive at the truth. God, being all goodness, allows you the merit of convincing yourselves through reason."*

C H A P T E R
XXIV

THE LAW OF EQUALITY

Natural Equality

803. Are all of us equal before God?

▲ *"Yes. All human beings tend toward the same goal, and God has made laws for the good of all. The saying 'the sun shines for all' reflects a broader truth than you imagine."*

Discussion: Everyone is governed by the same natural laws. Everyone is born with the same fragility and is subject to the same sufferings. The body of the wealthiest person is destroyed as utterly as the body of the poorest one. God gives natural superiority to no one, either by birth or in death. In God's sight, all of us are equal.

The Inequality of Talents

804. Why hasn't God given the same amount of talent to all of us?

▲ *"God created all spirits equal, but each one has lived a varying number of lives and has evolved in accordance to them. Differences—including the wide diversity in talents—can be accounted for by the sum of their incarnate experiences and by the extent of their will power. This diversity is absolutely necessary: because of it, each individual contributes to God's plan according to his or her ability. Furthermore, the solidarity that exists among the many worlds makes it possible for more advanced spirits to come and live on Earth and, in doing so, to set positive examples that enhance your progress."*

805. Does a more evolved spirit retain all of its faculties when it passes from a more to a less advanced world?

▲ *"Yes, since they cannot regress. But prior to reincarnating, a spirit may choose to live in a body with certain shortcomings, or else come into a trying situation as a way of mastering new lessons and furthering its progress."*

Discussion: The wide variety of human talents is a function of stages in spiritual development rather than of differences in the process of creation. God has not created spirits with unequal gifts. The coexistence of spirits of diverse evolutionary levels makes it possible for more evolved spirits to assist less advanced ones. Through our mutual need for each other, we practice the art of love which one day will unite us all.

Social Differences

806. Are social inequalities part of natural law?

▲ *"No, they are human constructions."*

—Will these inequalities vanish in time?

▲ *"Nothing but the laws of God are eternal. But don't you see these inequalities decreasing a little every day? As pride and self-centeredness are gradually eliminated from Earth, social differences will disappear. In time, the only remaining inequality will be that of personal merit. A day will come when you will stop evaluating each other by noble bloodlines and social status, when you will realize that it is the rightness of your thoughts and actions that constitutes your true value."*

807. What should we think of people who, strictly for personal benefit, use their social position to oppress others?

▲ *"They are to be deplored. Think how sad their futures will be when they have to live with the consequences of those acts. They will have to endure in another lifetime the hardship they have imposed on others."*[1]

Economic Inequalities

808. Aren't differences in income the result of people's differing talents, some of which are more valued by society than others?

▲ *"In some cases, yes; in others, no. You also have to consider that wealth can be ill-gotten."*

—In other words, hereditary wealth may be tainted?

▲ *"This is always hard to tell without investigation. But it is less important to*

....

1 *See question 684 on the consequences of worker exploitation.*

discuss the origin of inherited money, which may or may not have been based on somebody's wrong-doing, than to realize what it is that drives you to seek wealth. It is your intention and motivation that matters."

809. Would heirs to a fortune based on illegal activities be held accountable for them?

▲ *"The heirs would not be responsible. They might not even know the origin of their wealth. It is important to note, too, that in many cases a fortune comes into a particular individual's hands to allow him or her to benefit others and, indirectly, to repair any injustices. It is a happy person who realizes this much. If he or she acts in the name of the person who committed the original wrong, both of them will receive credit, since the latter will (from the spirit-world) have had a hand in bringing the reparation about."*

810. Often people write wills that distribute their assets more or less equitably among their loved ones. After passing on, are these people held accountable for any possible consequences of their dispositions?

▲ *"Every seed bears its fruit, but the fruit of the good seed is always sweeter. Remember this."*

811. Is absolute equality of wealth possible, and has it ever existed?

▲ *"No, it is impossible. The diversity in human talent and character prevents it."*

—Then those individuals who advocate absolute equality in the distribution of wealth as a solution to our social problems are wrong?

▲ *"They are visionaries. They fail to understand that the equality they dream of would be short-lived. Our advice is to concentrate on combating selfishness, which is the greatest wrong, rather than dwelling on chimeras."*

812. Does economic inequality imply that we will never enjoy the same level of well-being on Earth?

▲ *"The sense of well-being is relative, though you would enjoy a high level of well-being if you made a sincere effort to truly comprehend each other. True well-being, emotional and economic, comes from engaging in activities you enjoy. Considering the many different talents available, no necessary work would be left undone if this approach were taken. Harmony is in the order of things, and it would rule earthly life if it were not for your misguided interferences."*

—Will the mutual understanding you allude to ever come to pass?

▲ *"You will come to this understanding when you practice conscientiously the law of justice."*

813. Should society be responsible for people who, because of their own failings, end up living in misery?

▲ *"Yes. As we told you earlier, society itself may be the cause of many of these failings.² Isn't society's responsibility to make sure that all its members are educated and are given the opportunity to develop their moral consciousness? Frequently, the personal tragedies that afflict many of the impoverished are the result of poor education and a twisted value system."³*

Wealth and Poverty as Trials

814. Why do some of us have wealth and power while others are poor?

▲ *"In order to provide different kinds of trials. Your trials were chosen by you before reincarnating."⁴*

815. In which one, wealth or poverty, is it harder to succeed?

▲ *"Both are difficult. Poverty often incites rebelliousness against God; wealth can lead to all kinds of excesses."*

816. If the wealthy person is more exposed to temptations, doesn't he or she also have more opportunities to do good?

▲ *"That is what the wealthy often fail to do. They become self-centered and proud. And they never seem to get enough. Their wants increase along with their fortunes, so in their eyes the fortune is always too little."*

Discussion: Power and social status are trials as difficult and risky as poverty. The greater our means and power, the more obligations we have to fulfill and the greater our opportunities to do both good and evil. The poor among us are tested for resignation; the rich, on what use they make of their wealth.

Wealth and power arouse all the instincts and appetites that bind us to matter and keep us distant from spiritual perfection. This is why Jesus said that it is easier for a camel to pass through the eye of a needle than for a wealthy man to enter the kingdom of God.⁵

....

2 Translator's Note: See the discussion that follows question 793 on social ills brought about by lack of social progress.

....

3 See the discussion to question 685 on the role of education in the creation of the proper environment for social and economic progress.

....

4 Translator's Note: See question 258 to 273 on Choice of Trials.

....

5 Translator's Note: Matthew 19:24, Luke 18:25, Mark 10:25.

Equal Rights for Men and Women

817. Are men and women equal before God, and are they entitled to the same rights?

▲ *"Haven't they been given equal understanding of good and bad? Don't they have the same ability to evolve?"*

818. Why do women have an inferior status in some societies?

▲ *"Among men of limited intellectual and moral development, might is mistaken for right. This is the result of deformed social institutions and the continual abuse of the weak by the strong."*

819. Why are women physically weaker than men?

▲ *"It's a matter of function. Men have evolved physically through taking on tasks that demand muscular strength; women have always been engaged in gentler activities. Together, the two have come to complement and help each other overcome the many trials of life."*

820. Doesn't the difference in physical strength make a woman naturally dependent on a man?

▲ *"God gave physical strength to one sex in order that it might assist—not abuse—the other."*

Discussion: In God's design, men and women are naturally fitted to the functions they perform in life. If women have less physical strength than men, they are endowed with superior emotional awareness, which is in keeping with the maternal function and the fragility of the infants they care for.

821. Are the functions assigned to women as important as those assigned to men?

▲ *"Yes, possibly more important. It is, after all, the woman who gives the man his first notions and experience of life."*

822. Should men and women be equal before human laws, as they are before the law of God?

▲ *"This is exactly the first principle of justice: 'Do to others what you would have them do to you.'"*[6]

—In order to be considered just, should human legislation ensure the equality of rights between men and women?

▲ *"Equality of rights, yes; but human legislation is unable to ensure the equality of gender roles. Women are generally perceptive to inner feelings;*

....

6 *Translator's Note: Matthew 7:12.*

men are more driven by external and physical stimuli. Thus, men and women play different roles according to their intrinsic characteristics. Nonetheless, human law can only be just if it grants the same rights to both genders. Special treatment of either is a violation of the law of justice. The emancipation of women follows the progress of civilization; their forced submission to men is a remnant of more primitive times. Moreover, sex only exists in the physical realm; the same spirit can incarnate in either sex. It's only natural, then, that men and women should have equal rights."

Equality in Death

823. Where does the desire to preserve one's memory through lavish funerals and prominent monuments come from?

▲ *"It is a last act of self-centeredness."*

—But isn't it, just as often, a desire on the part of relatives to honor the dead?

▲ *"In such cases it is an ostentatious display of the family's wealth and status. Often these demonstrations have nothing to do with the departed; they are simply a way for the survivors to gratify their own vanity. Do you believe that the memory of the poor is less revered by their loved ones because they cannot afford to erect fancy stones in a cemetery? Do you believe that a luxurious memorial will save from oblivion the name of someone who led a useless life on Earth?"*

824. In this case, should we condemn elaborate funerals?

▲ *"No. When the memory of a good person is honored you set the person up as a role model."*

Discussion: The cemetery is the meeting point for all of us, and the place where all distinctions end. To try to perpetuate a memory by building stately memorials is an illusion. Time will destroy these monuments, just as it ages and wears out our bodies. This is the will of Nature. The memory of our deeds, both good and bad, will last longer than the cemetery in which we are interred. The splendor surrounding a funeral will not cleanse away our wrong-doing or make us rise one inch in the spiritual hierarchy.[7]

....

7 *See question 320 to 329 for additional considerations on the experience of death and dying from the spirit's viewpoint.*

XXV

THE LAW OF LIBERTY

Natural Liberty

825. Are there any conditions under which we experience absolute freedom?

▲ *"No, because all of you, from the greatest to the least, need each other."*

826. What would be the lifestyle of someone with absolute freedom?

▲ *"The same as a hermit's in a desert. As soon as two people find themselves together, they have reciprocal rights and duties to respect. They are, therefore, no longer absolutely free."*

827. Doesn't always respecting the rights of others deprive us of the right of personal freedom?

▲ *"Not at all—you hold that right from nature."*

828. Some people hold liberal opinions. Yet, in their own houses and among people who work for them, they are regular tyrants. How can we reconcile this contradiction?

▲ *"Intellectually they are aware of the laws of nature, but their awareness is colored by their pride and self-centeredness. In some instances, their behavior simply gives the lie to their words—they are duplicitous. In other instances, they lack the will power to do what they should."*

—Will the principles they hold be of any help to them in the afterlife?

▲ *"The more clearly a principle is understood by the intellect, the more inexcusable is the failure to put it into practice. The person who is sincere, though simple, is farther advanced on the road toward God than the one who tries to appear what he or she is not."*

Slavery

829. Are there people who, by their nature, are intended to be the property of others?

▲ *"The absolute subjection of any human being to another is contrary to the law of God. Slavery is an abuse of strength, and it will disappear with progress, as will all other abuses of human rights."*

Discussion: The human law that sanctions slavery is against natural law because it reduces individuals to the level of beasts and degrades them physically and morally.

830. When slavery has been established in a place for a long time, are the slaveholders to blame for conforming to a custom that seems natural to them?

▲ *"Wrong is always wrong. No amount of clever self-justification can change a bad deed into a good one. But the responsibility for wrong-doing always depends on the comprehension of the wrong-doer. The person who profits by the institution of slavery is always guilty of violating the natural law. But in this, as in everything else, the degree of guilt is relative. If slavery has become rooted in the minds and habits of some peoples, they may practice it in good faith, as something that appears entirely right and natural to them. But once their reason has developed more fully, they must recognize that their slaves are their equals in the sight of God. From that time, their slaveholding can no longer be excused."*

831. Some peoples have advanced more than others, with the result that their talents and skills have placed them in a position of superiority to others. Should less advanced people be dependent on more advanced ones?

▲ *"Yes, but only so that they can raise themselves to a higher level. The fact that some societies have attained greater progress is never a justification for the domination and exploitation of a less developed one. Throughout history, there have been peoples who have regarded the members of other races as little more than workhorses that they have the right to use. They believe themselves to be of purer blood. But they are fools who can see only matter. It is not the blood that is more or less pure—it is the spirit!"*[1]

832. Some people treat their slaves humanely, let them want for nothing, and argue that freedom would expose them to greater privations. How are we to interpret these claims?

▲ *"They only have a better understanding of their own interests. They take the same good care of their cattle and horses—hoping to get a better price for them on the market. They are not as guilty as the slaveholders who mistreat their slaves. But, in treating other human beings as merchandise, they deprive them of the right of personal freedom."*

....

1 *Translator's note: See question 361 on why people differ in their ethical qualities, and question 803 on the issue of equality.*

Freedom of Thought

833. Is there anything in us that escapes constraint and in which we can enjoy absolute liberty?

▲ *"Yes, in thought. In thought, there are no obstacles; you can enjoy an unlimited freedom. And while the action of thinking can be hindered for a while, it cannot be annihilated."*

834. Are we responsible for our thoughts?

▲ *"You are responsible to God. God alone has a full awareness of your thoughts and deplores or approves them according to the dictates of Divine justice."*

Freedom of Conscience

835. Does freedom of conscience arise naturally from freedom of thought?

▲ *"Yes, the two go in tandem with each other."*

836. Does anyone have a right to set up barriers to the freedom of conscience?

▲ *"No more than to freedom of thought. Only God has the right to intervene in matters of conscience. Human laws regulate relations among human beings; natural laws regulate those between human beings and God."*

837. What effect do obstacles to freedom of conscience have?

▲ *"They cause people to act differently from the way they think, making hypocrites of them. Consequently, freedom of conscience must be taken as one of the characteristics of true civilization and progress."*

838. Is every belief to be respected, even if it is known to be false?

▲ *"Every belief is worthy of respect when it is sincere and leads to the practice of goodness. The only beliefs you should condemn are the ones that lead to wrong-doing."*

839. Is it ever right to offend people whose beliefs are not the same as our own?

▲ *"To do so is to lack compassion and to infringe on others' freedom of thought."*

840. Does it infringe on freedom of conscience to put controls on beliefs that can lead to social turmoil?

▲ *"You can only repress actions; belief is inaccessible."*

Discussion: Forbidding acts that result from certain beliefs is not an infringement on the freedom of conscience if those acts are harmful to others. Such prevention still leaves the person free to hold the belief.

841. Should we, out of respect for freedom of conscience, allow the spread of dangerous ideas? Or may we, without infringing on this freedom, try to convince people that they have been deluded by those ideas?

▲ *"Not only may you—you should try to do it. But be sure to follow the example of Jesus in your attempts. Use gentleness and persuasion. And never resort to force, which would be worse than the false beliefs of the people you want to convince. If there is anything you should impose on the situation, it is goodness and fraternity. We do not advise that you ever resort to violence to convince anybody: conviction cannot be imposed."*

842. All doctrines aspire to be the sole expression of the truth. How can we recognize one that can rightfully be presented as true?

▲ *"The truest doctrine will be the one that produces the fewest hypocrites and the greatest number of truly ethical people (in other words, people who practice the law of love and compassion in its greatest purity and its widest application). This, in fact, is the only sign of the truth of a doctrine. Any belief that has as its consequence division and separation among God's children is both false and dangerous."*

Free Will

843. Do human beings have freedom of action?

▲ *"Since you have freedom of thought, you have freedom of action. Without free will, you would be a machine."*

844. Do we have free will from birth?

▲ *"You have it from the moment you develop the will to act in a conscious and deliberate way. In infancy and early childhood, free will is almost non-existent. It develops and changes its objectives with the development of the intellectual faculties. The child applies its free will to the needs associated with its age."*

845. Don't some people have instinctive predispositions that present obstacles to their exercise of free will?

▲ *"A person's present innate predispositions derive from his or her pre-incarnate existence. The kinds of acts a person is inclined to perform, then, result from the spirit's level of progress. In doing wrong the person may be seconded by spirits who enjoy partaking in such activity. However, no temptation is irresistible when there is a will to resist. Where there is a will there is a way."[2]*

846. Doesn't the body have influence over our actions, and if so, doesn't this influence constitute an infringement on the spirit's free will?

....

2 Translator's Note: See question 361 on the origin of ethical imperfections.

▲ *"Spirits suffer the influence of matter. This is why, on less material worlds, the faculties are manifested more freely. But the body does not lend faculties to the spirit. In addition, you must distinguish, when considering this question, between the moral and intellectual faculties. If an individual has a predisposition toward murder, it is without question the spirit that possesses it, not the physical organs. Likewise, someone who deadens his or her intellectual life, becoming solely occupied with the desires and appetites of the body, lowers him or herself closer to the animals. In a fundamental sense, this person fares even worse than an animal because he or she consciously surrenders to the instinctual nature and does so out of his or her free will."*[3]

847. Does mental illness or physical damage to the brain deprive us of our free will?

▲ *"If your mind becomes impaired, no matter what the cause, you are no longer the master of your actions and thereafter are no longer able to express your will freely. Mental infirmity, incidentally, is often a trial for spirits who in another life may have been too self-centered and contemptuous of others or made bad use of their minds. These spirits may be reborn in the bodies of the mentally handicapped, just as the dictator may be reborn in the body of a slave or the tight-fisted multi-millionaire in that of a homeless person. As a spirit, the mentally ill person is aware of its trials."*[4]

848. Since drunkenness distorts the mental faculties, can it be considered an extenuating circumstance in the commission of a crime?

▲ *"No. People who get drunk have voluntarily deprived themselves of their reason as a way of satisfying their lower nature. In doing so, they commit not one crime but two."*

849. What faculty has a more important role in the primitive state—instinct or free will?

▲ *"Instinct. This does not prevent primitive people from acting with entire freedom in certain situations, though they use that freedom primarily to satisfy their physical needs. Their free will necessarily grows with the development of their intellectual faculties. Also remember that, while you might have a more enlightened conscience than a primitive person, you are also held more accountable for your actions."*

850. Doesn't social status sometimes put limits on the use of free will?

....

3 *The influence of the body on human action is examined also in questions 367 to 370.*

....

4 *The spiritual implications of mental illnesses are also discussed in questions 371 to 378.*

▲ *"Without any question, society has its demands. But God, who is just and takes everything into account, will still hold you responsible if you put forth no effort to overcome such obstacles."*

Fate

851. Are there some life events that are fated—that is to say, preordained—and, if so, what becomes of free will?

▲ *"Apart from the life events that were the object of the spirit's choice before reincarnating, there is no 'fate', as that term is commonly understood. The choice of specific trials, though, creates a sort of fate for the spirit since it will have to undergo them. This is true at least for physical trials. As for moral trials, a spirit preserves its freedom to choose between good and bad and is always able to yield or resist. Seeing an incarnated spirit hesitate, a good spirit may naturally come to its aid; but it cannot influence the spirit to the extent of eclipsing its will. Likewise, a bad spirit may try to trouble or alarm it by making suggestions that exaggerate its anxieties. But regardless of the circumstances, the incarnated spirit always retains total freedom of choice."*

852. Some people seem to be pursued by a fate that is independent of their own actions. Don't the misfortunes of these individuals result from predestination?

▲ *"Their misfortunes may be purifications, which they are undergoing as result of choices made in the spirit-state. However, more often that not, the destiny to which you attribute certain events is in fact nothing more than the consequence of your own actions. Yet in the midst of these difficulties, if you can keep a clear conscience, you will find in it a source of consolation."*

Discussion: The truth or falseness of our perceptions causes us to succeed or fail in our endeavors. Often, rather than assume responsibility for mistakes, we blame our failures on destiny, in order to preserve our self-esteem. But if spiritual influences contribute to a certain result in some situations, it is nonetheless true that we do not have to accede to their suggestions. It is always in our power to repel negative ideas.

853. Some people fall into one danger after another. It seems that death is always staring them in the face. Isn't fate involved in such cases?

▲ *"There is nothing 'fatal' in the true meaning of the word but the time of death. When that time comes, no matter what form death takes, you cannot escape it."*

—Then if our hour has not come, we won't die, regardless of the danger we might be in?

▲ *"No, you will not be allowed to die. You have thousands of examples to prove this fact. But when your hour has come, nothing can save you. God, of course, knows the manner of your death. And it is often known by your spirit, too, since it may have become aware of the circumstances while planning its earthly existence."*

854. Are we to conclude, then, that precautions taken to avoid danger are useless?

▲ *"No. They are suggested to you specifically to keep you away from danger. They are one of the means Providence uses to prevent premature death."*

855. What purpose could Providence have in making us face serious dangers that really will not affect us?

▲ *"A risky situation may warn you away from a destructive path and stimulate you to better yourself. It can cause you to think more seriously about changing your ways. Also, through life-threatening experiences you are reminded of the fragility of your existence. And your spirit during such times is more sensitive to the advice of higher spirits. More often than not, unfortunately, you return to your old thoughts and feelings once the danger is past, and convince yourself that you will be able to come out unharmed again the next time. But if you take the time to examine carefully the cause and nature of the danger you escaped, you will often see that it arose from some fault or negligence of your own. Consider it a warning to look into your heart and seriously focus on the task of self-transformation."[5]*

856. Does a spirit know the kind of death it will have beforehand?

▲ *"The life the spirit chooses gives it a sense that one end is more likely than another. It also has a sense of the challenges its life will be exposed to and feels that it will prevail until its appointed time."*

857. Some soldiers brave the dangers of the battlefield, totally convinced that they will survive. Is there any foundation for this confidence?

▲ *"Just as some people have a premonition of their death, they can also foresee that the hour of death has not come. These premonitions may come from an intuition of the life path the spirit has chosen or the mission it has accepted. In addition, they may be the work of spirit-guides, who either want to ready someone for the great journey or instill courage in times of crisis. The spirit has an inner realization that it will not depart the body until its purpose has been fulfilled."[6]*

858. Why do people who have premonitions of their death generally dread it less than others?

----

5 *See questions 526 to 532 on the subject of spirits' intervention in human life.*

----

6 *See questions 411 on foreknowledge of death and 522 on the role of spirit-guides in premonitions.*

▲ *"It is the physical person, not the spirit, who dreads death. Someone who has had a premonition of death thinks of it in spiritual rather than human terms. In other words, the person understands that it will be a deliverance and will calmly wait for it."*

859. If death is inevitable when the time comes, can we say the same about all the accidents that happen to us in the course of a lifetime?

▲ *"We generally try to warn you through your intuition and direct you away from the majority of them. We do not like to see you suffer. But on the whole these accidents are unimportant in the life path you have chosen. In its purest sense, fate only applies to the time when your are born and the time you are scheduled to leave your physical body."*

—Are there incidents that must occur in a life and that spirits will not avert?

▲ *"Yes, the ones you planned in the spirit-state as part of your life. But you must not suppose that everything that happens to you is, as people say, 'written.' Frequently, events are the result of actions taken on Earth of your own free will. If you burn a finger, it isn't because it was preordained; it is the result of your own carelessness, and the pain it causes is the result of natural laws. Only the great sorrows and significant events of your life, the ones that profoundly affect you as a spirit, are, so to speak, foreordained."*

860. Can we, through our will and actions, prevent certain foreordained events from taking place?

▲ *"Yes, if the change is compatible with your life path, especially if it is a good deed or an effort at preventing wrong-doing."*

861. Does a murderer know, in choosing a life plan, that he or she will commit murder?

▲ *"No. All that can be known for certain is that choosing a particular kind of life incurs the risk of killing a fellow human. There is no telling whether someone will or will not murder because there is almost always deliberation in someone's mind before such an act. And where there is deliberation, a person is always free to act or not to act. If individuals knew beforehand that they would commit a murder while incarnated, they would of course be predestined to do so. But no one is ever predestined to commit a crime. A crime like any other action is, as a rule, the result of deliberation and free will.*

"You are all too apt, we note, to confound the events of material life and the acts of moral life. If there is sometimes a sort of fate, it is only in those events of your material life whose cause is beyond your action and independent of your will. As to the acts of the moral life, they emanate from you alone; consequently, you always retain freedom of choice. In those acts, there can be no fate."

862. There are people who never succeed in anything, who seem to be pursued by an "evil genius" in all their undertakings. Isn't there something that can be called fate in such cases?

▲ *"You can call it fate, if you like. In fact, it results from the choices those people made in the spirit-state. They wanted to test their own patience and resignation by a life of disappointment. But do not suppose that this is a definite rule. Sometimes this life condition comes about because the person insists on taking an unsuitable path or one for which he or she lacks the intelligence or skills. Someone who tries to cross a river without knowing how to swim stands a very good chance of drowning. You can say the same about most of the events of your life. If you only undertook tasks that were in harmony with your abilities, you would almost always succeed. But pride and greed draw you out of your proper path, and you mistake for a vocation what is only a desire to satisfy your ambitions. Then when you fail, you blame your 'star' rather than take responsibility for your faults. You might have been a good workman and earned your bread honorably in that capacity; instead, you preferred to write bad poetry and die of starvation. If only you could content yourself with your rightful place, there would be a place for every one."*

863. Don't society's values often lead us to follow one career rather than another? The choice of a profession is often influenced by the opinions of our friends and relations. Isn't this pressure to accede to the judgment of other people an obstacle to our free will?

▲ *"Human beings make social habits, not God; and if human beings submit to them, it is because it suits them to do so. On the other hand, anyone can refuse to adopt these habits. Your submission, therefore, is an act of free will. Why complain, then, and blame society for your private choice to follow the crowd?*

"God will always value your efforts to overcome pride and vanity. But who is going to applaud you for yielding to public opinion? Note that we do not mean to say that you should defy public opinion unnecessarily: that is the way of people who value mere unconventionality over real convictions. In the end, it is just as foolish to make yourself a freak or a laughingstock as it is wise to descend, willingly and uncomplainingly, when you find that you cannot maintain a position atop the social ladder."

864. If there are some people whom fortune treats unkindly, others seem disproportionately favored by it and succeed in everything they try. To what can we attribute this?

▲ *"In many cases, to the skillful management of their affairs. But, strange as this might seem to you, it may also be a kind of trial. People are often intoxicated by their success. They put excessive trust in their 'stars.' But when they fail to put their resources to good use, they may have to pay for that trust in the form of reverses that a little social responsibility might have prevented."*

865. How do we account for the run of luck that sometimes happens, for instance, in games of chance, where will and intelligence have nothing to do with the outcome?

▲ *"Individuals may have chosen certain experiences beforehand. The luck that favors them is a temptation, a test of their power to resist greed and pride. The person who wins in the material sense in these games, may in fact lose out as a spirit."*

866. In other words, what looks like fate in the shaping of our material destinies is really the result of our free will?

▲ *"You yourself have chosen your trial. The more difficult it is and the better you bear it, the higher you rise spiritually. Those individuals who seek lives of selfish enjoyment of plenty are weakling spirits. They remain stationary. Thus, on Earth, the number of the unfortunate is much greater than that of the fortunate because spirits generally choose the trials that will be most useful to them. They see clearly the futility of earthly splendors and amusements. Besides, even the most fortunate and sorrow-free life is not exempt from challenges and stress."[7]*

867. Where does the expression "born under a lucky star" come from?

▲ *"From an old superstition that connected the stars with human destiny. It is a symbolic expression, but some people still naively take it for literal truth."*

Foreknowledge

868. Is the future ever revealed to us?

▲ *"As a rule, the future is hidden. It is only in rare and exceptional cases that the future is revealed."*

869. Why should it be hidden?

▲ *"Knowledge of the future would interfere with your ability to act in the present and with your freedom to make choices. The thought that a particular event must happen would lead you to give up searching for a solution, or it might drive you to find some way of preventing the event.*

   "God wants each of you to concur in the accomplishment of the Divine plan, even when you would prefer to thwart it in some instances. Consequently, without knowing it, you yourselves pave the way for the events that will happen in the course of your life."

870. Since it is useful for the future to be hidden, why does God sometimes permit it to be revealed?

· ·

7 *The issue of fate and the spirits' intervention in human life is addressed in question 525 and the ones that follow it.*

▲ *"Because in those cases foreknowledge will expedite a particular end by influencing someone to act differently from the way he or she had intended. Also, foreknowledge may be a trial. The idea that a certain event is eminent often stirs up either wrong or virtuous thoughts in an individual. If you become aware, for instance, that you are to be the beneficiary of an inheritance you had not expected, your greed and craving for pleasure might well tempt you to wish for your benefactor's early death. On the other hand, the prospect of such an inheritance might stimulate only good and generous thoughts in you. How you react is your choice. Finally, the way you bear up under the disappointment of an unfulfilled prediction becomes another trial. (You will, however, be accorded the merit or demerit for any thoughts you held in anticipation of the event.)"*

871. Knowing everything, God knows whether someone will or will not fail in a given trial. What is the purpose of a trial if God has nothing to learn about that person?

▲ *"You might as well ask why God did not create human beings already accomplished and perfect.[8] Or why you have to pass through childhood before becoming an adult. The purpose of a trial is not to enlighten God about your accomplishments—God knows exactly what they are—but to leave to you the entire responsibility for your growth. Through these trials you acquire the strength to resist temptations. God is just and rewards solely according to a person's actions."*

Discussion: The same principle is at work in human society. For example, no matter how qualified a degree candidate may be or how confident we are of his or her success, that person will not receive a grade without taking an exam—that is to say, without being tested. Similarly, a judge only passes sentence on someone whose criminal activity has been proven, not on the simple presumption of guilt.

The more we think about the consequences of foreknowledge, the more clearly we see the wisdom of Providence in keeping the future hidden. If we were certain of future good fortune, we would become inactive; if we learned of a misfortune, we would be plunged into depression. In both cases our will would be paralyzed. For this reason, the future is presented to us as an end that we

·····························

8 *The issues discussed in this answer are corroborated by the replies to questions 119, 158, and 379.*

must reach through our own efforts and without advance knowledge of the steps that will be required. Foreknowledge would deprive us of initiative and the full use of our free will. We would let ourselves be drawn passively down the slope of circumstances, without using our energies and capabilities. When an event is sure, we tend not to busy ourselves about it.

Theoretical Summary of the Motivations of Human Action

872. We are in a position now to sum up the question of free will. First, we are not inevitably led into wrong-doing. Our actions are not written down beforehand; the crimes we commit do not result from any decree of destiny. We may have chosen, as a trial or purification, an existence in which our surroundings and circumstances tempt us to do wrong. But we always remain free, once incarnate, to act on the temptation or resist.

Second, our spirit exercises free will in the spirit-life by choosing its next existence and the kinds of trials to which it will subject itself. By the same token, the spirit exerts free will in the physical body by choosing to yield to or resist the temptations it has voluntarily chosen. The duty of education in this life is to combat the tendencies toward wrong-doing that a spirit brings into its new existence—a duty that will only be fulfilled when we come to a deeper and truer understanding of our spiritual nature. Then, through our knowledge of the laws that govern life, we will be able to change our inner nature, just as we enhance our intelligence through the process of education.

Third, each spirit chooses its future incarnate life based on the degree of purification it has already attained. It is in the power to make choices about the future that free will mainly consists. Incarnation does not, by any means, curtail free will. If the incarnated spirit yields to the influence of matter, it will always yield in the context of its previously chosen trials. The spirit is always free, however, to call on the assistance of God and good spirits to help it overcome that influence.

Lacking free will, we could neither be held responsible for doing wrong nor receive any merit for doing right. This principle is so fully recognized that people generally dispense blame or praise for an act in accordance with the intention behind it—that is to say, with the will of the doer. Will is synonymous with freedom. We cannot seek an excuse for our wrong-doing, therefore, in our physical organism. To do so would be to abdicate our reason, our very condition as human beings, and to assimilate ourselves to the condition of animals. The same situation would hold true concerning our right actions. But whenever we do something right, you will notice, we take care to claim the credit for it and never think of attributing that credit to some mechanical operation of our brains or other organs. Instinctively, we refuse to renounce the most glorious privilege of our species: our free will.

Fate, as commonly understood, supposes that all the events of human life, whatever their importance, have been previously and irrevocably ordained. But if this were the true order of things, we would be machines, without wills of our own. And if all our acts were invariably ruled by the power of destiny, what use would our intelligence be to us? If the doctrine of preordination were true, in fact, it would be the destruction of all our freedom of choice. Human responsibility would not exist; neither would good or bad, positive values or negative ones. God, being sovereignly just, could not admonish us for faults we did not have or reward us for virtues for which we could claim no real merit. Preordination would be, moreover, a negation of the law of progress since, if we were dependent on fate, we could make no attempt to better our position. Indeed, we would see our actions as both futile and unnecessary.

On the other hand, fate is not an empty word. As far as our situation on Earth and the roles we play here are concerned, it really does exist— though only as the result of our early, pre-incarnate choices. Because of these, we are destined to face situations that vary from a correction, to a trial, to a mission. But here the influence of fate comes to an end. Everything thereafter hinges on our will to succeed or fail. There are, of course, other factors that influence our decisions on earth: among them, the circumstances that our previous actions have created, and the influences to which we yield.[9] Therefore, where our moral decisions are concerned, fate simply does not exist. The spirit chooses beforehand its experiences on Earth, and when incarnate it makes personal decisions in full use of its free will. Only in death can we say that we face an absolute and inexorable fate, since we can neither evade the time nor change the manner of our death.

According to the general belief, we derive all our instincts from our physical organisms or from our psychological nature, for which (it has been claimed) we are not responsible. This, if true, would give us a valid excuse for our imperfections. It would allow us to claim justly that what we are has nothing to do with the choices we have made.

The Spiritist Doctrine takes a more ethical view. It admits the full extent of our free will. It shows us that when we do wrong we are yielding to lower suggestions, either internal or external to the individual. In doing so, the Doctrine leaves us with the entire responsibility for our decisions. It is within our power to combat these suggestions—which is much easier than repelling the commands of our "human nature." Accordingly,

....

9 *The issue of external influences is examined also in question 459.*

no temptation is irresistible. We can always close our mental life to the suggestions of our subconscious, just as we block our ears to the sounds of a human voice. We can always withdraw from negative suggestions by exerting our will, asking God for strength, and calling on good spirits to help us. This is what Jesus teaches in the Lord's Prayer: "Don't let us fall into temptation; but deliver us from evil."[10]

This theory of the causal forces of human action stems naturally from the teaching received from the spirit-world. Such teaching is not only morally sublime, but also eminently fitted to enhance our self-respect. It shows us that we are free to shake off the yoke of spiritual intruders, just as we close our homes to an unwelcome presence. It demonstrates that we are not machines, set in motion by impulses independent of our wills. It tells us that we are reasoning beings, with the power of listening to, weighing, and choosing freely between opposing counsels. We should add that at no moment during this kind of counseling are we deprived of our free will. What each of us does, we do through the activity of our spirit which, though temporarily incarnate, is in full control of its actions and preserves all its good and bad qualities.

The mistakes we commit have their origin in the imperfections of our spirits, which have not yet achieved the moral excellence we will all come to in the course of time. The incarnate life is given to us precisely so that our spirits can purge themselves of these imperfections through earthly trials. And it is precisely those imperfections that weaken us, that make us susceptible to the suggestions of other imperfect beings—beings who take advantage of our weakness in order to make us fail in completing our tasks. If we persevere and emerge victorious, our spirits attain a higher degree. If we fail, we remain stationary, no better and no worse, but with the unsuccessful trial to be lived through again, a repetition that can greatly retard our progress. Still, the more of our imperfections we can eliminate, the more our weaknesses diminish and the less susceptible we become to lower temptations. As our moral strength increases, misguided influences eventually stop interfering in our lives.

The human race contains a diverse population of spirits—some wrong-doers, others highly ethical. Enough corruption still exists that our planet remains relatively backward, and the proportion of less evolved spirits in relation to higher ones is still significant. Let us do our utmost, then, not to return here. Instead, let us seek admission into those realms where goodness reigns supreme. There, we will remember our sojourn on Earth only as a brief period of exile.

....

10 *Translator's Note: Matthew 6:13, Luke 11:4.*

THE LAW OF JUSTICE, LOVE AND COMPASSION[1]

Natural Rights and Justice

873. Are we born with a sense of justice, or is it something acquired by education?

▲ *"This sense is so natural that you often feel disgusted at an act of injustice. Education may foster it, but it doesn't create it. Even in the most primitive communities, you will find persons whose notion of justice is far more developed than that held by many in more advanced societies."*

874. If the notion of justice is so natural, why do different people understand it so differently? Very often, what seems just to me is seen as a grave injustice by someone else.

▲ *"Very often you allow your worldly ambitions to blur your true sense of justice."*

875. How would you define justice?

▲ *"Justice is respect for the rights of others."*

—What determines these rights?

....

1 *Translator's Note: The word in the French original is "charité." According to Le Petit Robert Dictionary of the French Language it is defined as (a) in Christian settings as "theological virtue consisting in the love of God and neighbor" (vertu théologale qui consiste dan l'amour de Dieu et du prochain en vue de Dieu), (b) "love of neighbor, altruism, beneficence, kindness, brotherly love, humanity, indulgence, mercy, philantropy" (amour du prochain, altruisme, bienfaisance, complaisance, fraternité, humanité, indulgence, miséricorde, philanthropie). In this work, the word charité has been primarily translated as "love," and secondarily as "compassion." We referred to The Oxford English Dictionary whenever questions arose regarding the equivalence of meanings.*

▲ *"Human as well as natural laws. But human law is just a reflection of the
social values accepted by a community. It changes as these values evolve. For
example, 'rights' deemed fundamental in the Middle Ages are outrageous by
your current standards. Why? Because rights established by human laws are
not always consistent with true justice. Also, many of your most private acts
go beyond the domain of human law. They are judged only by the tribunal of
conscience, where natural law prevails."*

876. According to natural law, what is the fundamental principle of justice?

▲ *"You will find it in the words of Christ which tell you to 'do to others as you
would have them do to you.'[2] The desire to see your own rights respected is
your best guide for understanding the true meaning of justice. When uncertain about the rights of your fellow human beings, put yourself in their shoes
and think of how you would like to be treated under the same circumstances.
That is how the Creator has placed the fundamental notion of justice in each
one of you; it lives in your consciences."*

Discussion: The true criterion for justice is to wish for others what we
would wish for ourselves. (Notice that this is not the same
as wishing for ourselves what we would wish for others.)
As it is not natural to wish harm for ourselves, we should
wish nothing but good for our neighbor.

In all ages and in all beliefs, human beings have sought
to enforce their personal rights. An inspiring implication of
the Christian doctrine is that this insistence on one's own
rights has become the basis for insisting on the rights of
others.

877. Does social life impose special responsibilities on us?

▲ *"Yes. As we told you, the first of these responsibilities is to respect the rights
of others. The just person is one who respects those rights. On your planet,
where so many neglect to observe this law, retaliation has become a response
of choice and a source of enormous social discord. Social life awards rights,
but it also imposes responsibilities."*

878. Sometimes we unknowingly overstep the boundaries of our own rights. How
can we tell when we've gone too far?

▲ *"Think of another person confronting the same circumstances you are facing
and consider how you would place a limit on that person's rights."*

—But if we all start attributing to ourselves the rights of our fellow men and
women, what becomes of the respect we owe to our superiors? Wouldn't the
course you are suggesting lead to insubordination and anarchy?

······························

2 *Translator's Note: Luke 6:31.*

▲ *"From the smallest to the greatest, all human beings are entitled to the same natural rights. You were all created equal and are regarded as such by your Creator. Your human-defined rights come and go as new social institutions replace old ones, but your fundamental natural rights are eternal and unchangeable. Deep inside, you are conscious of your strengths and weaknesses, and will sense when to defer to and show respect for those whose wisdom or virtues set them apart. This indicates to you the virtues and accomplishments that will also make you deserving of deference. When superior wisdom is truly appreciated, insubordination will no longer be an issue."*

879. Suppose someone really lives up to the true meaning of justice. Could you tell us something about that person?

▲ *"This is the truly noble person, whose life follows in the footsteps of Christ. Real justice can only be exercised when compassion and love for others are also present."*

Property Rights

880. Which is the most important among our natural rights?

▲ *"The right to life. No one has the right to take the life of another person or to do anything that might compromise somebody else's existence."*

881. Given our right to life, do we also have the right to accumulate wealth so that, for example, we may live comfortably when we're no longer able to work?

▲ *"Yes, but the accumulation of wealth should be the result of honest work, and a selfless stance toward life and family. In the working of a beehive, nature teaches a lesson in prudent foresight."*

882. Do we have the right to defend the possessions we have accumulated through hard work?

▲ *"Don't your books say: 'Do not steal'? Hasn't Jesus said: 'Give to Caesar what is Caesar's'?"*[3]

Discussion: The product of your honest work is your rightful property, which you are entitled to defend. The natural right to such property is as fundamental as the right to life and work themselves.

883. Is the desire to possess natural to us?

▲ *"Yes, but when it is simply for yourself and your personal enjoyment, it is selfishness."*

— What if we want to have more so we won't be a burden to others?

....

3 Translator's Note: Matthew 22:21, Mark 12:17.

▲ *"Some people are greedy and accumulate material things without benefit to anyone else, merely satisfying their own desires. Do you suppose that is why you were created? On the other hand, if the product of your work is put to the common good, then you are practicing the law of love and charity, and your work has the blessing of God."*

884. How do you define "rightful property"?

▲ *"No property is legitimate unless acquired without injury to others."*[4]

Discussion: When it cautions us against doing to others what we would not want others to do to us, the law of love and justice implicitly rejects all means of acquiring property that violate this principle.

885. Are there any limits to the right to property?

▲ *"All things that have been legitimately acquired constitute rightful property. But your laws are not perfect and often define rights that are inconsistent with natural justice. Such inconsistencies, however, will tend to disappear as your society evolves. What seems right in one era appears barbarous in another."*[5]

Love of One's Neighbor

886. What did Jesus really mean when he used the word "love"?

▲ *"Compassion for everyone, tolerance for the imperfections of others, and forgiveness of all offenses."*

Discussion: Love and compassion are complements of the law of justice. To love our neighbor is to do him or her all the good in our power, all that we wish might be done for ourselves.

According to Jesus, compassion is not restricted to giving money to the needy. It relates to all our relationships, regardless of the rank and social position involved. By fostering tolerance, compassion recognizes that all of us, without exception, are in need of tolerance.

Compassion teaches us not to look down on those who have less than we do. All too often, we are quick to lavish

....
4 *See question 808 on economic inequalities.*

....
5 *Translator's Note: The relativity of human legislation is also examined in question 795.*

deference on the rich, while making no effort to be at least courteous to the needy. Such social ineptitude only adds humiliation to lives that already carry considerable hardships. The truly charitable person makes a genuine effort to treat as equals even those whom worldly conventions place at the lowest end of the scale.

887. Jesus also said: "Love your enemies."[6] Doesn't that sound inconsistent with human nature? Isn't hostility just the result of lack of affinity between spirits?

▲ *"Obviously, it would not be realistic to expect a person to feel a tender and ardent affection for his or her enemies. That is not what Jesus had in mind. 'Love your enemies' means to forgive them and to return good for wrongdoing. This principle makes you better than your foes. By seeking revenge, you place yourself beneath them."*

888. What is your opinion of giving alms?

▲ *"Begging implies mental, as well as physical, degradation. If your society were based on natural law and justice, it would have the means of assisting the needy without humiliating them. Appropriate standards of living would be assured to those who cannot provide for themselves and who are presently at the mercy of chance and individual good will."*

—Do you condemn giving handouts?

▲ *"No, what we object to is the way many of you do it. Charity, in the sense used by Jesus, means seeking out those in need without waiting for them to hold out their hands.*

"The charitable person is gentle, benevolent, and pays as much attention to the way a need is eased as to the need itself. When a charitable deed is performed with discretion and tact, it is doubly beneficial. However, if your giving carries with it arrogance and indifference, those who need your favors may accept them out of necessity; but their hearts are not touched by your deeds. If you only give so that others can praise your generosity, you have no merit in God's eyes. Remember Jesus's words: 'Do not let your left hand know what your right hand is doing.'[7] Do not tarnish your charitable acts with pride and self-centeredness.

"You must also distinguish between simply giving handouts and true beneficence. The neediest person is not always the one who begs on the sidewalk. Many of the really poor are restrained from begging by the dread of humiliation; they suffer silently and in secret. The humane person seeks out

....
6 *Translator's Note: Matthew 5:44, Luke 6:35.*

....
7 *Translator's Note: Matthew 6:3.*

this hidden misery and discreetly relieves it.

"'Love one another' is the natural law that applies to all realms in the universe. Love is the law of attraction for thinking beings; attraction is the law of love for matter.

"Never lose sight of the fact that every spirit, regardless of how advanced it may be, is always placed between a superior, who serves as guide and counselor, and an inferior, toward whom it has the same responsibilities. Therefore, be charitable, not just by throwing some change to a beggar who happens to be in your way but by seeking out those who suffer in privacy. Be tolerant with the flaws of your fellow human beings; instead of despising the ignorant and unworthy, enlighten them, strive to make them better. Be gentle and considerate to those around you; treat everyone the same and you will be in harmony with the natural law established by God."

(St. Vincent de Paul)

889. Aren't there cases where beggars have no one but themselves to blame for their misfortunes?

▲ *"Oh yes. But with appropriate guidance and a sound moral education they would not have made the mistakes that caused their ruin. It is mainly by making such guidance available to everyone that the improvement of the Earth will ultimately be brought about."*[8]

Motherly and Filial Love

890. Is motherly love a virtue, or is it an instinctive feeling common to humans and animals?

▲ *"It is both. Nature has endowed the mother with love for her offspring in order to ensure their preservation. Among animals, maternal affection is limited to the provision of material needs; it ends when this care is no longer needed. In the human race, this affection lasts throughout life. It assumes a character of unselfish devotion that raises it to the rank of a virtue. In fact, motherly love survives death and follows the life of the child from beyond the grave. As you see, there is in this affection something more than the maternal connection that exists among animals."*

891. If motherly love is such a natural feeling, why do some mothers hold an aversion toward a child even from before its birth?[9]

▲ *"The absence of motherly love may be a trial chosen by the spirit of the child;*

....
8 *The answer to question 707 also addresses this issue.*

....
9 *See questions 386 to 391 for a broader discussion on human relationships.*

or a redemption if, in a previous life, it had been a bad parent or a bad child. In all cases, an uncaring mother can only be the incarnation of a less evolved spirit whose actions and attitudes constitute a trial for the child. However, the mother's violation of the laws of nature does not go unnoticed. In addition, the spirit of the child will benefit from overcoming the obstacles associated with its ordeal."

892. Can't parents be excused for not feeling the same tenderness for children who cause them a great deal of sorrow?

▲ *"No. Parents have been entrusted with the education of their children. Their mission is to make every possible effort to bring their children back onto the right path.[10] Also, the unhappiness of parents is often the result of the bad habits they have allowed their children to develop. It is like harvesting the sour fruits they themselves have sown."*

....

10 *See questions 582 and 583 for a complementary discussion on parenting and parents' responsibilities.*

XXVII

MORAL PERFECTION

Virtues and Faults

893. Which is the greatest virtue?

▲ *"All virtues are signs of an evolving consciousness. Consequently, all of them have merit, particularly the ones involved in acts of resistance to base tendencies. But the very highest virtue consists in sacrificing self-interest for the good of others. In short, it is the one that takes the form of the most disinterested expression of Christian love."*

894. With some people goodness seems to be second nature. Others, apparently, have to fight themselves to act generously. Do the actions of the two have the same merit?

▲ *"People for whom goodness is second nature have already made enough progress. In the past they've struggled and triumphed over themselves, and their generosity no longer requires an effort. They have acquired the habit of kindness. They are like war veterans who have won their medals on the battlefield.*

"The truly good stand out, at your level of progress, because their behavior provides such a strong contrast to the norm. But what is an exception for you is the rule on more advanced realms. There, goodness is natural. The inhabitants are more evolved, and even to consider a mean idea is perceived as abnormal. It is the prevalence of goodness that constitutes the happiness on these planets. One day on Earth, when the transformation is complete, the situation will be the same: everyone will come to understand and live by principles of genuine Christian love."

895. Certain attitudes are obvious signs of a corrupted moral sense. At a deeper level, what is the most characteristic sign of moral imperfection?

▲ *"Selfishness. Many people make a show of goodness, but it is like gilt on copper: it cannot stand up under the touchstone.[1] A great many people possess qualities that the world takes for virtues. But they often lack the resilience to resist trials, and the slightest blow to their self-esteem is sometimes enough to reveal the real character underneath. In fact, absolute disinterestedness is so rare on Earth that it approaches the miraculous. Attachment to material things indicates, in any event, a low level of progress. The more you care for the things of the world, the less you understand your destiny. By contrast, detachment shows that a person has arrived at a wider and clearer view of the future."*

896. Some quite generous people nonetheless lack the ability to make effective decisions and end up lavishing their money without doing any real good. Do their actions have any merit?

▲ *"Well, at least they have the merit of disinterestedness. They lose, of course, the merit for any good that might have come through wiser planning. Careless spending indicates, to say the least, a lack of judgment. Wealth is not given to be thrown away any more than it is given to be locked up in a safe. It is a deposit, and the trustees will have to account for it, for all the good they might have done but neglected, for all the tears they might have dried but turned away from."*

897. Can someone be blamed who does good only in the hope of rewards or advantages in the spirit-world? Does this kind of calculation delay our progress?

▲ *"You should act from motives of Christian love—that is, of disinterest."*

—Nonetheless, the desire to grow and free ourselves from suffering is natural. Spirits themselves teach that we should live righteously to achieve this end. Is it wrong to hope that through good deeds we will live a better life in the hereafter?

▲ *"Certainly not. But the person who does good spontaneously, selflessly, simply for the sake of pleasing God and helping a neighbor out of a bad situation, has already achieved some illumination. Obviously, this individual is much nearer spiritual fulfillment than one who acts out of self-interest."*

—Very well. Still, shouldn't we make a distinction between doing good for others and working to correct our own faults? We understand that there isn't much merit in doing good as a way of benefiting in the future life. But does it indicate a lack of progress to try to change ourselves, to overcome destructive emotions, to correct our dispositions, in the belief that we will raise ourselves spiritually?

▲ *"No, definitely not. It is true that when you calculate the interest every good deed will yield, you act selfishly. But there is no selfishness in working out your own improvement in the hope of getting closer to God. Actually, this should be the aim of every act."*

························

1 *Translator's Note: Touchstone: a black siliceous stone used to test the purity of gold and silver by the color of the streak produced on it by rubbing the touchstone with either metal.*

898. Given the temporary nature of our physical existence and the importance of our future life, is it useful to acquire scientific knowledge when this knowledge only concerns the physical life?

▲ *"Knowledge is never useless, since it contributes to your progress. Besides, acquiring new knowledge expands your intellectual capacity and quickens your development in the spirit-world. There you will learn in one hour what might otherwise have taken you many hours to understand. Greater knowledge, when put to proper use, also gives you an opportunity to help others. The journey toward perfection is based on achieving an all-encompassing knowledge; thus, everything you learn promotes your development."*

899. Two equally wealthy individuals use their wealth entirely for their own personal satisfaction. One was born to an affluent family and never wanted for anything; the other became rich through hard work. Which one is guiltier?

▲ *"The second. It is worse to have known suffering and then refuse to relieve it."*

900. Can someone who constantly accumulates wealth, but without doing good to anyone, excuse it on the ground of leaving a larger fortune to his or her heirs?

▲ *"This is nothing but an attempt to appease one's own guilty conscience."*

901. Consider two misers. One denies self the necessities of life and dies of starvation in the midst of plenty. The other is lavish in providing for self and gratifying personal desires but refuses to make the smallest sacrifice for a neighbor or help a worthwhile cause. When someone asks for a favor, this person is always short of funds. When indulging a personal whim, he or she always has money. Which of the two is guiltier, and will he or she be the worse off in the spirit-world?

▲ *"The one who spends solely for personal enjoyment is, in fact, more selfish than miserly. The first individual is already undergoing a part of the punishment for selfishness."*

902. Is it wrong to want riches in order to do good?

▲ *"When the desire is pure, it is commendable. But is it always quite disinterested? And does it never cover any secret thought of interest? Usually the first person you want to help out in these cases is yourself."*

903. Is it wrong to study other people's flaws?

▲ *"Yes, if you do it simply to criticize them or reveal their flaws to others. Then you show a lack of compassion. If you study with a view toward learning and correcting your own faults, though, you could find it useful. Never forget, in any case, that showing understanding for the faults of others is an act of compassion. And never reproach someone for a fault without first considering whether he or she might be able to accuse you of the same thing. In real-*

ity, the only reason for this kind of study is to try to acquire the opposite qualities. Is he miserly? Be charitable yourself. Is she proud? Be humble and modest. Is he harsh? Be gentle. Is she shabby and petty? Be generous. In short, act so that no one can say of you that you—in the words of Jesus—'see the mote in your brother's eye, but do not see the beam in your own eye.'"[2]

904. Is it wrong to investigate and expose social ills?

▲ *"It depends on your motive for doing it. If you only want to create a scandal or satisfy some personal grudge by showing the worst in a society, then it is wrong. Most people are aware of society's problems. A writer who takes pleasure in portraying wrongs for their own sake is going to be held responsible for any corruption his or her works bring about."*

—How can we judge an author's sincerity and purity of intent in these instances?

▲ *"You don't always have to. If good things get written, profit by them; if the writing is degrading, ignore it. An author, bent on proving his or her sincerity, must start by becoming an example of sincerity."*

905. There have been books of the highest artistry that have aided human progress through the power of their uplifting message. The authors themselves, though, have not always been particularly upright individuals. Will the good those authors have done through their writings be counted to them once they are in the spirit-life?

▲ *"High moral principles without practice are like seeds that have not been sown. What good is a seed if you do not make it multiply and feed you? These authors are all the more reproachable because they have keen minds. By not practicing the virtues they preach, they fail to reap the harvest that would naturally be theirs."*

906. Is it wrong for someone who does good to be conscious of that goodness and to inwardly acknowledge it?

▲ *"Since you are conscious of the wrong you do, you must also be aware of the good. It is the testimony of conscience that tells you whether you have done good or bad. By weighing your actions on the scales of Divine law (which are anchored in perfect justice and love), you perceive how good or harmful your actions are. It is not wrong, then, to acknowledge the action as long as it doesn't become a point of vanity."*[3]

---

2 *Translator's Note: Matthew 7:4, Luke 6:41.*

---

3 *See question 919 for additional comments on self-awareness.*

Passions[4]

907. Many of our passions have their roots in our instinctual nature. Are they therefore bad by definition?

▲ *"No, it is excessive indulgence in them that is bad, since all excess implies a weakness of will. Passions are built into you to spur you on to greater things. It is only their abuse that does harm."*

908. How can we identify the limit at which they stop serving their useful purpose?

▲ *"Passions are like spirited horses: they are useful when under control, dangerous when unbridled. Fail to govern a passion and it will become harmful, causing you to injure either yourself or others."*

Discussion: Passions are levers that increase our powers tenfold and that aid us in accomplishing the designs of Providence. But where we allow ourselves to be governed by them, we slip into every sort of excess. The force that was a lever for our progress ends up crushing us.

Passions are not bad per se. They are essential elements of human nature. A passion, strictly speaking, is a powerful intensification of an impulse or feeling. It is the excess that corrupts us and leads to unfortunate consequences. Desires of an extremely physical nature obviously bring us closer to the animal nature and impair our spiritual development. But we also have passions, powerful aspirations that raise us above the animal nature and carry us forward on the path to perfection.

909. Are our own efforts always enough to overcome the urges of our lower nature?

▲ *"Yes. Most of the time only very small efforts are needed. Unfortunately, you usually lack the will power to make even that. How few of you seriously try to subdue these impulses!"*

910. Can spiritual friends help someone trying to cope with such tendencies?

··························

4 *Translator's Note: The word in the French original is "passions," defined in the Le Petit Robert Dictionary as "an emotional and intellectual state powerful enough to impact the consciousness, by the intensity of its effects, or the permanence of its actions"* (etat affectif et intellectuel assez puissant pour dominer la vie de l'esprit, par l'intensité de ses effets, ou la permanence de son action). *Though in English the word "emotion" carries some similar connotations, the equivalence is insufficient. For lack of a better solution, we have employed the English equivalent, passion, with its significance of "powerful feelings, compelling psychological drive, motivation" rather than its more popular association with lust or sexual desire.*

▲ *"Yes, with heartfelt prayers to God. Spiritual guides will then come to the person's aid. It is their mission to do so."*[5]

911. Aren't there passions and appetites that are sometimes too strong to withstand?

▲ *"Many of you say 'I will' from the lips only. When you cannot control your passions, it is because you still take pleasure in them. But if you honestly struggle to rein in these instincts, you begin to understand your spiritual nature. You come to realize that every small victory is a triumph of the spirit over matter."*

912. What is the best way to deal with the predominance of our physical nature?

▲ *"Restraint and the practice of service."*

Selfishness

913. What is the fundamental cause of the faults found in human nature?

▲ *"If you study all your faults, you will find that their common foundation is selfishness. Ridding yourself of all the others requires that you attack selfishness at its root. Concentrate on this end. Selfishness is a kind of social gangrene, and moral progress depends on purging every selfish feeling from the human heart. Selfishness is incompatible with justice, love and compassion, and neutralizes every good quality."*

914. Since selfishness has its basis in self-interest, is it possible to eliminate it totally?

▲ *"As you become more aware of your spirituality, you attach less value to material things. In freeing yourselves from the chains of matter, you will start reforming the institutions that defend and foster selfishness. This should be the purpose of education."*

915. Since selfishness seems to be inherent in the human race, won't it always obstruct the reign of goodness on Earth?

▲ *"Selfishness is not a characteristic of humans but of the spirits incarnated on Earth. As these spirits purify themselves through reincarnation, they rid themselves of every imperfection, including this one. You have among you more people than you realize who have cleansed themselves of every vestige of selfishness and who practice absolute Christian love. They are anonymous, however; their virtue does not lend itself to the glare of popularity. But if there is only one with these qualities, why should there not be ten? And if there are ten, why not a thousand, and many more to come?"*

916. Far from diminishing, selfishness increases with civilization, which seems to feed and make it stronger. This brings up a problem. How can the effect (selfish-

....

5 *See question 459 on the spirit's influence on our actions and thoughts.*

ness) be destroyed by the cause (civilization)?

▲ *"The more obvious the social ills bred by human selfishness are, the more repulsive it becomes in your eyes. But sometimes selfishness must inflict enormous harm before you gain the willingness to fight it. Remember, though, that when you have finally discarded it from your hearts, you will truly begin living like brothers and sisters, doing each other no harm, and helping each other out of feelings of pure fellowship. Then, the strong will support the weak, and no one will lack the necessities of life. Everyone will honor the law of justice. It is indeed this reign of goodness that the enlightened spirits are helping to prepare."*

917. How can selfishness be eliminated?

▲ *"It is, certainly, the most difficult imperfection to root out. It is deeply ingrained in your physical nature, in your social structures, and in your educational systems. But its influence will gradually weaken as the knowledge of the future that Spiritist philosophy offers becomes clear and as its principles awaken you to a higher moral and spiritual life. Moreover, when properly understood, the Doctrine will help mold new habits, customs, and social relations. Selfishness, as you should have realized by now, is based on the magnification of narrow self-interest. The Spiritist Doctrine, on the contrary, forces you to look at everything from a higher vantage point, where the concept of personal interest becomes identified with principles of cooperation. In this way, it destroys the feeling of self-importance and openly combats selfishness.*

"Human beings often become selfish as a reaction to the selfishness of others. When you see that others always think of themselves first and rarely of you, you begin to think of yourself first, too. You create your own shield of selfishness, so to speak, as a protective device. But once the principles of Christian love and brotherhood become the basis of social institutions, and of the legal relations between nations and individuals, you will think less of your own personal interests. You will see that your concerns have been considered by others; and through many excellent examples and a good education, you will adapt to higher moral values. In the current climate of selfishness, of course, you need a great deal of virtue to sacrifice your own interests, especially when others respond with so little gratitude to your offering. But if you possess this virtue, the kingdom of heaven will be open to you. The happiness of the elect is assured, while at the final day of reckoning those who have thought only of themselves will be put aside and left to suffer loneliness."[6]

(Fénelon)

Discussion: Today, many praiseworthy efforts are being made that will

....

6 *The answer to this question is reiterated in the reply to question 785.*

assure the progress of the human race. More than in any other era, we are now encouraging and honoring good feelings and attitudes. Yet selfishness remains the plague of our society. It is a social disease of which we are all victims, and it should be combated with the same determination as any other epidemic. To this end we must take our cue from the physician and begin by tracing our sickness to its source. In every department of the social fabric—from family relationships to those among nations, from cottage to palace—we should seek its causes and influences, both apparent and secret, and everything that sustains and nurtures it. When those causes are discovered, the remedy will spontaneously present itself and, through our common efforts, this disease will gradually be eradicated.

The cure may indeed be slow, given the many causes of the sickness; but it is not impossible. In fact, we will bring it about most readily when we make education universal and when we make sure that education imparts not only factual information but also instills values and molds behavior.

Education, rightly understood, is the key to our ethical progress. When we can train our moral nature with the same degree of effectiveness as we do our intellectual one, we will be able to straighten a crooked nature as surely as we straighten a crooked sapling. But training of this kind requires tact, experience, and profound observation. Theoretical knowledge alone will never be enough for a teacher to exercise it successfully.

At present, no one who observes the life of a child (whether rich or poor), noting all the pernicious influences on it, the ignorance and negligence of the adults around it and their usually disastrous attempts to teach it correct values, will wonder why the world is so full of bent and corrupt people. But once we bring the proper skills and care to the development of the moral nature, we will find that, even though some natures will prove resistant, most will need only to be suitably cultivated in order to yield good fruit.[7]

Human beings seek happiness. It is a desire that prompts us to work hard to improve our lot on Earth and to discover the causes of the wrongs that afflict us. In self-

<hr />

7 *These issues are examined also in question 872.*

ishness we find one of the chief causes of affliction. Selfishness engenders the pride, ambition, greediness, resentment, enmity, and jealousy that continually annoy us; it troubles all our social relations—provoking dissension, destroying confidence, turning friends into enemies, and driving each of us to be constantly on guard against our neighbors. Eventually we must see how incompatible it is with our happiness and security. In addition, the more we have suffered from it, the more urgently we feel the necessity of fighting it, as we fight pestilence, dangerous animals, and every other disaster—out of our own interest.[8] Selfishness is the source of all our moral faults, just as compassion is the source of our virtues. To destroy the former and nurture the latter should be the aim of everyone who wants to ensure human happiness, both in the present and in the future.

Characteristics of the Good Person

918. How can we recognize those individuals who have made enough progress to rise in the spiritual hierarchy?

▲ *"By how their actions conform to the law of God and by their understanding of the spiritual life."*

Discussion: The truly good among us honor the laws of justice, love, and compassion in their greatest purity. When examining their consciences they ask whether they have done anything wrong, performed all the good in their power, and whether anyone has a reason to complain of them. They also ask whether they have done for others everything that they would wish others might do for them. Being filled with compassion, they do good for its own sake, without hope of reward, and are willing to sacrifice their own interest for the sake of justice.

The truly good are kind, benevolent, and humane. They see a brother or sister in every human being, regardless of race or belief. If God has given them power and riches, they take these gifts as trusts confided to them for the general good. Nor are they proud of their position and wealth since they know that God, the giver, can take these away at a moment's notice.

....

8 *See question 784 for a related discussion.*

If their social position means that others depend on them, the good treat those persons with equality, kindness and benevolence. They use authority to raise people, never to exploit them. In addition, they are tolerant of the weaknesses of others, knowing that they too need tolerance, reflecting in this the words of Christ "If anyone of you is without sin, let him be the first to throw a stone."[9] Above all, they are not vindictive. Following the example of Jesus, they forgive all offenses, knowing that they will be forgiven in the same proportion as they have forgiven. They respect the rights of others as scrupulously as they desire that their own rights be respected.

Self-Knowledge

919. In the present life, how can we guarantee our own moral progress and our ability to resist our lower tendencies?

▲ *"One of your wise men has told you, 'Know thyself.'"*[10]

—We agree with the maxim. But knowing the self is difficult. How should we go about it?

▲ *"At the close of each day, examine your conscience, review everything you have done, and ask yourself whether you have not failed in some duty, whether someone might not be within their rights to complain of you. Through this method you will come to knowledge of yourself and discover what there is about you that still needs reforming. If you examine your actions in this way every evening and pray for increased insight into your motives, you will find the strength to improve—for God will assist you. Ask yourself what you have done and what your aims were in doing it. Examine whether you have done anything that you would criticize in someone else or that you would be ashamed to be known as having done. Also ask yourself this question: 'If I were to die now, would I have to dread the sight of anyone?' Further, consider sincerely anything you might have done against God, your neighbors, or yourself. The answers to these questions will either put your conscience at rest or show you some of the moral weakness you still have to eliminate.*

"Self knowledge is the key to individual transformation. But, you will ask, 'How are we to evaluate ourselves? Isn't each of us subject to the illusion of self-love, which diminishes and excuses our faults? Doesn't the miser think he is simply practicing economy and foresight? Doesn't the proud

....

9 *Translator's Note: John 8:7.*

....

10 *Translator's Note: Statement inscribed on the temple of Apollo at Adelphi; Plato, in* Protagoras, *attributes the saying to the seven wise men.*

woman think of her pride only as dignity?' This may be true. But you have the right means of determining the facts. When you are in doubt about the rightness of an action, ask yourself what your opinion would be if it were done by someone else. If you would condemn it in another person, you must condemn it in yourself as well. Try also to learn what others think of you; and don't automatically reject the opinion of your enemies—they usually do not disguise the truth.

"If you are firmly resolved to improve yourself, examine your conscience in order to root out your lower tendencies, as you would pull up the weeds in a garden. Every night total up your moral accounts, just as the store-keeper totes up the day's profits and losses. If, after your assessment, you can say that the balance is positive, you can sleep peacefully and wait without fear for your awakening into the other life.

"Make your questions clear and precise, and never hesitate to ask them. A few minutes of inner dialogue may give you access to a happiness that will last forever. After all, you work every day in order to ensure security in your old age. It is one of the chief reasons that you endure the fatigues and priva-tions of your life. But between a few days of rest, usually attended by infir-mities, and the endless enjoyment that awaits the good, there can be no com-parison. Isn't this worth making a little extra effort, then?

"Many, of course, will say 'the present is certain, while the future is uncertain.' This is precisely the misconception that we are trying to remove from your minds as we demonstrate beyond doubt the future that is reserved for you. This is why, after producing the physical manifestation that appealed mainly to your senses, we now appeal to your reason through these teachings, which you are equally expected to spread the world over. It is for this reason that we have dictated The Spirits' Book.*"*

(St. Augustine)

Discussion: Often many of our faults go unnoticed. If we make use of Saint Augustine's advice more often, questioning our con-science and our motivations, we will determine more accu-rately when we slip without noticing. This question and answer format is more direct than relying on maxims, which we rarely apply to ourselves in any case. It requires objective answers—yes or no—without any room for excuses. By the sum of each, we can assess more easily how much good and bad we carry within us.

PART IV
HOPES AND SOLACE

CHAPTER XXVIII

EARTHLY JOYS AND SORROWS

Relative Happiness and Unhappiness

920. Can we enjoy perfect happiness on Earth?

▲ *"No. The incarnate life is designed to be either a trial or a purification. It is entirely up to you, and within your reach, to lighten your lot on Earth, and to be as happy as you can be on Earth."*

921. Once the human race is transformed, we can foresee that our happiness will be nearly complete. But in the meantime, can't we hope for a limited form of happiness?

▲ *"More often than not, you are the designers of your own unhappiness. Our advice is to put the laws of God into practice. You will not only spare yourself a great deal of grief, but you will also assure yourself as much happiness as you can have on the earthly plane."*

Discussion: When we rightly understand our destiny, we see incarnate life as no more than a short interlude at a shabby hotel where we have stopped on a long journey to new and exquisite quarters. In view of the end, we can easily console ourselves for life's passing annoyances.

We suffer when we fail to observe the laws governing our existence and when we overly indulge ourselves. If we trace the origin of our "earthly unhappiness," we will find that, for the most part, it is the result of a detour from the proper path, a move that has led us into a faulty road and, thereafter, into great anguish.

922. Each person views happiness on Earth differently. The hardship of one turns

on the happiness of someone else. Is there a common measure that will let us gauge happiness?

▲ *"In the material sense, it is having the necessities of life. Where the spiritual life is concerned, it is a clean conscience and faith in the future."*

923. Can't it be said that what one person finds a luxury another will see as a necessity of life, and vice versa? Doesn't it all depend on the economic situation?

▲ *"Yes—at least according to your earthly views. (As you come to see the truth of things, all these notions will be properly dealt with.) There is no doubt that if you have been living on a substantial income and then see it drastically reduced, you are going to consider yourself very unfortunate. You can no longer cut a grand figure socially or keep the indispensables of your status—vehicles, vacations, servants—simply to indulge your desires. You are going to see yourself, in fact, as lacking the necessities of life. But are you really a victim when so many other people are dying of cold and hunger, when they are homeless? Imitate the wise here: compare yourself with the people below you, never with those above, except when their superiority is spiritual and you can raise your soul toward the Infinite by modeling yourself after them."[1]*

924. Still, don't bad things happen even to the best of us—things that are independent of our conduct? Isn't there some way of sparing ourselves from them?

▲ *"In these situations, you should resign yourself without complaint—that is, if you really want to progress. As a consolation, you always have the hope of a happier future."*

925. Why does God give fortunes to people who obviously don't deserve them?

▲ *"Wealth appears to be a gift only if you are looking at the present. But remember that it is often a more dangerous trial than poverty."[2]*

926. Isn't civilization, in creating new needs and desires, the source of new problems?

▲ *"Your difficulties in this world reflect the artificial needs you create for yourselves. If you could learn to control your desires and live within your means, you would spare yourself many disappointments. The richest person is the one who has the fewest needs.*

"You envy the happiness of people who seem to be the favorites of fortune. But you don't know what their learning plan is. If they use their wealth only for themselves, they are selfish; in that case, a tough reversal awaits them. So pity, don't envy them. Sometimes the undeserving are allowed to prosper. Yet

....

1 *See question 715 on distinguishing between wants and needs.*

....

2 *Question 814 discusses wealth as a form of trial for the spirit.*

their happiness may be only apparent; nobody knows the bitter tears they shed in secret. Finally, if a good person experiences misfortune, it comes as a trial which, if faced with confidence, will be rewarded handsomely. Remember Jesus's words: 'Blessed are those who mourn, for they will be comforted.'"[3]

927. We understand that non-essential things are not indispensable to happiness. But the same is not true for basic necessities. Isn't it real misfortune to be deprived of them?

▲ *"Yes, you really are unfortunate when you don't have the bare essentials. Sometimes these situations result from your wrong-doing, and you have only yourself to blame. At other times, someone else is at fault, and that person will be responsible for it."*

928. Our talents are indicative of a vocation. Don't many of the troubles we have in life come from not pursuing that vocation?

▲ *"Yes. Often parents, out of pride or ambition, will force their children from the path nature laid out for them, and so will jeopardize their happiness. It is misguidance the parents will be held accountable for."*

—You would approve, then, of the child of wealthy parents taking up shoe repair, for instance, if this was her natural talent?

▲ *"Well, that is a bit of an exaggeration. Civilization has many needs. Why would a wealthy young person choose to fix shoes if she can do other important things? She may use her aptitudes in other endeavors—that is, if they don't run counter to common sense. For instance, instead of being a second-rate lawyer, she may instead become a good engineer, a technician, etc."*

Discussion: One of the most frequent causes of failure and disappointment in life is the placement of people in careers for which they lack any real ability. Unfitness of this kind is an inexhaustible source of setbacks; and, with pride preventing many people from taking lesser positions, suicide becomes an exit, a way of escaping what they see as humiliation. If such people had sounder moral structures, they would overcome any social prejudices and never allow themselves to be caught in such a quandary.

929. Even in the midst of wealthy communities we find people who lack the most basic necessities and who seem to have only death to look forward to. What should they do in such circumstances—allow themselves to die in destitution?

▲ *"You should never put yourself in a position where that is a choice. You can*

---

3 *Translator's Note: Matthew 5:4.*

always find means of getting food if you don't allow pride to come between your need and work. An old saying has it that 'There is no shame in honest work.' It is an adage, though, that one is more likely to apply to one's neighbor than oneself."

930. It is obviously social pressure that keeps some of us from getting work, especially when we have to take a less well-paid and lower-ranked position than our previous one. But aren't there some people who have no personal prejudices, who have put pride behind them, and yet are still genuinely incapable of providing for themselves? What about people who become sick, for instance, or meet some other circumstance beyond their control?

▲ *"In a society built on Christian principles of solidarity and compassion, no one would die of hunger."*

Discussion:　　In a society organized with wisdom and foresight, we would never slip into destitution except through our own fault. Though in some cases disease or other natural disasters may affect our plight, we should not in the long run despair over such possibilities. When all of us begin to live in accordance with the Divine laws, we will benefit from a social order founded on justice and cooperation; and we will find ourselves intrinsically better as people.[4]

931. In modern societies, it seems that most people struggle to make ends meet, while a small upper-class lives a happy life. Why is that?

▲ *"No class is perfectly happy. What looks like happiness and prosperity from the outside is often a 'facade.' Suffering is found everywhere. But to answer your question—we will state that what you call 'the underclasses' are more numerous because Earth is a place of purification and trial. When you have transformed it into a place where goodness is widespread, then there will be no more unhappiness and Earth will become a paradise for its inhabitants."*

932. Why do the wrong-doers of this world so often have authority over the good?

▲ *"This results from lack of assertiveness by the good. The wrong-doers are intriguing and bold; the good are too conciliatory. But a time will come when the good will find the determination to change things and the scenario will reverse itself."*

933. Do we design our moral tests in the same way we do our physical ones?

▲ *"Even more so. Physical suffering is often independent of one's action; moral sufferings are self-inflicted. Wounded pride, disappointed ambition, anxieties brought about by avarice, envy, jealousy, human desire—all these are the torments of the soul.*

....

4　*See question 793 for further ideas on the evolution of social order.*

"Envy and jealousy! If you don't know them, consider yourself happy. They are gnawing worms. Where they exist, serenity and peace wilt. Suffering from them, you endure longings, hatreds, rages that pursue you without rest even in your sleep. Envy and jealousy are fiery volcanoes that burn you from the inside. Is it such a surprise that, when you lose yourselves in their fires, you transform your life and Earth itself into a living hell?"

Discussion: Many of our colloquial expressions vividly picture the effects of certain harmful feelings. Someone is, we will say, "puffed up with pride," "dying with envy," "bursting with spite," "eaten up by jealousy," etc. These pictures accurately represent the states these emotions engender.

In many cases, such feelings have no real object. There are people, for instance, who are naturally jealous of anyone who succeeds or does anything out of the ordinary—even when their own interest is not at stake—simply because they can't have the same success themselves. Any evidence of superiority on the part of others offends them. We can safely say that if they had their way society would revel in mediocrity.

Our unhappiness invariably results from the undue importance we attach to material things. Selfishness, conceit, and greed make up a considerable part of our troubles. But when we aim beyond the narrow circle of material life and raise our thoughts towards our destiny, the Infinite, our difficulties seem petty and infantile to us, like the tears of a child crying over a broken toy that at the time represents its entire world.

If we look for happiness only in the gratification of desires, we will be disappointed; they don't bring real fulfillment. On the other hand, when we are able to put aside our hunger for "more" and "bigger" and "best," we can find enjoyment in circumstances other people would consider misfortune.

We are speaking here especially of modern societies, where the average person has more complex wants and therefore greater incitements to envy than those who lived in more primitive times. We tend to mull over our frustrations, so that they affect us all the more painfully. Yet we have the ability to figure out our feelings and to seek the solace we need. One source of solace is the Christian ideal, which gives us the hope of a better future; and in the Spiritist philosophy, which makes this future a certainty.

The Loss of Loved Ones

934. Isn't the death of a loved one a legitimate source of grief, since the loss is both irreversible and independent of our wishes?

▲ *"It is suffering that affects rich and poor alike. It's a learning experience and a trial for the survivors. Take heart, however, in the fact that communication with the departed is not at all closed. Indeed, there will come a day when this communication will become commonplace and even evident to your normal senses."*

935. Some people consider communicating with spirits blasphemous. How should we view this opinion?

▲ *"When there is a reverent concentration of thought and affinity and you approach the communication in good faith, there is no disrespect. The proof of this is found in the fact that spirits who love you take pleasure in coming to you. They are pleased that you remember them, that they can talk with you. The only blasphemy occurs when the communications are frivolous."*

Discussion: Communicating with spirits provides great comfort, since it allows us to speak with our departed relatives and friends. It draws them closer to us; they come to our side, hear us, reply to us. Death, in short, is no longer an impossible wall between them and us. On their part, they help us with advice and assure us of the pleasure they receive when we remember them. On ours, we have the satisfaction of knowing they are happy, of learning about the details of their new life, and of gaining the certainty that we will rejoin them when our turn comes.

936. What effect does uncontrollable grief of surviving relatives have on newly departed spirits?

▲ *"Spirits are touched by the sustained memory and deep regret of their loved ones. However, persistent and excessive grief causes them considerable distress. They see in it a lack of faith in the future and confidence in God. The survivors' grief could even prevent the departed spirit from a peaceful adaptation to its new reality."*

Discussion: Spirits, once free of the body, are happier than they were on Earth. When we regret their change of life, then, we also regret their happiness. Consider this comparison. Two friends are being held in the same prison. Both of them are scheduled to be set free, but one is released before the other. Now, it would be ungenerous for the friend who is left behind to regret this release. It would indicate selfishness, not affection, to wish for the friend to stay behind bars and suffer any longer. The same situation holds true for two people who love each other on Earth. The departed one is the first to be delivered; the one who remains ought to rejoice in that deliverance and patiently wait the moment of his or her own release.

We can illustrate this subject by another comparison. You have a friend whose situation, as long as she lives in your area, is difficult. Her health or interests require her to go to another country, where she will be better off in every respect. She will no longer be near you at every moment, of course, but the two of you will still be able to write each other. The separation between you will be only in your daily life. Should you anguish over her departure, since it is for her good?

The Spiritist Doctrine offers us the most effective consolation for this most distressing life experience. It provides us with proofs of the reality of the future life. It gives us the assurance of spiritual presences around us, and of the continued affection and care of those we loved on Earth. It shows us the way to maintain relations with them. It does away with solitude and separation. Finally, it proves that even the most isolated human being is always surrounded by friends, with whom it is possible to hold intimate and affectionate conversations.

At times the suffering may seem absolutely unbearable, and we may doubt our strength to overcome it. Yet, if we withstand the pain with courage, and if we silence our cries of self-pity, we will be glad we have undergone them when we finish our earthly career. In this matter, we should be like the patient who, finding out about her cure, celebrates the decision to have undergone a painful course of treatment.

Disappointments, Ungratefulness, Ruined Friendships

937. The disappointments caused by ungratefulness and the fragility of human friendships are another source of sadness to our hearts, are they not?

▲ *"Yes. But we teach you to pity the ungrateful and your insincere friends. Their unkindness will harm them more than it does you. Remember that ungratefulness originates in selfishness. The selfish person will sooner or later meet someone with a heart as hard as his or her own. Consider, too, the many people who have done more good than you have, who are worthier than you are, and yet whose kindness has likewise been repaid with thanklessness. Remember that Jesus himself during his lifetime was mocked, despised, and treated as a criminal and an impostor. You should not be surprised, then, when you are treated the same way. Let your awareness of the good you have done be your repayment in your present life, and don't concern yourself with the attitudes of the people you have helped. Ungratefulness serves to test your persistence in doing good. As for the ungrateful themselves, they will experience correction in the future, and with more or less severity depending on the extent of their ingratitude."*

938. Is it possible that the disappointments that ungratefulness brings about cause us to harden our hearts?

▲ *"It would be wrong to think this way. If you are generous, you are always glad to have done good. You know that if the beneficiaries of your kindness don't remember it in the present life, they will in a future one—and will feel shame and remorse for their lack of appreciation."*

—Still, this knowledge doesn't prevent us from being acutely pained by their ungratefulness in the here and now. Doesn't this pain often make us wish we were less sensitive in this area? Would we be happier?

▲ *"Yes, but it would be a selfish, hollow happiness. You should understand that ungrateful friends who desert you aren't worthy of your friendship and that you have made a mistake in your assessment of them. If you look at it this way, you won't regret their loss. Others, who understand you better, will take their place. In the meantime, pity them—they planted the seeds of their own sorrow—and don't allow yourselves to be influenced by their misconduct. This attitude will help you to keep your peace."*

Discussion: Nature has implanted in us the need to love and be loved. One of the greatest joys on Earth is to meet with friendly hearts. This empathy provides us with the first glimpses of the happiness that awaits us in the world of perfected spirits, where love and kindness reign. This is a joy the selfish will never know.

Incompatible Marriages

939. Friendly spirits are spontaneously attracted to each other in the spirit-world: this we can safely assume. How, then, do you explain that among us on Earth, affections are often one-sided, or meet with rejection and indifference. Also, how does a relationship that starts with the most loving feelings change into dislike, even hatred?

▲ *"You should realize that this is usually a form of correction and that such a state of affairs is temporary. Many people imagine they are desperately in love with each other because they judge entirely by appearance. Later, when they actually have to live together, they discover that their affection was based only on a passing impulse. It is not enough, you see, to be infatuated with someone who pleases you and whom you invest with all kinds of won-*

derful qualities. Live with this person for a while; you will soon find out what the appearances that captivated you are really worth.

"On the other hand, many marriages in which the partners seemed completely incompatible at first have developed into tender and lasting relationships based on the esteem created by a better acquaintance with each other's good qualities. You must not forget that it is the spirit who loves, not the body; and when the illusion of physical attraction disappears, one discovers the true qualities of a partner.

"There are two kinds of affection—one of the body, the other of the soul. But the two are often mistaken for each other. The affections of the soul, when pure and understanding, are lasting; those of the body perish, like the body itself. This is why people who thought they loved with eternal affection often end up despising each other after the initial attraction is gone."

940. Can't we say, too, that incompatibility between persons destined to live together is also a genuine source of suffering, made all the more bitter because it poisons an entire lifetime?[5]

▲ *"Very bitter, without question. But frequently you cause your own problems in this area. First, your divorce laws are inadequate. Do you really suppose that God would require people who dislike each other to live together forever? Second, you often place your own personal pride over and above your mutual happiness. Accordingly, you experience the consequences that naturally follow from these motives."*

—But isn't it true that an innocent victim is generally involved in such cases?

▲ *"Yes, in many cases. Usually this is the partner for whom separation is a major trial. If spirit-minded, this person will collect herself or himself and find comfort and understanding in faith. However, the person whose decision engenders the suffering will eventually be answerable for it. Finally, as you grow in understanding of yourselves and eliminate narrow-minded laws, these personal dramas will disappear."*

The Fear of Death

941. The fear of death is puzzling. How do we explain it, given that it originates with people who claim to believe in an afterlife?

▲ *"It is a groundless fear, but entirely predictable. Most people have been, from childhood, thoroughly indoctrinated into the belief that there is a Hell and a Heaven. And since under such a belief system nearly everything connected to human natural behavior is considered a sin, they consider that they will most likely go to Hell. Naturally, they are afraid. They anticipate a fire that*

---

5 *Translator's Note: At the time of the writings (1850s), divorce was considered a socially unacceptable alternative, particularly in France and other Catholic countries.*

will burn them forever without destroying them. Other people, somewhat more discriminating, throw aside their religious beliefs when they grow up. But their inability to assent to the doctrine of hell-fire lands them in a quandary really no better than the first. They become atheists and material- ists. Reacting to their old teaching, they come to believe that there is nothing beyond the present life.

"On the other hand, if you are a principled and spirit-minded person, death should hold no fear for you. Your faith gives you the certainty of a future life; and if you lived with love and compassion, you are assured of not meeting anyone in the spirit-world whose recognition you will dread."[6]

Discussion: When a person is materially minded, more attracted by the physical than the spiritual life, he identifies himself pri- marily with the pains and pleasures of earthly existence. His only happiness comes from the elusive satisfaction of his physical desires. This person, constantly preoccupied with the demands of material life, becomes tortured by perpetual anxiety. In this context, the thought of death is terrifying because he doubts the future and because he realizes that in dying he must leave all his affections and aspirations behind.

By contrast, when a person becomes spiritually minded, she raises herself above the illusory wants created by mate- rial desires; and she experiences, even on this earthly plane, enjoyments the materially minded person cannot conceive of. The moderation of desires gives her calmness and serenity of spirit. Involved in the good she has done, she finds no great disappointments in life, and its annoy- ances pass lightly over her without leaving lasting impres- sions.

942. Many people will consider your prescriptions for happiness to be somewhat commonplace, mere truisms. Couldn't anyone say, after all, that the true secret of happiness lies in our ability to bear up under our troubles?

▲ *"A good many people will take this view. But many of them are like the stub- born patient for whom a doctor prescribes a diet. They demand to be cured, but they refuse to change their habits and instead continue to gorge them- selves at the table."*

....

6 *See question 730 for a complementary examination of the fear of death.*

Disenchantment with Life; Suicide

943. Some people feel a deep weariness of life without any apparent reason. Where does this feeling come from?

▲ *"Idleness, a lack of conviction, sometimes boredom. Generally speaking, when you use your talents in the pursuit of something worthwhile, you will find pleasure in your work. Then the time passes quickly. You are able to bear the obstacles of life with patience and resignation, and to look at life with optimism."*

944. Do we have the right to terminate our own lives?

▲ *"No. The right to put an end to life belongs to God alone. The person who deliberately commits suicide repudiates the providential ordering that granted him or her a life in the earthly realm."*

—Isn't all suicide deliberate?

▲ *"No. If you kill yourself while insane, you really have no idea of what you are doing."*

945. What should we think of people who commit suicide because they are disenchanted with life?

▲ *"They are unfortunate but foolish. If they had used their time doing some useful work, life would not have been such a trial for them."*

946. And should we view in the same light people who resort to suicide in order to escape their troubles and failings?

▲ *"Poor spirits. They lacked the courage to bear the challenges of life. It is true that God helps those who face their trials with determination. But those who lack the will power to cope with their problems distance themselves from God. The tribulations of life are learning experiences. Face them with faith and resolution and the rewards for bearing them with the right attitude will be great. Pity those, however, who lacking faith, leave the solution of their problems entirely to their luck and to the circumstances. To use their own premise, they may ride their good luck for a while, but sooner or later they will have to face the emptiness of their stance."*

—Will someone who has driven another person to suicide be held accountable for that act?

▲ *"Yes. They will have to answer for it as for a murder."*

947. Some people become disheartened by their struggles, give up on themselves, and die in despair. Is this suicide?

▲ *"It is self-abandonment and indeed a form of suicide. But the people who contributed to it or were in a position to prevent it are often at greater fault. Such mitigating circumstances are taken into account. Don't suppose, though, that this is a blanket excuse. If this person had been firm and persevering, had made the best use of a good mind to pull him or herself out of those struggles, this outcome could have been prevented. The responsibility will be even greater for the person whose mind has been paralyzed by pride— who refuses, for instance, to earn a living through manual labor and would rather die of starvation than take a few steps down on the social ladder. It is infinitely more noble and dignified to bear up under hardship, to put up with the mockery of the vain and snobbish who reserve their good will for the well-off and turn a cold shoulder to anyone who really needs help. To throw away one's life on account of such people is doubly absurd, since they will be perfectly indifferent to the sacrifice."*

948. Is suicide wrong when it is committed out of shame for the harm the suicidal person has inflicted on others? Is this more justifiable than an act prompted by despair?

▲ *"Suicide doesn't cancel out responsibility in these cases. On the contrary, it adds a second wrong to the first. If you had the courage to do the wrong in the first place, you should have the courage to bear the consequences. Nonetheless, Divine justice weighs each case on its merits, taking into account all determining factors."*

949. Can suicide be excused when the person wants to avoid bringing disgrace on his or her children or family?

▲ *"An individual who commits suicide in the belief that it is for the best is wrong. Fortunately, Providence will take note of the motive and see the suicide as a self-imposed correction. In this case, motive lessens the fault; but it always remains a fault. Ultimately, when you get rid of your social misconceptions and abuses, you will have no more suicides."*

Discussion: People who take their own lives in order to escape shame and disgrace prove that they place more value on the esteem of human beings than on the esteem of God. Consequently, having abandoned the means of personal purification, they return to the spirit-world in the same state in which they left it. Fortunately, God—always more merciful than we are—forgives those of us who sincerely regret our faults, and takes into account all our efforts to repair what we have done. But nothing is ever repaired by suicide.

950. Occasionally we hear of people who kill themselves in hopes of entering a happier existence more quickly. What should we make of them?

▲ *"Their acts are not very intelligent. If they were to do good instead, they would be far surer of reaching that state. Suicide only delays their entrance into it. Once back in the spirit-world, they will understand this and ask to return to Earth to complete the kind of life they have cut short. The truth is that the sanctuary of the good cannot be opened by a fault, no matter what the motive behind the fault."*

951. But there is nobility, isn't there, when we sacrifice our lives in order to save the lives of others or to be useful to them?

▲ *"Done with this end in mind, it is not a suicide, but a sublime act. What is deplorable is the self-sacrifice that benefits no one, specially when it is motivated by pride. Sacrifice of one's own life is admirable when one's motives are disinterested. Where the end is selfish, its value is diminished."*

Discussion: Sacrifice at great personal cost is an expression of selfless love and supremely worthy in the sight of God. Life is the earthly possession to which we attach the greatest value and losing it for the sake of others would hardly be a crime. Nonetheless, before deciding on this course, we should consider carefully whether our life might not be more useful than our death.

952. There are some people whose excessive indulgence, as they well know, will bring on an early death. Their habits become addictions that they cannot control. Is this considered suicide?

▲ *"It is a suicide of sorts. Their lack of will and complete surrender to their appetites only distance them from Providence. You should realize that in these cases they are doubly responsible."*

— Are they as guilty as people who kill themselves out of despair?

▲ *"Guiltier, because they have had time to consider the suicidal nature of their pursuits. When suicide is committed on the spur of the moment, the person sometimes experiences a degree of bewilderment that borders on madness. As a result, this type of suicide will carry less personal responsibility than the ones we are talking about now. The correction a crime entails always depends on the awareness of wrong-doing that accompanies the act."*

953. Are we wrong to take our own lives in order to shorten sufferings that are going to lead to our death anyway?

▲ *"It is always wrong not to wait for the appointed moment of death. Besides, how can you tell whether the end of your life has arrived? Some help may come unexpectedly at the very moment you supposed would be your last."*

— We admit that under ordinary circumstances suicide is highly objectionable. But how would you approach the case in which death is inevitable, in which life would only be shortened by a short while?

▲ *"Even in these instances, suicide denotes a certain lack of respect and submission to the Divine Will."*

—In such a case, what are the consequences of suicide?

▲ *"The same as in all the others. It will entail a correction corresponding to the seriousness of the fault and the circumstances under which it was committed."*

954. Is there any guilt when negligence accidentally leads to a loss of life?

▲ *"Where there is no conscious intent to do harm, there is no guilt."*

955. In some countries, women used to voluntarily burn themselves to death on the funeral pyres of their husbands.[7] Were they considered suicides and did they have to undergo correction for that crime?

▲ *"They were acting according to age-old beliefs and customs. And of course they were victims of social circumstances and often had no say in the matter. Usually, they believed they were performing a duty, so their actions did not really fall under the category of suicide. Their unawareness excused them for their act. As civilization develops and spreads, this kind of practice disappears."*

956. Some people kill themselves because they cannot bear the loss of loved ones and want to be with them in the next life. Do they succeed in their intent?

▲ *"Just the opposite. Instead of reuniting with their loved ones, they find themselves separated from them, sometimes for a very long time. God cannot reward an act of ethical cowardice or grant a favor to someone who challenges Divine providence. Their moment of foolishness will, sad to say, bring them more intense grief than the moments of sorrow they hoped to shorten. They will not have the satisfaction they hoped for."[8]*

957. What is the state of the spirit after suicide?

▲ *"The consequences vary according to circumstances, but the one penalty that no suicide escapes is disappointment. Some suicides, it is true, face the expiation for their fault at once; others do so in a new earthly life harder to bear than the one they cut off."*

Discussion: Observation confirms the statement that the consequences of suicide are not the same in all cases. It also shows us that some consequences are identical in all cases of violent death. Foremost among these is the greater persistence, along with all its unfortunate effects, of the link that unites the spirit and body. In nearly all these cases, this link is in its full strength when it is suddenly snapped, whereas it weakens gradually when death results from natural causes and often breaks before life is completely extinct. The con-

....

7 *Translator's Note. A reference to the Hindu practice of* suttee, *a former Indian custom wherein a widow burned herself to death on the funeral pyre of her dead husband. The custom possibly had links with ancient beliefs that a man needed his companions in the afterlife as well as in this world. It was abolished in India by the British in 1829, but instances of it continued to occur in Indian states for more than 30 years.*

....

8 *See question 934-936 for additional perspectives on the issue of loss of loved ones.*

sequences of a violent death are, first, the prolongation of the mental confusion that usually follows death, and, second, the illusion that causes a spirit to believe that it is still living its earthly life.[9]

The affinity that continues to exist between the spirit and the body produces various repercussions. Thus, the spirit may be forced to watch the process of bodily decay, a sight it may be bound to witness for a long time—in certain cases, for the length of time it had left to live on Earth. This is not a general rule; but the suicide sooner or later will have to account for its actions. Many spirits who led miserable lives in their last incarnation have said that they volunteered for those trials in order to acquire resignation, the lack of which had led to suicide in a previous life.

In other cases the repercussion takes the form of an attachment to the physical body from which the suicide struggles in vain to free itself. In still other instances, it takes the form of acute regret at having done something so utterly useless and disappointing.

Religion, ethics and philosophy all condemn suicide as contrary to the laws of nature. All assert the principle that we have no right to shorten our lives voluntarily. But why don't we have that right? Why aren't we free to put an end to our sufferings? The Spiritist Doctrine explains, through the example of spirits who surrendered to the temptation, that suicide is not only a sign of weakness and an offense against the moral law (though some people will not give this aspect much importance) but that it is also an act at once witless and irresponsible, since no benefit can possibly come from it. The arguments of the Spiritist Doctrine on this subject are not merely theoretical: they place the facts of the case before our eyes.

....

9 *Translator's Note: See question 155 on the separation between body and soul and question 165 on the spirit's temporary state of confusion immediately after death.*

CHAPTER XXIX

FUTURE JOYS AND SORROWS

The After Life

958. Why do we instinctively reject the idea of annihilation?

▲ *"Because no such thing exists."*

959. Where do we get our instinctive sense that there is a future life?

▲ *"From the knowledge your spirit had before its incarnation. In the flesh, it retains a vague memory of that knowledge."*[1]

Discussion: From ancient times human beings have been concerned about the future beyond the grave. It is a very natural preoccupation. We attach a great deal of importance to our present life, but we cannot help considering how short and uncertain it really is, and how it can be cut off at any moment. Why shouldn't we worry, then, about our future condition? In preparing to move to a foreign country, don't we try to find out as much about it as possible? This is, quite naturally, our attitude toward the spirit-world as well.

What becomes of us after the fatal moment? It is a serious question, since it involves not only a few years but all Eternity.

Instinctively, we reject the idea of complete annihilation. Even if we have had no cares, we will ask ourselves, at the

....

1 *The knowledge and intuitions we carry from our previous incarnations are discussed in question 393.*

moment of our death, what is going to happen to us; and
we involuntarily envision hope. The expectation of a better
life lies in the inner consciousness of all of us, and God
would not have placed it there unless it had a purpose.
Indeed, it makes no sense to believe in God without also
believing in a future life and the preservation of our individuality after death. What good would it do to survive the
body if our spiritual essence were to be lost in the ocean of
Infinity? This would be equivalent to total annihilation.

The Intuition of Future Joys and Sorrows

960. The belief in future joys and sorrows is found among all people. Where does
it come from?

▲ *"All of you hold this conception. It is a premonition of certain realities trans-*
mitted by your higher self. You should listen frequently and carefully to the
inner voice of the self; it has a purpose when it speaks to you."

961. What is the predominant feeling most people experience at the moment of
death? Is it doubt, fear, or hope?

▲ *"Doubt for hardened skeptics, fear for the guilty, and hope for the good."*

962. Since we have these innate spiritual perceptions, why are there so many
skeptics?

▲ *"There are fewer skeptics than you might suppose. Many of them are arro-*
gant and make a pretense of skepticism when alive and healthy. But at the
moment of death their skepticism vanishes."

Discussion: Our notions of ethical responsibility are founded on a
belief in a future life. Our sense of justice tells us that when
it comes to the joys we are all striving for, the good person
and the wrong-doer cannot be equally rewarded. Our conviction of a just and compassionate God rejects such a possibility. Consequently, we should have no doubt that some
day each of us will reap the fruits of our deeds. It is in this
sense that our innate sense of justice points us to an intuitive concept of future joys and sorrows.

God's Intervention in Our Joys and Hardships

963. Is God personally concerned with each of us? Isn't God much too important,
and we much too small to be consequential in the sight of the Divine?

▲ *"God is concerned about all beings, however insignificant they might seem*
to be. Nothing is too unimportant for the goodness of God."

964. Does God need to know each of our actions to "reward" or "punish" us?
Aren't most of our actions too insignificant?

▲ *"God's laws apply to all your actions. If you violate them, you suffer for it and must take responsibility for your suffering. When you commit a wrong, God does not take time to judge you by saying, for example, 'You are a glutton and I'm going to punish you.' Nature sets a limit to your appetites. When you overstep that limit, sickness, even death, ensues. The so-called punishments are, in every case, the consequence of violations of natural law."*

Discussion: All our actions are subject to God's laws, regardless of how petty they seem. When we break God's laws and find ourselves in trouble, we alone are culpable. We are the architects of our own future happiness or misfortune. This truth becomes evident in the following story:

"A father educated his son, instructing him in how to make his way in life. He gave him a piece of land to farm and told him, 'Here are all the tools you need to till this field. It will provide you a good living in the future. Here are the directions to follow in cultivating it. I have given you all the instruction you need to understand the directions. If you follow them, you will have a good harvest every year. If you don't, the field will fail to produce and you may starve.' Having said this, he left him to act on his own."

Now, if the son cared for and cultivated that piece of land properly, isn't it true that it would produce accordingly? And if he neglected it, wouldn't he suffer the loss of his crops? How carefully he followed the directions his father gave him would ultimately determine his happiness or misfortune in old age.

God is far more careful of us, constantly advising us about the quality of our moves through envoys, the good spirits. These messages constantly inspire us, though we frequently don't listen to them. There is still another difference between our situation and the son's: God, unlike the earthly father, gives each of us a new chance to redeem our past mistakes through another reincarnation.

The Nature of Future Joys and Hardships

965. Do the suffering and happiness of the soul after death have anything material in them?

▲ *"They cannot be material because the nature of the soul is not material. Common sense tells you that such suffering and happiness are not physical, although they are considerably more vivid than physical impressions. When liberated from matter, the senses are far more acute; matter dulls them."*[2]

966. Why are our ideas about our future trials and happiness so often childish and absurd?

▲ *"Your intelligence is not developed enough for a more accurate perception. A child does not understand in the same way as an adult, does it? Your ideas of the future life often come down to you through faulty teachings—teachings that are in urgent need of reform. And your language is quite incapable of expressing anything that lies beyond your intellectual reach. This is why it has been necessary to make use of comparisons, though you have in the past mistaken symbols for realities. But as your understanding grows, you will begin to realize things that words cannot communicate."*

967. In what ways are more advanced spirits happy?

▲ *"First, their knowledge is more extensive. Second, they do not hate, grow jealous, envious, or ambitious, or experience any of the emotions that engender unhappiness. Nor do they experience any material needs, hardships, or grief. They are happy in their endeavors, and their mutual affection is a source of supreme joy for them.*

"The happiness of spirits always depends on the extent of their progress. But while only the most advanced ones can enjoy complete happiness, this doesn't mean that all others are unhappy. With infinite degrees of perfection between less and more advanced spirits, the extent of happiness is always relative.

"Finally, spirits of the intermediary ranks have glimpses of the happiness of spirits in the ranks above them and strive to reach that state. They have a reason to emulate more evolved spirits, but they do not envy them. They know that reaching their objective depends on their own efforts. Their consciences are peaceful and clear, and they feel fortunate in not having to endure the hardships of the less advanced."

968. You tell us that a condition for spiritual happiness is freedom from material needs. Isn't the satisfaction of these same needs a source of pleasure for us?

▲ *"Yes, of physical satisfaction. And certainly you suffer when you can't satisfy these needs."*

969. How should we interpret the statement that pure spirits are united in the bosom of God and are continually busy singing God's praises?

▲ *"It is an allegory, intended to give you an idea of their understanding of God's perfections. They see and comprehend God. But you should not take the words literally. Everything in Nature, from the grain of sand upward, sings—that is, proclaims the power, wisdom and goodness of God. The spirits of the highest order do not, however, remain in eternal contemplation.*

....

2 *See questions 237 to 257 for a discussion of the sensorial capacity of spirits.*

This would be a dull and mindless state—and utterly selfish, since it would lead to everlasting uselessness.

"The most advanced spirits no longer suffer the trials of incarnate life, and that is naturally a great source of happiness for them. And as we said, their knowledge and comprehension are very extensive; and with the help of this powerful intelligence, they serve the progress of other spirits. This is their occupation, which they very much enjoy."[3]

970. In what ways do less advanced spirits suffer?

▲ *"Their sufferings, which are as various as the causes that produce them, depend on the extent of the spirits' imperfections, just as the joys of the higher spirits depend on the extent of their perfection. We can summarize these sufferings as follows: less advanced spirits crave the things they need in order to be happy, many of which are beyond their reach. They can imagine happiness but cannot attain it. They have feelings of resentment, jealousy, anger, remorse, and an indefinable anguish. They long for every kind of pleasure but are tortured by their inability to satisfy those longings."*

971. Is the influence that spirits exercise over each other always good?

▲ *"It goes without saying that such influence is always good in the case of good spirits. But the imperfect ones spend their time seeking ways to hold down those they think are most receptive to their influence. Their victims are, in some cases, people whom they beset during their incarnate life."*

—Then we are not free of temptations after death?

▲ *"No, but the influence of less advanced spirits over other spirits is significantly reduced from what it was in the incarnate state. This is because spirits are not subject to physical desires."*[4]

972. If they aren't subject, how can they be tempted?

▲ *"Although they no longer exist in a physical sense, desires linger on in the minds of more materially minded spirits. Imperfect spirits arouse these desires by taking the spirits to places where they can see them acted out or showing them things that will be likely to excite them."*

—But what is the good of rousing desires that can not be satisfied?

▲ *"This is precisely part of their plight: the miserly spirit sees gold it cannot possess; the hedonistic spirit watches orgies in which it cannot participate; the arrogant spirit encounters honors that it envies but cannot share."*

973. What are the worst hardships that wrong-doing spirits endure?

---

3 *Translator's note: See Chapter 14, especially question 562, on occupations and missions of spirits.*

---

4 *See question 996 on the spirits' ability to influence each other.*

▲ *"To describe the mental torments that come with certain violations would be impossible. The spirits who experience them have real difficulty describing them. But unquestionably the most terrible is the spirit's impression that it is condemned for all eternity."*

Discussion: Conceptions of the state of the soul in the hereafter vary according to the person's intellectual development. The more logical the person's thinking is, the more precise and free of symbolism these conceptions become. Reason says that, since the soul is incorporeal, its sufferings and sorrows must be of a non-physical nature. Therefore, release from the material world does not bring exemption from pain. Sensations are no longer of a material nature, but for the same reason, no less real.[5]

These communications from the spirits are designed to show us the future state of the soul as a reality rather than as a theory. They tell us of incidents that befall spirits in the afterlife, and present them as the natural consequences of acts and intentions the spirits willed while on Earth. Such incidents are devoid of imaginative fantasy, but they are no less painful for the spirits who misused their abilities. The number and kinds of such incidents are infinite, but we can make some generalizations. Each spirit receives correction according to the wrongs it committed. Some spirits are chastised by the persistent vision of their crimes; others through their remorse, fears, shame, doubt, loneliness, darkness, separation from loved ones, etc.

974. Where does the doctrine of eternal fire come from?

▲ *"From popular symbology. Like many other ideas this, too, was misinterpreted as reality."*

—But can't the fear of such a symbol result in some good?

▲ *"Check to see if it puts limits even on the people who teach it. If you teach something that is contrary to reason, the impressions you produce will be neither lasting nor healthy."*

Discussion: Seeking to express adequately the nature of the suffering that a spirit may experience in the afterlife, human beings could find no more powerful comparison than that of fire, the cruelest punishment imaginable for earthly crimes and a symbol of potent and dynamic activity. This explains why the belief in eternal fire reaches back into antiquity

....

5 *See question 237 on sensorial perception in spirits.*

and why later generations adopted it from their ancestors. It is also the reason that fire is such a commonly used metaphor—as when we say "the fire of passions," "burning with love," "burning with jealousy," etc.

975. Do less advanced spirits understand the happiness of the good?

▲ *"Yes. And it is a source of suffering for them since they realize that they have deprived themselves of the same happiness. This is why a spirit, once free of matter, wants to reincarnate. It knows that by handling itself well it will cleanse its consciousness and earn the rights to similar happiness. That is why it chooses trials that will help its purification.*

"You should also know that a spirit is responsible for all the bad it has committed or indirectly caused; for all the good that it could have done but did not; and for all the bad resulting from the good that it neglected to do.

"In the realm of spirit, consciousness is no longer veiled. As if the spirit had come out of a dense fog, it can now see how far it needs to progress in order to achieve happiness. In addition, its anguish increases because it realizes the full extent of its failings. The spirit is no longer under any illusion and sees things as they really are."

Discussion: Free from matter, the spirit has extended perception and is able to foresee the future promised to it. It realizes what it has failed to do in past lives and anticipates what it must accomplish in order to reach its goals. Like the traveler who has reached the top of a mountain, it sees the path by which it has already come and knows how far it must travel to arrive at its destination.

976. Does the sight of unhappy spirits upset the more advanced ones? Does it disturb their happiness?

▲ *"More advanced spirits do not feel distressed at these tribulations because they know that they will have an end. Moreover, they are committed to assisting their needy brothers and sisters in their efforts to evolve and take great pleasure in the success of the work."*

—We can understand that this might be true when they do not know the unhappy spirits or take no special interest in them. But isn't the sight of the pain and suffering of those they loved on Earth distressful for them?

▲ *"The very fact that they see your troubles shows that they do take a special interest in you. Yes, as some religions will tell you, evolved spirits do consider your suffering but from a very different point of view than you do. They know that your trials are useful for your progress, provided you accept them as such. What troubles them most is not so much your earthly hardships— which they know are only temporary—but your attitude in facing them."*

977. If spirits cannot hide their thoughts from each other and all their actions are transparent, does an offending spirit always view its victim?

▲ *"Your common sense tells you this must be the case."*

—Are the disclosure of its shameful acts and the constant memory of its victims a source of pain for a spirit?

▲ *"Greater than you realize. But the anguish will go away as the spirit makes amends for its wrong-doing. This purification can take place either in the spirit-world or on Earth in a new reincarnation."*

Discussion: When we return to the spirit-world, our entire past is revealed, along with all our good and bad deeds. The spirit who has acted wrongfully in life may try to escape the vision of the suffering it caused others, but without success. Such memories are a source of incessant pain and remorse until the spirit makes up for its errors. By contrast, the spirit who has done well will be received with friendly and open arms.

For a wrong-doer there is no greater torment than having to face her victims. How much more disturbing it will be, in the spirit-world, to be face-to-face with them. There, when the veils of matter have been lifted, she will understand the true extent and consequences of the wrong she has done. She will see her most secret actions disclosed, her lies unmasked, and will have the impression that nothing can be done to make this sad state of affairs come to an end. Then, she will at last be overcome by shame, regret, and a most poignant remorse. All the while, the victim enjoys peace.

978. Doesn't the memory of faults committed in a more backward time disturb the happiness of an advanced spirit?

▲ *"No, because it has redeemed its faults and emerged successfully from the trials it endured for that purpose."*

979. Does the thought of the trials that it still has to endure to reach perfection interfere with a spirit's happiness?

▲ *"To the extent that it is still influenced by material concerns, yes. This is why it can enjoy perfect happiness only when it becomes completely purified. But the anticipation of future trials is not painful for spirits who have reached a reasonable level of awareness."*

Discussion: The spirit who has attained a moderate level of awareness already enjoys some true happiness. It feels a warm sense of satisfaction, enjoying what it sees and all that surrounds it. The veil that covers the marvels and mysteries of creation is gradually lifted, and Divine perfection is revealed in all its magnificence.

980. Are the ties of fellowship that link spirits of the same order a source of happiness for them?

▲ *"Spirits whose affinity is cemented by lofty ideals find in their union a source of great joy since they are not afraid that it will be clouded by selfishness. They form families who are attracted by common ideals: it is in this pure and sincere devotion that their happiness consists. No false or deceitful beings can be found in their midst."*

Discussion: We enjoy the first fruits of such happiness on Earth when we find souls with whom we are compatible gathering in cordial and noble unity. When we reach more evolved states, we will enjoy a transcendent and unlimited happiness because we will only find like-minded souls who are completely unselfish. It is this love for each other that is true life, while selfishness only spreads destruction.

981. Is there a difference in the future condition of an individual who was afraid of death and one who looked on it indifferently or even with relief?

▲ *"The difference can be considerable. However, what matters are the causes that produced the fear or the desire. It is obvious, for example, that those who want to die only to end their trials are, in fact, rejecting Providence and seeking to avoid valuable learning experiences."*

982. Is it necessary to accept the tenets of the Spiritist Doctrine and to believe in spirit manifestations to be assured of a favorable situation after life?

▲ *"If this were true, everyone who does not believe in it or who has never heard about the Spiritist Doctrine would be doomed. This is an absurd idea. It is your good deeds that guarantee your happiness in the future. Good is always good, whatever path has led to it."*[6]

Discussion: The acceptance of the Spiritist philosophy helps us improve ourselves to the extent that it provides us with guidance about our future state. In showing us how to envision our future, it helps to speed along our progress, and so sustains and enlightens us. The spirit instructors teach us to endure our trials with patience and resignation, and discourage us from committing acts that could delay our future happiness. Their teachings contribute to our happiness by explaining all these things. No claim has ever been made, however, that a person cannot attain happiness without subscribing to the principles of the Doctrine.

....

6 *See questions 165 and 799 for additional comments on the relationship between belief systems and life after death.*

Earthly Sufferings

983. Is it correct to say that a free spirit endures tribulations of a mental nature while an incarnate one experiences those of a physical nature?

▲ *"It is true that while in a physical body, the spirit experiences physical hardships, but not exclusively. The hardships may also be mental. Strictly speaking, the body experiences distress of a physical nature while the spirit experiences distress of a mental nature. Contrary to the views of many, death does not necessarily bring an end to a person's anguish, which when deep-rooted, may follow it well into the afterlife and sometimes even into a future incarnation. Therefore, according to its need to cleanse itself the spirit may ask to come back in a new life that will be even harder than the one it just quitted. A rich person who misused money could come in an impoverish condition, subject to all kinds of deprivations. The proud person will most likely be subject to humiliations. Someone who overstepped authority and treated subordinates harshly and scornfully might be forced to obey someone far more relentless. To put it briefly, when your trials are not the results of mistakes in the present life, they come as purifications for wrong-doing in previous lives. When you leave the physical realm you will understand this better.[7]*

"A spirit who chooses a physical life without any significant trials risks falling into a sort of complacency that is not conducive to progress. If it is able to satisfy its wants it might even say that it has found happiness on Earth. But this happiness is only a temporary illusion. Sooner or later, it will have to return to the path of progress, which requires productive experiences in the physical realm."

984. Do all the major difficulties of our physical life result from mistakes in the present life?

▲ *"Generally speaking, no. As we have said, these hurdles may have been designed by Providence or be the result of your own choice. They are means for you to correct or provide redress for faults you committed yourself. In addition—though this is less frequent—they could be part of a mission of love. But every transgression of the laws must be neutralized by an equivalent corrective effort, be it in the present or in a future lifetime. Accountability is of the law. Consequently, when a good person has a life of hardship, she may be working to correct her own mistakes from this or a previous life."[8]*

....

7 *See related discussion in questions 273, 393, and 399.*

....

8 *See question 393 for a discussion of the connection between present and previous lives.*

985. Can we consider it a reward when someone reincarnates on a more advanced world?

▲ *"This happens because the spirit has evolved. As they advance on the evolutionary path, spirits incarnate in successively more evolved worlds. This process continues until the influence of matter is completely discarded. Thereafter, they enjoy the happiness reserved for pure spirits."*

Discussion: On worlds where conditions are less material than on Earth, the needs of the inhabitants are less pronounced, and the physical demands on them less poignant. They no longer manifest the negative tendencies that caused them so much trouble on less developed worlds. They live in peace because they practice the law of justice, love and charity, and have no reason to hate or be jealous. They know nothing of the worries and anxieties that come from envy, pride, and selfishness.[9]

986 Can a spirit who made considerable progress while on Earth still reincarnate here?

▲ *"Yes. If it has an unfinished task to accomplish, it may ask for a new incarnation. But this is no longer for the purpose of correction; it is, rather, a mission for the purpose of service."*[10]

987. What happens to us when we avoid doing wrong but do nothing to free ourselves from material attachments?

▲ *"If you have made no effort to progress morally, the conditions of your next incarnation will be similar to your current one, which means that your trials will be prolonged. You will have remained stationary."*

988. We find many people whose life flows smoothly, who are free from all cares. Do these comfortable circumstances indicate that they have nothing from the past to deal with?

▲ *"Do you know 'many' people like that? You are mistaken if your answer is yes. Such lives often only appear to be calm. These individuals may have chosen such an existence; but when they leave it, they realize that they have not progressed and will regret having wasted the time.*

"We want to stress that a spirit cannot acquire knowledge and evolve except through effort. If a spirit remains inactive, it does not evolve. It is like certain people who, according to your customs, need to earn their living but decide instead to have a good time or take to their beds to avoid working.

"We would also like to emphasize that each one of you will be account-

....

9 *See questions 172-182 for a discussion of the conditions of life in different worlds.*

....

10 *This point is reiterated in question 173.*

able for any voluntary inaction during your life. A useless life adds nothing to your spiritual growth. In fact, that happiness is equal to the sum of the good you have done. And the sum of your future misfortune is equal to your wrongs and the heartache you have spread."

989. There are people who, though not completely bad, spread unhappiness because of their tempers. What will happen to them?

▲ *"They will carry with them vivid memories of the distress they provoked, which will be a source of anguish for them. In a later life they may have to endure the grief they caused others."*

Rehabilitation and Repentance

990. Does repentance occur in the physical or in the spiritual state?

▲ *"In the spiritual state. But it can occur in the physical state, if you come to understand the difference between right and wrong."*

991. What are the consequences of repentance for a free spirit?

▲ *"It brings about a desire to reincarnate so that it can continue on its path of progress. The spirit, aware that its imperfections prevent its fulfillment, is always anxious to rid itself of faults in a new life."*[11]

992. And what happens when we repent while in the physical state?

▲ *"You start advancing faster and, time on Earth permitting, you will strive to repair your faults and mend your ways. When your conscience points out your imperfections, you have started on the road of inner-transformation."*

993. Don't some people have tendencies only toward evil-doing and refuse to repent?

▲ *"We have already said that progress is continuous. Someone who has only evil dispositions in this life will eventually acquire good ones in some other life. This is the reason you must be reborn so many times. Everyone must evolve. Some will do this faster than others, depending on their efforts. If someone has only good tendencies, that person's spirit is already far along the path, but it too had negative tendencies in other lifetimes."*[12]

994. In the case of a perverse person who stubbornly denies her wrongs, will she accept them after death?

▲ *"Yes, the spirit will always recognize them; such awareness of the bad things it has done or caused is a source of suffering. Its repentance may not always be immediate, however. Some spirits hang on to their malicious ways despite*

....

11 *Translator's note: For a discussion of aspects of the preparation to reincarnate, see also questions 332 and 975.*

....

12 *See also question 894 on the development of innate tendencies.*

their sufferings, though sooner or later they come to see their errors and repent. Good spirits, in the meantime, work to enlighten them—a work you yourself may come to perform one day."

995. Are there spirits who, without showing ill-disposition, are unconcerned about their own fate?

▲ *"There are spirits who are passive and unengaged. This passivity eventually becomes a sore for them. Since evolution is in the order of things, their very frustration becomes the instrument that will prod them to advance."*

—Don't such spirits want to shorten their trials?

▲ *"Undoubtedly they do, but they have enough will power to move on with their existences. Aren't there people among you who prefer to die destitute rather than work?"*

996. Since spirits can see the harm their imperfections cause them, why do some of them aggravate and prolong their state by doing wrong in the spirit-state—by misleading humans, for instance?

▲ *"They are slow to repent. And if they are full of resentment, they may be lured into the wrong path by spirits even less advanced than themselves."*[13]

997. We see spirits who, though relatively unevolved, are still open to good thoughts and to prayers made on their behalf. How do you explain the fact, then, that other spirits, while giving the impression of being more knowledgeable, are hard and cynical?

▲ *"Your thoughts and prayers are beneficial for those already willing to reconsider their ways. They will have no effect on the hard-of-heart, and the rebellious. They will only be helped when, one day, a flash of conscience enlightens them."*[14]

Discussion: We should never forget that physical death does not bring about a sudden transformation. If a person's life on Earth was objectionable, death does not remedy that situation. The spirit continues to persist in its ways until at length it develops a new awareness through suffering, study, and reflection.

998. Does atonement occur in the physical or the spiritual state?

▲ *"In both. On the physical plane, it comes through the trials you undergo; on the spiritual plane, through the mental suffering that comes from the realization of your faults."*

999. Is sincere repentance during physical life enough to erase our faults and

....

13 *See question 791 on the influence spirits have on each other.*

....

14 *See question 664 on the effect of prayer on spirits.*

deserve God's grace?

▲ *"Repentance does help to improve the spirit's condition, but it still must amend its past."*

—Suppose a criminal says: "It may be true that I will have to make up for my wrong-doing, but I see no need to regret anything I did." What would you say to this person?

▲ *"If he clings stubbornly to a vile mind-set, he will only have more misdeeds to make amends for in the future."*

1000. Can we make amends in our present life?

▲ *"Yes, but don't think that you can do it by simply depriving yourself of some trivial comforts or even by donating your possessions after your death when they are no longer of any use to you. Such actions are easy displays of repentance, but in the eyes of God they are no more useful than breast-beating over your wrongs. The loss of a finger while helping someone else erases more faults than a lifetime of self-imposed restrictions that benefit no one.[15] A bad action is not amended except by a good one, and a sacrifice has no value without making inroads into your pride or your material interests.*

"It does little good to give away assets after you are dead—when you no longer have use for them. It does no good either to deprive yourself of a few small pleasures and trifling posessions (in penance), if the harm you engendered is not undone. In short, what is the use of humiliating yourself before God if you continue to play for image on Earth, acting in a prideful and self-centered manner?"[16]

1001. Isn't there any value in deciding that our possessions will serve a useful purpose after we are gone?

▲ *"It is better than nothing, so it has some merit. The problem is that people who make these generous endowments and legacies are usually more selfish than generous. They want all the honors for an act of generosity which cost them only minor privation. It is true that, if individuals deprive themselves in life, they will have a double merit: first for the personal sacrifice and second in the satisfaction of seeing the happiness of the people they helped. But selfishness will often whisper, 'Whenever you give, you deprive yourself of your own pleasures.' And because selfishness speaks louder than disinterestedness and charity, people keep the money for themselves instead of giving it away, using their personal needs as an excuse. Pity them. People who ignore the pleasure of giving miss one of humanity's greatest and tenderest pleasures. The satisfaction in being generous, a form of happiness available to you in the present life, is a compensation God offers you for submitting to*

....

15 *See question 726 on the futility of self-inflicted hardships.*

....

16 *For a discussion of the value of giving, see also questions 720-21.*

the tempting trial of wealth." [17]

1002. What can a person do who faces immediate death and has no chance to make amends? Is it enough to repent?

▲ *"Repentance will hasten his or her rehabilitation, but it will not provide purification by itself. The future always lies ahead for this person."*

The Length of Corrections

1003. Is the length of the future trials experienced by a person with a guilty conscience arbitrary or does it follow some rule?

▲ *"God never acts in an erratic manner. Everything in the universe is ruled by laws that reveal supreme wisdom and compassion."*

1004. What determines the length of our trials?

▲ *"The time required for your improvement. Your spiritual state depends on your level of awareness. The length and nature of your trials depends, then, on what still needs to be done to complete your transformation. As you progress and your feelings become more sublimated, your trials will decrease and their nature will change."*

(St. Louis)

1005. To a suffering spirit, does time seem longer or shorter in the spirit-world than in the physical one?

▲ *"It seems longer. Remember that sleep does not exist for it. Only when spirits reach a certain degree of awareness is time, as defined on Earth, fused, so to speak, with Infinity."* [18]

1006. Can a spirit's sufferings be eternal?

▲ *"If it remained a wrong-doer eternally—that is, if it could never repent and change—the answer would be yes. But God didn't create beings that remain imperfect forever. They were made simple and ignorant, and all of them progress in time, depending on their own free will. A spirit can delay its own progress, but sooner or later it will feel an irresistible need to abandon the wretched spheres and be happy. Consequently, the law that regulates the length of trials is remarkably wise and benevolent. It subordinates the duration of sufferings to the efforts of the spirit's ever present free will. It is only when the spirit misuses its will that it pays a price."*

(St. Louis)

1007. Are there spirits who never repent?

....

17 *For a complementary perspective on the trial of wealth, see also question 814.*

....

18 *The concept of time in the spirit-world is also the subject of question 240.*

▲ *"There are spirits who take a very long time to repent. But to assume that they will never improve would be to contradict the law of progress and to maintain that a child cannot become an adult."*

(St. Louis)

1008. Does the length of the spirit's trials always depend on its will, or are some of them imposed on it for a prescribed amount of time?

▲ *"There are trials that can be imposed for a set length of time. But God, Who desires only good, always takes into consideration a spirit's repentance; the desire to improve is never wasted."*

(St. Louis)

1009. According to the above, would the trials imposed never be eternal?[19]

▲ *Saint Augustine: "Use your common sense, and ask yourself whether eternal condemnation for a few moments of error is not a negation of God's goodness. What is the length of a human life, even if someone lives a hundred years, relative to Eternity? Eternity! Do you have any idea of what this word really means? And if you do, doesn't your reason reject the idea of suffering endless and hopeless torture solely because of a few faults?*

"It is understandable that ancient people would have imagined God to be terrible, jealous, and vindictive: they were unaware and so attributed human emotions to the Divine. But this is not the God that Jesus Christ extolled in his teachings, which place love, charity, compassion, and forgiveness of offenses above all other virtues. Could the virtues imposed as a duty on God's children be lacking in God?

"Isn't it also a contradiction to attribute infinite compassion and infinite revenge to God? You believe that God is, above all, just. But justice doesn't exclude compassion, and God would be merciless if people were condemned to excruciating and perpetual punishment. God's actions provide a perfect standard of justice, or God could not oblige us to practice justice.

"Besides, isn't justice most sublime when it is combined with compassion and when it orders that the length of a trial must depend on the efforts of the offender to rehabilitate? This is where we find the truth of the maxim: 'To each according to his own deeds.'"[20]

▲ *Lamennais: "Try by all the means at your disposal to erase from your minds the idea of eternal punishment; it is a contradiction of the justice and compassion of God. It is also the greatest source of skepticism, materialism, and indifference that has overtaken humanity since its intelligence began to develop.*

....

19 *Translator's Note: This question was answered individually by different spirits.*

....

20 *Translator's Note: Matthew 16:27*

"A spirit who has evolved even to a small extent soon becomes aware of this monstrous injustice and rejects it, though it frequently confuses the situation by rejecting both the imaginary punishment and the God to whom it is erroneously attributed. From this situation arises all your countless social ills, and it is for this that we have come to bring the cure.

"Our task should be all the easier because the defenders of this belief have avoided expressing a formal opinion in support of it. Neither the Councils nor the Church Fathers have definitely settled the question. If, according to a literal interpretation of the gospels, God threatened the guilty with inextinguishable fire, there is absolutely nothing in Christ's words to indicate that they will have to be there to the end of time.

"You are like hapless sheep that have gone astray. The Good Shepherd is approaching you and, far from wishing to banish you from his presence forever, comes to lead you back into the fold. Prodigal children—renounce your voluntary exile. Come back. God waits for you with open arms and will always welcome you to your true home."

▲ *Plato: "When will you ever get enough of these wars of words? Haven't you shed enough blood because of them? Must the fires of the stake be lit again for the sake of mere words? You disagree about the expressions 'eternal punishments' and 'everlasting fires.' But realize that what you now understand as Eternity was not perceived by ancient peoples in the same way. Let the theologians consult the texts at their source, and like the rest of you, they will realize that the Hebrew text did not use the words that have been translated into Greek, Latin, and modern texts to mean 'endless punishment.'*

"Eternal punishment is the equivalent of eternal evil: as long as evil exists among you, suffering will continue. It is in these relative terms that you must interpret the sacred writings. The eternity of suffering is not absolute. The day will come when all of you, through your repentance, will don the robes of innocence; and on that day there will be no more 'weeping or gnashing of teeth.'[21] Admittedly, your human reason is limited. But, such as it is, it represents a gift from God; and with its help, there will not be one person of good faith who does not eventually understand the relative nature of the concept of eternal punishment.

"Evil is not eternal. God is eternal and, being perfect in goodness, God could not have created an eternal evil. If this were not so, we would have to deprive God of the most magnificent of Divine attributes, sovereign power, because a God Who leaves intact an element that destroys the work of the universe cannot be considered sovereignly powerful.

"Humanity, no longer look for punishments in the depths of the Earth. Repent your mistakes but take hope in the thought that you can redress

....

21 *Translator's Note: Matthew 13:42*

them. Take comfort in the idea of a God who is infinitely loving, absolutely powerful, and just."

▲ *Paul the Apostle: "The ultimate goal of human existence is oneness with the Divine Being. Love, justice, and knowledge are the means of attaining this goal. Hatred, injustice, and ignorance are hurdles to it that must be overcome. You distance yourself from God whenever you attribute to Divine law a harsh quality that it does not have. By doing so you attribute to the Infinite Being less compassion, tenderness, and love than you do to your own kind.*

"The notion of Divine retribution should be as repulsive and inadmissible to you as the horrendous tortures and executions of the Middle Ages. The principle of indiscriminate reprisals, common in that era, has nowadays been decisively banished from your civil law. How could you possibly conceive a Divine Being who is less merciful than your own justice system?

"Please believe me, brothers and sisters. It is time to modify your long-held dogmas or to let them die out. Open your minds to the benevolent influences of your spirit-guides and let your actions reflect those influences.

"The notion of Hell, with its burning fires and boiling cauldrons, might have had some credibility in the Iron Age, but not in the present. In this century, the idea is comparable to imaginary ghosts that were used to frighten children; but children quickly outgrow such fears and so should you. By persisting in these terrifying mythological images, you encourage disbelief, a scourge that eats away at the very fabric of society. The end result will be a state of social disorder, the thought of which breaks my heart.

"All of you whose faith is dynamic and enthusiastic, join your efforts and let go of outdated and discredited allegories. When you sincerely embrace the true meaning of Divine justice, you will find it in perfect harmony with your feelings and with the more enlightened customs of your time.

"What, in fact, is a 'sinner'? Someone who has strayed from the ultimate goal in order to pursue ephemeral whims; someone who has forgotten that, like all human beings, he or she is on Earth to live in harmony and to revere the beautiful and the good, as exemplified by the Christ.

"What is 'punishment'? It is the natural result of pursuing those whims—it is a trigger device that helps offenders realize the deviant nature of their acts. The anguish that overcomes the 'sinner' is the sting that stimulates the soul to reassess its goals; it has no purpose other than to rehabilitate the soul. To hold that such anguish is eternal would be to deny the offending soul a reason to exist.

"I urge you to stop placing an eternal separation between the goodness of God and the fallibility of your human condition. Instead, think of your many lifetimes as renewed opportunities to lessen your sufferings and to

strive towards perfection. That is the merciful justice system that promotes oneness with God."

Discussion: The idea of future joys and sufferings is an important element in urging us on to moral excellence and in discouraging us from wrong-doing. But if the idea of future suffering is forced on us in a way that defies reason, the very notion of accountability for our actions falls short of its objective. If, on the other hand, the future is presented to us in a rational way, we will more readily accept the concept of joys and sufferings. The Spiritist philosophy provides us with judicious explanations regarding this subject.

The doctrine of eternal punishment, taken in its absolute sense, makes of the Supreme Being an implacable God. Could we assert, and remain logically consistent, that a king is very good, very kind, very indulgent, and wishes only for the happiness of his subjects, and at the same time claim that he is envious, vengeful, inflexible, and harsh? Could we accept the idea, without any thought of its inadequacy, that he punishes three-fourths of the people with the stiffest tortures for any offense or infraction against his laws, even though some of those people acted out of ignorance? Aren't all these notions contradictory? Very well: can God be less indulgent and less rational than we are?

The doctrine presents another contradiction. God, foreseeing everything, must have known, at the creation of our spirits, that we would violate Divine laws. From the beginning, in other words, our spirits were destined to eternal misery. Is this either admissible or rational?

But if we admit a doctrine that ties our sufferings to the extent of our faults, everything becomes consistent with reason and justice. God certainly knew that our spirits, having been created simple and ignorant, would err. But through our own imperfections, God provides us with the means to learn. This learning occurs when we experience the consequences of our earthly wrong-doing. To improve, we must rectify our errors. Following this course of events, we are never denied hope. The moment of our deliverance from suffering depends on the amount of effort we make to become better, more ethical. If the doctrine of future joys and suffering were presented under this aspect, few would doubt its truth.

The word "eternal" is ordinarily used in a symbolic manner to designate anything of long duration, the end of which cannot be foreseen, although we know very well that an end will eventually occur. We say, for example: "the eternal snows of the mountain peaks and polar regions," although we know that the physical world has an end and that climatic conditions could change by a displacement of the Earth's axis or by a cataclysm. The word "eternal," in this case, doesn't mean "infinite duration."

When we suffer a long illness, we say that our sickness is eternal. It is not so surprising then that spirits who suffer for years or centuries should express themselves in this manner. Neither should we forget that their unenlightened state prevents these spirits from foreseeing the end of their trials, causing them to believe that they will suffer forever—a misconception that is itself a result of their relative imperfection.

The doctrine of a material fire, of furnaces and tortures borrowed from the Tartarus[22] of Greek mythology, is completely disregarded by most modern theologians. Unfortunately there are still children who are taught that these terrifying allegorical pictures are positive truths. Those who persist in teaching such notions are more zealous than enlightened. They make a serious mistake, however, because their young audience, once free from their terror, are likely to join the ranks of the skeptics.

Modern theology admits that the word "fire" is used in a symbolic sense in the Bible and should be understood as referring to a mental experience.[23] Nonetheless, people like ourselves, who are aware of incidents of life in the hereafter, have ample proof that these sufferings are excruciating even if their nature is not physical.

Even in regard to the length of sufferings, many theologians are beginning to accept the restriction indicated above and to consider that the word "eternal" may refer to a principle of accountability. In short, it is the affirmation of an immutable law rather than the implication that individuals will endure suffering for an endless time.

When the teaching of traditional religion freely admits such an enlightened interpretation, and many others that

....

22 Translator's Note: In classical mythology, Tartarus, located below Hades,—i.e., the underworld—was the place where the wicked were punished and where Zeus imprisoned the Titans.

....

23 See question 974 on the notion of eternal fire.

reflect the thinking of an advanced age, it will bring back a belief in God and the future life to many who are presently lost in the maze of materialism.

The Resurrection of the Body

1010. Does the doctrine of the resurrection of the body actually refer to the doctrine of incarnation taught by spirits?

▲ *"How could it be anything else? The expression 'resurrection of the body' is ridiculous in the eyes of people who suppose that it must be taken literally or not at all. It leads to skepticism. But if you give it a reasonable interpretation, the persons you call free-thinkers will easily accept it, precisely because they are used to rationalizing. Don't be mistaken—free-thinkers are eager to believe. Perhaps even more than others, they feel apprehensive about the future but are unable to accept something that science has rejected.*

"The doctrine of many successive lives complies with God's justice, and it alone can explain the inexplicable. Do you wonder then that it can be found in many religions?"

1011. Then, through the dogma of the resurrection of the body, the church is teaching the doctrine of reincarnation?

▲ *"Clearly. Reincarnation clarifies many things that are misunderstood, and in time you will recognize that the Holy Scriptures imply and endorse it. As you know, the spirits did not come to subvert religion, as some contend, but to confirm and sanction it through irrefutable proofs. Because the time has now come to replace the use of symbolic language, the spirits speak without allegories to give their words a clear and explicit meaning and to avoid any false interpretation. Hence, the number of people who are sincere believers [in their own religions] will only grow."*

(St. Louis)

Discussion: Physical science demonstrates the impossibility of resurrection interpreted in its traditional sense. For the body to come back to life, its organic components would have to remain intact so that, though dispersed, they could at some future time reunite as a living whole. Things don't occur in this way, however.

The body is formed of various elements—oxygen, hydrogen, nitrogen, carbon, etc.—and when it decomposes, these disperse and form new bodies. The same atoms of carbon in our present bodies will, for example, become part of the composition of many thousands of different bodies after we die. An individual may have in his or her body atoms that belonged to our earliest ancestors. And those same organic molecules that you absorb in your food may be composed of atoms that come from the body of an individual you once knew, and so on. This happens because matter is finite in quantity but unlimited in the number of its transformations. How, then, could each of our bodies be reconstituted using those same elements? It would be physically impossible.

We cannot rationally admit the resurrection of the body except as an image symbolizing the reincarnation phenomenon. Interpreted in this way, it offers nothing to contradict scientific knowledge because it is perfectly rational.

According to theological dogma, the resurrection does not occur except on the "Last Day." According to the Spiritist Doctrine it occurs every day. But the idea of the Last Judgment hides a beautiful and noble metaphor, one of those immutable truths: the principle of individual responsibility.

After meditating on the Spiritist theory regarding the future state of our souls and on the different experiences they will undergo, we find it self-evident that the Judgment (as a form of assessment) that brings about our spiritual rehabilitation is not a fiction, as skeptics think. It is the natural adjunct to the theory of reincarnation and the existence of many worlds while, according to the traditional doctrine of the Final Judgment, we have only one life and the Earth is the only inhabited planet.

Heaven, Hell, and Purgatory

1012. Are there places in the universe that are reserved for the punishment or reward of spirits, according to their merit?

▲ *"We have already answered this question. Sorrow and happiness and the extent thereof depend on each spirit's degree of progress. Spirits carry within themselves the principle of their own happiness or misfortune. Moreover, in the spirit-world, spirits are everywhere; no place has been closed off and especially set aside for them. As to incarnate spirits, they are relatively happy or unhappy, depending on the level of evolution of the planet on which they live and on their own individual progress."*

— According to this view, Hell and Heaven do not exist in the manner we usually conceive of them. Is that right?

▲ *"They are merely symbols. There are happy and miserable spirits everywhere, and they gather together because of their intrinsic compatibility."*

Discussion: Fixed places for punishments and rewards only exist in the human imagination. They result from our tendency to materialize and circumscribe things that we cannot conceive of.

1013. How are we to understand Purgatory?

▲ *"As physical and mental suffering; as time for reevaluation and the beginning of rehabilitation. It is almost always on Earth that you create your own Purgatory and where you make up for your faults."*

Discussion: What we call Purgatory is also a symbol and should be interpreted as such. It is not a defined place but the state of imperfection of spirits who must address their own consciences. The conscience is purified in the course of many reincarnation experiences. The purgatory, so to speak, consititutes all the many challenges and frustrations of physical life.

1014. What prompts some spirits, who seem to be of the higher orders, to answer questions regarding Hell and Purgatory in the commonly understood sense that you have told us is wrong?

▲ *"Their answers may depend on the awareness of the people questioning them. Some people have certain preconceived ideas, and the spirits avoid a blunt reply to prevent offending their convictions. If a spirit were to tell, say, a Muslim, without proper precautions, that Mohammed was not correct in some point, that person would be insulted and reject Spiritist ideas altogether."*

—We can understand such precautions on the part of spirits who want to instruct us. But how do you explain that some spirits, when they are asked about their condition, answer that they are suffering the tortures of Hell or Purgatory?

▲ *"When they are of limited awareness and not completely dematerialized, spirits hold on to part of their earthly ideas, translating their impressions into terms familiar to them. They find themselves in an environment that does not allow them to delve into their futures, except indistinctly. This is the reason why spirits recently freed from the flesh speak just as they would have done during physical life. In a more figurative view, Hell would be understood to mean a life of extremely harsh trials, marked by uncertainty of an end to it. Likewise, Purgatory would be a life of trials, but with the awareness of a better future.*

"This is a matter of language. When you undergo intense physical or mental distress, don't you say that 'life is hell'? Such expressions are always meant to have a symbolic meaning."

1015. What should we understand by the phrase, "a tormented soul"?

▲ *"A wandering soul, uncertain of its future, to whom you can provide the relief it frequently asks for when it happens to communicate with you."*[24]

1016. In what sense should we understand the word "Heaven"?

▲ *"Well, it is not a place like the Elysian Fields of the ancients, where all the good spirits gather together, with nothing to do but enjoy Eternity in a state of passive bliss. No. It is the universal space; it is the planets, the stars, and all the more elevated spheres where spirits exercise and enjoy all their abilities without the trials of the material world or the pain common to undeveloped states."*

1017. Some spirits have stated they inhabit the fourth or the fifth heaven. What do they mean by this?

▲ *"You asked them what heaven they inhabited because you have the idea of many heavens placed one on top of the other like floors in a multi-story building. They simply replied according to this idea. But for them the words "fourth or fifth heaven" express different degrees of purification and happiness.*

"It is the same when you ask a spirit whether it is in Hell. If the spirit is unhappy, it will say 'yes,' because for it Hell means suffering. But it is quite aware that it is not in a furnace. A spirit of pagan origin would have replied that it was in 'Tartarus.'"

Discussion: The same phenomenon occurs with similar expressions, such as "the city of flowers," "the city of the elect," "the second and third sphere," etc. These are allegorical expressions that spirits will use either as symbols or because they simply ignore the reality of things, sometimes even the most elementary scientific principles.

As for places of punishments and rewards, these are limited notions, no longer seriously considered. They belong to the same world view that conceived of Earth as the center of the universe, over which the sky formed a dome, an area for the stars. Heaven was placed above, Hell below. This is the origin of the expressions "to ascend to Heaven," "to be in the highest Heaven," "to be cast down into Hell."

Astronomy has since revealed Earth's history and its constitution. It has shown us that Earth is a very small planet among many billions of celestial bodies and devoid of any special importance. It has also proved that space is infinite and that there are no high or low places in the universe. As a result, we must relinquish the idea that there is a Heaven above the clouds and a Hell below the Earth. The

24 *See question 664 on the beneficial influence of prayer for suffering spirits.*

same applies to Purgatory; no definite location can be assigned to it.

The Spiritist Doctrine proposes to provide, with respect to all these points, an explanation that is at once, and in the utmost degree, rational, sublime, and comforting. It is our duty, too, to show that we bring our Hell and our Heaven with us, and find our Purgatory during our physical life and throughout our many different incarnations.

1018. How should we understand Christ's words: "My Kingdom is not of this world"?[25]

▲ *"Christ replied in a symbolic manner. He wanted to say that he does not rule except over pure and unselfish hearts. He is present wherever love of good prevails, whereas individuals who are fascinated by material possessions and attached to worldly interests distance themselves from him."*

1019. Will goodness ever rule on Earth?

▲ *"Goodness will prevail on the Earth only when the number of its enlightened inhabitants exceeds that of its spiritually and morally unaware ones. At that time love and justice, the true sources of goodness and happiness, will prevail.*

"Through your moral progress and practice of Divine laws, you will attract more evolved spirits to Earth, while simultaneously repelling unenlightened ones. But these backward spirits will leave finally only after pride and selfishness are forever banished from your hearts.

"The transformation of the human race has been predicted since ancient times, and you are gradually approaching the critical age when it will come about. All those who work for human progress are helping to speed along the coming of this new age, which will occur through the reincarnation of more progressive spirits, who will establish a new order on Earth.

"At that time, imperfect spirits and those who try to prevent progress from occurring will be excluded from Earth since they will be unfit to live among more evolved individuals whose happiness they would disturb if they stayed. These spirits will be assigned to less advanced planets where they will undergo their own difficult trials. While working for their own advancement on those planets, they will also assist in the progress of their less evolved associates, the planets' original inhabitants.

"In the exclusion of these hardened spirits from the transformed Earth, you find the origin of the sublime symbol of the 'Paradise Lost.' You can see that the advent of the human race on Earth occurred under similar conditions of exile. The ancient peoples brought within themselves the traces of

....

25 *Translator's Note: John 18:36.*

their old emotions, evidence of their relative unawareness. This is the real meaning of the myth of the fall of Adam and Eve, a fall that brought in its wake the 'sinfulness' of their descendants. When considered in this light, 'original sin' symbolizes the as-yet-imperfect nature of humanity, whose members are individually responsible for themselves and for their own faults, not for the faults of their distant ancestors.

"We ask, then, that you work at the immense task of transforming the planet with zeal and courage. If you do, you will reap the seed you have sown a hundredfold.

"As for those who close their eyes to the light, they are preparing long centuries of darkness and despair for themselves. Pity them. Those who center all their pleasures in material possessions will suffer more privations than any pleasures they presently enjoy. Pity them as well. Above all, pity the selfish who in the future will find no one to help them carry the burden of their sufferings."

(St. Louis)

CONCLUSION

I

People who see magnetism only in terms of the magnetized toy ducks that swim around in water basins will find it difficult to understand that these toy-figures contain the secret of the mechanism of the universe and the movement of the planets.[1] The same hesitancy is characteristic of individuals whose knowledge of the Spiritist Doctrine is confined to early table-turning phenomena—the starting point of modern spiritual manifestations—which they regard simply as a social pastime. They cannot appreciate how such a simple and ordinary phenomenon, known to the ancients and even to our modern indigenous people, can be connected with the deepest questions of psychological life and the social order. The superficial observer finds little connection between a table that moves around on the floor, guided by unknown forces, and the moral condition and future destiny of the human race. But just as the age-old phenomenon of boiling water has given rise to steam-powered engines, ordinary table-turning, though many disdain it, has given rise to a new philosophy that furnishes the solution to problems no other has been able to solve.

I appeal to all honest adversaries of the Spiritist Doctrine to demonstrate whether their criticism is based on a sensible understanding of the subject, since their position has no value otherwise. To ridicule things about which we know nothing, which we have not studied and analyzed conscientiously, is not to criticize but to open oneself to the charge of levity and poor judgment. Obviously we could have presented this philoso-

....

1 *Translator's Note: The reference to the toy duck is connected to experiments that were performed since the publication of William Gilbert's work "De Magnete" (On The Magnet) in 1600. "De Magnete" offered the first rational explanation to the mysterious ability of the compass needle to point north: the Earth itself was magnetic. "De Magnete" opened the era of modern physics and astronomy. As for the 'secret of the mechanism of the Universe' the author refers to Gravity and Electromagnetism, the only known interactions known at the time. Gravity is the force responsible for the formation of stars and the solar systems, including the Earth, and for the orbits of objects around each other. Electromagnetism is the force that acts between all particles with electric charge, governing phenomena on a scale ranging from atoms to microscopic objects. Together with the nuclear force (quantum matter), discovered in the Twentieth Century, they constitute the fundamental forces of nature.*

phy as the product of a human mind; in which case, it would have met with much less rejection than it has and would rightly be considered deserving of patient examination by scientists and scholars. But it claims to have originated from spirits, and so they cry, "What an absurdity!" It is thought hardly worth a glance by people who judge the work simply by its title, as the monkey in the fable judges the nut by its husk. But leaving aside the issue of its intellectual origins, let us assume that the book is the work of a human being. Can anyone, after having carefully read it, say in all truth and honesty that there is anything in it to laugh at?

II

It is not surprising to have materialists as adversaries: the Spiritist Doctrine is unquestionably a threat to their position. Philosophical materialism is, of course, a doctrine most people choose not to proclaim openly. Generally, their attacks come cloaked under the mantle of reason and science.

Odd as it may seem, however, many of the most extreme attacks have appeared in the name of religion, of which the attackers understand little. They aim their arrows especially at the supernatural. According to them, since the Spiritist Doctrine is based on the paranormal, it can be nothing more than a ridiculous delusion. They do not consider that, in unequivocally denying the possibility of the "marvelous" and the "supernatural," they deny religion itself. Religion is founded, after all, on revelation and miracles; revelation itself is no more than a synonym for supra-human communication. Haven't all the sacred writers, beginning with Moses, referred to this kind of communication? And what are miracles if not facts of a marvelous and supernatural kind since they are, according to the liturgy, departures from the laws of nature? Thus, in rejecting the marvelous and the supernatural, these adversaries reject the very basis of all belief.

But it is not from this point of view that we should consider the subject. Belief in spirit evidence does not necessarily settle the question of miracles—that is to say, whether God does or does not, in certain cases, abrogate natural laws. Indeed, it leaves the question entirely open to interpretation. The Spiritist Doctrine says, and shows, that the phenomena on which it is based are supernatural only in appearance, that they only seem to be supernatural to some people because they are unusual and unlike any other facts before them. It is our position that they are no more supernatural than any other phenomena that modern science is explaining, though these too were believed to be miraculous in the past. All supernatural phenomena are, without exception, the consequence of general laws; they reveal to us one of the powers of nature, a power we did not know or at least did not understand previously but which our observation has shown us is included in the scheme of things. Spiritist philosophy, therefore, is founded less on the marvelous and the supernatural than is traditional religion itself; and those who attack it on this score do so because they do not know what Spiritism really is. As for those who oppose it in the name of science, we say to them, however knowledgeable they are, "If your science, which has taught you so many things, has not taught you that the domain of nature is infinite, you are only half-learned."

III

The materialists claim that naiveté, a virus that threatens to infect our century, must be eliminated. Still, would it be preferable to see the world dominated by their skepticism? It is to the very absence of belief that we can attribute the general disintegration of family-ties and the greater part of the disorders that are now undermining society. By demonstrating the existence and immortality of the soul, on the other hand, the Spiritist Doctrine revives faith in the future, raises the courage of the depressed among us, and enables us to bear the trials of life with resignation. Do you call this an evil? We are confronted here with two opposing doctrines: one denies the existence of a future life, the other proclaims and proves it. One explains nothing, the other explains everything, and, in doing so, appeals to our reason. One provides a justification for selfishness; the other offers a firm basis for justice, compassion, and love toward our fellow human beings. One shows only the present and abolishes all hope, the other consoles us by showing us the vast enterprise of the future. Which of the two is more harmful?

Among the most skeptical critics of the Spiritist Doctrine are those who refer to themselves as apostles of universal brotherhood and progress. Universal brotherhood, however, implies selflessness and sacrifice. Why would they, then, destroy human hope and purpose by professing that death is the end of everything, that tomorrow the human being will be no more than a worn-out machine, a piece of rubbish? If this were true, what would stand in the way of each individual indulging him or herself at the expense of every other person? The natural end of this position, stripped of its fine phrases, would be self-gratification, carried on at every minute of every day of our brief lifetime on Earth; and, along with self-gratification would come a constant striving to accumulate enough money to assure the most enjoyment possible. Wouldn't such a mindset automatically arouse in us jealousy of people who own more than we do? And would there ever be any more than a single step from jealousy of them to stealing from them? What would prevent it? The law? But the law can only deal with a limited number of cases. Conscience? The sense of duty? But what, from their point of view, is conscience, and on what do they base the sense of duty? Would this sense have any motive or aim if it were true that everything ends for us with our present life? Reasonably, this belief can only admit to one maxim: "Every man for himself." Despite the claims, universal brotherhood, conscience, duty, humanity, even progress, are empty words in this doctrine. The people who promote it have no idea of how much harm they do to society and how many crimes they assume responsibility for. But what of responsibility? Nothing of the kind exists for the skeptic, who owes allegiance only to matter.

IV

Human progress results from the practical application of the law of justice, love, and charity, which is founded on certainty of the future: remove the certainty and you take away the corner-stone of the law. Consider that all other laws originate in this law. It comprises all the conditions of human happiness. We can cure our social ills through it alone. We see this in the gradual improvement in social conditions that has taken place as the law has become better understood and more widely observed. If a partial and incomplete application of it has been enough to produce a noticeable effect on social conditions, we have no doubt of the positive impact it will have when it becomes the basis of all social institutions. Is such a result possible? Yes. The human race has already taken ten steps forward—proof that it can and will take twenty steps, and many more afterwards.

We can infer the future by analyzing the past. We see that hostility among different nations has begun to melt away, that the barriers separating them are being overthrown as civilization progresses, that hands are joining from one end of the world to the other. A larger measure of justice has been introduced into international law; wars occur less frequently and, when they do break out, are waged with less savagery than before. Consistency is being gradually established in human relations. Distinctions of race and class are disappearing, and people of different religious beliefs have begun to stop their sectarian squabbling in order to unite in adoration of one and the same God.[2] We speak here primarily of the nations that lead the civilized world.[3]

....

2 *Translator's Note: One might object to this point on the basis that since this was written, humanity has experienced two world wars and untold numbers of civil wars, racial and religious clashes, and other ethnic and factional conflicts. These tragedies are evidence that human beings still have a long way to go before achieving the ultimate goal of oneness with God, but they do not deny the fact that moral progress is taking hold, albeit at a gradual pace. To be sure, the Cold War is now a fixture of the past; and social practices that were generally tolerated even in Allan Kardec's time—such as slavery and unequal legal rights to men and women—are now viewed as social aberrations by the civilized world.*

....

3 *See questions 789-793 for a complementary perspective on the issue of human progress on Earth.*

In every respect we are still far from being perfect, and many old ruins must be pulled down before the last remnants of barbarism are cleared away. Can those ruins withstand the irresistible action of progress, this living force that is itself a law of nature? The present generation is more advanced than the last; we cannot doubt that the next will be more advanced still. It must be so; the force of things demands it. In the first place, each generation, as it passes away, carries with it some of the adherents of society's worst vices, and thus society is gradually reconstituted with new elements that have thrown aside antiquated ideas. Second, when we really begin to want progress, we earnestly focus our energies and overcome any hurdles along the way. With the progressive movement of human society certain, there can be no doubt that we will continue to move forward.

All of us want to be happy, it is our nature to do so. Through progress we experience an increase in our sense of well-being; otherwise, progress would have no value. Later, as we enjoy the fruits of our economic advances, we come to see that the happiness of the whole is impossible without progress in social relations. But the long term stability of the social order depends on the ethical transformation of individuals generally. And again, the force of things will lead us to work toward that end—an end that, in the Spiritist Doctrine, we have an effective means of attaining.

V

As if to proclaim the power of the ideas articulated by the Spiritist Doctrine, there are people who complain that these ideas are spreading in all directions and threatening society. But only a philosophy founded on reason and fact can aspire to the level of general acceptance. Therefore, if Spiritist notions are spreading everywhere, creating followers in every rank of society and especially among the educated, it is evident that they must be based on truthful principles. This being so, the efforts of its detractors must be in vain; their attempts at ridicule will only give the Doctrine new life. The advice of our spirit-friends supports this fact; they have repeatedly said: "Do not allow opposition to make you uneasy. Whatever is done against you will turn to your advantage, and your bitterest opponents will serve your cause in spite of themselves. Against the will of God, the ill-will of human beings is helpless."

As a moral philosophy, the Doctrine will help humanity to attain a new evolutionary phase. Wherever it is accepted, an advance in moral principles will inevitably follow. The rapid expansion of Spiritist ideas should, then, cause no surprise. It results from the profound satisfaction those ideas give to people who embrace them intelligently and sincerely.

Interest in these ideas develops in three distinct phases. The first phase is curiosity, stimulated by the strangeness of the phenomena produced at Spiritist gatherings; the second phase is an engagement in reasoning and philosophical inquiry; the third is the application of Spiritist principles. The period of curiosity goes by quickly. Curiosity has a very short existence; the mind, once satisfied that it has understood a novelty, immediately abandons it for something else. But where a subject awakens deeper thought and appeals to judgment, the mind lingers. At this point, the second phase has already begun; the third will certainly follow.

As the principles and goals of the Spiritist Doctrine have become clear, it has quickly grown in acceptance. Unquestionably, it touches the most sensitive nerve in the human heart, the desire for happiness. This is the secret force that will bring about its triumph. It offers inner fulfillment to anyone who delves deeply into its principles. How many a Spiritist, without ever having witnessed psychic phenomena, has thought: "Beyond the phenomena, there is its philosophy, which explains what no other philosophy ever has. With rigorous logic the Doctrine furnishes me with solutions to problems of vital importance to my future. It furnishes me with calmness, security, and confidence. It frees me from the anguish of uncertainty. Compared to these results, the question of psychic demonstration is of secondary importance."

To attackers of this philosophy, we reply: "Would you like to have a means of repudiating it successfully? Bring forward something better; find a more comprehensive solution to the problems it addresses; give us a greater source of certainty that will make us even happier. But you must thoroughly understand the meaning of the word 'certainty,' since human beings will only accept as certain what appears logical to them. And you must not content yourselves in your attacks simply by saying that things are not so. You must prove—not by negation, but by facts—that what we assert as existing has no existence, has never existed, and cannot exist. In addition, you must tell us what you have to offer in its place. Further, you must prove that the Spiritist Doctrine does not make human beings better and therefore happier, and that this improvement does not derive from the practice of the purest of ethical systems—the sublime and simple ethic of the Gospel, which so many praise and so few practice. When you have done all this, you will have a right to attack the Doctrine."

The Spiritist Doctrine is robust because it is based on principles common to the great religious philosophies: God, the soul, future joys and sorrows. It attracts followers because it demonstrates that joys and sorrows are the natural consequence of earthly life; and because, in the picture it presents of the future, it offers nothing a logical mind would regard as contrary to reason. We ask those critics, skeptics by choice, whose whole doctrine consists in the negation of the future: "What compensation can you offer for the sufferings of the present life? You base your teachings on incredulity. The Spiritist Doctrine is based on confidence in God. While your views offer the annihilation of consciousness in the future and self-ishness as a means of coping with the present, the Spiritist Doctrine invites people to live with hope, good fellowship, and joy in the present. While your assertions lack substantive evidence, the Spiritist Doctrine presents rational explanations and clear evidences. How can you expect that the world will hesitate to choose between the two doctrines?"

VI

The idea that the Spiritist Doctrine depends on supranormal phenomena and would decline if they stopped altogether is preposterous. Its strength lies in its philosophy and in the appeal it makes to reason. In ancient times its concepts were studied as part of the "mysteries" and carefully hidden from ordinary people. Today, they are treated in a clear, direct manner, without allegories, mysticism, or complicated symbols. The time has come for making the truth known in a language everyone can understand. This new revelation, as this work has shown, is intended for all humanity. And it does not ask for blind acceptance but urges everyone to examine the logical grounds for believing it. Once this is done, it will become quickly apparent that it is sounder than any of the theories that defend annihilation as our ultimate spiritual state.

Yet, one might wonder, can spirit phenomena be suppressed? The answer is no. Such an attempt would have the combined effect of all per-secutions—i.e., it would excite curiosity and the desire to learn about a forbidden subject. If spirit manifestations were the privilege of a single individual, it could be stopped simply by preventing that person from producing them. Unfortunately for our critics, these manifestations are within everyone's reach. They are now being experienced by great num-bers of people, from the highest to the lowest, from the palace to the cot-tage. It might, of course, be possible to prevent their production in pub-lic; but, as is well known, it is not in public but in private that they are most successfully demonstrated. Moreover, anyone may be a medium. How would it be possible to prevent each family in the privacy of the home, each individual in the silence of his or her room, each prisoner, even in his or her cell, from holding communication with the invisible beings around them, despite the presence of persons who try to keep them from doing it? If mediums were forbidden to exercise their ability in one country, how would it be possible to stop them elsewhere? In order to silence all the mediums, it would be necessary to incarcerate half the human race. Also, if it were possible to burn all the Spiritist books in exis-tence, they would at once be reproduced because the source from which they emanate is beyond the reach of attack and because it is impossible to imprison or burn the spirits who are their real authors.

The Spiritist Doctrine is not the work of any one person; no one can claim to have created it. It is as old as creation itself. Its fundamental principles are found in all religions and in the Catholic religion even more than in others. Indeed, Catholicism[4] contains all the principles found in the Spiritist Doctrine: admission of the existence of spirits of every degree; the spirits' relations, both occult and overt, with humanity; guardian-angels, reincarnation (under the guise of resurrection), the freeing of the soul during normal physical life, second-sight, visions, manifestations of every kind (including tangible apparitions). As for what the church calls "demons," they are what we call misguided spirits. Except for the belief that the so-called demons are doomed forever while all the others have a path of light before them, the only difference between these two conceptions is a name.

The unique contribution of the Spiritist Doctrine has been to make a coherent whole of what has, until now, been scattered. It has been, further, to explain in clear and precise terms what has previously been obscured by the language of allegory, and to eliminate the products of superstition and ignorance from human belief, leaving only what is real and actual. This is its mission. It does not propose any new paradigm but seeks rather to make ideas that are already established clear and distinct. Primarily, it integrates concepts that are found in all cultures and ages. Who, then, could be so arrogant as to hope that he or she could stifle it, either by ridicule or persecution? If it could be proscribed in one place, it would shortly reappear in another or on the very spot from which it had just been banished. It exists in the constitution of things. And no one can annihilate what is, in fact, one of the powers of nature or veto what exists by Divine decree.

Yet what reasons could there be for opposing the spread of Spiritist ideas? Those ideas, it is true, are a protest against abuses springing from pride and selfishness. Such abuses, while benefiting a few, are harmful to the many; and the Doctrine would, therefore, have the people on its side, leaving only the exploiters of humanity as its adversaries. When widely felt, certainly, its influence will make human beings less greedy, more benevolent toward one another, and more in harmony with the dictates of Providence. In a broader context, it will help bring more order and tranquillity to society.

·····························

4 *Translator's Note: The singling out of the Catholic religion is likely explained by the fact that the book was originally written in Nineteenth-Century France, a predominantly Catholic country.*

VII

The Spiritist Doctrine has three essential dimensions: communications between the physical and spiritual realms, the moral philosophy deduced from these communications, and the application of that philosophy to daily living. Its adherents comprise three groups: (a) those who believe in the reality and genuineness of spirit manifestations and confine their activities to scientific experiments regarding them; (b) those who understand the Doctrine's philosophical and moral structure; and (c) those who practice, or at least try to live by, its moral principles. But from whatever perspective—scientific or spiritual—the phenomena are considered, everyone realizes that they have ushered in an entirely new order of ideas, an order that must necessarily have an impact on human life and clearly a positive one for anyone who really understands its premises.

Our critics also fall into three groups. In the first group we find those people who systematically reject anything new and speak without a solid understanding of the subject. People in this group admit nothing beyond the testimony of their senses. They have not seen anything, do not wish to see anything, and are unwilling to delve into the subject in any depth. Their unwillingness to see clearly may result from the fear of having to acknowledge a mistake: they have declared the whole subject to be chimerical, insane, utopian, and without real existence. These are the willfully incredulous. With them we may include those individuals who have condescended to glance at the subject in order to be able to say, "I have tried to see something in it and failed," but who do not realize that a half hour's attention is not enough to acquaint them with a new field of study. In the second group we discover people who, although perfectly aware of the authenticity of the phenomena, oppose the matter from personal prejudice. They know the Doctrine is sound but fear its consequences and attack it as an enemy. In the third group we include those persons who dread the Doctrine's moral principles because those principles constitute a rebuke to their acts and desires. Taken seriously, the Doctrine would inconvenience them; yet they neither reject nor accept it, preferring instead to close their eyes. The first group is swayed by pride and presumption; the second by prejudice; the third by selfishness. We would look in vain for the fourth group—that is, individuals who base their opposition on a careful and conscientious study and who try to bring forward positive and irrefutable evidence of the Doctrine's flaws.

It would be hoping too much of human nature to imagine that it could suddenly be transformed by Spiritist ideas. Undoubtedly, the extent to which these ideas penetrate will vary greatly. But, however slight the penetration may be, the Spiritist Doctrine will raise the level of humanity's spiritual awareness and push back materialist notions. This outcome follows from mere exposure to paranormal phenomena. It will have much greater value for those who pass beyond the phenomena and experience its beneficial moral effects.

The first and most general of these effects is the development of a religious perspective, even in people who, while not materialists, are unmindful of spiritual things. It is a perspective that leads to a degree of indifference toward death, to a temperate and rational acceptance that will allow believers to deal with death without revolt or sadness, and as something they need not fear. This attitude grows out of the assurance of what follows death.

The second effect of the Spiritist Doctrine is resignation in the face of life's trials. The Doctrine leads us to consider everything from an elevated point of view, thereby diminishing the importance we attach to life on Earth and making its hardships less painful. Consequently, we have more courage in difficult times, are better able to control our desires, and become more firmly opposed to the idea of suicide, which we know will not bring us the consolation we seek. The certainty of a future in which we can assure our own happiness, and the possibility of re-establishing relations with those who were dear to us, are the highest motivations of the Spiritist. Further, we view the exercise of living from a deathless and mystery-free perspective.

The third effect is a greater tolerance for the flaws and needs of others. Tolerance, it is true, often runs headlong against selfishness, one of the most tenacious and difficult human flaws to eradicate. Generally, we are willing to make sacrifices provided they impose no real privations on us. Unfortunately, few people today use the word "tolerance" without associating it with the self. Thus, the willingness to sacrifice one's self-interest is the most visible indicator of progress.

VIII

It is sometimes asked whether the spirits teach us anything new in the way of ethical principles, anything superior to the teachings of Christ. Further, the question arises as to what use the Spiritist Doctrine is if its moral teachings are the same as those of the Gospels. This type of reasoning recalls Caliph Omar[5] who said, in speaking of the Library at Alexandria, "If it contains only what is found in the Koran, it is useless, and in that case must be burned; if it contains anything that is not found in the Koran, it is bad, and in that case, it must also be burned." Spiritist ethics do not differ from those of Jesus. But we must ask, in turn, whether humanity did not, before Christ's time, have the law God gave Moses?

....

5 *Translator's Note: Caliph Omar or Umar I, in full Umar Ibn Al-Khattab (c. 586-644), the second Muslim caliph (from 634), under whom Arab armies conquered Mesopotamia and Syria and began the conquest of Iran and Egypt.*

The doctrine of Christ, after all, can be found in the Ten Commandments. Can we argue, therefore, that the moral teachings of Jesus are useless? We must also ask those who deny the value of the Spiritist philosophy why Christ's teachings are so little practiced, and why it is that those who proclaim the sublimity of Christianity are often the first to violate its foremost law, that of universal love. The spirits come not only to confirm the tenets of Christian philosophy but also to show us its practicality. They make understandable truths that have been taught only in allegorical form, and they provide solutions to abstract problems of human psychology.

Jesus came to show us the road of true goodness. God sent him to awaken human beings to the Divine law they had forgotten. Why then should God not send spirits to remind us once again, in clear terms, of principles we seem at present to have overlooked in our devotion to pride and material gain? We cannot set bounds to the power of God or dictate the Divine will. We cannot say with certainty that the promised time has not arrived when truths, unknown or misunderstood until now, are to be openly proclaimed in order to accelerate human progress. Isn't there something providential in the fact that spirit manifestations are presently occurring all over the globe? Nor is it a single person, an isolated prophet, who comes to arouse us. Light is breaking forth on all sides, and a new world is opening up before our eyes.

As the invention of the microscope disclosed the world of the infinitely small to us, a world we did not suspect existed, and as the telescope showed us a multitude of stars and planets, likewise once hidden, the spirit-communications of the present day reveal the existence of an invisible world that surrounds and engulfs us. It is a world that is continuously in contact with us and that takes part in everything we do, although we have been unaware of it until recently. Yet, within a short time, the existence of this world, which is our final destination, will be as incontestable as the infinite numbers of worlds we see through the lenses of microscope and telescope. Is it without purpose that this new world has been made known on Earth, that humanity has been initiated into the mysteries of life beyond life? It is true that these discoveries, if we can so describe them, are contrary to certain long accepted ideas. But all great scientific discoveries have changed, and even overthrown, widely held notions, and forced their defenders to swallow their pride. The same will hold true for the Spiritist Doctrine; it, too, via the fields of knowledge it will clear the way for, will take its place among the branches of human endeavor.

Communication with the departed allows us to understand better what is to come. And it prepares us for the joys and sorrows that await us according to our merits. Thus it brings spirituality back into a society that has come to see in the human being only matter, only an organized machine. We feel justified therefore in asserting that the facts on which the Spiritist Doctrine is based will give a death-blow to materialism. If Spiritism had done nothing more than this, it would be entitled to the gratitude of everyone who values social harmony. However, it does much more: it shows us the inevitable result of wrong-doing, and the necessity of goodness. The number of people in whom it has instilled better attitudes, whose corrupt tendencies it has neutralized, and whose wrong-doing it has deflected, is larger than generally supposed; and it grows with every passing day. Hearing the spirits share their joys or repent for what they did on Earth makes the future more real; it is no longer a vague fantasy. Anyone witnessing these communications must reflect on what this reality means personally to him or her, and must feel the need of self-examination and self-transformation.

IX

The fact that differences of opinion exist among certain Spiritist streams regarding particular doctrinal points has been used by opponents to attack the Doctrine. It is not unheard of, however, that contrary interpretations will arise at the outset of a new discipline, when the inventory of observations is still incomplete. A more exhaustive study of the facts has already led to the rejection of most contravening opinions—for example, the view that held that all spirit communications were with unevolved spirits (as if God could not have sent higher ones). This supposition is both absurd, since it goes against the evidence, and impious, since it denies the power and goodness of the Divine. Our spirit-teachers have advised us not to trouble ourselves about differences of opinion among Spiritists, assuring us that unity will eventually be established. In fact, it has already developed in regard to most points at issue, and other discrepancies are being resolved daily.

At one point this question arose: "On what basis can an impartial person arrive at a conclusion about the relative merits of the various theories the spirits put forth when doctrinal unity has not been established?" The spirits gave the following reply:

"The purest light is the one unobscured by any cloud; the most precious diamond is the one without a flaw. Judge our communications in the same manner—by the purity of our ideas. Do not forget that there may be spirits who have not yet freed themselves from their earthly ideas. Learn to distinguish us by our language. Judge us by the sum of what we tell you. See whether there is a logical sequence in the ideas we suggest; whether there is, in our statements, anything that reveals ignorance, pride, or malevolence. In a word, determine whether our communications always bear the stamp of wisdom that attests true superiority.

"If your planet were free of error, it would be perfect, which is far from being

the case. You must still learn to distinguish error from truth. Above all, you need to learn from experience, which will allow you to exercise your judgment and so progress. Doctrinal unity will evolve from the stream in which good is clear and untainted. People will gather spontaneously at those points in the stream where they can catch the brightest glimpses of the truth.

"What do a few differences of opinion matter when they deal more with form than substance? The fundamental principles of the Spiritist Doctrine are well established and should unite humanity in compassionate service to others and in love for God. Whatever you suppose the path of progress and the condition of your future life to be, the principle aim does not change, which is, to do good. All this is already contained in the Doctrine."

Although differences of opinion over some points may exist among Spiritists, all of them agree on the fundamental principles. At this level, unity already exists. The exception may be the small number who still do not accept the action of spirits in psychic phenomena and who attribute the phenomena to purely physical causes—a view contrary to the axiom, "Every intelligent effect must have an intelligent cause"—or explain it as a product of the intellect, which finds no support in the evidence. There may, then, be different streams of thought or ways of seeking light on specific points of doctrine. There should not, however, be sects set up in opposition to each other. Antagonism should only exist between those who work for the good and those who desire the bad.

No one who has sincerely adopted the broad moral principles laid down in this work can wish his or her neighbor ill-will, regardless of the opinions they hold on matters of secondary importance. If any of these streams is in error, honest inquiry will eventually clarify them. After all, the different currents have a common direction. If a current leads to the goal, the specific path it takes does not matter. Nor should anyone try to impose an opinion by force, whether physical or mental; and any group acting with deliberate hostility toward another is clearly in the wrong, since it can only be acting under the influence of negative forces. The only power an argument has is its intrinsic rationality; and moderation will do more to ensure the triumph of truth than tongue-lashings poisoned by envy and jealousy. Good spirits preach only union and the love of one's neighbor. Nothing malevolent or uncharitable can ever proceed from a pure source.

Bearing on these remarks, and as a fitting conclusion to the present work, we offer the following message from the spirit of Saint Augustine— a message giving advice that all readers will find worth knowing by heart: *"For long enough human beings have torn each other to pieces, cursing one another in the name of a God of peace and mercy, whom they only insult by this sacrilege. The Spiritist Doctrine will eventually constitute a bond of union among them by showing them the difference between truth and error. But for a long time to come, there will be scribes and Pharisees who reject the Doctrine, as they rejected Christ. Would you like to know the nature of the spirits who inspire the world's various religious denominations? Judge them by their actions and by the principles they profess. Good spirits do not instigate wrong-doing. Neither do they advise or condone murder or violence; nor excite factional hatreds, the thirst for riches and honors, or desire for earthly things. Only those who are kind, humane, and benevolent are counted as friends by spirits of high degree. They are counted as friends by Jesus, for they follow the road that leads to him."*

(Saint Augustine)

GLOSSARY

Action and Reaction – see Cause and Effect.

Afterlife – the life after the physical life; the state to which the spirit returns after existence in the physical realm.

Angel – a being that has attained the state of pure spirit. Angels have passed up through all the degrees on the scale of progress and freed themselves from all the impurities of the material world.

Animism – situation in which the medium's subconscious mind, rather than another spiritual individuality, is the source of a mediumistic message. The term is also used to identify religious practices based in the belief that all living things have a soul. However, only the former notion is recognized in the Spiritist literature.

Astral Body – see Perispirit.

Attachment (spirit) – a temporary situation in which spirits of limited awareness seek connection and enjoy living in close relationship with an incarnate person.

Aura – A field of energy that surrounds human beings. The aura is a form of radiation emitted by the spirit. It should not be confused with the bio-energy that radiates from the human and animal body.

Automatic Writing (Psychography) – the process of receiving written communications without the control of the conscious self. Writing of truly automatic kind, when the arm and hand are under spirit control, is rare. More often the writing is the product of mind-to-mind communication between the medium and the communicating spirit. By its very nature, the process may be more or less affected by the medium's mind.

Bio-Energy – the vital life force that sustains physical life (see also Vitalism).

Cause and Effect (Action and Reaction) – a law of nature according to which every effect must have a generating cause. In the moral realm, every conscious human action produces an effect. Logically, good actions are likely to generate good reactions, and vice-versa. In the ultimate sense, however, the effect is more than just an equivalent outcome. For instance, a person who seriously harms another doesn't need necessarily to experience the same form of harm, because the person may neutralize the negative effect by doing good to others. This interpretation of the principle of Cause and Effect is more attuned with Jesus' instruction "For she loved much, her sins are forgiven" (Luke 7:47), and the concept of Divine Justice.

Cord (Spiritual) – see Silver Cord.

Catalepsy – A condition in which consciousness and feeling are suddenly, temporarily lost, and muscles become rigid; it may occur in epilepsy and schizophrenia.

Clairaudience – A paranormal perception in which the person 'hears' spirit communications and perceives events taking place in the spirit realm.

Clairvoyance – A paranormal kind of perception in which the human mind perceives images, more or less well defined, of events, scenes, or objects in the spirit realm.

Christianity – Christian beliefs or practices; Christian qualities or character. In the Spiritist tradition, Christianity defines a mental attitude and a relationship with life in all its expressions, rather than a religion in the conventional sense of the word.

Christian Spiritist – the person who sympathizes with or embraces the spirit philosophy and is committed to the work of personal transformation following the ideal defined by Jesus Christ.

Cosmic Principle – the subtle, fundamental, unifying substance that gives rise to phenomena such as heat, magnetism, and electricity, and to matter itself.

Cult – A religion or religious sect regarded as unorthodox, with its followers often living in an unconventional manner under the guidance of an authoritarian, charismatic leader.

Death – The exhaustion of the bodily organs and with that the complete liberation of the spirit from the physical body.

Demon – spirits of scanty moral progress who nurture hatred and harbor base sentiments and inclinations.

Destiny – predetermined course of events in human life. The Spiritist Doctrine does not endorse the view that the circumstances of a person's life were scripted beforehand. They are usually the result of a person's own actions, or choices made before incarnation. Human beings are the creators of their own destiny.

Determinism – the notion that every event, including human choices and decisions, have sufficient causes. The Spiritist philosophy does not support this view in all that regards the moral and spiritual aspects of human life.

Devil – same as Demon.

Divine Justice – The system of laws and norms that flow from God. They are eternal and unchanging. The Divine Justice assures that every person receives according to his or her merit. It is not a strict system of punishments and rewards. God always considers the causes of our actions and does not punish any one. Love is the fundamental essence of the Divine Justice.

Dream – Dreams are often the recollection of what the spirit experiences and happen during sleep of the body. The spirit is never inactive during the bodily rest. The dreams referred to in the original works of the Spiritist Doctrine are known, in modern dream literature, as psychic dreams.

Ectoplasm (From the Greek: ektos, external and plasma: substance) – Visible substance that exhales from the body of certain mediums in the production of materializations.

Ecstatic Trance – A state of profound inner concentration in which the person shows little awareness of the immediate environment. In this state the person may have visions and manifest special mediumistic powers. It is distinguished by an intense feeling of joy.

Euthanasia – the act of interrupting human life in a painless manner to, supposedly, relieve the pain and suffering of a terminal illness. From a continuous life perspective, euthanasia generates a complex stream of consequences that may bring more suffering than what the person still had to endure.

Evil Spirits – same as Demons.

Evolution (Spiritual) – the process of development of the spirit. Spirits were created simple and in a state of unawareness. They develop and grow through experiences in this and various other spheres of life. The spirit's evolution is a continuous and progressive movement. Evolution is a forward movement, it never regresses. Every spirit has to tread the path of evolution; none is left behind or condemned to unawareness.

Exorcism – ritual ceremonies or formulas used by certain religions to remove a harmful or disturbing spirit from a place or a person's life.

Expiation – the means and circumstances by which a person atones, provides reparation, for wrongs done to self or others. Used in the Spiritist literature to refer to experiences in which there is a great deal of suffering or difficulty unconnected to a person's past actions or choices.

Family (Spiritual) – any group of spirit beings that share mutual affection, and have affinity of ideas and values. They may choose to be born in the same family of kin. Their connections have roots in past life experiences. This affinity may draw these spirits together in the physical life. Their ties strengthen with their progress.

Fatalism – same as Determinism.

Fate – same as Destiny.

Free Spirits – The temporary state of spirits between incarnations.

Free Will – the notion that human action expresses personal choice, rather than the intervention of divine forces. Free will is a fundamental right of the human consciousness. Without free will, human life would be a either a series of predetermined movements or a sequence of random events. As a spirit progresses, the exercise, so to speak, of its free will expands, i.e., the spirit takes responsibility for a wider range of choices.

Gender (in spirits) – spirits have no gender.

Gift (Spiritual) – a special sensorial ability, usually identified as paranormal, that allows a person to interact with subtler dimensions of life, i.e., spirit reality.

God – The Supreme intelligence of the Universe, the First Cause of All things.

Ghost – in the popular culture, word used in reference to the soul of a dead person that wanders among or haunts living persons. Such occurrences are indeed the sighting of the spiritual body, or perispirit, of those persons who after their physical death are temporarily unable to adjust themselves to the spirit realm.

Golden Rule – 'do to others as you would have them do to you' (Luke 6:31).

Guardian Angel – same as Guide.

Guide (Spiritual) – A spirit who has achieved a high stage, relatively speaking, of moral and intellectual development. They may be identified as teachers, guides, or counselors. They take interest in the growth of an individual or group. Other schools of thought call them angels, and spiritual masters.

Healing (Spiritual) – treatment of physical or spiritual illnesses by means of bio-energy transfer and prayer. Through cleansing or replenishing the energies of the spiritual body, the physical body is able to restore itself to health. The healer works in close association with spiritual beings. The therapy is based on the power of prayer, faith, and love.

Healing Energy – the energy that enables spiritual healing to take place. It is the energy produced through prayer and faith during the spiritual healing therapy. See also Healing.

Hell – in traditional Christian theology, the place in which the evil doers are condemned to live for all eternity. The Spiritist philosophy rejects the notion of Hell as a place of perpetual punishment because all God's creatures are destined to progress and attain happiness. In the Spiritist literature the word Hell is employed only as metaphor to describe a place where distraught, rebellious, and anger souls gather temporarily.

Hypnotism – the science of dealing with the induction of hypnosis, an artificially induced state resembling sleep in which the subject is highly susceptible to suggestion.

Hypnotic Power – the power held by certain individuals, as well as spiritual beings, to induce another into a hypnotic state.

Incarnate spirit – A spirit that is temporarily wearing the garment of a physical body; the soul of a living person.

Induced Trance – usually a self-induced trance in preparation for mediumistic, psychic practice.

Inner Transformation – the renovation of moral values, views, and behavior that constitutes the essential purpose of incarnate life. It is the striving to acquire the perfections inspired by becoming conscious of God. The enlightened spirits who dictated the Spiritist Doctrine considered inner transformation as the fundamental task of the spirit in the course of time, and have presented Jesus as our divine point of reference.

Inner Voice – the voice of conscience in its purest expression. St. Francis of Assisi used this expression to identify the Christ voice that guided him in critical decisions.

Intelligent Principle – one of the essential principles of the universe; the core constituent of the spirit.

Intuition – The ability to understand a situation or draw conclusions about complex events without the use of rational process. Also, a form of presentiment about future events. For some spiritually sensitive persons, the ability to sense the ideations of enlightened spirits who take interest in a particular area of human development.

Invocation – the act of invoking a spiritual being, Jesus, or God, for aid, protection, inspiration, or guidance.

Jesus – in the words of the enlightened spirits who laid the basis of Christian Spiritism as a philosophy of life, 'the most perfect example that God has offered to us as a guide and model.'

Last Judgment – according to the traditional dogma, 'the final trial of all mankind.' This notion is not supported in the Christian Spiritist philosophy because the doctrine views the process of life and evolution as continuous and infinite.

Laying On Of Hands – a form of spiritual healing in which the healer, in a state of profound meditation or prayer, places hands over the patient's head without physical touch. In this state the healer gives off the bioenergy that replenishes or helps rebalance the patient's energy field. This is the purest form of spiritual healing as it was practiced by Jesus.

Karma – Hindu and Buddhist ethical doctrine of "as one sows, so shall one reap" in this or in a future reincarnation. According to the law of karma, every conscious human action—in thought, word, or deed—leads to consequences, good or bad, depending on the quality of the action. Karma implies strict causality. A positive act will lead to a positive result. Accordingly, the result will directly correspond to the nature of the cause. In the Christian Spiritist application the notion of direct causality between the action and the result of the action is amended with Jesus' precept '"For she loved much, her sins are forgiven" (Luke 7:47). See Cause and Effect.

Kirlian — A photographic method that captures bio-fields of persons or objects through a high voltage discharge process. The process of Kirlian photography is named after Seymon Kirlian, a Russian inventor. The interpretation of the coronas that surround the animate objects photographed is open to controversy. Some researchers argue that they are a paranormal phenomenon, the aura. Others counter that they show nothing more than electricity being discharged which can be produced under certain conditions. Although we are far from a conclusive interpretation, there is growing evidence that energy flows in the body are influenced by mental states, medical conditions, healing treatment, prayer, etc.

Levitation – the raising of a person or object through psychic or paranormal methods.

Magnetic Healing – similar to Spiritual Healing but reliant only on the energy and mental power of the healer (as opposed to healing with the assistance of spiritual guides, and prayer).

Materialism – the philosophical principle that matter is the only reality and all phenomena, including thought and feeling, can be explained in terms of matter and physical processes. Alternatively used to signify the attitude that possessions are the greatest good and highest value of life, and that spiritual values are not relevant.

Materialization – It is one of the several types of mediumistic phenomena produced by conscious or unconscious mediums who possess such a gift. During materialization, a spirit takes a visible form to make itself materially visible.

Medium (From the Latin: medium, intermediate) — a person endowed with a superior   sensitivity who serves as an intermediary for communication between the physical and spirit world.

Mediumship – The faculty of mediums. There are many types of mediumship. The more common are: Trance, Automatic Writing, and Clairvoyance.

Mentor – same as Guide.

Mesmerism – A healing method developed by F. A. Mesmer (1733-1815) involving the induction of hypnotic trances and the transfer of physical energy, originally named animal magnetism, from the therapist to the patient. People in trance often showed paranormal abilities.

Metempsychosis – the ancient doctrine by which a soul (spirit) may enter another human body or that of an animal according to its deeds in a previous life.

Miracle – A physical event that appears inexplicable by the known laws of nature and is considered of divine or supernatural cause. Christian Spiritism proposes that the so-called miracles, even the more amazing healing and paranormal phenomena, appear so as the result of our still limited understanding of the laws of nature.

Mission (spiritual) – the kind of assignment trusted to more advanced spirits, as opposed to the trials and expiations experienced by the majority of the souls on Earth. Missions are attributions that impact a large circle of people, rather than just the individual or the individual's immediate family.

Moral Conscience – A well developed ability to understand right from wrong coupled with a resilient willingness to act accordingly. To act in such a manner requires cultivation of emotions and integration of spiritual values in the management of physical needs and desires.

Obsession – in Spiritist studies, the temporary influence exercised by an ill-meaning spirit over a person. The causes range from a person's own behavior all the way to mutual hatred between the besetting spirit and its victim, and may have origin in this as well as in a previous lifetime. It is a condition that requires spiritual treatment, behavior change, and inner transformation. In severe cases it may cause physical and mental ailments.

OBE – Out-of-Body Experience - the temporary freedom obtained by an incarnate spirit during deep trance or sleep to travel outside the human body. The spirit may visit places or friends on Earth, travel to places in the spirit realm, or take part in benevolent endeavors under the guidance of a spiritual mentor.

Occult – related to magic, astrology, and other disciplines that rely on secret, mysterious, or supernatural forces

Original Sin – in traditional Christian theology, the sin committed by Adam, the first man. As a consequence of this first sin, we are all born with a tendency to be evil. This notion is not endorsed by the Spiritist

Doctrine, which postulates that all spirits are created equal, with the same propensity for good and evil.

Paranormality – deals with events beyond the range of normal sensorial experience or scientific explanation; for instance, a medium's intuition of a future event.

Perispirit – From the Greek, *Perí* means surrounding. It is the subtle body of the spirit. It serves as interface between the spirit and the physical body. Also known as spiritual body, astral body or double.

Poltergeist – a paranormal phenomena involving the movement of objects, rapping, and sounds produced by spiritual entities. Usually the presence of a person with the proper type of sensitivity is necessary for the phenomena to occur.

Possession (spiritual) – an aggravated spiritual obsession (see Obsession) in which the ill-meaning spirit is able to have a controlling influence over a person's actions. Spiritual possession tends to have a longer course. Deep-seated hatred or vengeance usually are the motivating forces behind these relationships. Cure requires spiritual assistance and specialized medical treatment.

Premonition – An intuitive anticipation of a future event.

Pure Spirits – beings that have reached the higher states of moral and intellectual perfection.

Purgatory – according to the theology of some traditional Christian denominations, the place of temporary punishment reserved for the penitent souls that had their sins forgiven on Earth. The Spiritist Doctrine does not subscribe to this view.

Psychometry – a psychic gift with which the medium is able to sense the history of an object by holding it, or the past of a person by simply touching or shaking hands with the person.

Regresssion (Past Lives) – psychological therapy by which persons under hypnotic trance access memories of events that have supposedly taken place in past lives. It has been successfully used in the treatment of phobias and a variety of traumatic experiences. Although not without controversy, this therapy is receiving increasing attention from the medical community.

Reincarnation – The notion that a spirit (soul) can be reborn in a new body, as part of the continuous progress toward higher levels of spiritual existence. The purpose of reincarnation is to offer the spirit opportunities to grow in awareness, love, and intellectual ability. In addition, reincarnation provides the time and circumstances for the spirit to provide reparation for wrongs committed in prior existences.

Remote View – a type of psychic technique in which the medium, or subject, is able to acquire information about a person, place, or event which is distant in time or space.

Resurrection – in traditional Christian theology, the belief that at a point in time there will be a final judgment and that God will then raise into heaven all the saved who have been dead. When this occurs, their physical bodies will rise from being dead and will be reunited with their souls. The Spiritist Doctrine does not subscribe to this view.

Revelation – The act of revealing divine truth, or that which is revealed by God to man. Revelation is the supernatural communication of truth to the mind of a teacher or writer, who, in traditional Biblical lexicon, is called a prophet. The Spiritist Doctrine was given to humanity by the ennobled intelligences who fulfilled a design of God. According to this notion, the Spiritist Doctrine is a revelation of our true spiritual nature, purpose, and destiny as eternal spirits. However, the Spiritist philosophy endorses the notion that revelation is a continuous process, and that the progress of humanity is accomplished by the incarnation of exceptional individuals with responsibilities in every major field of human endeavor to reveal or expand continuously the frontiers of our knowledge (see question 622). The Doctrine in no way claims to have access to the absolute truth. This enlightened stance is cemented in the motto: "The Only Unshakeable Faith Is That Which Can Withstand Reason, Face to Face, In Every Stage Of Humankind's Development." Besides, Allan Kardec made it a cornerstone of the Spiritist thought that the Doctrine is dynamic and that its evolution should occur always in agreement with the development of scientific knowledge.

Ritual – The repeated performance of ceremonial acts prescribed by tradition or religion. Religious rituals are dependent upon some common belief system. Rituals are part of the fabric of every human society.

Second-sight – same as Clairvoyance. It gives the medium the ability to see spirits and perceive events and circumstances of the spirit world. It is a complex and difficult gift in which the medium is responsible for interpreting and communicating what is seen. Because of this element of intellectual interpretation, which opens the doors to personal biases and beliefs, the issue of reliability is always a concern.

Seer – a person endowed with the gift of Clairvoyance or Second-sight.

Silver Cord – the metaphorical link between the spiritual and the physical body. When the cord is broken, the physical body dies, and the spirit is free to continue life in the spirit world.

Sin – in religious theology, willful and deliberate transgression of divine law, the violation of some religious or moral principle.

Sin (Original) – see Original Sin.

Soul – An incarnate spirit (question 134 in this book). Before uniting to the body, the soul is one of the many distinct beings inhabiting the invisible world.

Spirit – The intelligent beings of Creation. They populate the entire universe and can be found beyond the boundaries of the material world.

Spirit World – the essential world that pre-exists and survives everything else. Spirits are everywhere in the universe. The spirit world has beauty, life, and harmony beyond anything that incarnate beings can conceive.

Spirit of truth (The) – in the Christian Spiritist perspective, a collective of enlightened spirits who represent the purest aspect of the Christian thought and ideal. The ideas proposed in messages signed by 'the Spirit of truth', in this book and other works, are divine in a logical sense, if one considers that these ideas were produced by beings who live in oneness with Jesus, and are inspired purely by their love of God. In the Spiritist Doctrine "the Spirit of truth" re-affirms the morality of the Gospel as the highest creation of human conscience, and encourages the quest for knowledge through science and reason.

Spiritual Body – see Perispirit.

Spiritist Doctrine or Christian Spiritism – The philosophy that deals with the nature, the origin and the destiny of Spirits, as well as their relationship with the corporeal world.

Spiritist (or Christian Spiritist) – A follower of the Spiritist Doctrine.

Spiritual Family – see Family.

Spiritualism – in philosophy, the notion that human beings are more than just matter. As a doctrine, Spiritualism denies that the contents of the universe are limited to matter and the properties and operations of matter. It maintains that the real being (spirit) is radically distinct in nature from matter. Plato is practically considered as the father of Spiritualism, as he articulated the distinction between the irrational, or sensuous, and the rational functions of the soul. For him the rational soul was related to the body merely as the pilot to the ship or the rider to his horse. In this sense, all religions which accept the existence in the human being of a principle independent from matter, are Spiritualist.

Spiritualism, in daily American and British usage, however, is commonly defined as a belief that the dead communicate with the living through mediums. In this case, the usage is more closely associated with the religion of Modern Spiritualism. While there are many parallels between Modern Spiritualism and the Spiritist Doctrine, the differences are very significant, and they should not be confused, or used as equivalents.

Spontaneous Trance – the individual is temporarily without control of his will or awareness; commonly observed in the religious ecstasy that accompanies the phenomenon of speaking in tongues.

Suicide – the deliberate taking of one's own life. Suicide is an act that carries profound and long lasting consequences for the spirit as it is a transgression of natural laws.

Table turning – the phenomenon where tables and other objects move without human contact. Table turning was very popular in the mid 1850's. The phenomenon was characterized by a table moving in irregular ways, in various directions, rising, and remaining suspended in the air. The invisible agents that produced the table movements later identified themselves as spirits. In the context of Modern Spiritualism and the Spiritist Doctrine, the tables provided the first and crudest form of communication with the spirit world. The methods of communication have since changed. Tables are no longer employed as means of communication, as other more reliable and accurate methods have become available; for instance, automatic writing, and clairvoyance.

Telepathy – communication between minds without the use of ordinary sensory channels.

Tiptology – A language of beats, raps or tilts. A name given to a kind of spirit communication system using beats or other noises. Alphabetical typology is the designation of letters (or ciphers) by raps or tilts.

Trance – This is an expanded state of consciousness characterized externally by apparent sleep or unconsciousness. During a trance the medium may willingly serve as an instrument for a spirit communication.

Transitional Worlds – Way stations that serve as resting places for free spirits.

Trial – a life or state of pain or anguish that tests patience, endurance, courage, or belief. In the Spiritist literature, two other conditions are discussed: life of expiation in which the spirit repairs the wrong or harm done in a previous life, and life of mission, in which the spirit is assigned a task that impacts the social, cultural, spiritual, scientific, or artistic progress of a group or society.

Vital principle – The principle that gives organic life to all beings; it has its source in the Cosmic Principle.

Vitalism – The doctrine that life processes arise from or contain a non-material vital principle and cannot be explained entirely as physical and chemical phenomena. The vitalist concept is at the heart of the Spiritist view of the origin of life. Christian Spiritism maintains that this vital force has its origin in God, the divine source, the First Cause of all things, and that life is not solely the result of biochemical processes and organic evolution.

BIOGRAPHICAL APPENDIX [1]

Augustine [Saint] (354-430). One of the foremost philosopher-theologians of early Christianity and, while serving (396-430) as bishop of Hippo Regius, the leading figure in the church of North Africa. He had a profound influence on the subsequent development of Western thought and culture and, more than any other person, shaped the themes and defined the problems that have characterized the Western tradition of Christian Theology. Among his many writings considered classics, the two most celebrated are his semi-autobiographical Confessions, which contains elements of mysticism, and City of God, a Christian vision of history.

de Paul, Vincent [Saint] (1580-1660). French priest, founder of numerous charitable organizations. Of peasant family, he began his work on behalf of the poor as a young priest by working to relieve the lot of galley slaves. He founded the Congregation of the Mission (the Vicentians or Lazarists; 1625) to preach to the rural poor and, with Saint Louise the Marillac, founded the Daughters of Charity (1633), composed of peasant women who, in ministering to the poor, were the first sisters to work outside the convent buildings in active service. Vincent also organized several seminaries to train young men for the priesthood and inaugurated the now-standard practice of a period of spiritual preparation for men about to be ordained to the priesthood. Canonized in 1737, he is the patron of all charitable works inspired by his example, including the famous lay organization, the St. Vincent de Paul Society.

Fénelon, Francois de Salignac de la Mothe (1651-1715). French archbishop, theologian, and man of letters whose progressive views on politics and education and whose involvement in a controversy over the nature of mystical prayer caused concerted opposition from church and state. His pedagogical concepts and literary works, nevertheless, exerted a lasting influence on French culture.

---

1 *Translator's Note: All biographical entries compiled from: The New Groliers Multimedia Encyclopedia - Release 6; Dictionary of Scientific Biography; Encyclopedia Britannica; Webster New Biographical Dictionary - 1983; Cambridge Biographical Dictionary 1990.*

Franklin, Benjamin (1706-1790). American printer and publisher, author, inventor, scientist, and diplomat, who is probably best remembered for his role in helping to frame the American Declaration of Independence and the U.S. Constitution. His greatest scientific contribution relates to his experiments in electricity. He invented the lightning rod.

John the Evangelist [Saint]. One of the twelve apostles of Jesus Christ. A Galilean fisherman, brother of Saint James. Author of five New Testament books: the fourth gospel, three Epistles, and the Book of Revelation.

Lammenais, Huges-Felicite Robert de, (1782-1854). French priest and philosophical and political writer who attempted to combine political liberalism with Roman Catholicism after the French Revolution.

Louis IX, King of France [Saint Louis] (1214-1270). The oldest son of the future king Louis VIII and Blanche of Castile, he came to the throne as a child in 1226. A man of great piety and a strong pacifist in dealing with fellow Christians, Louis was less tolerant of heretics and non-Christians, against whom he led two major crusades. In his later years, Louis promoted internal reforms and made international treaties that were intended to establish permanent, peaceful relations. Admired for his prowess, his piety, and his strong sense of justice, Louis was revered as a saint well before his canonization in 1297.

Plato (c428-348 or 347 BC). Greek philosopher. Disciple of Socrates and teacher of Aristotle, with them laid the philosophical foundations of Western culture. His written works are in the form of dialogues, in each of which his master Socrates takes the leading role. These include The Republic (regarded as his greatest work; a search for justice in construction of an ideal state), Laws (on the same theme), Symposium (on ideal love), Phaedrus (on rhetoric), Timaeus (a theory of the universe and story of the lost Atlantis), Apology (purporting to give Socrates's speech in his own defence at his trial), Phaedo (on the immortality of the soul).

Saint Augustine (see Augustine [Saint])

Saint John the Evangelist (see John the Evangelist [Saint])

Saint Louis (see Louis IX, King of France)

Saint Vincent de Paul (see de Paul, Vincent [Saint])

Socrates (c.470-399 BC). Greek philosopher. Developed the Socratic method of enquiry and instruction, consisting of a series of questions designed to elicit a clear expression of something supposed to be implicitly known by all human beings. Left no writings. His philosophy is known through the writings of his disciple, Plato.

Swedenborg, Emmanuel (1688-1772). Swedish scientist, philosopher, and religious writer, published Sweden's first scientific journal in 1716. Also published other scientific works. Starting in 1747 devoted himself to psychical and spiritual research; wrote numerous works on the interpretation of the Bible. Although he himself never tried to preach or to form a religious sect, his followers founded a regular ecclesiastical organization known as the Church of New Jerusalem.

SUBJECT INDEX

For more information on other works by Allan Kardec
or to start or join a study group write to:

Allan Kardec Educational Society
P.O. Box 26336
Philadelphia   PA 19141
Phone 215 3294010

AKES – Book Distribution Center
P.O. Box 30692
Phoenix   AZ 85046
Phone 602 9963123

or visit our website: www.allan-kardec.org